Canary Islands

Damien Simonis

Canary Islands

1st edition

Published by
Lonely Planet Publications
Head Office: PO Box 617, Hawthorn, Vic 3122, Australia
Branches: 150 Linden Street, Oakland, CA 94607, USA
10a Spring Place, London NW5 3BH, UK
71 bis rue du Cardinal Lemoine, 75005 Paris, France

Printed by
Colorcraft Ltd, Hong Kong

Photographs by
Damien Simonis

Front cover: Windmill, Lanzarote (Anselm Spring, The Image Bank)

Published
August 1998

Although the authors and publisher have tried to make the information as accurate as possible, they accept no responsibility for any loss, injury or inconvenience sustained by any person using this book.

National Library of Australia Cataloguing in Publication Data

Simonis, Damien.
Canary Islands.

1st ed.
Includes index.
ISBN 0 86442 522 8.

1. Canary Islands – Guidebooks. 1. Title.

914.490483

Damien Simonis

Damien is a London-based journalist. With a degree in languages and several years' newspaper experience on, among others, *The Australian* and *The Age*, he left Australia in 1989. In between stints on several London papers, including *The Guardian*, *The Independent* and *The Daily Telegraph*, he has also worked and travelled widely in Europe, the Middle East and North Africa. In addition to this book he has also worked on Lonely Planet's *Jordan & Syria*, *Egypt & the Sudan*, *Morocco*, *North Africa*, *Spain* and *Italy* guidebooks, and is working on a *Barcelona* guide.

From the Author

As always, behind the face in the very attractive photo on this page lies an ocean of people who, in one way or another, have helped in the construction of this guide.

Keith Harris of Books on Spain, in the UK, was kind enough to help out with problems of bibliography.

I owe a large debt of thanks to John Noble and Susan Forsyth, my colleagues on Lonely Planet's guide to Spain, whose work has helped smooth my path in the preparation of the Facts for the Visitor chapter.

Staff at various tourist offices, but in particular at the Oficina de Turismo de Santa Cruz de Tenerife, have been most helpful.

The guys at Lonely Planet's London office, and especially Sara Yorke and Angie Bjelogrlic for their expertise in matters volcanic, are worth their weight in pints.

Michèle Nayman has been a great friend and source of support through some interesting moments.

In Santa Cruz de Tenerife a special thanks to Isabel Álvarez, who sight unseen rolled out the red carpet simply because her sister in London, Carmen, ordered her to do so!

From the Publisher

This book was edited in Lonely Planet's Melbourne office by Rowan McKinnon, with much help from Sarah Mathers, Ada Cheung, Mary Neighbour and Bethune Carmichael. The maps were drawn by Helen Rowley who also laid out the book and designed the colour pages. Trudi Canavan drew the illustrations, Mick Weldon drew the cartoons and the cover was designed by Margie Jung, who also drew the back-cover map. Special thanks to computer boffin Andrew Tudor for his trusty templates, and to Michelle Bennet for additional research.

Warning & Request

Things change – prices go up, schedules change, good places go bad and bad places go bankrupt – nothing stays the same. So, if you find things better or worse, recently opened or long since closed, please tell us and help make the next edition even more accurate and useful.

We value all of the feedback we receive from travellers. Julie Young coordinates a small team that reads and acknowledges every letter, postcard and email, and ensures that every morsel of information finds its way to the appropriate authors, editors and publishers.

Everyone who writes to us will find their name in the next edition of the appropriate guide and will also receive a free subscription to our quarterly newsletter, *Planet Talk*. The very best contributions will be rewarded with a free Lonely Planet guide.

Excerpts from your correspondence may appear in new editions of this guide; in our newsletter, *Planet Talk*; or in updates on our Web site – so please let us know if you don't want your letter published or your name acknowledged.

Contents

Boxed Asides

Map Legend

BOUNDARIES

.... International Boundary

.... Provincial Boundary

ROUTES

A25 ..... Freeway, with Route Number

.... Major Road, with Tunnel

.... Minor Road

.... Minor Road - unsealed

.... City Road

.... City Street

.... City Lane

.... Steps on Street

.... Cable Car or Chairlift

.... Walking Tour

.... Ferry Route

.... Walking Track

AREA FEATURES

.... Building

.... Cemetery

.... Sand

.... Market

.... Park, Gardens

.... Reef

.... Urban Area

HYDROGRAPHIC FEATURES

.... Coastline

.... Creek, River

.... Flow

.... Lake, Intermittent Lake

.... Rapids, Waterfalls

.... Salt Lake

.... Swamp

SYMBOLS

◉ **CAPITAL** ...... Provincial Capital

● **CITY** .... City

● **Town** .... Town

● Village .... Village

■ .... Place to Stay

Å ...... Camping Ground

⌂ .... Shelter

▼ .... Place to Eat

♬ .... Pub or Bar

✈ .... Airport

..... Ancient or City Wall

θ .... Bank

⌐ .... Beach

Ä .... Castle or Fort

⌒ .... Cave

⊞ .... Church

.... Cliff or Escarpment

◣ .... Dive Site

⊙ .... Embassy

⌐ .... Golf

⊕ .... Hospital

�énlighthouse .... Lighthouse

❋ .... Lookout

⚑ .... Monument

▲ .... Mountain or Hill

🏛 .... Museum

← .... One Way Street

🄿 .... Parking

)(......................... Pass

🅿 .... Petrol Station

○ .... Point of Interest

★ .... Police Station

✉ .... Post Office

❖ ...... Shopping Centre

🏛 .... Stately Home

▭ .... Swimming Pool

☎ .... Telephone

❶ .... Tourist Information

⊖ .... Transport

⟷ .... Two-Way Street

Å .... Volcano

Note: not all symbols displayed above appear in this book

Map Index

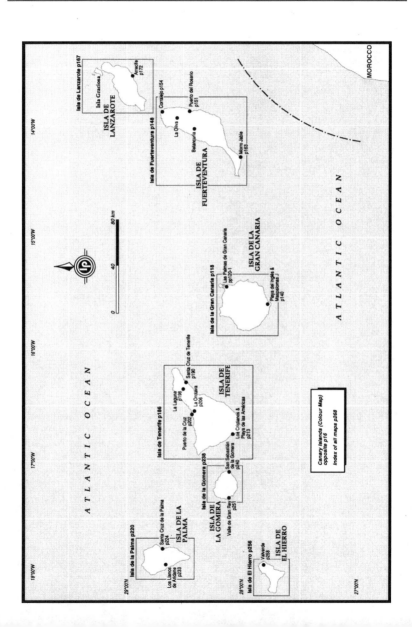

ATLANTIC OCEAN

ATLANTIC OCEAN

29°00'N

28°00'N

27°00'N

18°00'W   17°00'W   16°00'W   15°00'W   14°00'W

0   40   80 km

Introduction

'Oh, surely you're not going to the Canary Islands!' travel snobs exclaim in horror. Sun and fun holiday package destination par excellence, the Canaries are seen by many as the last winter refuge of British lager-louts, German hippies and pensioners from across northern Europe.

To write off the islands in this cavalier and uninformed fashion, however, is to do them, and yourself, a great injustice. The Canary Islands, a Spanish archipelago little more than 100km from the coast of Saharan Africa, are in fact a fascinating and multi-faceted destination for travellers. You don't have to stray too far from the main beach resorts to discover an absorbing, multi-faceted culture.

The island of Gran Canaria alone is often described as a continent in miniature, its countryside an ever-changing pastiche: sub-tropical and fertile to the north, more arid and reminiscent of the desert in the south. Tenerife is still more interesting. The three small western islands, mountainous, green and dotted with occasional brief strands of black sand, present a startling contrast to the desertscapes and sparkling white beaches of their easternmost counterparts, Lanzarote and Fuerteventura. A rich and often bizarre indigenous flora thrives right across this chain of volcanic islands.

Exploring the islands, the back roads and villages bring you in touch with a unique side of Spanish culture, reflecting an unusual mix of influences far removed from the mainland.

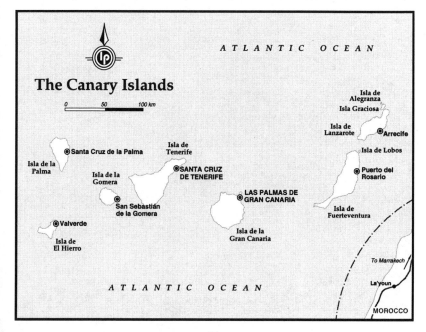

Amid the melting pot of Andalucían, Berber, Portuguese, Italian, French and even British migration, los Guanches, the native islanders displaced by the Spanish conquest in the 15th century, also left their mark.

And just as Canarios migrated in search of a better life to Latin America, so in later years South American influences have wafted back across the Atlantic, best sampled in the cuisine and music.

This fascinating mix can be easily and relatively cheaply explored – just put aside your preconceptions and go.

Facts about the Islands

HISTORY

The origins of the Canary Islands and its earliest inhabitants are enveloped in thick mists of myth and uncertainty. The islands themselves are estimated to be 30 million years old, relatively young by the planet's standards.

The existence of the islands was known, or postulated, in ancient times. Plato (428-348 BC), in his dialogues *Timaeus* and *Critias*, spoke of Atlantis, a continent destroyed and sunk deep into the ocean floor in a great cataclysm which left only the peaks of its highest mountains above the water. Whether Plato believed in the lost continent's existence or had more allegorical intentions remains a matter of conjecture. In the centuries since Plato's death, those convinced of the existence of Atlantis have maintained that Macronesia (ie the Canary Islands, the Azores, Cape Verde and Madeira), are the visible remains of the lost continent.

Legend also has it that one of the 12 labours of Hercules (Heracles to the Greeks) was to go to the end of the world and bring back golden apples guarded by the Hesperides ('daughters of evening'), offspring of Hesperis and Atlas, the latter a mythical Mauritanian king who gave his name to the Atlantic Ocean and the Atlas mountain ranges in Morocco. Hercules supposedly had to go beyond the Pillars of Hercules (the modern Strait of Gibraltar), which came to be known as the Garden of the Hesperides, to reach the paradisical home of these maidens. Hercules carried out his task and returned from what many later thought could only have been the Canary Islands – about the only place to fit the ancients' description.

And so the islands gained a reputation, passed down from one classical writer to the next, as a Garden of Eden. Homer identified the islands as Elysium, a place where the righteous spent their afterlife. For all their story-telling, there is no concrete evidence that either the Phoenicians or Greeks ever landed in the Canaries. It is entirely possible, however, that early reconnaissance of the North African Atlantic coast by the Phoenicians and their successors, the Carthaginians, took in at least a peek at the easternmost islands of the archipelago. Some historians believe a Phoenician expedition landed in the islands in the 12th century BC, and that the Carthaginian Hanno turned up there in 470 BC.

The expanding Roman empire defeated Carthage in the Third Punic War in 146 BC, but the Romans appear not to have been overly keen to investigate the fabled islands. Indeed, only shortly after the birth of Christ did the Romans receive vaguely reliable reports on them, penned by Pliny the Elder (23-79 AD) from accounts of an expedition carried out around 40BC by Juba II, a client king in Roman North Africa. In 150 AD, Ptolemy fairly accurately located the islands' position with a little dead reckoning, tracing an imaginary meridian line marking the end of the known world through El Hierro.

The Guanches

That the Canary Islands were inhabited before the birth of Christ is undisputed. But by whom? Carbon-dating of the sparse archaeological finds has pushed back the known date of settlement to around 200 BC, although earlier settlement is conceivable. For a long time, learned observers maintained that the islands were first inhabited by Cro-Magnon man, the Neolithic predecessor of *Homo sapiens*. Such conclusions have emerged from the comparison of ancient skulls of indigenous inhabitants with Cro-Magnon remains discovered in the Mediterranean.

Historians tend to wrinkle their noses up at the idea now, although the evidence either way is so flimsy that it cannot be

Dogs & Purple Prose

To the ancient Greeks, the fabled islands beyond the Pillars of Hercules were known as the Hesperides or Atlantes, after the daughters of Atlas supposedly visited by Hercules. Long thought to be abundant in every possible kind of fruit, the islands were also often referred to as the Garden of Hesperides. Elysium, the field of perfect peace where the ancient Greeks supposed the good and great spent the afterlife, has also been associated by some writers with the Canaries.

Canaries took their name from the islands rather than the other way around

The Romans, who apparently never set foot on the islands, knew them as the Insulae Fortunatae (Fortunate Isles). The Spaniards, when they set about conquering them in the 15th century, also tended initially to refer to them as the Islas Afortunadas.

Juba II, the North African king who gave Pliny the Elder an account of the Islands, referred to them as the Insulae Purpuriae (Purple Isles), because of the purple dyes extracted from the orchil lichen on Fuerteventura and Lanzarote. Juba's report can't have been all fiction, as he at least got the number of islands right – seven. The Romans gave them the following names: Canaria (Gran Canaria); Nivaria (Tenerife); Capraria (Lanzarote), Planaria (Fuerteventura), Junonia Mayor (La Palma), Junonia Minor (La Gomera) and Pluvialia (El Hierro).

When the Europeans began to occupy the islands in earnest, they found the locals had their own names for the islands, some of them still preserved: Achinech (Tenerife); Tamarán (Gran Canaria); Tyterorgatra (Lanzarote); Maxorata (Fuerteventura); Benahoare (La Palma); Gomera (La Gomera) and Hero (El Hierro).

Why Canaria? One improbable tale talks of an adventuresome Latin couple, Cranus and Crana, who went off in search of a challenge, bumped into what is now Gran Canaria and liked it so much they stayed. They dubbed the island Cranaria, which was later simplified to Canaria.

Another theory suggests the name came from the Latin *canere* (to sing) in reference to canaries, thought by some to be native to the islands. Most ornithologists claim the bird took the name from the islands, rather than the other way around.

Others who prefer dogs to birds say the name came from the Latin word for dog (*canus*), because Juba's expedition found the island was home to what they considered unusually large dogs. On the other hand, there was a school of thought that the natives of the island were dog-eaters!

It is probable that none of these fanciful solutions to the riddle is even remotely correct. Another theory claims that the people of Canaria, who possibly arrived several hundred years before Christ, were in fact Berbers of the Canarii tribe living in Morocco. The tribal name was simply applied to the island and later accepted by Pliny. Canaria became 'great' (*gran*), according to some chronicles, after its people put up a tough fight against the Spanish *conquistadores*. Equally unclear is at precisely what point the islands came to be known collectively as Las Islas Canarias, although probably this came with the completion of the Spanish conquest of the islands at the end of the 15th century.

completely ruled out. It throws the doors of speculation wide open, since Cro-Magnon man came onto the scene as long as 40,000 years ago.

A disconcerting clue is provided by European descriptions of locals in the wake of conquest in the 15th century. They found, mainly on Tenerife, tall and powerfully built people, blue eyed and with long fair hair down to their waists. These lanky blond islanders were known as Guanches (from *guan*, 'man', and *che* or *achinch*, meaning 'white mountain' in reference to the snow-capped Teide volcano).

The Tenerife Guanches fascinated the Europeans (and ultimately put up the most tenacious resistance to them), but their origin is an open question. If they were not descendants of Cro-Magnon man, where did they come from? Some suggest they were Celtic immigrants from mainland Iberia, and even related to the Basques. More fancifully, it is tempting to see a drop of Nordic blood in the Guanches – did Norse raiding parties land here in the 8th or 9th centuries?

Whatever the explanation, the term Guanche came to be used of all the Canary Islands' indigenous people, although not all of them fit the description. In the eastern islands in particular, the original inhabitants were almost certainly Berber migrants from nearby Saharan Africa. Place names and the handful of words of the Canary Islands languages (or dialects) that have come down to us bear a striking resemblance to Berber tribal languages. It has also been noted that the occasional case of blue eyes and blondish hair occurs among the Berbers too. This would lend still more credence to the feeling that the islands' original inhabitants were all Berber migrants, and so dispel more imaginative speculation of the kind mentioned above.

When and in what number these people occupied the islands remains a mystery, but it appears certain that they came from several tribes. One of them may have been the Canarii tribe, which could explain the islands' present name. Certainly, by the time European swashbucklers started nosing around the islands in the Middle Ages, they were peopled by a variety of tribes often more hostile to one another than to visiting strangers.

Guanche Society

For all their differences, the tribes of the Canary Islands had much in common. They all led a primitive existence, their Stone-Age economy reliant on limited farming, herding, hunting and gathering. The main sources of meat were goats (imported from North Africa?) and fish. Barley was grown and, ground and toasted, formed *gofio*, the basic staple which in one form or another is still eaten today.

The women made pottery, often decorated with vegetable dyes. Implements and weapons were fashioned roughly of wood, stone and bone. Goat-skin leather was the basis of most garments, while jewellery and ornaments were largely restricted to earthenware bead and shell necklaces.

The majority of islanders lived in caves, mostly artificial. In the eastern islands (now the province of Las Palmas) some built simple low houses, with rough stone walls and wood-beam roofs covered with stones and caked with wet earth.

Oddly enough, the Guanches seem to have known nothing of sailing, at best using simple dugouts for coastal fishing or to move occasionally between the islands.

Among the Guanches' primitive weapons were the *banot* (lance), rocks and the *tenique*, a stone wrapped up in animal hide and used as a mace.

The Guanches worshipped a god, known as Alcorac in Gran Canaria, Achaman in Tenerife and Abora in La Palma. It appears the god was identified strongly with Magec (the sun). Tenerife islanders commonly held that Hades was in the Teide volcano, directed by the god of evil, Guayota.

For a people who regarded death and gore with some disdain, they went to enormous trouble to facilitate one's passage from this life to the next. Although not as expert as the Egyptians, the Guanches mummified their dead chiefs and nobles before laying them out in burial caves – usually in barely accessible locations. The embalmers were treated as untouchables, excluded from community life.

The head of a tribe or region was the *mencey*, although in Gran Canaria the more common chief's title was *guanarteme*. His rule was almost absolute, although justice was administered through a council of nobles (*achimencey*), sometimes known as a *taoro* or *tagoror*. A little like the ancient Basque parliament which used to sit beneath the Árbol de Gernika (the Tree of Guernica), the taoro would usually gather under the ancient branches of a dragon tree (*Dracaena draco*). Between them, the chief and aristocrats owned all property, flocks and the like, leaving the *achicaxna*, or plebs, to get along as best they could. Although essentially a patriarchal society, women did have some power. On Gran Canaria in particular, succession rights were passed through the mother rather than the father. But when times got tough, they got tougher still for women. Infanticide was practised throughout the islands in periods of famine, and it was girls who were sacrificed, never boys.

The island clans were not averse to squabbling and by the time the European conquest of the islands got underway in the 15th century, Tenerife was divided into no less than nine tiny fiefdoms. Gran Canaria too had been a patchwork of minor principalities, but by the 15th century these had merged to form two kingdoms, one based around the town of Gáldar, another around Telde. Fuerteventura was another island divided in two, and tiny La Palma boasted an astonishing 12 cantons. The other islands were each ruled by one mencey.

The First Encounters

Virtually no written record remains of visits to the Fortunate Isles until the 14th century. Rumour has it that Ireland's St Brendan turned up in the 6th century after a remarkable voyage in search of the 'promised land of saints' (immortalised in the 10th-century epic *Navigatio Brendani*). For centuries sailors tried in vain to find 'St Brendan's Island' in the Atlantic.

There is circumstantial evidence that Arabs operating out of Muslim Portugal in the 10th century not only landed in the islands, but left behind some settlers.

The first vaguely tenable account of a European landing comes in the late 13th or early 14th century, when the Genoese captain Lanzarotto (or Lancelotto) Malocello bumped into the island that would later bear his name: Lanzarote. From then on slavers, dreamers searching for the Río de Oro (the 'River of Gold' route for the legendary African gold trade that many thought spilled into the Atlantic at about the same latitude as the islands), and missionaries bent on spreading the Word all made excursions to the islands.

Of these missions, the most important was the Italian-led and Portuguese backed expedition of 1341. Three caravels charted a course around all seven islands and took note even of the tiniest islets: the Canary Islands were finally, more or less accurately, on the map.

The Conquest Begins

On 1 May 1402, Jean de Béthencourt, Lord of Granville in Normandy (France) and something of an adventurer, set out from La Rochelle with a small and ill-equipped party for the Canary Islands. The avowed aim, as the priests brought along for the ride would testify, was to convert the heathen islanders. Uppermost in de Béthencourt's mind was more likely the hope of glory and a fast buck. He and his partner, Gadifer de la Salle, may have hoped to use the Canaries as a launch pad for exploration of the African coast in search of the Río de Oro. That project never got off the ground, and the buccaneers decided to take over the islands instead. So commenced a lengthy and inglorious chapter of invasion, treachery and bungling. Many Guanches would lose their lives or be sold into slavery in the coming century, the remainder destined to be swallowed up by the invading society.

Canary Islands

0   40   80 km

ELEVATION

0
200m
500m
1000m
1500m
2000m

Ruta de los Volcanes
Hike along the mountain ridge, through the heart of the island's volcanic territory

La Laguna
Discover the beauty and eccentricity of Canarian urban architecture - 18th-century mansions with bright balconies and shady patios

Cueva Don Justo
An enormous underground cavity accessed through 6km of volcanic tunnels

Parque Nacional de Garajonay
Ancient laurel forests in a UNESCO World Heritage Site

Pico de Teide
Spain's highest peak, reached by cable car in 8 minutes

Jameos del Agua
A 500-seat concert hall around an underground lake deep within volcanic caverns

Montañas del Fuego
More than 50 sq km of volcanic activity, with ground temperatures soaring to 100°C

Playa de Sotavento de Jandía
The most beautiful beaches in the Canaries - long white stretches of sand shipping gently into the Atlantic

Parque Arqueológico del Bentayga
Preconquest history, including sacred sites and Guanche granaries, preserved in this superb national park

ISLA DE EL HIERRO
Valverde
Malpaso (150m)
Tanausada (113m)
Puerto de la Estaca

ISLA DE LA PALMA
Los Llanos de Aridane
Volcán San Antonio (657m)
Santa Cruz de la Palma

ISLA DE LA GOMERA
Valle de Gran Rey
Alto de Garajonay (1487m)
San Sebastián de la Gomera

ISLA DE TENERIFE
Puerto de la Cruz
La Orotava
La Laguna
SANTA CRUZ DE TENERIFE
Pico del Teide (3718m)
Los Cristianos & Playa de las Américas

ISLA DE LA GRAN CANARIA
Puerto de las Nieves
Pico de las Nieves (1949m)
Mogán
Pico del Viento (67m)
La Isleta
LAS PALMAS DE GRAN CANARIA
Maspalomas

ISLA DE FUERTEVENTURA
Morro Jable
Betancuria
La Oliva
Corralejo
Puerto del Rosario
Isla de Lobos

ISLA DE LANZAROTE
Timanfaya (510m)
Arrecife

Isla de Alegranza
Isla Graciosa
Aguas Grandes (266m)
Batata (479m)

ATLANTIC OCEAN

MOROCCO
El Aaiún
To Marrakech

DAMIEN SIMONIS

View from Ermita de San Sebastián, Santa Cruz de la Palma, Isla de la Palma

De Béthencourt's motley crew landed first in Lanzarote, at that stage governed by Mencey Guardafía. There was no resistance, and de Béthencourt went on to establish a fort on Fuerteventura.

That was as far as he got. Having run out of supplies and with too few men for the enterprise, he headed for Spain, where he aimed to obtain the backing of the Castilian crown. What had started as a private French enterprise thus became a Spanish imperialist adventure.

De Béthencourt returned in 1404 with ships, men and money. Fuerteventura, El Hierro, and La Gomera quickly fell under his control. Appointed lord of the four islands by the Castilian king Enrique III, de Béthencourt encouraged the settlement of Norman farmers and began to pull in the profits. He returned home to Normandy in 1406, where he died 16 years later, leaving his nephew Maciot in charge.

Squabbles, Bungles & Stagnation

What followed could hardly be described as one of the world's grandest colonial undertakings. It was characterised by continued squabbling and the occasional mutiny among the colonists, and the European presence did nothing for the increasingly unhappy islanders in the years following de Béthencourt's departure.

Maciot soon revealed how ugly colonial administration could be. The islanders were heavily taxed, and many sold off into slavery; he also recruited them for numerous abortive raids on the remaining three independent islands. Maciot capped it all off by selling his rights – inherited from his uncle – to the four islands to Portugal, a move which prompted a tiff with Spain, that was eventually awarded rights to the islands by Pope Eugene V. This contretemps bubbled along on a low heat for years, and Portugal only recognised Spanish control of the Canaries in 1479 under the Treaty of Alcáçovas. In return, Spain agreed that Portugal could have the Azores, Cape Verde and Madeira.

Maciot died in self-imposed exile in Madeira in 1452; there then followed a string of minor Spanish nobility, all eager to sell on their rights to the islands almost as soon as they had acquired them.

Numerous commanders undertook the business of attacking the other islands, but with extraordinarily little success. Whilst better armed than their Stone-Age adversaries, the Spaniards were repeatedly confounded by their enemies' guerrilla tactics.

Landing a force was rarely a problem, but making any headway into the interior was quite another matter. Guillén Peraza died in an attempt to assault La Palma in 1443. In 1464, Peraza's brother-in-law Diego de Herrera, appointed Lord of La Gomera, attempted a landing on Gran Canaria and another near present day Santa Cruz de Tenerife, both ending in failure. By 1466 he had managed to sign a trade treaty with the Canarios, the people of Gran Canaria, and won permission to build a defensive turret in Gando bay. Intermittent clashes continued over the ensuing years, but the Spaniards made no real progress.

The Fall of Gran Canaria

In 1478 a new commander arrived with fresh forces (including for the first time a small cavalry unit) and orders from the Catholic monarchs of Spain, Fernando and Isabel, to finish the Canaries campaign off once and for all. Juan Rejón landed at the site of modern Las Palmas and dug in. He was immediately attacked by a force of 2000 under Doramas, guanarteme of the island's Telde kingdom. Rejón carried the day, but fell victim to internal intrigue by making an enemy of the spiritual head of the conquered territories, Canon Juan Bermúdez, accussing him of incompetence.

An investigator sent from Spain, Pedro de Algaba, sided with Bermúdez and conspired to have Rejón transported to Spain in chains. Rejón in turn convinced the authorities in Spain that he'd been badly treated and was given carte blanche to return to the Canaries to re-establish his control. One of his first acts was to have Algaba arrested and executed, and this act of vengeance proved his final undoing, as Queen Isabel believed the punishment unwarranted and had Rejón replaced by Pedro de Vera.

De Vera continued the campaign and had the good fortune to capture the island's other guanarteme, Tenesor Semidan (known as Don Fernando Guanarteme after his baptism), in an attack on Gáldar by sea. Tenesor Semidan was sent to Spain, converted to Christianity and returned in 1483 to convince his countrymen to give up the fight. This they did on 29 April, and de Vera subsequently suggested some might like to sign up for an assault on Tenerife. Duly embarked, de Vera committed the umpteenth act of treachery that had marked the long years of conquest: he packed them off to be sold as slaves in Spain. But the Canarios learnt of this and forced the ships transporting them to put in at Lanzarote.

After the frightful suppression of a revolt in La Gomera in 1488 (see the San Sebastián section in the chapter on La Gomera), de Vera was relieved of his post as Captain-General of the conquest.

The Final Campaigns

De Vera's successor was a Galician soldier of fortune, Alonso Fernández de Lugo, who in 1491 received a royal commission to conquer La Palma and Tenerife. He began in La Palma in November, and by May the following year had the island under control. This he achieved partly by negotiation, though the last mencey of La Palma, Tanausú, and his men, maintained resistance in the virtually impregnable crater of the Caldera de Taburiente. Only by enticing him out for talks on 3 May, and then ambushing him, could de Lugo defeat his last adversary on the island. For La Palma, the war was over.

Tenerife proved the toughest for the Spaniards to gain control. In May 1493, de Lugo landed in Tenerife, near the site of modern-day Santa Cruz, with 1000 infantry soldiers and a cavalry of 150, among them Guanches from Gran Canaria and La Gomera.

In the ensuing months the Spaniards fortified their positions and attempted talks with various of the nine menceys, managing to win over those of Güímar and Anaga. Bencomo, mencey of Tahoro and sworn enemy of the invaders, was sure of the support of at least three other menceys, while the remaining three wavered.

In spring of the following year, de Lugo sent a column westwards. This proved a disaster. Bencomo was waiting in ambush in the Barranco de Acentejo ravine, and there the Spanish force was decimated at a place now called La Matanza ('the slaughter') de Acentejo. The survivors beat a hasty retreat, and although foiling a Guanche assault on their positions, de Lugo thought better of the whole operation and left Tenerife.

By the end of the year he was back, and engaged in the second major battle of the campaign, at La Laguna on 14 November 1494. Here he had greater success, but the Guanches were far from defeated and de Lugo fell back to Santa Cruz.

The stalemate was broken by an unexpected ally. At the beginning of the new year a plague known as the *modorra* began to ravage the island. It seemed hardly to affect the Spaniards, but soon took a serious toll of the Guanches.

When de Lugo finally moved again from his base at Santa Cruz in December 1495, the mood of the islanders was subdued. On 25 December, 5000 Guanches under Bencomo were routed in the second battle of the Acentejo. The spot, only a few kilometres south of La Matanza, is still called La Victoria ('victory') today. By the following July, when de Lugo marched into the Valle de la Orotava to confront Bencomo's successor Bentor, the diseased and demoralised Guanches were in no state to resist. Bentor surrendered and the conquest was complete. Pockets of resistance took two years to mop up and Bentor, aghast at the loss of his realm, eventually committed suicide.

Four years after the fall of Granada and the reunification of Christian Spain, the

Catholic monarchs could now celebrate one of the country's first imperial exploits – the subjugation in only 94 years of a small Atlantic archipelago defended by Neolithic tribes. Even so, the Spaniards had some difficulty in fully controlling the Guanches. Many refused to settle in the towns established by the colonists, preferring to live their traditional lives out of reach of the authorities. Their agility and cunning in their own land would keep this proud minority a step ahead of the Spaniards for many years to come.

Nevertheless, the Guanches were destined to disappear; whilst open hostilities had ceased, the *conquistadores* continued shipping them as slaves to Spain – a practice that had enticed some of the Europeans here in the first place. Remaining Guanches were converted en masse to Christianity, taking on Christian names and the surnames of their new Spanish godfathers. Some of the slaves, themselves sooner or later brought to conversion, would be freed and permitted to return to the islands. Although the bulk of them were dispossessed of their land, they soon began to assimilate with the colonisers. Within a century their language had all but disappeared: except for a handful of words, all that comes down to us today are the many Guanche place names of the islands.

Economic See-Saw & Foreign Challenges

As the 16th century dawned, the prospects for the Canary Islands seemed quite rosy. Gran Canaria and Tenerife in particular attracted a steady stream of settlers from Spain, Portugal, France, Italy and even Britain. Each island had its own local authority, or *cabildo*, although increasingly they were overshadowed by the royal court of appeal, established in Las Palmas in 1526. Sugar cane had been introduced from the Portuguese island of Madeira, and soon sugar became the Canaries' main export. Until the mid-16th century the islands prospered.

The 'discovery' in 1492 of the New World by Columbus, who called in to the archipelago several times en route to the Americas, proved a mixed blessing. Whilst it brought much passing trade it also soon became clear that sugar could be more cheaply produced in the Americas. The local economy was really only saved by the growing export demand for wine produced mainly in Tenerife – *vino seco* (dry wine), what Shakespeare called Canary Sack, was much appreciated in Britain.

Poorer islands, especially Lanzarote and Fuerteventura, remained backwaters, their unfortunate inhabitants making a living from smuggling and piracy off the Moroccan coast – the latter activity part of a tit-for-tat game played out with the Moroccans for centuries.

Spain's control of the islands did not go completely unchallenged. Moroccan troops occupied Lanzarote in 1569 and again in 1586, but they were fairly quickly dispatched on each occasion. Sir Francis Drake engaged in some gunboat tactics off Las Palmas in 1595, but he too was seen off. A Dutch fleet tried to repeat the effort four years later, and managed to reduce the city to rubble.

The most spectacular success went to Admiral Robert Blake, one of Oliver Cromwell's three 'generals at sea'. In 1657, a year after war had broken out between England and Spain, Blake annihilated a Spanish treasure fleet (at the cost of only one ship) at Santa Cruz de Tenerife. British harassment culminated in 1797 with Admiral Horatio Nelson's attack on Santa Cruz. Sent there to intercept yet another treasure shipment, he not only failed to storm the port town, but lost his right arm in the fighting.

Island Rivalries

Within the Canary Islands, a bitter feud developed between Gran Canaria and Tenerife over supremacy of the archipelago. The fortunes of the two rested largely with their economic fate. As demand for Canaries' sugar fell and wine rose, Tenerife, with land much better suited to the vine, inevitably took the lead. As its exports grew, so too did its ports and overall trade turnover.

When the Canaries were declared a province of Spain in 1821, Santa Cruz de Tenerife was made the capital. Bickering between the two main islands remained heated, and Las Palmas frequently demanded the province be split in two. The idea was briefly but unsuccessfully put into practice in the 1840s.

Gran Canaria was in any case beginning to redress the economic imbalance. As wine in its turn began to drop off as a major revenue earner, cochineal production was introduced as an export commodity. At the same time, Sir Alfred Lewis Jones set up the Grand Canary Coaling Company in Las Palmas – the port was soon every bit as busy as that of Santa Cruz.

Gran Canaria's politicians continued to lobby for division of the region, and in 1911 managed to resurrect the old island cabildos. Santa Cruz's overall control of the archipelago was sapped by the restoration of local island governments.

In 1927, Madrid finally decided to split the Canaries into two provinces: Tenerife, La Gomera, La Palma and El Hierro in the west; Fuerteventura, Gran Canaria and Lanzarote in the east.

Flight to the Americas

The cochineal boom was followed by bust in the 1870s as chemical dyes came on to the market. So the Canary Islands turned to other raw export products: bananas, and to a lesser extent, tomatoes and potatoes.

Again, the boom-bust cycle upset all the

A Little Liberté in Tenerife

The French Revolution was not for the faint-hearted. When Jean-Baptiste Drouet, son of a postmaster in Sainte Menehould in Champagne, saw the fleeing carriage of King Louis XVI pull up on 21 June 1791, he got word to the revolutionary authorities who stopped the royal runaway in Varennes.

Drouet was elected a deputy of the Convention a year later and voted with those wanting to see the king put to death. The French had good reason to be wary of the British in those heady days, and Drouet advocated the hunting down and execution of every English man, woman and child resident in France, an idea that was left in abeyance. Captured in 1793 by the Austrians, he was back in action on the Council

of Five Hundred in 1795. Imprisoned for conspiracy a year later, he escaped to Tenerife.

In 1797, fighting in the defence of Santa Cruz against Admiral Horatio Nelson's landing attempts, he finally got the opportunity to kill a few Englishmen. A musket ball shattered Nelson's right elbow as he attempted to come ashore; he was rescued and shortly after had his ship's surgeon amputate his arm just below the shoulder.

Thereafter life in sunny Santa Cruz was pleasant, but for Drouet there was no place like home; he returned to France after Napoleon had established the empire.

A Brief & Bitter Exile

The feeling of some Canarios that perhaps they have more in common with Africa than Europe is perhaps not entirely spurious, although they'd prefer to be part of Spain than join, say, Morocco.

Back in 1895, the last of the proud Bantu warrior kings, Gungunhana, arrived in the Canaries a dispirited and broken man. Aged only 45, he had attempted to protect his kingdom of Gaza, in modern day Mozambique, by playing off the various European powers against one another. It worked for a while, but in the end he and his men were overwhelmed in battle by the Portuguese. He found asylum in the Canaries, but lived for only another year.

rosy calculations. WWI and the British sea blockade of the continent wrecked international trade and suddenly the banana seemed more like a lemon. This time Canarios voted with their feet, choosing to migrate to Latin America; emigrants shipped out to join their forbears in Cuba, Venezuela, Uruguay, Nicaragua, Mexico and Guatemala.

Civil War & Franco's Spain

The islands' economy picked up slowly after WWI, but more shocks were in store. In 1931, the second republic was declared in Madrid, heralding a period of hope ultimately dashed by chaos. As the left and right in mainland Spain became increasingly militant, fears of a coup grew. In March 1936, the government decided to 'transfer' General Franco, a veteran of Spain's wars in Morocco and beloved of the tough Spanish Foreign Legion, to the Canary Islands.

Suspicions that he was involved in a plot to overthrow the government were well founded, and when the pro-coup garrisons

of Melilla (Spanish North Africa) rose prematurely on 17 July, he was ready. Having seized control of the islands virtually without a struggle (the pro-Republican commander of the Las Palmas garrison died in mysterious circumstances on 14 July), Franco flew to Morocco on 19 July. Although there was virtually no fighting in the islands, the Nationalists wasted no time in rounding up anyone vaguely suspected of harbouring Republican sympathies.

Francoism thus came to the Canary Islands from the outset, but the war on the mainland lasted three years. The postwar economic misery of Spain was shared by the Canary Islands, and again many opted to emigrate. In the 1950s the situation was so desperate that 16,000 Canarios migrated clandestinely, mainly to Venezuela, even though by then that country had closed its doors to further immigration. A third of those who attempted to flee perished in the ocean crossings.

Tourism & 'Nationalism'

The Canary Islands' latest monoculture has proved the most astounding. When Franco decided to open up the doors of the country to northern European tourists – sun-starved and on tight budgets – the Canaries benefited as much as the mainland. Millions of holiday-makers now pour into the islands year-round.

Not everyone was satisfied with the suntan-lotion-led recovery. Always a fringe phenomenon, Canaries nationalism started to resurface in opposition to Franco. MPAIC, founded in 1963 by Antonio Cubillo to promote secession from Spain, embarked on a terrorist campaign in the late 1970s; Cubillo was expelled (he was later allowed to return).

In 1978, a new constitution was passed in Madrid with devolution as one of its central pillars. Thus the Canary Islands became a *comunidad autónoma* (autonomous region) in August 1982, but remained divided in two provinces.

The main force in Canary Islands politics since its regional election victory in 1995 has been the Coalición Canaria (CC). While not bent on independence from Spain (which would be unlikely), the CC nevertheless puts the interests of the islands before national considerations (see also the Government section below). Indeed, the 'nationalists', along with their Basque and Catalan counterparts on the mainland, were essential to the right-wing Partido Popular's (PP) accession to government in Madrid in March 1996. And they make their support conditional on consideration given to their wants. Disillusion with the Partido Socialista Obrero Español (PSOE), which was enveloped in a series of scandals in the 1990s, distrust of the PP and a general feeling that the islands are treated as a backwater by the big national parties may just keep the CC in the pilot's seat in the foreseeable future.

GEOGRAPHY

The Canary Islands, an archipelago of seven islands and six islets 112km from the Atlantic coast of North Africa, lie 1120km south-west of Spain.

The archipelago lies between the 28th and 29th parallels, and the seven main islands have a total area of 7447 sq km.

Their total area may not be great, but packed into them is just about every imaginable kind of landscape, from the long sandy beaches of Fuerteventura and dunes of Gran Canaria to the majestic Atlantic cliffs of Tenerife and mist-enveloped woods of La Gomera; from the almost Saharan desertscape of the easternmost islands to the rock-wall spectacle of the Caldera de Taburiente in La Palma. The highest mountain in all of Spain is the Teide peak (3718m) which dominates the whole island of Tenerife.

None of the islands have rivers, and lack of water remains a serious problem. Extracting funds from Madrid for waterconservation projects is always high on the list of priorities of Canarios politicians in the Spanish capital. Instead of rivers, webs of *barrancos* (ravines) cut their way from the mountainous interior of most of the

islands to the coast. Water flows along some, but others remain distressingly dry.

Lanzarote and Fuerteventura, the two most easterly islands, would be quite at home if attached to the nearby coast of continental Africa. Volcanic in origin – like the entire archipelago – their landscapes are otherworldly. Although both hilly, neither island is blessed with impressive mountains. The highest point is the Jandía peak (807m) in southern Fuerteventura. Long stretches of beach are Fuerteventura's greatest tourist drawcard. Lanzarote was last rocked by a volcanic eruption in 1824, but the 1730 blasts gave the island its present appearance. Eruptions are scary, but the lava can be good news for farmers, creating fertile ground where before there was nothing. Today Lanzarote still produces a wide range of crops including cereals, vegetables and wine grapes, grown mostly on volcanic hillsides. The Montañas del Fuego in the Parque Nacional de Timanfaya still give off plenty of heat, enough to fry an egg. And the island's fine black sand beaches are an attraction. North of the island are clustered five of the archipelago's six little islets (the other is Isla de Lobos, just off the northern tip of Fuerteventura), of which Isla Graciosa is the largest. It is home to a few hundred people.

Gran Canaria is roughly a circular-based volcanic pyramid, its northern half surprisingly green and fertile, and still to some extent dominated by the now eclipsed banana business. South of the peak of Pozo de las Nieves (1949m), the territory is more arid, reminiscent of Gran Canaria's eastern neighbours. Tourists coming to the southern sandy beaches and dunes have brought more wealth to the island than banana plantations could ever have done. For the variety of its geography, flora and climate, the island is often dubbed a 'continent in miniature'.

Gran Canaria's big brother, at least in terms of size, is Tenerife, the last redoubt of the Guanches and every bit as much a 'mini-continent'. Almost two-thirds of the island is made up of the rugged slopes of the volcanic mountain peak and crater Teide (3718m). A further string of mountains, the Anaga range, spreads to the north-east. The only real lowlands are right in the north around La Laguna and parts of the coast. The staggering cliffs of the north coast are occasionally lashed by Atlantic rain squalls, arrested by the mountains in such a way that the south-western and south-eastern coasts present a more serene weather picture.

The remaining western islands have much in common with one another. Better supplied with spring and/or rain water, they are green and ringed by rocky, ocean-battered coastlines. La Palma is dominated by the yawning funnel known as the Caldera de Taburiente, whose highest peak is the Roque de los Muchachos (2426m). The centre of La Gomera's high *meseta* (plateau) is covered by a UNESCO-listed laurel forest – the Parque Nacional de Garajonay. El Hierro, the tiniest of the Canary Islands, is mountainous (the highest peak is Malpaso at 1501m) with, again, a coastline that seems designed as a fortress.

GEOLOGY

The Canary Islands are little more than the tips of a vast volcanic mountain range that lies below the Atlantic. They have this in common with other Atlantic islands like Madeira, the Azores and Cape Verde islands. Viewed this way, the highest peak in the Canaries, Tenerife's Teide, is about a 7000m climb from the Atlantic floor!

The volcanoes were thrown up millions of years ago, about the time the Atlas Mountains were formed in North Africa. Behind this event was the movement of great slabs of the Earth's crust, known as tectonic plates. Basically, as the plate on which Africa rests pulled away from that which bears South America and pushed up against Europe, the earth crumpled and folded along what is now a series of mountain ranges, including the Atlas Range in Morocco. At the same time, great blocks of rock were thrown up within the Atlantic along much the same latitudes, and up

through the cracks in and around these blocks flowed streams of liquid rock. The power of the forces at work below the crust, contributing to the rise of the volcanic islands of the Atlantic, is difficult to fathom.

Nowadays in the Canary Islands you can best get a feel for the rumblings below the surface on Lanzarote, where the Montañas del Fuego still bubble with vigour. Of the remaining islands, not an eruptive peep has been heard from Fuerteventura, Gran Canaria, La Gomera or El Hierro for centuries. Tenerife's last display was a fairly innocuous affair in 1909, and La Palma hosted the most recent spectacle, a fiery outburst in 1971. Lanzarote's last eruptions took place in 1824.

Of course, there is plenty of activity across the floor of the Atlantic Ocean, and many peaks lie out of sight below the surface. Occasionally new volcanic islands are puffed up into the light of day, but they are generally little more than feeble mounds of loose ash and are quickly washed away.

For centuries the angry Teide mountain loomed menacingly in the imagination of the Guanches, and later their Spanish overlords. A rumbling god of the underworld was thought to live in its bowels, occasionally giving vent to extreme displeasure by belching up his molten bile from the deepest infernal chambers of the mountain. Teide is indeed an impressive work of nature. Not only is it Spain's highest peak, it is the third largest volcano in the world, after Hawaii's Mauna Loa and Mauna Kea.

All three are what is known as shield volcanoes. They are characterised by their enormous size and rise up in a broad cone at an angle of rarely more than 6° to the summit which contains a steep-walled crater with a flat base. Teide, like the Hawaiian volcanoes, is principally of basalt.

Sometimes such volcanoes, or similar ones known as stratovolcanoes, really blow their tops. Massive explosions cause the whole summit to cave in, emptying the vent, spewing forth the upper levels of the magma chamber and so blasting away an

Volcanic Origins

Volcanoes are formed by magma (molten rock), which comes from the earth's mantle, beneath the crust. There are various theories about the origins and composition of magma: hot, fluid and largely made of basalt, it cannot reach the earth's surface except by way of fissures or cracks. The opening of such a vent brings a drop in temperature and lessens the viscosity of the magma, after which it is more fluid and has less trouble making its ascent; in doing so, it helps to decrease the surrounding pressure, leading to a release of gaseous material (from which the forming magmatic chamber will derive much of its eruptive force). Dropping pressure leads to a fall in the magma's specific gravity, which, when it falls below that of surrounding rocks, gets an added upward push.

Magma also has a habit of working sideways, squeezing through strata of different materials, effectively making use of a lateral fault. This lateral progression sometimes leads to the creation of so-called volcanic tubes or tunnels. The liquid rock would push its way through weakened rock heated to extraordinary temperatures. When the lava flow passed on, the rock walls were still hot enough to be molten, and bits would drip off onto the lava floor before cooling. The best example you are likely to see of this is at the Cueva de los Verdes in northern Lanzarote.

The magma chambers thus formed become the launch site of subsequent eruptions. Your average volcano evolves from an existing one ejecting highly basaltic magma, in often not so violent effusions, from cracks and other vents to one with changed, more acidic magma, tending towards more violent and spectacularly explosive eruptions.

Among the materials vomited up by volcanoes over the centuries is nephelinite, a silica-poor lava, exclusively from the Tertiary era, containing nepheline and pyroxene. It is usually crystalline and, although abundant in the Canary Islands (along with the Azores and Cape Verde), is a comparatively rare rock. It contains a host of minerals, including titanium-rich augite.

Volcanic landscape of Lanzarote

enormous crater. The result is known as a caldera, within which it is not unusual for new cones to emerge, creating volcanoes within volcanoes. There are several impressive calderas on Gran Canaria, most notably the Pico de Bandama and the Caldera de Tejeda, the latter formed five million years ago. Oddly enough, the massive Caldera de Taburiente on La Palma does *not* belong to this group of geological phenomena (although it was long thought to, and the generic term 'caldera' was first coined in the 19th century by a German geologist).

Turning back to Teide for a moment, the Las Cañadas depression was similarly formed by the combination of the emptying of a high level magma chamber and the resultant collapse and lateral movement of the summit.

Although seemingly quieter than Italy's Vesuvius, Etna and Stromboli, all of which still have it in them to cause quite a fright, Teide is by no means finished. Above Etna, in Sicily, there is a constant cloud of steam, pushed up through a fairly narrow vent (formed by lava build up and minor belches over the centuries). Although not as obvious, wisps of hot air can be seen around the peak of Teide too. Where the lava is fairly fluid in such cases, steam pressure can build up to the point of ejecting lava and/or ash in an eruption through the narrow vent. If sufficient pressure builds up, that vent can simply be blown off.

When they do erupt, they belch out all sorts of things: ash, cinders, *lapilli* (small, round bombs of lava) and great streams of molten rock. Volcanic eruptions, however, don't just come through one central crater. Often subsidiary craters form around the main cone, or lava and other material crack fissures into the mountain and escape that way.

All the Canary Islands are made of volcanic rock, dating at least from the Tertiary era, that is anything up to 65 million years ago (great rock blocks below the surface of Fuerteventura and Lanzarote have been estimated at up to 40 million years old). Basalt is the common denominator through-out the islands – it forms much of their bedrock and the mighty walls of the Caldera de Taburiente on La Palma, for instance, are made of basalt. It is a material occasionally used in the public buildings of the islands. Other minerals found include iron, sulphur and copper.

The Canary Islands are far from having exhausted their potential for fireworks. Geologists predict that the islands of La Palma and Tenerife are the most likely candidates for future eruptions.

CLIMATE

The Canary Islands enjoy a particularly benign climate. Indeed, it seems to be endlessly spring, with mean temperatures ranging from 18°C in the winter to about 24°C in summer. Daily highs can easily reach the mid-30s°C in summer. Even on a hot day at the beach, it can be pleasantly cool higher up, and the snow atop the Teide mount is a clear enough sign that, in winter at any rate, some warm clothing is essential. This is especially the case if you intend doing any hiking in the mountains.

With the exception of Lanzarote and Fuerteventura, the northern side of the islands is sub-tropical, while the south (including the first two mentioned isles) is generally drier, more arid and marginally hotter.

Rainfall is slight (rarely more than 250mm annually, except on parts of the windblown northern coasts, where it can be as much as 750mm), and what there is tends to fall mainly on the north side of the more mountainous islands. Rain and cloud are carried in off the Atlantic by trade winds (*alisios*) blowing in from the north-east and prevented from reaching across all the islands by the mountains and hills. Higher alisios from the north-west – predominantly dry trade winds which caress all the islands – tend to cap the north-easterlies, adding to the pressure which keeps them embracing the hills in a mantle of fog.

Highest rainfall occurs in winter (from November to February), when it is feasible to be stretched out on a sun-drenched beach

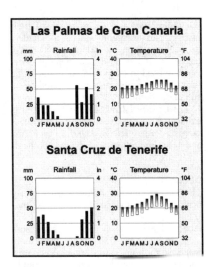

Las Palmas de Gran Canaria

Santa Cruz de Tenerife

In the Canaries bronchitis sometimes does well ... Rheumatism, neuralgia, Bright's disease, gout, scrofula, venereal and other diseases find the climate most suitable. The first and second stages of consumption show material improvement ... If strength permits, excursions should frequently be made to the hills or to the mountains, the change of air, even if only for a few hours, being of great advantage. All hotels will provide luncheon in a basket.

Because all the islands drop away fairly steeply into the ocean, the Gulf Stream moves easily from the north-west through deep channels around and between the islands, although with less force in the eastern islands. Counteracting the warmth of the stream is the chillier Canary Current, which embraces the islands as it flows by the African coast towards Senegal, before looping west into the mid-Atlantic. This keeps the average water temperature to a little below what might be expected in these latitudes – 18°C in winter and 22°C in summer. The further west you go, the warmer the water gets.

in the south of Tenerife or Gran Canaria, while to the north it's grey, cool and maybe wet! La Palma in the west is the most blessed of the Canaries when it comes to rain, while the bare and comparatively flat Lanzarote and Fuerteventura receive hardly a drop. This is not so much, as is often assumed, because they lie closest to Saharan Africa, but more due to their lack of mountains.

Occasionally, especially in summer, a broiling *sirocco* (the hot wind off Africa) howls in from the Sahara, bearing swathes of dust and desert sand. Locally known as the *kalima*, it turns the day into twilight, leaving the sun a dull, ineffectual disk in a grey pall. The ocean is agitated and at the end of the day you can feel the grime plastered into your skin. It's a case of, if you won't go to the Sahara, the Sahara comes to you. It's at its worst in the most eastern islands.

This is the exception rather than the rule and in fact the islands have long had a reputation as a place for health cures. A Samler Brown, in his *Madeira, Canary Islands & Azores*, first published in 1889, noted on the subject of the islands' invigorating clime:

ECOLOGY & ENVIRONMENT

As in mainland Spain, the 1960s saw the first waves of mass sea-and-sun tourism crash over the tranquil shores of the Canary Islands. As Franco and his cohorts rubbed their hands in anticipation of filling up the state coffers with easy tourist dollars, no one much gave any thought to what impact the tourists, or the mushrooming coastal resorts, might have on the environment.

Tourism, Construction & Pollution

The near unregulated building and expansion of resorts well into the 1980s has created some monumental eyesores, particularly on the southern side of Tenerife and Gran Canaria. Great scabs of holiday villas, hotels and condominiums have spread across much of the two islands' southern coasts. And the problem is not restricted to the resorts – hasty cement extensions of towns and villages mean that even the interior of the islands is being increasingly spoiled by property developers and speculators. Politics and influence-peddling are often the unsavoury background to a frequent tendency to turn a blind eye to these activities. For most foreign visitors, the ugliness is offset by the chance to party in the sun in winter, when most of Europe lies huddled beneath its thick, cold, grey mantle.

The massive influx of visitors to the islands over recent decades has brought or exacerbated other problems. Littering of beaches, dunes and other areas of natural beauty, both by outsiders and locals, remains a burning issue. Occasionally ecological societies organise massive clean-ups of rubbish along beaches and the like – worthy gestures but equally damning evidence of the extent to which the problem persists.

For the islands' administrators, it's a conundrum. Tourism has come to represent an essential pillar of the Canaries' economy, which quite simply cannot do without it. They argue that profits from the tourist trade are ploughed back into the community. However, this is still fairly haphazard, and there have long been calls for more regional planning.

Some of the damage done over the years, especially to the coastline, may not be reversible, but the regional government is considering an *ecotasa* (eco-tax) to be levied on visitors and channelled into infrastructure and environmental protection.

Water

One of the islands' greatest and most persistent problems is water, or rather the lack of it. Limited rainfall and fresh water springs have always helped restrict agriculture in the islands, and it is a commodity still in short supply.

Desalination appears to be the way forward for the Canaries, which already accounts for two per cent of the world's desalinated water production. Pretty much all the drinking water on Lanzarote and Fuerteventura is desalinated sea water.

In summer, the corollary of the perennial water problem is the forest fire. With almost clockwork regularity, hundreds of hectares of forest are ravaged every summer on all the islands except the already bare Lanzarote and Fuerteventura.

Nature Reserves

Only since the late 1980s have real steps been taken to protect the islands' natural diversity. The 1987 law on the Conservación de Espacios Naturales (preservation of nature areas) delimited 42% of territory earmarked for some form of protection. The law passed in 1994 from being a mere declaration of intent to an enforceable regulatory mechanism. The islands' four national parks, for instance, are largely protected from human interference by rules banning visitors from free camping or straying from defined walking paths (see the following National Parks section). You can contribute to keeping all parks and the countryside clean by obeying the rules on where you are permitted to hike and keeping all your trash with you – what you take in you should also take out.

Whales & Dolphins

Several species of whale and dolphin used to think the Canary Islands such a friendly place that they'd often hang about just 20m off the coast. But then the islands began to fill with curious visitors who soon started heading out to sea to get a closer look. The more they came, the greater the distance these magnificent mammals put between themselves and the islands. In spite of it all, a colony of pilot whales (*ballenas pilotos*) is based off the south coast of Tenerife. As many as 26 whale and dolphin species (a third of the world total) have been observed off the Canary Islands. The most common of them, apart from the pilot whales, are sperm whales (*cachalotes*) and bottlenose dolphins (*tursiones*).

Whale observation is a lucrative business, and often aggressive, with boatloads of tourists jostling for position around schools of these animals – after all, for many people the Canaries present a unique opportunity to see whales in their natural habitat.

In 1996 a new law aiming to regulate observation of sea mammals went into effect. The idea is to limit the number of boats heading out to follow schools at any one time and curb unpleasant practices such as using sonar and other devices to attract whales' attention. Four small patrol boats attempt to keep a watchful eye on these activities. There has been much talk of establishing a single marine centre from which all excursions would be organised. It seems extraordinary that, if there is real concern about leaving these animals as undisturbed as possible, such a measure has not already been taken.

There is nothing intrinsically wrong with joining excursions to go whale-watching. Where possible, try to join an outfit that respects the regulations. You could also contact the Whales & Tales organisation in Tenerife (see Environmental Organisations below).

Should you happen, by the way, to come across a beached whale or dolphin, call ☎ 922 25 00 02 or 922 25 63 44.

Environmental Organisations

The islands are swarming with environmental action groups, some more active than others. Most are members of the Federación Ecologista Canaria Ben-Magec (☎/fax 928 31 10 04), Calle de las Botas 5, Las Palmas. Some of the individual groups (the word 'Apdo' followed by number indicates a post box number only) you'll find on the islands include:

Gran Canaria
  ASCAN (Asociación Canaria de Amigos de la Naturaleza) – Calle del Presidente Alvear 50, 2, Las Palmas (☎ 928 27 36 44)
Fuerteventura
  ASCAN – Calle de Juan Tadeo 6, Puerto del Rosario (☎ 928 85 20 71)
Lanzarote
  Asociación Cultural y Ecologista El Guincho – Apdo 365, 35580 Arrecife, (☎ 928 81 54 32; fax 928 81 54 30)
Tenerife
  ATAN (Asociación Tinerfeña de Amigos de la Naturaleza) – Apdo 1015, 38080 Santa Cruz de Tenerife (☎/fax 922 27 93 92)
  ADES (Asociación para la Defensa del Surf) – Calle de Imeldo Seris 17, Santa Cruz de Tenerife
  Whales & Tales – Apdo 7, 38080 La Laguna (☎ 922 82 05 59). This German-founded group works to protect whales and other sealife in the Canaries, as well as organising whale observation trips and ecologically sensitive excursions on various islands.
La Palma
  Asamblea Irichen – Apdo 170, 38700, Santa Cruz de la Palma (☎ 922 44 06 62)
La Gomera
  Asociación Ecologista y Cultural Guarapo – Apdo 74, 38800 San Sebastián de la Gomera (☎ 922 80 07 10)
El Hierro
  ADNIH (Asociación para la Defensa de la Naturaleza e Identidad del Hierro) – Calle de la Ola 7, La Restinga (☎ 922 55 82 19)

FLORA & FAUNA
Flora

A combination of rich volcanic soil and the varied altitude of the more mountainous islands supports a surprisingly rich diversity of plant life, both indigenous and imported. Despite their small area, the Canary Islands are home to about 2000 species, about half of them unique to the islands. The only brake on what might otherwise be a still more florid display in this largely sub-tropical environment is the distinct shortage of water. However, budding botanists will have a field day here (see also the Books section of the Facts for the Visitor chapter for some suggested reading).

Up until an altitude of about 400m, the land is home to plants that thrive in hot and arid conditions. Where farmland has been irrigated, you'll find bananas, oranges, coffee, sugar cane, dates and tobacco. In the towns, bougainvillea, hibiscus, acacia, geraniums, marigolds and carnations all contribute to the bright and colourful feast for the eyes. Of the more exotic specimens, the strelitzia, with its enchanting blue, white and orange blossoms, stands out. Colourful though they are, these exotics have all been introduced to the islands. The dry and uncultivated scrublands near the coast, the so-called tabaibales, host various indigenous plants.

At elevations of around 700m, the Canaries' climate is more typical of the Mediterranean, encouraging crops like cereals, potatoes and grapes. Where the crops give way, there are stands of eucalyptus and cork that take up the baton. Mimosa, broom, honeysuckle and laburnums are also common sights.

Higher still the air is cooler and common plants and trees include holly, myrtle and

---

The Dragon Tree

Among the more curious trees you will see in the Canary Islands is the drago (dragon tree; *Dracaena draco*), which can reach 18m in height and live for centuries. The sap, predictably known as dragon's blood, was long used in various medicines. The tree is one of a family of up to 80 species (*Dracaena*) which survived the Ice age in tropical and sub-tropical zones of the Old World, and is one of the last representatives of Tertiary era flora.

---

the laurel. The best place to explore forest land is in La Gomera's Parque Nacional de Garajonay, host to one of the world's last remaining Tertiary era forests and declared a UNESCO world heritage site. Known as laurisilva, it is made up of lichen-covered laurels, holly, linden and heather, often swathed in swirling bands of mist.

Up until 2000m the most common tree you're likely to encounter is the Canary pine, which manages to set down roots on impossibly steep slopes which would defeat most other species. It is a particularly hardy tree, whose fire-resistant timber makes fine construction material. The highest points of Tenerife and La Palma are too harsh for any but the hardiest of Alpine vegetation.

Up in the great volcanic basin of the Parque Nacional de las Cañadas del Teide are some outstanding flowers. Apart from the feisty high-altitude Teide violet, one of the floral symbols of the Canaries is the *tajinaste*, or Teide viper's bugloss. Every two years in spring it sprouts an extraordinary conical spike of striking red blooms, not unlike an ear of corn in appearance.

Although much of the vegetation is common across the islands, there are some marked differences. Fuerteventura, Lanzarote and the south of Gran Canaria distinguish themselves from the rest with their semidesert flora, where saltbush, Canary palms and other small shrubs dominate. Concentrated in a couple of spots – the cliffs of Famara in Lanzarote and Jandía in Fuerteventura – you will find more abundant flora. This includes the rare cardón de Jandía, a cactus-like plant, several species of daisy and all sorts of odd cliff plants unique to these islands.

Fauna

The Fortunate Isles are not overly endowed with indigenous animal life. Apart from introduced animals (such as rabbits, mice, North African hedgehogs and domesticated animals), about the most interesting land-going beasty is a rather large (up to 1m long), ancient and ugly lizard (lagarto del Salmor) found only on the island of El

Not Just a Pretty Frond

The palm tree is as common in the Canary Islands as it is in North Africa and the Middle East. Apart from the native Canary palm (*Phoenix canariensis*), the islands boast a fair population of date palms. The latter were largely imported after the Spanish conquest – La Gomera, for instance, had none until Hernán Peraza, the island's ill-fated governor, decided to import some from North Africa. A third hybrid between the two has also taken firm root in the islands.

Even when not cultivated for dates, this graceful tree, which grows more than 20m tall, provides fine, sturdy timber. The ribs of its leaves can be used in furniture, while the individual leaf strands are handy for basketware. The base of the leaves was traditionally used for fuel, while the fruit stalks and fibre could be used to make rope and other packing material. Palm leaves also come in handy for celebrating the Christian feast of Palm Sunday and the Jewish Feast of Tabernacles.

And the palms without dates can still provide sustenance. The Gomeros, for example, extract what they call palm honey from the *guarapo*, or sap, of the palm, boiling it into a dark, sticky and sweet liquid.

Spanish missionaries thought the palms so handy that they took samples of the Canarian version to Latin America in the 18th century.

Hierro. Its ancestors are thought to have grown as large as 9m, but until recently it was deemed extinct. There may be as many as 200 in circulation, but you'd be lucky to catch a glimpse of one in the wild.

A couple of bat species send up the occasional night patrol – of the islands' bats, only the *orejudo canario* is endemic.

Reaching for the sky are more than 200 species of bird, although many of these are visitors rather than home-grown. Among indigenous birds are the canary (those in the wild are a muck-brown colour, not the sunny yellow colour of their domesticated cousins), and a couple of types of large pigeon, the *rabiche* and *turqué*. Common throughout the islands are quails, crows, partridges, sparrows, blackbirds, warblers, blue tits, chaffinches, kestrels, various types of owl and green finches.

Several species are seen only in Lanzarote and Fuerteventura. The *hubara* bustard is one, as is the black oyster-catcher.

The odd eagle or vulture can also be seen. One to look out for is the *hoopoo*, whose black-and-white wing patterns, curved beak and striking crest are hard to miss.

See also Whales & Dolphins in the preceding Ecology and Environment section.

Marine Life

The waters around the Canary Islands host 350 species of fish, five of them known only here, and about 600 species of algae.

The famous Monk Seals no longer hang about Lanzarote and Fuerteventura – the nearest colonies are in Mauritania – but there is talk of attempting to reintroduce them to the archipelago. Out at sea, several species of whale and dolphin can occasionally be spotted cruising about, and there is no shortage of organised trips for this purpose (see also Whales & Dolphins in preceding Ecology & Environment section).

There are dive centres on all the islands – see the Activities section in the Facts for the Visitor chapter.

National Parks & Other Reserves

With 42% of their territory falling under one of eight categories of parkland, the Canary Islands are one of the most extensively protected territories in all of Europe – at least in theory.

At the top of the tree are the four *parques nacionales*, administered at a state level from Madrid through ICONA (Instituto Nacional para la Conservación de la Naturaleza). The Parque Nacional de las Cañadas del Teide has as its centrepiece Spain's highest mountain, the volcanic peak of the Teide; the Parque Nacional de Garajonay in La Gomera is a splendid rainforest relic from the Tertiary era; for active volcanic activity visitors head for the Montañas del Fuego in the Parque Nacional de Timanfaya on Lanzarote; and the enormous eroded-rock cauldron at the heart of La Palma's Parque Nacional de la Caldera de Taburiente encloses another world.

Beyond the national parks, the responsibility for the administration and protection of parks and other natural areas of interest rests with Spain's regional governments. A 1994 regional law identifies seven other divisions of territory worthy of protection in the Canary Islands. Of these, the *parques*

naturales form the second and most extensive tier. They generally betray a greater level of human intrusion (villages, farms, roads etc) than the *parques nacionales*, making them ineligible for consideration as national parks by international criteria.

The remaining six categories are: *parques rurales*; *reservas naturales integrales*; *reservas naturales especiales*; *monumentos naturales*; *paisajes protegidos*; and *sitios de interés científico*.

GOVERNMENT & POLITICS

Even before the Canary Islands were declared a single province of Spain in 1821, competition for primacy between the two main islands, Tenerife and Gran Canaria, had long been intense. The election of Santa Cruz as the provincial capital infuriated

Nice Dog, Good Dog

If you come across a solid looking dog with a big head and stern gaze, you are probably getting to know the Canary Dog, known in Spanish as the *presa canario*. This beasty is right up there with the Pit Bull as a tenacious guard dog, loyal and chummy with its human owners but rarely well disposed to outsiders.

Also known as the *verdino* (from a slightly greenish tint in its colouring), opinion is divided on the dog's origins. Probably introduced to the islands in the wake of the conquest in the 15th century, and subsequently mixed with other breeds, the Canary Dog has been used for centuries in the islands to guard farms and cattle. When it comes to stopping human intruders in their tracks, none is so full of fight as this dog. It is prized by owners for its fearlessness and loyalty.

One can only speculate about the dogs mentioned in Pliny's description of ancient King Juba's expedition to the islands in 40 BC. They too were said to be exceptionally robust. There are those who are convinced that the verdino's ancestors were indeed present in the islands 2000 years ago. But as usual, the accounts are conflicting. Some academics maintain that the conquistadors were none too taken with these animals when they arrived in the 15th century and eventually set about having the majority of them destroyed, considering them wild and dangerous. Other accounts suggest that the Spaniards found no such animals on their arrival, and hence later introduced their own. Whatever the truth, the Canary Dog is prized now as a local island breed, a living canine symbol of the 'differentness' of the Canary Islands.

politicians and other worthies in Las Palmas, the main city on Gran Canaria, and marked the beginning of a long fight to have the province split in two. That idea was tried and shelved in the 1840s, and it only became reality in 1927. Lanzarote, Fuerteventura and Gran Canaria formed one province, with Las Palmas as capital, while Tenerife, La Palma, La Gomera and El Hierro were grouped under the leadership of Santa Cruz de Tenerife.

The historic electoral victory of the socialists in Madrid in 1982 was accompanied by the declaration of the Canary Islands as a *comunidad autónoma*, one of 17 autonomous regions across Spain. The region's flag is a yellow, blue and white tricolour – to which the few militant *independentistas* add seven stars to represent the islands. The provincial division remains intact, as does the bitter rivalry between the two. So much so that the regional government has offices in both provincial capitals, which alternate as lead city of the region every four years, to coincide with regional elections. All citizens over the age of 18 are entitled to vote.

Article 148 of the national constitution grants considerable power to the regional government, which covers areas ranging from agriculture through transport and tourism to health and local policing. The comunidad raises its own taxes, topped up by contributions from the central state's coffers. In the case of the Canary Islands, a special deal on investment and taxes has to be negotiated with the European Union every few years. The Canary Islands government, usually with Madrid's support, argues that their geographical position creates certain disadvantages with respect to the rest of the Union, and so requires compensation in the form of its exceptional status. So far this has not caused a problem.

To the ordinary Canarios the most important level of government is the *cabildos* (individual island administrations), which were resurrected in 1912 and are directly responsible for each of the islands. The islands are further subdivided into town and district municipalities, or *municipios*. As can be imagined, these five tiers of government inevitably lead to some bureaucratic doubling up.

After Franco's death, the Partido Socialista Obrero Español (PSOE) rose to become the strongest national party in the Canary Islands, while the right-wing Partido Popular (PP) tended to run a distant second. There was no shortage of local parties fighting for scraps of the electorate, but most struggled through the 1980s. Occasionally, however, one or other grouping managed to swing enough votes to go into coalition with the major parties.

Since the early 1990s, these splintered forces have been able to bury their assorted hatchets (among them the age-old rivalry between Gran Canaria and Tenerife politicians) and form what is today the most powerful political force in the islands, the Coalición Canaria (CC), which has also gone by the name of Coalición Nacionalista. Its concern is first and foremost to improve the deal the Canaries get from Madrid.

In the 1995 regional elections the CC became the single biggest force in the Canaries with 33% of the vote. The PP came in on 31% and the PSOE, by now reeling under a spate of scandals, on 23%.

In the 1996 general Spanish elections which saw the demise of the socialists in Madrid and the victory of the PP, the CC was one of three 'nationalist' parties (the others were the Basque PNV and Catalonian CiU parties) to profit from the closeness of the vote, promising their support for the new prime minister José María Aznar only in return for concessions to their demands for greater autonomy.

The CC's platform in 1996 was wide-ranging, and among their high-minded objectives were the control of crime and drug abuse, elimination of waiting lists in hospitals, improved finances for education and a host of other socially laudable goals. From Madrid they demanded cheaper transport between the islands and the mainland

CRUZ

Top Left: Doorway, Ermita de San Sebastián de la Gomera
Top Right: Detail, Casa de Colón in Plaza del Pilar Nuevo, Las Palmas de Gran Canaria
Bottom Left: 16th-century façades, Avenida Marítima, Santa Cruz de la Palma
Bottom Right: Calle de la Cruz, Teguise, Isla de Lanzarote

DAMIEN SIMONIS

DAMIEN SIMONIS

DAMIEN SIMONIS

DAMIEN SIMONIS

DAMIEN SIMONIS

Tiling
Left: Tiled seats and fountain, Plaza del 25 de Julio, Santa Cruz de Tenerife
Top Right: Sign, Plaza de la Constitución, Santa Cruz de la Palma
Bottom Right: Sign for barrio, Puerto del Rosario, Isla de Fuerteventura

and complete local control of ports, airports, public utilities and other enterprises.

In the Canaries themselves, the situation in Madrid is exactly reversed. For there the CC governs with support from the PP. The regional premier, Manuel Hermoso, and Aznar play an interesting game. The socialists have lately tried to convince the local PP to join them in dumping Hermoso. Such a move would see the CC withdraw support from Aznar in Madrid and so in turn threaten his position. All of this obliges Aznar to try to reign in the Canaries PP in order to keep his own political skin intact!

In late 1997, however, Aznar dealt something of a blow to the Canary Islands by agreeing to a slightly watered-down agreement with Brussels on the REF (Régimen Económico y Fiscal). This regulates the islands' exceptional status within the EU, and time limits were imposed on certain kinds of investment aid. Grumble as some of the Canarios might, there was little they could do – Hermoso's opponents, especially the PSOE, were doing everything they could to depict the agreement as a complete failure of the regional government and an added reason for dumping Hermoso.

All the laments aside, it was estimated that 70 billion ptas (about US$460m) in aid would arrive in the Canaries from EU coffers in the course of 1998.

ECONOMY

The fortunes of the Canary Islands have, since the time of their conquest by Spain in the 15th century, always been precarious. An obligatory stop on the old Spanish trade routes to South America, the islands' economy was based on cash crops. Over the centuries sugar, wine grapes, cochineal (used in the production of natural dyes) and bananas were the backbone of the islands' export economy. Predictably, this made the islands and their often struggling inhabitants prey to the vagaries of world markets and boom-bust cycles. Crisis often triggered waves of emigration, mostly to Latin America.

Agriculture and light industry respectively account for about 4.5% and 9% of the islands' gross domestic product, while the services sector (of which a large chunk is tourism-related) represents a whopping 80% of the total. With in excess of 7.5 million tourists (staying on average 10 days) flooding into the islands every year it is easy to identify the islands' latest cash crop. Indeed, in 1997 the islands smashed all their own records with 8.4 million visitors! Exporting bananas and tomatoes is a poor earner by comparison. Tourism is such a pillar in the islands' economy that one rather wild local estimate claimed the Canaries account for 25% of worldwide tourism (a trifle hard to believe, but it gets the point across!). Aside from the big oil refinery at Santa Cruz de Tenerife and some food processing, secondary industry is barely in evidence.

The islands' exports are fairly limited. Of the total annual income of less than US$1m from products sold abroad, a little over half comes from fruit and vegetables, with seafood coming in a distant second, representing a sixth of the income. A great deal of the islanders' (and tourists') needs are met by imports worth US$6m annually.

Special tax breaks and regulations are aimed to act as a magnet to business and residents in the islands. There are all sorts of tax discounts and the like for businesses (local or foreign) aiming to operate here, while low indirect taxation acts as an incentive to residents to remain in the islands. While IVA (*impuesto sobre el valor añadido*), the Spanish version of VAT, can run up to 16% in mainland Spain, the Canary Island equivalent, IGIC (*impuesto general indirecto canario*), is a flat 4.5%, compensating for the higher base cost of imported goods and generally resulting in cheaper retail shopping than on the mainland. Petrol, alcohol and tobacco are subject to special low taxes too.

All of this may or may not have a positive effect on the islands' economy, and the local statisticians can point to a per capita GDP only a little way behind the Spanish national average. But average wages in the islands are lower than on the mainland (the most recent statistics put the average mainland wage at 217,000 ptas a month and 182,000 ptas a month in the Canary Islands) and officially 16.5% of the islands' workforce is jobless, higher than the national average of 13%. Keep in mind that the official figures can be deceptive. Unofficially the jobless rate in the islands has been estimated as high as 27%, compared with a national rate of about 24%. Also worth remembering is that, by some estimates, the Spanish minimum wage is the lowest in the European Union.

POPULATION & PEOPLE

The total resident population of the Canary Islands at the turn of the century was 364,414, and now stands at 1,605,400, growing at the slow rate of 1.15% annually. For every Canary Islander, or Canario, five foreigners visit the islands each year!

The bulk of the population is concentrated in the two main islands, Gran Canaria (714,139) and Tenerife (665,562). Of the remaining islands, the population ranges from 81,521 in La Palma to just 8338 in El Hierro. With an average of 215 people per sq km, the Canary Islands are considerably more crowded than mainland Spain, where there are only 77 people per sq km.

Only a fraction of all the people who visit the Canaries decide to stay for good. At the last count, 54,000 foreigners called the Canaries home. The Germans (12,000) and Brits (11,000) were by far out in front. Of the 7700 from the Americas, many are descendants of Canarios who migrated there generations ago. Venezuelans (2000) and Cubans (1200) are the best represented, and both countries were favoured destinations for migrants from the often less than fortunate isles.

Although the term Canario has come to designate all the islanders, it once referred more strictly to the people of Gran Canaria alone (now more often as not referred to as Grancanarios or Canariones). The people of Tenerife are Tinerfeños; those of Lanzarote are Lanzaroteños; Fuerteventura Majoreros

(from the Guanche name for much of the island, Maxorata), La Gomera Gomeros; La Palma Palmareños; and El Hierro Herreños.

Most of the locals have the classic Mediterranean looks of the Spaniards (with perhaps a little Berber mixed in) – dark hair, flashing eyes and olive complexion. But talk to them for a while and you might not find they think of themselves so much as Spaniards.

The godos (Goths), as the Canarios refer to Spaniards from the peninsula, are not automatically thought of as being part of the family, and while mainlanders like to joke about the Canarios being African, there are some in the islands who actually prefer to think of themselves as African (at least insofar as this distinguishes them from the rest of Spain). After all, they are a lot closer to Africa than Spain.

EDUCATION

Education is free and obligatory in the Canary Islands from the age of six to 14. About a third of pupils attend Catholic schools, which are often subsidised by the state. Upon matriculation, students must also sit entrance exams for university. Students study for six years or so, taking out qualifications such as the diplomada after three years and the licenciado after another two or three years' study.

There are 33 universities across Spain, but until recently there was only one in the Canary Islands, at La Laguna in Tenerife. Many Canarios find themselves heading for the mainland to pursue their preferred courses. Argument raged for years about whether a second university should be established in Gran Canaria. Long considered by Tinerfeños as an extravagant doubling up of La Laguna, which started as a modest outpost of learning in 1701, the vocation-oriented Universidad de Las Palmas de Gran Canaria was finally set up in 1989.

ARTS
Painting
Guanche Cave Art The Guanches left behind cave paintings in various parts of the

islands, particularly in the cuevas (caves) of Barranco de Balos, Agaete, Gáldar (all on Gran Canaria), Belmaco and Zarza (La Palma) and the Cuevas de El Julán (El Hierro). The paintings appear to date back at least to the 13th and 14th centuries, the period immediately preceding the beginning of the Spanish invasion. Some of them depict human and animal figures, while others (such as in the Cueva Pintada de Gáldar) are foremost geometric figures and decorative designs. Circles and ovals seem to have been the preferred symbols and figure among funerary inscriptions in Lanzarote and La Palma.

From Conquest to the 19th Century It was quite some time after the conquest of the Canary Islands before any painters of note began to appear.

Gaspar de Quevedo from Tenerife was the first major painter to emerge from the Canary Islands in the 17th century. Quevedo was succeeded in the 18th century by Cristóbal Hernández de Quintana (1659-1725), who left work behind in the Catedral de la Laguna, Tenerife. More important was Juan de Miranda (1723-1805), among whose outstanding works is *La Adoración de los Pastores* (The Adoration of the Shepherds) in the Iglesia de la Concepción in Santa Cruz de Tenerife. His best known acolyte was Luis de la Cruz y Ríos (1776-1853), born in La Orotava and above all a portraitist.

Valentín Sanz Carta (1849-98) was among the first Canarios to produce works depicting the land in the 19th century. Others of his ilk included Lorenzo Pastor and Lillier y Thruillé, whose work can be seen in the Museo de Bellas Artes in Santa Cruz de Tenerife.

The 20th Century The Canary Islands' main exponent of Impressionism was Manuel González Méndez (1843-1909), whose *La Verdad Venciendo el Error* hangs in the Ayuntamiento de Santa Cruz de Tenerife.

Néstor Martín Fernández de la Torre

(1887-1938) whose speciality was murals, is best represented by his *Poema del Mar y Poema de la Tierra* (Poem of the Sea and Poem of the Earth). This and other works can be seen in the gallery dedicated to him in Las Palmas de Gran Canaria.

The Cuban-Canario José Aguiar García (1895-1976), who grew up in Cuba of Gomero parents. He was a prolific painter, and again it is in his mural works that he reached the apogee of his craft. His works are spread across the islands; the *Friso Isleño* hangs in the casino in Santa Cruz de Tenerife.

All the great currents of European art filtered through to the Canary Islands. Of the so-called Coloristas, names worth mentioning include Francesc Miranda Bonnin (1911-63); and Jesús Arencibia, who did the big mural in the Iglesia de San Antonio de Tamaraceite on Gran Canaria.

The first surrealist exposition in Spain was held on 11 May 1935 in Santa Cruz de Tenerife. The greatest local exponent of surrealism, Tinerfeño Óscar Domínguez (1906-57), ended up in Paris in 1927 and was much influenced by Picasso. Cubist Antonio Padrón (1920-68) now has a museum dedicated to his works in his birthplace, Gáldar (Gran Canaria). Others of the period include Felo Monzón (1910-89) and Jorge Oramas (1911-35).

Leading the field of abstract artists is Manuel Millares (1921-72), native of Las Palmas. Lanzarote's César Manrique (1919-92) also enjoyed a degree of international recognition.

Canarios currently working hard at the canvas include Cristino de Vera (1931-), who displays elements of a primitive expressionism in his paintings, and María Castro (1930-). José Luis Fajardo (1941-) uses just about any materials which come to hand in his often bizarre works.

Sculpture
The roll call of important sculptors is rather short in the Canaries. Two names you may come across are José Luján Pérez (1756-1815) and Fernando Estévez de Salas

(1788-1854). The former's most important works are the *Cristo* in the Catedral de Las Palmas and the *Cristo de la Columna* (Christ at the Pillar) in the Iglesia de Teror (Gran Canaria). Estévez is at his best in *Jesús Preso* (Christ Captured). *Nuestra Señora de las Angustias*, the masterpiece of Miguel Arroyo (1920-), stands in the Iglesia del Pilar in Santa Cruz de Tenerife.

More recently, Eduardo Gregorio (1903-74) and Plácido Fleitas (1915-72) are two of the more outstanding modernists. Martín Chirino (1925-) remains an icon of abstract sculpture, heavily influenced by African and Guanche art. He now spreads his time between the Canary Islands and the USA.

Architecture
Before the Conquest The Guanches lived more often than not in caves, and of the rudimentary houses they built nothing remains today.

Gothic & Mudéjar Spaniards, Portuguese, French, Flemish, Italian and even English masters all injected something of their own architectural wealth into the Canaries. It is worth bearing this in mind when contemplating the styles of architecture briefly described below. There is little that can be considered architecturally 'pure' in the handful of outstanding monuments the islands possess.

By the time the conquest of the islands was completed at the end of the 15th century, the gothic and mudéjar styles already belonged more to the past than the present. The Catedral de Las Palmas is nevertheless a fine example of what some art historians have denominated Atlantic gothic. The bell tower of the Basílica de la Virgen del Pino (Teror, Gran Canaria) retains its Portuguese gothic identity. Don't include the Catedral de Arucas (Gran Canaria) in the equation however – this magnificent edifice, with all the soaring power and complexity of the style, is in fact a neogothic imitation.

The mudéjar style which characterises a swathe of churches and public buildings throughout mainland Spain is barely present in the islands. A hangover from the years of Muslim rule, the use of brick rather than stone, and exquisite wooden ceilings (*armaduras*) set Christian Spanish monuments apart from anything else in Europe. Often mudéjar influences would be combined with other styles imported and adapted from across the Pyrenees. Only a few scraps of mudéjar influence made it to the islands. Probably the best examples are the fine ceilings (in this case known as *artesonado*) in the Iglesia de la Concepción in La Laguna, Tenerife. Not far behind are those of the Iglesia de Santa Catalina, in Tacoronte, on the same island.

Plateresque & Baroque In mainland Spain, a rather particular style of decorating monuments marked the arrival of the Renaissance. Known as plateresque, it has its single greatest repository in the Castilian city of Salamanca, whose extraordinary edifices drip with controlled detail, busts and swirling motifs. An almost imperceptible taste of it can be had at the Catedral de Las Palmas and the Iglesia de la Concepción in La Laguna, Tenerife – the latter a veritable reference work of styles from the gothic through the mudéjar to the plateresque. The Casa de Colón in Las Palmas also has plateresque features. The trademark of the 17th century, baroque, left several traces across the archipelago and is best preserved in the parish church of Betancuria (Fuerteventura), built on the ruins of an earlier gothic church which was destroyed by pirates late in the 16th century.

Modern Times Neoclassical, neogothic and other styles typical of a perhaps less creative era, from the late 18th century on, are represented in imposing public buildings of the bigger cities, but as with their continental counterparts, warrant less interest than their predecessors. The Catedral de Arucas, already mentioned, is an impressive piece of neogothic – it's a shame it's not the genuine article.

Modernism, with its use of glass and

wrought iron, makes an appearance in such constructions as the Mercado del Puerto in Las Palmas de Gran Canaria, along with private houses in areas like Las Palmas' Triana district and Las Ramblas in Santa Cruz de Tenerife.

Military Architecture Apart from churches, the single most common construction efforts from the earliest days of conquest went into castles and forts. This lasted until well into the 18th century. The bulk of these forts were and are rough-and-ready affairs, and few have particular artistic merit. Among those to look out for though are the Torre del Conde (San Sebastián de la Gomera), Castillo de la Luz (Las Palmas de Gran Canaria) and the Castillo de San Juan (Santa Cruz de Tenerife).

Popular Architecture Rural houses were and are, of course, simple affairs. The outstanding element was usually the internal courtyard, or *patio*, in which a great deal of family life was played out. Another singular element about these houses, usually brilliantly whitewashed, was the wooden balcony protruding from windows in those houses consisting of two or more floors. At their most elaborate, such balconies are intricately carved works of art.

Private houses and mansions in the towns and cities might incorporate various styles with, say, a plateresque (or plateresque-like) entrance, wooden balconies of various types and a striking variety of broad windows. The windows are in some cases true works of art, multi-paned and with varied combinations of wooden shutters, frames and panels. The patio, again, remains a paramount element – usually the most striking and beautiful part of Canario houses. The mix in many cases bears signs of Portuguese and Andalucían influence. If you were to seek out these urban jewels only once, you should do so in La Orotava and La Laguna (Tenerife).

Literature

Before the arrival of the conquering Spani-

ards in the 15th century, the Guanches appear not to have known writing. Something of a frontier world even after the conquest, the Canaries were not an immediate source of writers of world renown. Little if anything that the islands have produced in the way of literature has made it into English translation.

This is not to say the islanders have been inactive. The Guanches themselves did not write down their verses, but an Italian historian, Leonardo Torriani, made efforts to translate some of their ballads. And with the conquistadores came storytellers to chronicle their exploits.

Various historians and poets followed, but the first of note beyond the islands was the Tinerfeño José de Viera y Clavijo (1731-1813), an accomplished poet but known above all for his painstaking history of the islands, *Noticias de la Historia General de Canarias*. His contemporary, Tomás de Iriarte (1750-91), born in Puerto de la Cruz, was for years something of a dandy in Madrid court circles. He wrote several plays, but his *Fábulas Literarias*, poetry and tales charged with a mordent wit, constituted his lasting work.

Ricardo Murphy (1814-40) led the way for Romantic poetry in the islands, and succumbed at an early age, like so many ardent poets of the time, to tuberculosis (which he contracted in London).

Nicolás Estévanez (1838-1914), spent much of his life outside the Canary Islands, as soldier and politician in Madrid, and then 40 years' exile in France. His poems, in particular one called *Canarias*, marked him as the motor behind the so-called Escuela Regionalista, a school of poets devoting themselves to themes less universal and more identifiable with the archipelago.

Another of the islands' great historians emerged about the same time. Agustín Millares Torres (1826-96) is remembered for his monumental *Historia General de las Islas Canarias.*

Benito Pérez Galdós (1843-1920), considered the greatest Spanish novelist since Miguel Cervantes and up there with Balzac and Dickens, grew up in Las Palmas, moving to Madrid in 1862. A prolific chronicler of his times, he produced 46 historical novels and numerous other books. Among his masterpieces is the four-part *Fortunata y Jacinta*, which recounts the lives of two unhappily married women of different social classes. Ángel Guimerá (1849-1924) was born in Santa Cruz de Tenerife but become one of Barcelona's great lyric poets and a leading figure in Catalan theatre.

Doctor Tomás Morales (1885-1921) became in his short life one of the islands' leading exponents of Modernist poetry. A contemporary of his, also of some note, was Alonso Quesada (1886-1925).

The year 1927 is marked out as the key point in another era of splendour in Spanish letters, and the poet Josefina de la Torre (1909-) was one of its most important figures in the Canaries. As the 20th century wore on, so the poets of the Vanguardia took the centre stage. Among them in the Canary Islands were Pedro Perdomo Acedo (1897-1977) and Felix Delgado (1904-36).

Isaac de Vega (1920-) has been one of this century's outstanding novelists in the Canaries. His *Fetasa* is a disturbing study of alienation and solitude.

Carmen Laforet Díaz's (1921-) *Nada*, written in the wake of the Civil War, is the partly autobiographical account of a young girl's move from her home in the Canary Islands to study in post-Civil War Barcelona, where she is obliged to live in squalor with her grandmother. She has followed this up with other novels of lesser impact and, in 1961, *Gran Canaria*, a guide to her home island.

One of the most creative talents to emerge among the post-modern poets of the 1980s was Yolanda Soler Onís (1964-). *Sobre el Ámbar*, written from 1982 to 1986, is a collection of pieces whose images are sourced largely from an exploration of island poetic traditions.

Other contemporary novelists to look out for are Roberto Cabrera and E Díaz Marrero.

Music
Traditional The symbol of the Canarios' musical heritage is the *timple*, a ukelele-style instrument of obscure origin. While many thought it was a variation on the Italian mandolin or the Spanish and Portuguese *guitarillo*, it now appears that Berber slaves shipped in for farm work by the early Norman invaders under Jean de Béthencourt might have introduced it to the islands.

It's a small wooden, five-string instrument with a rounded back (it is said the original Berber version was made of a turtle shell), with a sharp tone. There is also a four-string version known as the *contra* or *requinto*, prevalent in Lanzarote.

The timple has travelled widely, as emigrants from the islands took it with them to Cuba and other Latin American countries, where it was incorporated into their instrumental repertory.

Whenever you see local traditional fiestas, the timple will be there accompanying such dances as the *isa* and *folía*, or if you're lucky the *tajaraste*, about the only dance said to have been passed down from the ancient Guanches.

If you especially like the timple, you could do worse than getting hold of a CD by Domingo Rodríguez Oramas, known as El Colorado.

Los Sabandeños is one of the most widely known folkloric groups in the Canary Islands, and their latest CD, *Gardel* is a good serving of this light, melodic music.

Verode is a popular group dedicated to traditional Canario music. With six singers, their repertoire includes sentimental island eulogies and melancholy recollections of emigrant life. The CD *Veinte Años* contains a collection of their best work. Watch out too for Taburiente. One of their better CDs is *Nuevo Cauce*. Other groups to bear in mind include Los Gofiones, Mestisay and Añoranza.

Over the centuries there has been no shortage of migration from Andalucía in the south of Spain, and with it came another musical tradition. Popular Andalucían dances such as the *malagueña* have become part of the local island folk tradition. Flamenco, however, is pretty much absent from the islands.

Contemporary In the mid-1990s a new star burst onto the Spanish music stage and by 1998 looked set to make in-roads into the world scene. Rosana Arbelo, born in Lanzarote in 1962, is a fine singer-songwriter whose first CD, *Lunas Rotas*, was a smash hit in Spain and elsewhere in Europe in 1996-97. Her lyrics tend to the melancholy, accompanied by an appealing mix of Cuban, Spanish and African rhythms.

However, the islands' most established *cantautor* (singer-songwriter), and one appreciated across all Spain, is Tenerife's Pedro Guerra. One of his best CDs is titled *Golosinas*.

Las Ratas are a popular rock band whose only CD so far is self-titled.

SOCIETY & CONDUCT

Politeness is a question of taste and habit, and what it is depends on where you come from. It is always easy to tell a foreigner (especially of the Anglo-Saxon variety) in a bar or shop by the excessive number of 'por favors' marking each and every request. Your average Canario (and mainland Spaniard), often dispenses with please and thank you and just gets to the point: 'Give me a carton of milk!'. How rude you might think, but then it's not customary for Anglos to routinely greet all and sundry when entering the same establishments with a cheery *buenos días*. Locals also, as they pass diners on their way out of a restaurant, have an almost distressing habit of smiling: *que aprovecheis* (bon appetit).

Making quick friends in these islands is often not difficult. You don't need to be overly outgoing to strike up a chat with people here (particularly if you speak passable Spanish), but don't expect it to go much further than that. Hearty farewells and promises of further meetings are, while not to be dismissed, to be taken with a sizeable grain of salt. Like anywhere else in the world, lasting friendships require spadework.

People socialise in the streets. Dinner parties and intimate gatherings in people's homes are the exception rather than the rule.

Canarios are a pretty relaxed lot but, again, relaxation is done in different ways. Like mainland Spaniards and most Latins, the Canarios like to dress well, at least when on show. The more extreme will dress to the nines just to head for the supermarket. No one expects foreigners to emulate this, but the down-at-heel-I-haven't-washed-for-a-week look favoured by some bedraggled tourists is sometimes inappropriate, particularly in restaurants and discos. A little common sense is a handy asset.

Questions of Time

The Canary Islands and the UK share the same time. So when Londoners are scrambling to make the Tube in the pre-dawn winter cold or cursing all known gods while crawling down the M-25, your average Canario in Las Palmas is probably still asleep. If not, he or she is also on the way to work, but with considerably less stress.

By 2 pm, most shops, business and government departments are shut and everyone is heading home for a meal with the family or down to their favourite restaurant for a long lunch with colleagues or friends. Lunch can last until 4 pm, and sometimes later. The much mythologised siesta is thus more often than not dedicated to eating, family and friends, although there's time for a quick nap too if you want. Your weather-beaten Londoner, at 2 pm, has probably just rushed back into the office after a sandwich and pint swallowed in haste at the nearest pub.

As offices and shops reopen (from about 5 pm) in the Canaries, Londoners are clock-watching, waiting to rush out into the dark evening traffic home. Although government offices, banks and the like tend to close in the afternoon in the Canaries, most shops and businesses carry on until about 8 pm. There's no need to rush to get home though, because those who want to go out have bars and restaurants at their disposal until the early hours – no 11 o'clock closing here.

Somehow these people seem more in control of their time. Although in many resorts restaurants and bars cater to foreign habits, locals tend to eat late, rarely arriving at a restaurant before 10 pm. Arrangements to meet in a bar at midnight for the evening's entertainment are the norm.

And Canarios are family-oriented. So where there's a *feria* or an outdoor café on a warm night, you'll almost see as many kids running about as adults – even at 3 am!

RELIGION

One of the primary concerns of the conquistadores from Spain was to convert the benighted heathen of these far flung islands to the one true faith. As the protracted and largely inglorious conquest proceeded, the indigenous inhabitants were swiftly converted to Christianity, usually as part of the terms of surrender. When armed resistance ended, the Guanches seem to have protested little at the conversion from their own once complex faith, about which precious little is known (see the History section earlier in this chapter).

Roman Catholicism quickly took hold in the islands, and as in the rest of Spain has left a deep-rooted impression. Although the depth of the average Canario's religiosity may be a subject of speculation, the Church still plays an important role in people's lives, at least *pro forma*. Most Canarios are baptised, have church weddings and funerals and attend church for important religious feast days, although fewer than half of the islanders regularly turn up for Sunday Mass. A good number of the colourful and often wild fiestas which take place throughout the year have some religious context or origin.

LANGUAGE

The language of the Canary Islands is Spanish (*español*), otherwise known more correctly as Castilian (*castellano*) to distinguish it from other mainland tongues such as Basque and Catalan.

Pronunciation

Pronunciation of Spanish is not difficult, given that many Spanish sounds are similar to their English counterparts, and there is a clear and consistent relationship between pronunciation and spelling. If you stick to the following rules you should have few problems in being understood.

Those steeped in the castellano of the central and northern mainland will be surprised by the Latin American lilt of the language spoken in the Canaries. It bears a closer resemblance to what you hear in Andalucía. The 'lisp' you would normally expect in 'z' and 'c' before vowels is pronounced more as a sibilant 's', and 's' is hardly pronounced at all, but rather aspirated – Las Palmas sounds more like Lah Palmah! Swallowing of consonants like this is a marked feature of Canaries Spanish, and even solid speakers of the language may find themselves wondering just how much they really understood on hearing a lively *charla* (chat) among Canarios.

The Spanish of the Canaries has several other peculiarities. The standard second personal plural pronoun *vosotros*, 'you', is rarely heard. Instead, the more formal *ustedes* is used.

Where more than one option appears for vocabulary items below, the first cited is the most common usage in the islands. The *-a/-o* endings of some words indicate feminine and masculine forms, eg an asthmatic woman is *asmática*, while an asthmatic man is *asmático*.

Vowels

Unlike English, each of the vowels in Spanish has a uniform pronunciation which does not vary. For example, the Spanish letter 'a' has one pronunciation rather than the numerous pronunciations we find in English, such as the 'a' in 'cake', 'cat', 'cart' and 'call'. Many Spanish words have a written accent. This acute accent (as in días) indicates a stressed syllable; it doesn't change the sound of the vowel. Vowels are pronounced clearly even if they are in unstressed positions or at the end of a word.

a	somewhere between the 'a' in 'cat' and the 'a' in 'cart'
e	as in 'met'
i	similar to the 'ea' in 'heat'
o	similar to the 'o' in 'hot'
u	as in 'put'

Consonants

Some Spanish consonants are the same as their English counterparts. The pronunciation of other consonants varies according to which vowel follows. The Spanish alphabet also contains the letter 'ñ', absent from the English alphabet. Until recently, the clusters 'ch' and 'll' were also officially separate consonants, and you're likely to encounter many situations – eg in lists and dictionaries – in which they are still treated that way.

b	somewhere between 'b' and 'v'; also (less commonly) like the 'b' in 'book' when initial or preceded by a nasal such as **m** or **n**
c	a hard 'c' as in 'cat' when followed by **a**, **o**, **u** or a consonant; as the 'th' in 'thin' before **e** or **i**
ch	like the 'ch' in choose, although in the Canaries it often sounds more like 'y' – 'Guanche' is often pronounced as 'Guanye'
d	as in 'dog' when initial or preceded by **l** or **n**; elsewhere as the 'th' in 'then'
g	as in 'gate' when initial or before **a**, **o** or **u**; elsewhere much softer. Before **e** or **i** it's a harsh, breathy sound, similar to the 'ch' in Scottish 'loch'
h	always silent
j	a harsh, guttural sound similar to the 'ch' in Scottish 'loch'
ll	similar to the 'y' in 'yellow'
ñ	a nasal sound like the 'ni' in 'onion'
q	'q' is always followed by a silent **u** and one of the vowels **e** (as in que) or **i** (as in aquí); the combined sound of 'qu' is like the 'k' in 'kick'

Don't Mumble, Give a Whistle

The American Indians had smoke signals, the Guanches had the whistle. On the small islands of La Gomera and El Hierro, the original inhabitants developed an ingenious way for getting messages to pals across deep ravines and other uncompromising territory. Where the complicated sounds of words could be confused over distance, the Guanches found that whistles were more readily picked up.

What perhaps began as a greeting or danger signal (a little like the Australian bush call 'coo-ee'), developed into a veritable language, known today as El Silbo Gomero. Placing different fingers into the mouth in various positions to produce different sounds, the Guanches more or less created a limited whistling alphabet. In an age before the telephone, these whistled messages could be heard up to 4km away across deep ravines.

According to more gruesome accounts, the language was developed after the Spanish conquest, among those Guanches who had their tongues removed by the authorities for misdemeanours.

It appears that Guanches on the other islands may have used the language too. In the wake of the Spanish conquest, a good deal of this 'language' fell into disuse. Only proper names and a few skeletal expressions survived. An Austrian expert on all things Canarian, Dr Dominik Wölfel, compiled all the known words that he could in 1940 and came up with a total of 2909!

Nowadays, there remain a few locals able to produce some of these whistled words. That the language survives at all is due more than anything else to tourism: it seems that visitors can't get enough of this kind of local colour.

r	a rolled 'r' sound; longer and stronger when initial or doubled as in 'send'
v	same as b
x	as the 'x' in 'taxi' when between two vowels; as the 's' in 'say' when preceding a consonant
z	as the 'th' in 'thin'

Basics

Hello.	*¡Hola!*
Goodbye.	*¡Adiós!*
Yes.	*Sí.*
No.	*No.*
Please.	*Por favor.*
Thank you.	*Gracias.*
That's fine/ You're welcome.	*De nada.*
Excuse me.	*Perdón/Perdone.*
I'm sorry. (forgive me)	*Lo siento/Discúlpeme.*

Small Talk

How are you?	*¿Cómo está?*
I'm fine, thanks.	*Estoy bien, gracias.*
What's your name?	*¿Cómo se llama?*
My name is …	*Me llamo …*
Where are you from?	*¿De donde es?*
I'm from …	*Soy de …*

Language Difficulties

I (don't) understand.	*(No) Entiendo.*
Do you speak English?	*¿Habla inglés?*
Could you write that down, please?	*¿Puede escribirlo, por favor?*

Getting Around

What time does the … leave/arrive?	*¿A qué hora sale llega … ?*
bus (city)	*el guagua/ autobús/bus*
bus (intercity)	*el guagua/ autocar*
Where is the … ?	*¿Dónde está …?*
bus stop	*la parada de autobús*
train station	*la estación de trenes*

I'd like a … ticket	*Quisiera un billete …*
one-way	*sencillo* (or *de sólo ida*)
return	*de ida y vuelta*

Directions

I want to go to …	*Quiero ir a …*
Can you show me (on the map)?	*¿Me puede indicar (en el mapa)?*
Go straight ahead.	*Siga/Vaya todo recto/derecho.*
Turn left …	*Gire a la izquierda...*
Turn right …	*Gire a la derecha …*
at the traffic lights	*en el semáforo*
at the next corner	*en la próxima esquina*

Around Town

I'm looking for …	*Estoy buscando …*
a bank	*un banco*
the … embassy	*la embajada de …*
the post office	*los correos*
the public toilets	*los servicios/ aseos públicos*
the telephone centre	*el locutorio*
the tourist office	*la oficina de turismo*

Accommodation

Where is a cheap hotel?	*¿Dónde hay un hotel barato?*
Do you have any rooms available?	*¿Tiene habitaciones libres?*
How much is it. ?	*¿Cuánto cuesta …?*
per night	*por noche*
per person	*por persona*
May I see it?	*¿Puedo verla?*
Is breakfast included?	*¿Está incluido el desayuno?*
youth hostel	*albergue de la juventud*
camping ground	*camping*
hotel	*pensión/hostal/hotel*

Food

breakfast	*desayuno*
lunch	*almuerzo/comida*
dinner	*cena*

Time & Dates

What time is it?	*¿Qué hora es?*
today	*hoy*
tonight	*hoy por la tarde*
tomorrow	*mañana*
yesterday	*ayer*
Monday	*lunes*
Tuesday	*martes*
Wednesday	*miércoles*
Thursday	*jueves*
Friday	*viernes*
Saturday	*sábado*
Sunday	*domingo*

Numbers

0	*cero*
1	*uno, una*
2	*dos*
3	*tres*
4	*cuatro*
5	*cinco*
6	*seis*
7	*siete*
8	*ocho*
9	*nueve*
10	*diez*

100	*cien/ciento*
1000	*mil*
10,000	*diez mil*
one million	*un millón*

Health

I'm ...	*Soy ...*
diabetic	*diabética/o*
epileptic	*epiléptica/o*
asthmatic	*asmática/o*
antiseptic	*antiséptico*
aspirin	*aspirina*
condoms	*preservativos/ condones*
diarrhoea	*diarrea*
medicine	*medicamento*
nausea	*náusea*
sunblock cream	*crema protectora contra el sol*
tampons	*tampones*

Emergencies

Help!	*¡Socorro!/¡Auxilio!*
Call a doctor!	*¡Llame a un doctor!*
Call the police!	*¡Llame a la policía!*
Go away!	*¡Vete!*

Facts for the Visitor

PLANNING
When to Go
When it comes to sunshine, the Canary Islands are caught in a kind of weather-warp, with an eternal spring-summer climate. It's a year-round destination and you can pretty much take your pick of when to go.

The winter months *are* a tad cooler but paradisiacal when compared with mainland Europe, the UK and North America (with the possible exception of Florida). This makes the December-February period predictably the islands' busiest, which can mean crowds and higher prices.

Summer is also busy, mainly because that's when mainland Spaniards elect to go (for your average Madrileño, the Canaries can seem refreshingly *cool* in the height of a scorching mainland summer). Thus May to October can also be considered high season, although package prices and air fares start coming down by the end of September.

The best periods to look for maximum value on air fares are from November to mid-December and, better still, March to May (with the notable exception of the intense Easter rush). Spring is a great time to be in the islands.

What Kind of Trip?
The bulk of tourists arrive with a package deal, usually covering flights, transfers and hotels. For those with limited budgets, this also usually means sticking to one of the islands and staying for a week or two.

This of course can suit. If you are just after some winter sun and/or some intense partying, opting to stay in the one spot is probably ideal.

Independent travellers moving around on a limited budget are less common in the islands, but there is no particular impediment. Forget about youth hostels and camping grounds (of the former there is

precisely one, and options for the latter are extremely limited), but you can often find quite affordable rooms in small hotels and apartments.

Those who wish to shun the crowds and enjoy the best the islands have to offer in nature can elect to stay inland, for instance in country houses, or *casas rurales*. There is no shortage of walking possibilities and you could easily spend a couple of weeks on hiking excursions, especially in the relatively low-key western islands.

Scuba diving is a popular activity and, with courses available, the Canaries could a make a pleasant spot for a diving holiday for both beginners and more experienced divers. Other aquatic activities, such as deep-sea fishing and sailing, could easily form the main theme around which to build a trip to the Canaries.

The Canaries are not terribly hard work. Independent travellers can trek, unaided as they might elsewhere in Europe, across the whole archipelago.

Maps
Regional Maps Among the clearest and best value maps of all seven islands is produced by Macmillan and the AA, which includes a few city plans and costs UK£3.95. Kümmerly & Frey and the AA do virtually the same map for double the price! The scale on both is 1:150,000. Firestone's *Islas Canarias*, also 1:150,000, is not a bad if you're driving around.

Spain's Ministerio de Obras Públicas y Urbanismo (MOPU) produces two maps at 1:200,000, one for each province – they look impressively thick until you realise that most of what is depicted is Atlantic Ocean!

Island Maps If you plan on staying on only one of the islands, then perhaps a more detailed island map is for you. Freytag & Berndt does some good ones, including

Teneriffa (German for Tenerife) at a scale of 1:75,000, *La Palma* (1:50,000) and *Gomera* (1:35,000).

Spain's Instituto Geográfico Nacional (IGN) has a series of detailed island maps too, drawn at 1:50,000 but perhaps too cluttered to be attractive to the average hiker. The Servicio Geográfico del Ejército produces still more detailed maps dividing each of the islands into bite-sized pieces at 1:25,000. These are not particularly up to date.

City Maps For finding your way around the few major cities and towns, the free maps handed out by tourist offices are often adequate. Otherwise, there are plenty of commercial maps available in bookshops and newsstands.

Distrimapas does a good map of Gran Canaria with detailed city maps of Las Palmas and the south coast resorts. The green Everest map of Tenerife, while not so hot on the island, has accompanying city plans to a host of places, *excluding* Santa Cruz, which is fine because the tourist office handout is, in this case, more than sufficient.

Where to Buy Maps You can buy the maps you need as you go through the islands. Outside the Canaries, specialist stores like Stanford's in London (see Books below) usually stock a fair range.

What to Bring
Bring as little as possible. You can buy pretty much anything you might need in the Canaries.

Luggage If you'll be doing any walking with your luggage, even just from bus stations to hotels, a backpack is the best bet. The ones with straps and openings that can be zipped inside a flap are the most secure and least clumsy. A small day-pack is handy.

Clothes & Shoes Although the weather is generally mild all year round, you should bring a light sweater for cooler moments, especially in the evenings, or if you intend to head inland and explore higher altitudes.

Although rainfall is slight, a poncho or some other kind of wet-weather gear is advisable if you intend to explore the northern sides and mountains of the islands (except the arid Fuerteventura and Lanzarote), particularly in the winter months.

See Climate in the Facts about the Islands chapter for the kind of temperatures and rainfall you can expect on your trip.

Pack a better set of clothes (other than jeans and T-shirts) for discos and smart restaurants. Unless all you want to do is hang around beaches and bars, you will need a pair of sturdy shoes, along with something light like sandals. For the nicer restaurants, bars etc, something other than grotty running shoes will be necessary.

Useful Items Apart from any special personal needs, consider the following:

- under-the-clothes money belt or shoulder wallet, useful for protecting your money and documents
- towel and soap, often lacking in cheap accommodation
- small Spanish dictionary and/or phrasebook
- Swiss army knife
- minimal unbreakable cooking, eating and drinking gear if you plan to prepare your own food and drinks
- medical kit (see Health)
- padlock or two to secure your luggage to racks
- adapter plug for electrical appliances
- torch (flashlight)
- alarm clock
- sunglasses

Basic drugs are widely available and indeed many items requiring prescriptions in countries like the USA can be obtained easily over the counter in the Canary Islands. If you require specific medication, it's easier to bring it with you.

SUGGESTED ITINERARIES
With seven islands to choose from, and considerable diversity among them, you can cobble together pretty much any itinerary –

from frenetic island-hopping to slothful beach combing. The following suggestions assume you want to explore in some depth whichever islands you choose to visit.

Short Trips

With only a week or two to spare, you should concentrate your efforts on one or two islands. Tenerife makes a good one-to-two week destination. You could combine excursions to the Teide peak and some hiking (around the volcano or parts of northern Tenerife like the Anaga mountains or the Masca gorge) with visits to the most interesting towns in the north (including La Orotava and Santa Cruz and the bright university town of La Laguna). When you've had enough of nature and culture, party animals can retire to the south for a few days' sea, sun and drinking after which you're unlikely to find extra time on your hands. The restless can embark on whale-spotting trips and shoot across to the lovely island of La Gomera for a day.

Another possibility might be a surf-and-travel tour of the easternmost islands, Lanzarote and Fuerteventura – plenty of ferries operate between the two, making getting around easy. There are lots of fine beaches for swimming, surfing and wind-surfing; and enough of interest inland, such as the Timanfaya national park, to keep your curiosity well stoked.

Digging Deeper

With a little more time, you can plan wider ranging trips. The three western islands (La Palma, La Gomera and El Hierro) are the least visited of the archipelago. This is largely due to their lack of long white beaches or hammering nightlife, and makes them a striking alternative to the standard holiday for which the Canaries are best known.

The three islands are rugged, offering rainforest-hiking possibilities, exploration of volcanoes and meanderings through verdant countryside and sleepy farming or fishing villages. The seaside is never far away, it's just that the beaches are mostly small, black, pebbly and sometimes a little difficult to get to.

Equally, you could attach one or more of these islands to a trip to one of the more popular ones in the east – Tenerife is the obvious candidate, but there is no reason why you should not spend a week on the great sand dunes of Maspalomas, Gran Canaria, and then switch to the 'backwaters' of the west.

A 'Grand Tour'

To get an impression of all the islands, you need to set aside at least a month, and preferably more like six weeks. Few visitors stay long enough to even consider trying to tackle the lot in one hit. If you do have the time (and the interisland travel costs are not prohibitive for your budget), there is plenty to keep you occupied, even without considering the myriad sporting activities like diving, fishing, golf and so on.

On the way, you might include: the Parque Nacional de la Caldera de Taburiente (La Palma); walks in the Parque Nacional de Garajonay (La Gomera); a hot volcanic experience in the Parque Nacional de Timanfaya (Lanzarote); excursions in Tenerife's Parque Nacional de las Cañadas del Teide and the ascent of the Teide peak (the highest in all Spain); the towns of La Laguna and La Orotava (Tenerife); Las Palmas de Gran Canaria; some of the smaller villages, like Masca and Garachico on Tenerife; the great sandy beaches of Maspalomas and Fuerteventura; and perhaps also a walking/driving excursion through the misty heart of El Hierro.

THE BEST & THE WORST

Coming up with a Top 10 hit list for the Canary Islands is difficult, but the following had definite appeal:

- The ascent of the Teide peak (Tenerife)
- Chilling out on the beaches of northern Fuerteventura
- Sunset in the village and gorge of Masca (Tenerife)
- Feeling the volcanic heat of Lanzarote's Montañas del Fuego

- *Barraquitos* (coffee with condensed milk, cinnamon and a shot of alcohol)
- The old town centres of La Laguna and La Orotava (Tenerife)
- Walking in the laurel forest of the Parque Nacional de Garajonay (La Gomera)
- The coast drive along El Golfo and around past Playa del Verodal (El Hierro)
- Fresh fish with *papas arrugadas y mojo picón* (wrinkly potatoes with spicy sauce)
- Walking the Ruta de los Volcanes (La Palma)

I felt I could live without a second dose of the following:

- Lager louts in Playa de las Américas (Tenerife)
- Rush hour and parking in Las Palmas (Gran Canaria)
- The high price of interisland air fares
- Puerto Rico (Gran Canaria)
- Gofio
- Tour-bus traffic on the road to Masca (Tenerife)
- Bananas (I never want see another banana tree again!)
- Valverde (El Hierro)
- Arriving in Santa Cruz de la Palma on the ferry after midnight
- Touts in the resorts

TOURIST OFFICES
Local Tourist Offices
Each island capital and many centres have what is generally called an Oficina de Turismo or Oficina de Información Turistica. Smaller towns often have a Centro de Iniciativas y Turismo (CIT). Opening hours vary, as does the quality of the information, although generally staff are obliging.

Tourist Offices Abroad
Information on the Canary Islands is available from the following branches of the Oficina Española de Turismo abroad:

Argentina
 (☎ 01-322 7264) Avenida Florida 744, 1°, 1005 Buenos Aires
Austria
 (☎ 01-512 9580) Mahlerstrasse 7, 1010 Vienna-I
Belgium
 (☎ 02-280 1926) Rue des Arts 21, 1040 Brussels

Brazil
 (☎ 011-655999) Rua Zequinha de Abreu 78, Cep 01250 São Paulo
Canada
 (☎ 416-961 3131) 102 Bloor St West, 34th Floor, Toronto, Ontario M4W 3E2
Denmark
 (☎ 33 15 11 65) Store Køngensgade 1-3, 1264 Copenhagen
Finland
 Mechelininkatu 12-14, 00100 Helsinki (☎ 09-441992)
France
 43 rue Decamps, 75784 Paris, Cedex 16 (☎ 1-45 03 82 50)
Italy
 Via del Mortaro 19, interno 5, Rome 00187 (☎ 06-678 3106)
 Piazza del Carmine 4, 20121 Milan (☎ 02-72 00 46 17)
Germany
 Kurfürstendamm 180, 10707 Berlin (☎ 030-882 6543)
 Grafenberger Allee 100 (Kutscherhaus), 40237 Düsseldorf (☎ 0211-680 3980)
 Myliusstrasse 14, 60325 Frankfurt/Main (☎ 069-725033)
 Schubertstrasse 10, 80336 Munich 15 (☎ 089-538 9075)
Japan
 Daini Toranomon Denki Bldg 4F, 3-1-10 Toranomon, Minato Ku, Tokyo 105 (☎ 03-34 32 61 41/2)
Netherlands
 Van Meerdervoort Laan 8-8a, 2517 AJ The Hague (☎ 070-346 5900)
Norway
 Ruselökkveien 26, 0251 Oslo-2 (☎ 22 83 40 50)
Portugal
 Av. Fontes Pereira de Melo 51-4° andar D, 1000 Lisbon (☎ 01-3541992)
Sweden
 Stureplan 6, 114-35 Stockholm (☎ 08-611 4136)
Switzerland
 15 rue Ami-Lévrier, Geneva 1201 (☎ 022-731 1133)
 Seefeldstrasse 19, CH 8008 Zurich (☎ 01-252 7930/1)
UK
 22-23 Manchester Square, London W1M 5AP (☎ 0171-493 5760)
USA
 666 Fifth Avenue New York NY 10103 (☎ 212-265 8822)
 8383 Wilshire Boulevard, Suite 960, Beverly

Hills, Los Angeles, California 90211 (☎ 213-658 7188)

Water Tower Place, Suite 915, East 845 North Michigan Ave, Chicago, Illinois 60611 (☎ 312-642 1992)

1221 Brickell Avenue, Miami, Florida 33131 (☎ 305-358 1992)

VISAS & DOCUMENTS

It may not look like it geographically, but the Canary Islands are a part of Spain. Hence all rules (on passports, visas, residence etc) which apply to Spain apply equally to the Canary Islands.

Passport

Citizens of the 15 European Union (EU) member states, Norway and Iceland can travel to Spain, and hence the Canary Islands, with their national identity cards alone. People from countries which do not issue ID cards, such as the UK, must have a valid passport. UK Visitor passports are not acceptable. All non-EU nationals (excluding those from Norway and Iceland) must have a full valid passport.

If you've had the passport for a while, check that the expiry date is at least some months off, otherwise you may not be granted a visa (if you need one). Also, if you travel a lot and your passport is nearly full, do yourself a favour and get a new one before you leave.

By law you are supposed to have your ID card (or passport) with you at all times in the Canaries, in case the police ask to see it. In practice this is unlikely to cause trouble. You will always need one of these documents for police registration when you take a hotel room.

Visas

For visits of up to 90 days, nationals of many countries require no visa at all. Those who do need a visa can find the process of acquiring one a little irritating. With the implementation of the Schengen Agreement in April 1995, the situation has, if anything, become more confusing.

Spain, along with Portugal, Italy, France, Germany, Austria, the Netherlands, Belgium and Luxembourg, form part of the border-free travel zone known as the Schengen Area. Sweden, Finland, Denmark and Greece are expected to join up soon. Travel *between* these countries normally entails no passport control on land frontiers, at ports or in airports, although spot checks are always possible. A common police data bank has been established and, to compensate for the dropping of internal controls, vigilance at all non-Schengen frontiers and for flights and vessels arriving from non-Schengen countries (including other EU countries) has been tightened, as have the requirements for visas. Extraordinarily, the member countries have *not* standardised their list of countries whose nationals require visas to enter.

Among those who need no visa for any Schengen country are citizens of the USA, New Zealand, Japan, Israel and Switzerland. Among those who require one for Spain (and thus the Canary Islands), but not necessarily the other Schengen countries, are Australians and South Africans (including those resident in another EU country *not* party to the Schengen Agreement). Residents of one Schengen country do *not* require a visa for another Schengen country. Possession of a visa for any Schengen state allows travel to *all* other Schengen countries, but technically you are supposed to apply for the visa at the consulate of your main destination country.

A traveller needing a visa could try to head for the Canaries by air from another Schengen country (such as Holland) for which they require no visa and take a chance on not being checked on arrival. In spite of the open borders policy, however, the chances of slipping through Canary Islands airports undetected are not high, as there are no separate channels for Schengen flights. The authorities will not hesitate to deport you whence you came should they catch you.

Types of Schengen Visa There are several types of Schengen visa. Various transit visas allow you to cross the Schengen Area in order to reach a non-Schengen country. They will be of no use to those heading directly for the Canary Islands.

Of interest to travellers are the 30-day and 90-day visas. In London they cost UK£17.75 and UK£21.30 respectively (single entry into the Schengen area). A 90-day multiple-entry visa costs UK£24.85. You are allowed to apply for only one 90-day visa of either type in any six-month period.

You need to fill in an application form and provide four passport-size photos. If you are resident in the country where you apply and do so in person, the process should take between 24 and 48 hours (never same day). Postal applications should include a self-addressed envelope stamped for registered mail and can take up to a month. You may also be asked for proof of solvency.

If you apply for the visa in a country where you are *not* resident, the process can be lengthy. Your request may be forwarded to Madrid (mainland Spain), and a reply could take weeks. In addition, you may be asked to present tickets for onward or return flights, evidence of hotel accommodation and solvency, or even an invitation from someone in Spain. Finally, it is unlikely you will be given the option of the 90-day, multiple-entry visa.

Visa Extensions & Residence Nationals of EU countries, as well as Norway and Iceland, can enter and leave the Canary Islands (and the rest of Spain) at will. Those wanting to reside and work on Spanish territory for longer than 90 days can apply for a *permiso de residencia* during the first month of their stay. The bureaucracy involved in getting the residence permit can be trying, although not nearly as much as in pre-EU days. You will need a work contract in the Canary Islands or the mainland and/or proof of adequate funds to support yourself. With the former, the process is long but the outcome assured. Your *tarjeta de residencia* entitles you to five years' res-

idence. Arm yourself with lots of photocopies of work contracts, passport pages, bank statements and passport-size photos. You will have to go the *comisaría* (police HQ) of the town you intend to stay in – count on making several visits.

The same goes for other nationals in the Canary Islands with work contracts or on study programs. In most cases the initial application has to be made at the Spanish consulate in your present country of residence. Non-EU spouses of EU citizens resident in Spain can apply for residence too. The process is lengthy, and those needing to travel in and out of the country in the meantime should ask for an *exención de visado* (visa exemption). In most cases, the spouse is obliged to make the formal application in his or her country of residence. A real pain.

Travellers wishing simply to extend their tourist visa can apply at their local *comisaría*, but don't count on being successful.

Photocopies

You'd be wise to keep photocopies of all the data pages of your passport and any other identity cards, and even your birth certificate if you can manage it. This will help speed up replacement if they are lost or stolen. If your passport does go astray, notify the police and obtain a statement, and then contact your embassy or consulate as soon as possible.

Other worthwhile things to photocopy include airline tickets, travel-insurance documents with emergency international medical-aid numbers, credit cards (and international card-loss phone numbers), driver's licence, vehicle documentation and any employment or educational qualifications you may need if you are considering work or study. Keep this, and the serial numbers of your travellers cheques, separate from the originals, and leave copies of all this stuff with someone reliable at home.

Some spare cash tucked away into a money belt, stuffed into a pair of socks or otherwise concealed could come in handy if you lose your wallet or purse.

Travel Insurance

You may never need travel insurance, but you'll be glad you've got it if you get into trouble. These papers, and the international medical-aid numbers that generally accompany them, are valuable documents, so treat them like air tickets and passports. Keep the details (photocopies or hand-written) in a separate part of your luggage. For more details, see the Health section below and the Getting There & Away chapter.

Driving Licence & Vehicle Papers

EU licences (pink or pink and green) are recognised in the Canary Islands. Other foreign licences should be accompanied by an International Driving Permit (in practice, your own driving licence will more often than not suffice) available from automobile clubs in your country and valid for 12 months.

If you happen to be chugging around the islands in your own vehicle, you will require its registration papers and an International Insurance Certificate (or Green Card). Your third-party insurance company will issue this. For further details, see the Car & Motorcycle section in the Getting There & Away chapter.

Hostel Card

If you desperately want to stay in the islands' only HI youth hostel, you'll need a valid HI card. You can get the card in your home country, or the hostel can issue one on the spot. Otherwise, the TIVE youth travel organisation, which has offices in Las Palmas de Gran Canaria and La Laguna (Tenerife), can issue one to foreigners for 1800 ptas.

Student, Teacher & Youth Cards

An ISIC (International Student Identity Card) or similar card will get you discounted entry into some museums and other sights, and can be an asset in the search for cheap flights out of the Canaries. It can also come in handy for such things as cinemas, theatres and other travel discounts.

The cards are available from many student and budget travel offices, including the following:

Australia
   Student Services Australia – 1st Floor, 20 Faraday St, Carlton 3053 (☎ 03-9348 1777)
Canada
   Travel Cuts – 187 College St, Toronto (☎ 416-977 3703)
   Voyages Campus – Université McGill, 3480 Rue McTavish, Montreal (☎ 514-398 0647)
UK
   Cards are best obtained from STA and Campus Travel offices – see Air in the Getting There & Away chapter
USA
   CIEE – 205 East 42nd St, New York (☎ 212-661 1414)
   1093 Broxton Ave, Los Angeles (☎ 213-208 3551)
   312 Sutter St, San Francisco (☎ 415-421 3473)

There are also similar cards for teachers (ITIC). They are good for various discounts and also carry a travel-insurance component.

If you're aged under 26 years old but not a student you can apply for a FIYTO (Federation of International Youth Travel Organisations) card or Euro<26 card (in Spain also known as the Carnet Joven), which give much the same discounts as ISIC.

The head office of FIYTO is in Denmark, at Islands Brygge 81, DK-2300 Copenhagen S, where you can write to request a brochure. Otherwise, the organisations listed above will issue the cards.

Both cards are issued by student unions, hostelling organisations and some youth-travel agencies (like Campus Travel in the UK). They don't always entitle you to discounts, but you won't find out until you flash the card.

In the Canary Islands, TIVE issues ISIC cards for 700 ptas and the Euro<26 for 1000 ptas. Addresses appear under appropriate city entries in the course of the guide.

EMBASSIES
Spanish Embassies

Here follows a list of Spanish embassies in

a selection of countries throughout the world:

Algeria
  46 Rue Azil Ali, Algiers (☎ 02-71 69 93/65/66)
Argentina
  Mariscal Ramón Castilla 2720, 1425 Buenos Aires (☎ 01-802 6031/2)
Australia
  15 Arkana St, Yarralumla, Canberra 2600, ACT (☎ 02-6273 3555, 02-6273918); consulates in Sydney and Melbourne
Brazil
  SES-Av des Naçoes, 44, 70429-900 Brasilia DF (☎ 061-244 2776, 244 2023)
Canada
  74 Stanley Avenue, Ottawa (Ontario) K1M 1P4 (☎ 613-747 2252/747 7293); consulates in Toronto and Montreal
France
  22 Avenue Marceau, 75381 Paris, Cedex 08 (☎ 1-44 43 18 00/53); consulates in Marseille, Bayonne, Hendaye, Pau and other regional cities
Germany
  Schlossstr. 4, 53115 Bonn (☎ 0228-217094/5)
Ireland
  17A Merlyn Park, Balls Bridge, Dublin 4 (☎ 01-269 1640/2597)
Morocco
  105 Ave Allal ben Abdellah, 3 Zankat Madnine, Rabat (☎ 07-707600, 707980)
New Zealand
  represented in Australia
Netherlands
  Lange Voorhout 50, 2514 EG The Hague (☎ 070-364 3814/5/6)
Portugal
  Rua do Salitre 1, 1296 Lisboa Codex (☎ 01-347 2381/2/3/4); consulates in Porto and Valença do Minho
Tunisia
  22 Avenue Dr Ernest Conseil, Cité Jardin, 2001 Tunis (☎ 01-280613, 281539)

UK
  Embassy: 39 Chesham Place, London SW1X 8SB (☎ 0171-235 5555)
  Consulates: 20 Draycott Place, London SW3 2RZ (☎ 0171-589 8989)
  Suite 1A, Brooks House, 70 Spring Gardens, Manchester M2 2BQ (☎ 0161-236 1233)
  63 North Castle St, Edinburgh EH2 3LJ (☎ 0131-220 1843)
USA
  2375 Pennsylvania Avenue, NW Washington, DC 20037 (☎ 202-452 0100); consulates in New York, Los Angeles, San Francisco, Chicago, Miami and other cities

Foreign Embassies in Spain

Most countries have diplomatic representation in Spain, but all the main embassies are located in Madrid. Some of these are listed here. A handful of countries also maintain consulates in the Canary Islands (see below).

Algeria
  Calle del General Oráa 12 (☎ 91 441 60 65)
Argentina
  Calle de Pedro de Valdivia 21 (☎ 91 562 2800)
  Consulate: Calle de José Ortega y Gasset 62 (☎ 91 402 51 15)
Australia
  Plaza del Cubridor Diego Ordás 3 (☎ 91 441 93 00)
Canada
  Calle de Nuñez de Balboa 35 (☎ 91 431 43 00)
France
  Calle de Salustiano Olozaga 9 (☎ 91 435 55 60)
Germany
  Calle de Fortuny 8 (☎ 91 557 90 00)
Ireland
  Calle de Claudio Coello 73 (☎ 91 576 35 00)
Italy
  Calle de Lagasca 98 (☎ 91 577 65 29)
  Consulate: Calle de Agustín Bethencourt 1 (☎ 91 534 69 09)
Morocco
  Calle de Serrano 179 (☎ 91 563 10 90)
  Consulate: Calle de Leizaran 31 (☎ 91 561 89 12)
New Zealand
  Plaza de la Lealtad 2 (☎ 91 523 02 26)
Portugal
  Calle de Castello 128 (☎ 91 561 78 00)
  Consulate: Paseo del General Martínez Campos 11 (☎ 91 445 46 00)
South Africa
  Calle de Claudio Coello 91 (☎ 91 435 66 88)
Tunisia
  Plaza de Alonso Martínez 3 (☎ 91 447 35 08)
UK
  Calle de Fernando el Santo 16 (☎ 91 319 02 00)Z
  Consulate: Calle del Marqués Ensenada 16 (☎ 91 310 29 44)
USA
  Calle de Serrano 7 (☎ 91 577 40 00)

Foreign Consulates in Las Palmas de Gran Canaria

Countries with consular representation in Las Palmas de Gran Canaria include:

France
    Calle de Néstor de la Torre 12
    (☎ 928 29 23 71)
Germany
    Calle de José Franchy Roca 5 (☎ 928 49 18 80)
Italy
    Calle de León y Castillo 281-283
    (☎ 928 24 19 11)
Morocco
    Avenida de José Mesa y López 8
    (☎ 928 26 28 59)
Portugal
    Calle de Alejandro Hidalgo 3 (☎ 928 23 31 44)
UK
    Calle de Luis Morote 6 (☎ 928 26 25 08)
USA
    Calle de Martínez de Escobar 3
    (☎ 928 22 25 52)

Foreign Consulates in Santa Cruz de Tenerife

Countries with consular representation in Santa Cruz de Tenerife include:

France
    Calle de José María de Villa 1
    (☎ 922 23 27 10)
Ireland
    Calle del Castillo 8 (☎ 922 24 56 71)
Italy
    Calle del Pilar 27 (☎ 922 27 57 09)
UK
    Plaza de Weyler 8 (☎ 922 28 66 53)

CUSTOMS

Although the Canary Islands are a part of Spain, for customs purposes they are not considered part of the EU (the same is true, for instance, of the Channel Islands in the UK). For this reason, you are allowed to bring in or take out a maximum duty free of 2L of still wine, 1L of spirits (or 2L of fortified wine), 60ml of perfume, 50ml of *eau de toilette*, 200 cigarettes and a maximum of UK£145 (or equivalent in other currencies) of other goods and gifts.

When returning to an EU country from the Canaries, you must use the green or red customs channels, not the blue EU-only channel.

MONEY

A combination of travellers cheques and credit cards is the best way to take your money.

Currency

Spain's currency is the peseta (pta), known in the plural slang as pelas and affectionately to some expats as 'potatoes'. The legal denominations are coins of one, five, 10, 25, 50, 100, 200 and 500 ptas, and notes of 1000, 2000, 5000 and 10,000 ptas.

A five ptas coin is widely known as a *duro*, and it's fairly common for small sums to be quoted in duros: *dos duros* for 10 ptas, *cinco duros* for 25 ptas, even *veinte duros* for 100 ptas.

When changing money, try to avoid being stuck with a bunch of 10,000 ptas notes, as they can be difficult to change.

Exchange Rates

Currencies of the developed world can be changed without problems in any bank or exchange office. Exchange rates fluctuate and, like most currencies, the peseta has lost a lot of ground against the US dollar and UK sterling since early 1997.

Australia	A$1	=	100 ptas
Canada	C$1	=	108 ptas
France	1FF	=	25 ptas
Germany	DM1	=	85 ptas
Japan	¥100	=	119 ptas
New Zealand	NZ$1	=	85 ptas
Portugal	100$00	=	83 ptas
UK	UK£1	=	258 ptas
USA	US$1	=	154 ptas

Costs

Daily living expenses in the Canary Islands are marginally lower than those in Europe. Although the islands are not a standard backpacker destination, a prudent traveller might get by on around 6000 ptas a day – sharing rooms in the cheapest *pensiones* and apartments, eating one simple restaurant meal a day, making sandwiches for lunch, and travelling slowly by bus and ferry (planes will burn big holes in your pockets).

A breakdown of average costs per person per day at this level might be: 1500 ptas for a bed in a double room (3000 ptas for two); 500 ptas for breakfast (juice, coffee and a *sandwich mixto* – toasted ham and cheese sandwich); 500-1000 ptas for lunch (make it yourself); up to 2000 ptas for dinner; and the rest on transport, the occasional sight and a couple of quick beers. Luckily, sights for which you pay are few on the ground, although one-time splurges such as the cable car up the Teide mountain on Tenerife (2100 ptas) can wreak havoc with your daily calculations if you are sailing this close to the wind. Theme and amusement parks are all pricey, and your costs will also rise if you want to go on boat excursions and the like.

A more comfortable budget would be 10,000 to 15,000 ptas a day. With this you could up your daily hotel allowance to 3000 ptas or even 4000 ptas, include a few days' car hire (say an average three days per week of travel time) and consider having a modest sit down lunch as well as your evening meal.

If money is no object, the sky's the limit. You can easily spend 5000 ptas or more per person on accommodation, and moderate to expensive restaurants can start coming in at 5000 ptas a head. Flying between the islands is expensive (see the Getting Around chapter for details) but enormously time-saving, and with a free-and-easy wallet you can let yourself go in the nightlife hot spots of the main resorts.

Cost-Savers You'll save a little money by avoiding the peak tourist season in December to February, when prices tend to sneak upwards (and when your choice of cheap accommodation may be limited).

Single occupancy of rooms almost always costs more per person than doubles, triples etc. In many of the cheapest *pensiones* you are charged for a double room even if there is only one of you. The only

way around this is to hook up with another traveller.

You can save a few pesetas on long distance mail by sending aerogrammes instead of standard letters or postcards (this does not apply to letters under 20g posted to Europe).

In many cafés it is up to 20% cheaper if you stand at the counter, although this is not a set rule.

More information on accommodation, food and travel costs can be found in the Accommodation and Food sections of this chapter and in the Getting Around chapter.

Carrying Money
Keep only a limited amount of your money as cash, and the bulk in more easily replaceable forms such as travellers cheques or plastic. If your accommodation has a safe, use it. If you must leave money and documents in your room, divide the former into stashes and hide them in different places. Lockable luggage is a good deterrent.

On the streets, especially in the cities and big resort areas, keep as little on you as necessary. The safest thing is a shoulder wallet or under-the-clothes money belt or pouch. External money belts tend to attract attention to your belongings; if you eschew the use of any such device, keep money in your *front pockets* and watch out for people who seem to brush close to you – there is an infinite number of tricks employed by teams of delinquents, whereby one distracts your attention and the other deftly empties your pockets.

Cash
Even if you're using a credit card you'll make most of your purchases with cash, so you need to carry some all the time. Obviously you don't want to carry too much, but bear in mind that you generally reduce your overall service charges for exchange by changing larger amounts in one hit (this applies mainly to travellers cheques) – so there may be times when you have more on you than you'd like.

Don't bring holiday funds in your home country's cash – if you lose it you're stuffed.

Buying a few pesetas before you come to the Canaries will save you a bit of time and hassle on arrival and you often get a better rate on the peseta at home. That said, it isn't necessary, as changing on arrival is pretty straightforward.

You can change leftover pesetas back into your currency, either on returning home or before you leave – you will get a marginally better rate if you change back on Spanish territory. Try not to be stuck with coins as they generally cannot be changed.

Travellers Cheques

These are safe and easily cashed at banks and exchange offices throughout the Canary Islands. Always keep the bank receipt listing the cheque numbers separate from the cheques and keep a list of the numbers of those you have already cashed – this will reduce problems in the event of loss or theft. Check the conditions applying to such circumstances before buying the cheques.

If your travellers cheques are in pesetas, you should pay no exchange charge when cashing them. Most hard currencies are widely accepted, although you may have trouble with the New Zealand dollar. Buying cheques in a third currency (such as US dollars if you are not coming from the USA), means you pay exchange charges twice; when you buy the cheques and again when cashing them.

Get most of your cheques in fairly large denominations (the equivalent of 10,000 ptas or more) to save on any per-cheque commission charges.

American Express exchange offices charge no commission to change travellers cheques (even other brands). For American Express travellers cheque refunds you can call ☎ 900 99 44 26, a Spain-wide number. Take along your passport when you go to cash travellers cheques.

Credit/Debit Cards & ATMs

Carrying plastic (whether a credit or debit card) is the simplest way to organise your funds. You don't have large amounts of cash or cheques to lose, you can get money after hours and on weekends, and the exchange rate is good if not always the absolute best. By arranging for payments to be made into your card account while you are travelling, you can avoid paying interest.

Major credit/debit cards, such as Visa, MasterCard, Eurocard, Cirrus, Plus, Diners Club, JCB, American Express, Citibank and Eurocheques cards, are widely accepted.

These cards can be used for many purchases (including in some supermarkets) and in hotels and restaurants (although smaller establishments tend to accept cash only). Cards can also be used in automatic telling machines (ATMs – or *cajeros automáticos* in Spanish) displaying the appropriate sign or, if you have no personal identification number (PIN), to obtain cash advances over the counter in many banks. Visa and MasterCard are among the most widely recognised for such transactions. Check charges with your bank, but as a rule there is none for purchases on major cards and a 1.5% charge on cash advances and ATM transactions in foreign currencies. Occasionally you may come across ATMs which don't accept your card or, rarely, that don't work at all. Card-eating ATMs are as rare in the Canary Islands as anywhere. Don't expect to find a hole in the wall in every village you visit – always stock up on money in the main towns.

Check with your card's issuer before you leave home on how widely usable your card will be, on how to report a lost card, on daily or weekly withdrawal/spending limits, and on whether your PIN will be acceptable (some European ATMs don't accept PINs of more than four digits). If you think you may go over your credit limit while away, you can make a deposit into your account before you leave to give you access to extra funds. American Express is also widely accepted (although not as common as Visa or MasterCard). American Express card holders can sometimes get cash or at least travellers cheques – up to various maximums depending on the type of card – from American Express offices (in Gran Canaria, Tenerife and Lanzarote) by writing a personal cheque drawn on their home bank account (check this with your bank before leaving home).

If you can, take more than one card and try to keep them separate in case one is lost or stolen. American Express cards tend to be the easiest to replace – you can call ☎ 91 572 03 03 or 91 572 03 20 (in Madrid) at any time. Other cards may not be replaceable until you get home, but you must report their loss straight away. You can report Visa, MasterCard or Access loss on ☎ 91 435 30 40 or 91 519 21 00 (Madrid). For Diners Club card losses call ☎ 91 47 40 00 (Madrid). Eurocard loss can be reported on ☎ 91 519 60 00.

Electronic Money

The travellers cheque may be on the way out. Visa now offers a new form of electronic cash, a prepaid disposable credit card known as Visa TravelMoney. You buy the card from selected banks or travel agencies (such as Thomas Cook) for amounts from UK£100 to UK£5000 and you are issued with a PIN number. Note that there is a 2% commission. It works for ATM withdrawals wherever the Visa sign is displayed. The first four withdrawals are free. If you haven't used up the money by then, any subsequent withdrawal carries a UK£1.50 fee. Enquire at Thomas Cook or call Visa before you travel.

International Transfers

To have money transferred from another country, you need to organise someone to send it to you and a bank (or a Western Union or MoneyGram money-transfer office) in the Canary Islands where you can collect it. If there's money in your bank account at home, you may be able to instruct the bank yourself.

For information on Western Union services, call free on ☎ 900 63 36 33. For MoneyGram, call ☎ 900 20 10 10. The latter only has one representative in the Ca-

naries, in Las Palmas de Gran Canaria, while Western Union is a little more widely represented (including by branches of Mail Boxes Etc). To send sums of up to US$400, the sender is charged US$20. The money can supposedly be handed over to the recipient within 10 minutes of being sent.

To set up a transfer through a bank, either get advice from the bank at home on a suitable pick-up bank in the Canary Islands, or check with a local bank on how to organise it. You'll need to let the sender have precise details of the Canary Islands bank branch – its name, full address, city and any contact or code numbers required. It's probably easiest to have the money sent in pesetas. A bank-to-bank telegraphic transfer typically costs the equivalent of about 3000 or 4000 ptas and should take about a week to clear.

It's also possible to have money sent by American Express.

Changing Money

You can change cash or travellers cheques at virtually any bank or exchange office. You'll find both at the main air and sea ports. Banks tend to offer the best rates, with minor differences between them. The Canary Islands has a surfeit of banks, many with ATMs. They're mostly open Monday to Friday from 8.30 am to 2 pm, and Saturday from 9 am to 1 pm – though some don't bother with Saturday opening. From May to the end of September almost no banks will open on Saturday.

In resorts and cities which attract swarms of foreigners you will also find exchange offices – usually indicated by the word *cambio* (exchange). Generally they offer longer opening hours and quicker service than banks, but worse exchange rates.

Travellers cheques generally attract a higher rate of exchange than foreign cash, but this can be deceiving – often commission is charged on cheques and none on cash. Rates offered *do* vary marginally, particularly from exchange booth to exchange booth, so shop around.

Wherever you change money, ask about

commissions and confirm that exchange rates are as posted. Every bank seems to have a different commission structure: commissions may be different for travellers cheques and cash, and may depend on how many cheques, or how much in total, you're cashing. A typical commission is 3%, with a minimum of 300 to 500 ptas, but there are places with a minimum of 1000 and sometimes 2000 ptas. Those that advertise 'no commission' may offer poorer exchange rates.

Tipping & Bargaining

In restaurants, the law requires menu prices to include service charge, and tipping is a matter of personal choice – most people leave some small change if they're satisfied, and 5% is usually plenty. It's common to leave small change at bar and café tables. The only places where you might bargain are markets (although even there fixed prices are generally the rule) and in some cheap hotels, particularly if you're staying for a few days.

Taxes & Refunds

The Canary Islands have a special tax regime setting them apart from the rest of Spain. On the mainland, value-added tax (VAT) is known as IVA (*impuesto sobre el valor añadido*) and reaches 16% on retail goods.

In the Canary Islands however, the equivalent is the IGIC (*impuesto general indirecto canario*). It is a flat rate 4.5% on retail goods and services, including hotel accommodation. Being so low, there is no tax-refund system for visitors.

POST & COMMUNICATIONS
Stamps & Post Offices

Stamps are sold at many newsagents and various other stores displaying the yellow-on-brown sign *Timbre*, as well as post offices (*oficinas de correos*).

Cities have quite a lot of post offices and most villages have at least one. The two main provincial post offices in Las Palmas de Gran Canaria and Santa Cruz de Tener-

ife are open Monday to Friday from about 8 am to 8.30 pm, and Saturday from 9 am to 2 pm. Most others open from 8.30 am to 2.30 pm Monday to Friday, and 9.30 am to 1 pm on Saturday.

Postal Rates

A postcard or letter weighing up to 20g costs 70 ptas to other European countries, 115 ptas to North America, and 185 ptas to Australia, New Zealand or Asia. Three A4 sheets in an air-mail envelope weigh less than 20g.

Aerogrammes cost 85 ptas regardless of the destination.

Certificado (registered mail) costs an extra 175 ptas for international mail. *Urgente* service, which means your letter may arrive two or three days faster, costs an extra 230 ptas for international mail. You can send mail both certificado and urgente if you wish.

Perhaps a day or two quicker than urgente service – but a lot more expensive – is Postal Exprés service, sometimes called Express Mail Service (EMS). This is available at most post offices and uses courier companies for international deliveries. Packages weighing up to 1kg cost 3780 ptas to the other EU countries or Norway, 6300 ptas to North America, and 8015 ptas to Australia or New Zealand.

Sending Mail

It's quite safe to post your mail in the yellow street-postboxes (*buzones*) as well as at post offices.

Mail to other western European countries normally takes up to a week; to North America allow up to 10 days; to Australia or New Zealand up to two weeks.

Receiving Mail

Delivery times are similar to those for outbound mail. Addresses in the Canary Islands have five-digit postcodes, use of which will help your mail arrive a bit quicker.

Poste restante mail can be addressed to you at *lista de correos* anywhere in the

Canary Islands that has a post office. It will be delivered to the city or town's main post office unless another one is specified in the address. Take your passport when you go to pick up mail. It's a fairly reliable system, although you must be prepared for mail to arrive late. It helps if people writing to you capitalise or underline your surname, and include the postcode. Postcodes that appear in the course of this guide are good for poste restante/lista de correos. A typical lista de correos address looks like this:

Jane SMITH
Lista de Correos
35080 Las Palmas de Gran Canaria
Islas Canarias
Spain

American Express card or travellers cheque holders can use the free client mail-holding service at the four Canary Islands branches of American Express offices in Gran Canaria, Tenerife and Lanzarote. Take your passport when you go to pick up mail.

Telephone

There is no shortage of the distinctive blue pay phones in the Canary Islands. They are easy to use for international and domestic calls. You have the option of using coins and/or phonecards (*tarjetas telefónicas*) and, in some cases, credit cards (including Visa, American Express and Diners Club). Phonecards come in 1000 and 2000 ptas denominations and, like postage stamps, are sold at post offices and *estancos*.

An alternative in some places, although being phased out in favour of pay phones, is the telephone centre. Usually called a *locutorio*, a telephone centre has a number of booths, where you do your own dialling, then pay someone sitting at a desk afterwards. These places can be useful if you don't have enough coins or a card, or if pay phones are in short supply. They also usually have a good stock of telephone directories (*guías telefónicas*).

Public phones inside bars and cafés, and phones in hotel rooms, are always a good

deal more expensive than street pay phones. Management set their own rates for these; always ask the cost before using one.

Costs The Canary Islands are not paradise as far as cheap phone calls are concerned. You can expect a three-minute pay phone or private-line call to cost around 30 ptas within your local area; 80 ptas to other places in the same province; 190 ptas from one of the islands' two provinces to the other, or to mainland Spanish provinces; 350 ptas to other EU countries; 600 ptas to North America; and 1100 ptas to Australia. Calls are around 15% cheaper between 10 pm and 8 am, and all day Sunday and holidays. To North America there is a 'super reduced' rate between 3 am and 8 am all week.

Domestic Calls Canary Islands telephone numbers all begin with 9 and consist of nine digits. The first three digits were, until April 1998, telephone area codes, but have since become incorporated into the number. So phone numbers in the Canary Islands that begin with 928 are for the province of Las Palmas (Gran Canaria, Fuerteventura and Lanzarote), and those that begin with 922 are for the province of Santa Cruz de Tenerife (Tenerife, La Gomera, La Palma, El Hierro). However you must dial all nine digits even if you are ringing next door. Mainland Spain phone numbers can be found in any telephone directory.

To speak to a domestic operator, including for domestic reverse-charge (collect) calls within the Canary Islands and Spain, dial ☎ 1009. A reverse-charge call is *una llamada por cobro revertido*. For directory enquiries dial ☎ 1003; calls cost about 45 ptas from a private phone but are free from a phonebox.

International Calls To make an international call dial ☎ 07 (this is due to become 00 in April 1999, bringing Spain into line with the rest of the EU), wait for a new dialling tone, then dial the country code, area code and number.

You can place reverse-charge international calls through an operator (☎ 1005 for Europe; ☎ 1008 for the rest of the world), but it is much easier, and often cheaper, to use the Country Direct service in your country. You dial the number and request a reverse-charge call through the operator in your country. Numbers for this service include:

Australia	☎ 900 99 00 61
Austria	☎ 900 99 00 43
Belgium	☎ 900 99 00 32
Canada	☎ 900 99 00 15
Denmark	☎ 900 99 00 45
France	☎ 900 99 00 33
Germany	☎ 900 99 00 49
Ireland	☎ 900 99 03 54
Israel	☎ 900 99 09 72
Italy	☎ 900 99 03 91
Japan (KDD)	☎ 900 98 09 81
Japan (IDC)	☎ 900 98 08 11
Japan (ITJ)	☎ 900 98 08 12
Morocco	☎ 900 99 02 12
Netherlands	☎ 900 99 00 31
New Zealand	☎ 900 99 00 64
Norway	☎ 900 99 00 47
Portugal	☎ 900 99 03 51
Sweden	☎ 900 99 00 46
Switzerland	☎ 900 99 00 41
UK (Telecom)	☎ 900 99 00 44
UK (Mercury)	☎ 900 99 09 44
USA (AT&T)	☎ 900 99 00 11
USA (MCI)	☎ 900 99 00 14
USA (Sprint)	☎ 900 99 00 13

For international directory enquiries dial ☎ 1025.

Calling the Canary Islands from other Countries The country code, as for Spain, is ☎ 34.

Voicemail Voicemail could be an efficient way to keep in touch with friends and family. In London, Travellers' Connections (☎ 0181-286 3065; netcomuk.co.uk/~travcons) offers such a service. It works like an answer phone. You are allotted a London phone number and a PIN. Whenever you call that number you can leave a greeting – the message can be as long as you like – and

retrieve messages left for you. There is no limit on the length or number of messages left for you and you can keep or delete them as you wish during the time for which you have paid for the service (which costs from UK£15 a month to UK£75 a year). Obviously you pay for a long distance call (call cheapest rate), and you also have to let your loved ones know what the number is before you hit the road!

Fax

Most main post offices have a fax service: sending one page costs about 350 ptas within the Canary Islands and Spain, 900 ptas to elsewhere in Europe, and 1700 to 2000 ptas to other countries. However you'll often find cheaper rates at shops or offices with 'Fax Público' signs.

Email & Internet Access

Those needing an email fix can try one of the few Internet cafés in the islands, or an 'Internet bureau' (often a locutorio with computer terminals). Access to the Internet generally costs 500 ptas per half hour.

Those travelling with their own computers will need access to a phone. The phone jacks in the Canary Islands are the standard American style RJ-11 variety, making modem connection easy. Be wary of plugging into hotel room phone outlets, as hotel PABX phone systems can fry your modem and computer. Unless you have access to one of the few international providers, you will need to consider joining a local service for your stay – for most people probably too much hassle to worry about. CompuServe as yet has nodes only in Madrid, Valencia and Barcelona, which means making long distance calls to log on.

Telegram

These dinosaurs can be sent from post offices or dictated by phone (☎ 22 20 00) and are an expensive but sure way of having important messages delivered by the same or next day. You can also send telexes from post offices, but they are expensive too.

BOOKS

Most books are published by different publishers in different countries. A book might be a rarity in one country and readily available in another. Bookshops and libraries search by title or author, so your local bookshop or library is best placed to advise you on a certain book's availability.

While there is a wealth of literature in English, Spanish and other languages on Spain, the pickings on the Canary Islands are rather slim. Indeed, outside the islands it is difficult to come by anything much besides … other guidebooks. Except for these, most of the titles listed below will require a good deal of hunting around.

Lonely Planet

Lonely Planet publishes a guide to Spain, and a comprehensive Spanish phrasebook.

Travellers' Tales

The Canary Islands, by Florence du Cane, came out in 1911 and is charming mostly because of the paintings by Ella du Cane. Even before the du Canes were wandering around the islands, Olivia Stone had published *Tenerife and its Six Satellites* in London in 1887.

Another early traveller to the islands was Charles Piazzi Smyth, whose colourful impressions were set down in *Tenerife, or the Advantages of a Residence Among the Clouds* in 1852.

History & People

Those who do not read Spanish will not find a great deal around on the history of the Canary Islands. Even those who do read Spanish will be underwhelmed by what's on offer. A quirky volume of at times dubious academic worth is *Las Islas Canarias a Través de la Historia*, by Salvador López Herrera and translated as *The Canary Islands Through History*. Herrera attempts to trace the story of the Guanches and then the Spanish conquest of the archipelago.

Felipe Fernández-Armesto, a leading authority on the islands' history, has produced *The Canary Islands After the Conquesta*, a fairly specialised work concentrating on 16th-century life in the islands. A classic history written in 1764 is George Glas' *History of the Canary Islands*.

A fairly straightforward summary of the islands' past is *History of the Canary Islands*, by José M Castellano Gil and Francisco J Macíos Martín. It is published in various languages by the Centro de la Cultura Popular Canaria.

The Guanches – Survivors and their Descendants, by José Luis Concepción, looks at the fate of the islands' first inhabitants. He also wrote a volume on customs, called *Costumbres, Tradiciones Canarias* (published in English and German).

In *La Religión de los Guanches*, author Antonio Tejera Gaspar attempts to piece together the puzzle of the islanders' beliefs.

Madeira & the Canary Islands, by A Samler Brown, was first published in 1889 as a precursor to the archetypal traveller's guidebook. Try to get a hold of a later edition of this book, because there is quite a lot of interesting, if highly dated, material in it.

In *Le Canaarien*, Alejandro Cioranescu has collected texts by the islands' initial conquerors, Jean de Béthencourt and Gadifer de la Salle.

Art

For quite a comprehensive review of art and architecture, high and low, in the islands, you might be interested in a series of volumes entitled *El Arte en Canarias*, published by La Biblioteca Canaria.

Flora & Fauna

Budding botanists should check out a series of brochures called *Plants & Flowers of …* (attach the name of whichever island appeals to you). The series is published by Discovery Walking Guides, which also does a series of (surprise, surprise) walking guides to all the islands bar Fuerteventura. In the Canary Islands themselves you should be able to track down numerous titles devoted to the archipelago's flora. *Flowers in the Canary Islands*, by Juan

Alberto Rodríguez Pérez, is available in English and German.

A Birdwatchers' Guide to the Canary Islands, by Tony Clarke and David Collins, is the perfect companion for a pair of skyward-pointed binoculars.

Food

Pleasures of the Canary Islands: Wine, Food, Beauty, Mystery, by Ann & Larry Walker, is one of the few introductions to Canaries cuisine in English. Look at it before you go, as you are unlikely to want to lug this hardback around with you.

More portable, but available only in the Canaries, is a paperback volume by various authors called *The Best of Canary Island Cooking*, published by the Centro de la Cultura Popular Canaria. Another possibility is *Typical Canary Cooking*, by José Luis Concepción.

If you get hooked on *mojo*, look out for *Todos los Mojos de Canarias*, by Flora Lilia Barrera Álamo and Dolores Hernández Barrera.

INTERNET RESOURCES

A search on key words like 'Canaria', 'Canarias' or 'Canary Islands' on any of the standard search engines will throw up a plethora of sites on the World Wide Web. As usual, you have to wade through an awful lot of dross to find anything useful, but some interesting things are swimming around out there. It will be a help if you read Spanish, as many sites are in this language only.

A key site is Canarian Internet Resources (canaryweb.es/). Here you'll find several hundred links to all sorts of other sites covering just about the whole gamut of Canary Islands-related subjects.

If you want to get an idea of the issues that move Canarios, you can read daily news from the Canaries on-line, have a look at Canarias 7 on step.es/canarias7.

Astronomy buffs wanting to know about the latest galaxy-busting developments at the observatories on Tenerife and La Palma can hook into the Instituto de Astrofísica de Canarias (IAC) Web site at iac.es.

For some general travel hints, you could browse through Excite City.Net (city.net/countries/spain), a search engine with links to cities of the world, including maps, sights and limited practical information.

All of the islands have Web sites devoted to tourist information (they can all be traced through the Canarian Internet Resources Web site). Tourist information on the Canaries can also be accessed through the Government tourist office at spaintour.com/canarias.htm. A German-language service is on infocanarias.com.

CompuServe's Spanish Forum has a data library where you can find information on the Canary Islands, or you can post messages asking for specific tips.

NEWSPAPERS & MAGAZINES
Local Press

There is no shortage of local rags in the islands. *La Gaceta de Canarias* and *Canarias 7* are perhaps the most interesting, although the Tenerife-based *Diario de Avisos* is also OK and provides local listings and information on air and sea timetables, etc. The *Diario de Las Palmas* is its equivalent on Gran Canaria. The islands' sporting journal is *Jornada Deportiva*. For the truly parochially inclined, each island gets its own edition of *La Isla*.

Spanish National Press

For a wider view on the world, you can turn to Spain's national press. The main dailies can be identified along roughly political lines, with the old-fashioned *ABC* representing the conservative right, *El País* identified with the PSOE (Spain's centre-left socialist party) and *El Mundo* a more radical, left-wing paper that prides itself on breaking political scandals.

For a good spread of national and international news, *El País* is the pick. One of the best selling dailies is *Marca*, which is devoted exclusively to sport.

Foreign-Language Press

International press such as the *International Herald Tribune*, *Time* and *Newsweek*, plus rafts of newspapers from all over western Europe, reach major cities and tourist areas within a day of publication.

Local Papers
The big British and German presence in the islands has led to the growth of several foreign-language rags. They include *Here and Now* and *Island Connections* in Tenerife, and *Island Sun*, published in Gran Canaria. *Canarian Weekly* is supposedly circulated in all the islands, but you'd be lucky to see it outside the main tourist centres. The Germans can pick up the *Wochenspiegel*. These are all weekly or fortnightly, carry useful listings information and occasionally even job adverts.

RADIO
The Spanish national network Radio Nacional de España (RNE) has four stations. RNE 1, with general interest and current affairs programs, and RNE 5, with sport and entertainment, are on AM (medium wave); RNE 2, with classical music, and RNE 3 (or 'Radio d'Espop'), with admirably varied pop and rock music, are on FM (VHF). Most listened to of all is the commercial pop and rock FM station 40 Principales. Broadcast frequencies vary from place to place.

There is no shortage of local radio stations across the islands, most of them on the FM band – even tiny La Gomera has three stations.

Reception quality varies considerably around the islands, and you may find you can pick up only a few stations clearly. Indeed, in the extreme north of La Palma about all you can get is Portuguese broadcasts from Madeira!

In the main resort areas you can also pick up local foreign language radio. For instance, the English-language music station Power FM broadcasts on 91.2 FM in the Playa de las Américas area in southern Tenerife. Oasis 101 FM is another one. While on Gran Canaria, you can tune into Radio Maspalomas.

The BBC World Service broadcasts to the Canary Islands mainly on 12,095 and 15,485kHz (short wave). Voice of America can be found on various short-wave frequencies, including 9700, 15,205 and 15,255kHz, depending on the time of day. The BBC and VOA broadcast for much of the day from about 5 am to after 9 pm, but the reception quality fluctuates considerably.

TV
Most TVs receive five main channels – two from Spain's state-run Televisión Española (TVE1 and La 2) and three independent (Antena 3, Tele 5 and Canal Plus). You may also be able to pick up local channels, such as Tenerife's Teidevision (channel 6) or TeleGC in Las Palmas. A government-run TV station for the entire archipelago was due to begin transmission in mid-1998.

News programs are generally decent, and you can occasionally catch an interesting documentary or film (look out for the old English-language classics late at night on La 2). Otherwise the main fare is a rather nauseating diet of soaps (many from Latin America), endless talk shows and almost vaudevillian variety shows (with plenty of glitz and near-naked tits). Canal Plus is a pay channel dedicated mainly to movies: you need a decoder and subscription to see the movies, but anyone can watch the other programs, such as news and sport.

Many private homes and better hotels have satellite TV. Foreign channels you may come across include BBC World (mainly news and travel), BBC Prime (other BBC programs), CNN, Eurosport, Sky News, Sky Sports, Sky Sports 2, Sky Movies, and the German SAT 1. Among Spanish satellite channels are Documenta and Canal Clásico, which have some good documentaries and arts programs.

PHOTOGRAPHY & VIDEO
Film & Equipment
A roll of 36-exposure 100 ASA Kodak film costs around 650 ptas. It costs up to 1700 ptas to have 36 exposures developed. A roll of 36 slides costs around 700 ptas and about the same to develop and frame. All the

major brands are available and generally the quality of processing is as good as anywhere.

Outlets where you can buy films and have your photos processed are numerous. A roll of film is most commonly called a *carete* but you will be understood if you ask for 'film'. Shop around a little, as all sorts of special offers crop up involving reduced processing costs, free copies or enlargements and so on.

Photography

Light is the key. As a general rule the midday sun is for mad dogs and not photographers – it is harsh and will lend your snaps a washed-out look. It follows that early and late in the day are the best times to shoot. Use the light's angle and shadows to effect. A basic rule for straightforward shots is to have the light source behind you (but take care not to get your own shadow in the shot!).

Video

Properly used, a video camera can give a fascinating record of your holiday. As well as videoing the obvious things – sunsets, spectacular views – remember to record some of the ordinary everyday details of life in the islands. Often the most interesting things occur when you're actually intent on filming something else. Remember too that, unlike still photography, video moves – so, for example, you can shoot scenes of the countryside rolling past the bus window, to give an overall impression which isn't possible with ordinary photos.

Video cameras these days have amazingly sensitive microphones, and you might be surprised how much sound you pick up. This can be a problem if there is a lot of ambient noise – filming by the side of a busy road might seem OK when you do it, but viewing it back home might simply give you a deafening cacophony of traffic noise. One good rule for beginners to follow is to try to film in long takes, without moving the camera around too much. Otherwise your video could well make viewers seasick! If

your camera has a stabiliser, you can use it to obtain good footage while travelling on various means of transport, even on bumpy roads.

Remember – you're on holiday – don't let the video take over your life and turn your trip into a Cecil B de Mille production.

Make sure you keep the batteries charged, and have the necessary charger, plugs and transformer for the Canary Islands. It is usually worth buying a few cartridges duty free before you start travelling.

Finally, remember to follow the same rules regarding people's sensitivity as for still photography – having a video shoved in their face is probably more annoying and offensive than a still camera. Ask permission first.

If you want to record or buy video tapes to play back home, you won't get a picture if the image registration systems are different. TVs in the Canary Islands, and nearly all pre-recorded videos on sale here and in Spain, use the PAL (phase alternation line) system common to most of western Europe and Australia. France uses the incompatible SECAM system, and North America and Japan use the incompatible NTSC system. PAL videos can't be played back on a machine that lacks PAL capability.

Airport Security

Your camera and film will be routinely passed through airport x-ray machines. These shouldn't damage film but you can ask for inspection by hand if you're worried. Lead pouches for film are another solution.

TIME

Like most of Europe, the Canaries operate on the 24-hour clock which for those accustomed to 'am' and 'pm' can take some getting used to.

The Canary Islands are on Greenwich mean time (GMT/UTC), plus an hour in summer for daylight saving time, and thus always an hour behind mainland Spain. The islands keep the same time as the UK,

Ireland and Portugal. Morocco is on GMT/UTC year round – so in summer it is an hour behind the Canary Islands, even though it's further east!

Daylight-saving (summer) time starts on the last Sunday in March, when clocks are put forward one hour. Clocks are put back an hour on the last Sunday in October. Ensure that when telephoning home you also make allowances for daylight-saving in your own country.

European cities such as Madrid, Barcelona, Paris, Munich, Berlin, Vienna and Rome are an hour ahead of the Canaries. Athens, Cairo and Tel Aviv are two hours ahead. When it's noon in Las Palmas de Gran Canaria, it's 4 am in San Francisco, 7 am in New York and Toronto, 8 pm in Perth, 10 pm in Sydney, and midnight in Auckland. Note that summer time start and finish dates in some countries vary from those in the Canary Islands.

ELECTRICITY

The electric current in the Canary Islands is 220V, 50Hz and plugs have two round pins, like Spain and Continental Europe.

Travellers from the USA need a voltage converter (although many of the more expensive hotels have provision for 110V appliances such as shavers). Make sure you bring plug adapters for your appliances. It is a good idea to buy these *before* leaving home as they are virtually impossible to get in the Canaries. If your appliance's voltage is the same, all you'll need is a European plug to fit onto the one you've brought with you from home.

WEIGHTS & MEASURES

The metric system applies in the Canary Islands. See the conversion table at the back of this book. Decimals are indicated with commas and thousands with points. You will sometimes see years written as 1.997.

LAUNDRY

Self-service laundrettes are extremely rare. Small laundries (*lavanderías*) are fairly common but not particularly cheap. You may find yourself paying as much as 600 ptas to have a pair of trousers done, 450 ptas for a shirt and 550 ptas for a simple skirt! They will be very clean and nicely folded, but how long does that last?

TOILETS

Public toilets are not too common and often little more inviting. The easiest option is to wander into a bar or café and use its toilet. The polite thing to do in this case is have a coffee or something before or after, but you're unlikely to raise too many eyebrows if you don't. Carry some toilet paper with you when out and about as many toilets lack it. If there's a bin beside the loo, put paper etc in it – it's there because the local sewerage system couldn't cope otherwise. Here and there you'll still find hole-in-the-ground squat toilets.

HEALTH

The Canary Islands are not exactly a haven for exotic diseases, and the worst many visitors pick up is an extended hangover from too much partying in the resorts. Other potential risks are sunburn, dehydration, insect bites, or mild gut problems at first if you're not used to a lot of olive oil.

Predeparture Planning

Immunisations No jabs are normally needed to visit the Canary Islands, but the story may be different if you're coming from an infected area – yellow fever is the most likely one. You can check with your travel agent or Spanish embassy.

A few routine vaccinations are recommended whether you're travelling or not. They include polio, tetanus and diphtheria, and sometimes measles, mumps and rubella (German measles). All these are usually administered in childhood, but some require later booster shots. For details, check with your doctor or nearest health agency.

All vaccinations should be recorded on an International Health Certificate, which is available from your physician or government health department. Among those you might consider before travelling are:

Hepatitis A The most common travel-acquired illness after diarrhoea, which can put you out of action for weeks. Havrix 1440 is a vaccination that provides long-term immunity (possibly more than 10 years) after an initial injection and a booster at six to 12 months.

Gamma globulin is not a vaccination but a ready-made antibody collected from blood donations. It should be given close to departure because, depending on the dose, it only protects for two to six months.

Hepatitis B This disease is spread by blood or by sexual activity. Travellers who should consider a hepatitis B vaccination include those visiting countries where there are known to be many carriers, where blood transfusions may not be adequately screened or where sexual contact is a possibility. It involves three injections, the quickest course being over three weeks with a booster at 12 months.

Diphtheria & Tetanus Diphtheria can be a fatal throat infection and tetanus can be a fatal wound infection. All travellers should have these vaccinations. After an initial course of three injections, boosters are necessary every 10 years.

Polio Polio is a serious and easily transmitted disease, still prevalent in many developing countries. Everyone should keep up to date with this vaccination. A booster every 10 years maintains immunity.

Yellow Fever Yellow fever is the only vaccine legally required for entry into many countries, although usually only enforced when coming from an infected area. Protection lasts 10 years and is recommended where the disease is endemic, eg Africa and South America. You usually have to go to a special yellow fever vaccination centre. Vaccination poses some risk during pregnancy; also people allergic to eggs may not be able to have this vaccine. Discuss with your doctor.

Health Insurance Travel insurance to cover theft, loss and medical problems is a wise idea.

EU citizens are entitled to free medical care in the Canary Islands under the Spanish national health system on provision of an E111 form, available in your home country before you come. Even with an E111, you will still have to pay for medicines bought from pharmacies, even if prescribed, and perhaps for a few tests and procedures. Your own national health system may reimburse these costs.

An E111 is no good, however, for private medical consultations or treatment in the Canary Islands, which includes virtually all dentists and some of the better clinics and surgeries. If you want to avoid paying for these, you'll need adequate medical as well as theft and loss insurance on your travel policy.

In Britain, E111s are issued free by post offices; all you need to supply is your name, address, date of birth and National Insurance number. In other EU countries ask your doctor or health service how to get the form.

Most, but not all, US health insurance policies stay in effect, at least for a limited period, if you travel abroad. On the other hand, most other non-European national health plans don't, so you must take out special medical as well as theft and loss insurance.

A wide variety of insurance policies is available and your travel agent will be able to make recommendations. The international student travel policies handled by STA Travel or other student travel organisations are usually good value. Always check the small print. For more hints on travel insurance turn to the start of the Getting There & Away chapter.

Medical Kit Medicines are easily available in the Canary Islands, and in fact many are cheaper than in countries such as the USA and Australia. Quite a few that would normally require a prescription in other countries can be obtained easily over the counter. In any event, you'd be wise to carry a small, straightforward medical kit. It could include:

- **Antibiotics** – useful if you're travelling well off the beaten track, but they must be prescribed; carry the prescription with you
- **Antihistamine** (such as Benadryl) – useful as a decongestant for colds and allergies, to ease the itch from insect bites or stings, and to help prevent motion sickness; antihistamines may cause sedation and interact with alcohol so

care should be taken when using them; take one you know and have used before, if possible

- **Antiseptic** such as povidone-iodine (eg Betadine) – for cuts and grazes
- **Aspirin** or paracetamol (acetaminophen in the USA) – for pain or fever
- **Bandages and Band-aids**
- **Calamine lotion** or **aluminium sulphate spray** (eg Stingose) – to ease irritation from bites or stings
- **Cold-and-flu tablets and throat lozenges** – pseudoephedrine hydrochloride (Sudafed) may be useful if flying with a cold to avoid ear damage
- **Insect repellent**
- **Loperamide** (eg Imodium) or Lomotil for diarrhoea; prochlorperazine (eg Stemetil) or metaclopramide (eg Maxalon) for nausea and vomiting
- **Multivitamins** – especially for long trips when dietary vitamin intake may be inadequate
- **Rehydration mixture** – for treatment of severe diarrhoea; particularly necessary if you're travelling with children
- **Scissors, tweezers and thermometer** (note that mercury thermometers are prohibited by airlines)
- **Sunscreen and chap stick**
- **Water-purification tablets**
- **Other Preparations** Make sure you're healthy before you start travelling. If you are going on a long trip make sure your teeth are OK. If you wear glasses take a spare pair and your prescription.

If you need a particular medication take a good supply; it may not be available locally. Take some packaging showing the generic name, which will make getting replacements easier. Take a legible letter or prescription from your doctor to show you legally use the medication.

Basic Rules

Water Domestic, hotel and restaurant tap water is safe to drink throughout the islands. In places with water shortages you might want to check; lowering of water tables might introduce some undesirable ingredients into the supply. Ask '¿Es potable el agua?' if you're in any doubt.

Water from public spouts and fountains is not reliable unless it has a sign saying 'Agua Potable'. Often there are signs saying 'Agua No Potable': don't drink here.

Natural water, unless it's straight from a definitely unpolluted spring, is likewise not safe to drink unpurified.

Safe bottled water is available everywhere, generally for 75 to 85 ptas for a 1.5L bottle in shops and supermarkets.

The simplest way of purifying any water you're uncertain about is to boil it vigorously for five minutes. If you can't boil water it should be treated chemically. Chlorine tablets (Puritabs, Steritabs or other brand names) will kill many pathogens. Iodine is also very effective in purifying water and is available in tablet form (such as Potable Aqua).

Medical Treatment

For serious medical problems and emergencies, the local public-health service provides care to rival that anywhere in the world. However, seeing a doctor about more mundane problems can be a highly frustrating business. If you want to see a

Nutrition

If your food is poor or limited in availability, if you're travelling hard and fast and therefore missing meals, or if you simply lose your appetite, you can soon start to lose weight and place your health at risk.

Make sure your diet is well balanced. Eggs, meat, pulses and dairy products are all safe ways to get protein. Fruit and vegetables are good sources of vitamins. Try to eat plenty of grains, including rice and bread.

In hot weather make sure you drink enough; don't rely on feeling thirsty to indicate when you should drink. Not needing to urinate, or very dark-yellow urine, is a danger sign. Carry a water bottle on long hikes. Excessive sweating can lead to loss of salt and therefore muscle cramping.

~~~~~~~~~~~~~~~~~~~~~~~~~~~~~~

Everyday Health

Normal body temperature is up to 37°C or 98.6°F; more than 2°C (4°F) higher indicates a high fever. The normal adult pulse rate is 60 to 100 per minute (children 80 to 100, babies 100 to 140). As a general rule the pulse increases about 20 beats per minute for each 1°C (2°F) rise in fever.

The respiration (breathing) rate is also an indicator of illness. Count the number of breaths per minute: between 12 and 20 is normal for adults and older children (up to 30 for younger children, 40 for babies). People with a high fever or serious respiratory illness breathe more quickly than normal. More than 40 shallow breaths a minute may indicate pneumonia.

~~~~~~~~~~~~~~~~~~~~~~~~~~~~~~

doctor quickly, or need emergency dental treatment, you could try the *urgencias* (emergency) section of the nearest hospital. Otherwise, the expense of a private clinic or surgery is often worth the saving in time and frustration. A consultation at such a clinic typically costs somewhere between 3000 and 6000 ptas (not counting medicines). If you have travel insurance you may well be covered for this expense. All dental practices are private in any case.

Take all imaginable documentation when you deal with medical services – passport, E111, insurance papers, ideally with photocopies too. Tourist offices, the police, and usually your accommodation, can all tell you where to find doctors, dentists and hospitals, or how to call an ambulance. Many major hospitals and emergency medical services are mentioned and shown on maps in this book's city sections.

Pharmacies (*farmacias*) can help with many ailments. A system of duty pharmacies (*farmacias de guardia*) operates so that each town or district of a city has at least one open all the time (although often only for filling prescriptions). When a pharmacy is closed, it posts the name of the nearest open one(s) on the door. Lists of farmacias de guardia are also often given in local papers.

Environmental Hazards

Fungal Infections Fungal infections occur more commonly in hot weather and are usually found on the scalp, between the toes or fingers, in the groin and on the body (ringworm). You get ringworm (which is a fungal infection, not a worm) from infected animals or other people. Moisture encourages these infections.

To prevent fungal infections wear loose, comfortable clothes, avoid artificial fibres, wash frequently and dry carefully. If you do get an infection, wash the infected area at least daily with a disinfectant or medicated soap and water, and rinse and dry well. Apply an antifungal cream or powder like tolnifate (Tinaderm). Try to expose the infected area to air or sunlight as much as possible and wash all towels and underwear in hot water, change them often and let them dry in the sun.

Heat Exhaustion Dehydration and salt deficiency can cause heat exhaustion. Take time to acclimatise to high temperatures, drink sufficient liquids and do not do anything too physically demanding.

Salt deficiency is characterised by fatigue, lethargy, headaches, giddiness and muscle cramps. Salt tablets may help, but adding extra salt to your food is better.

Heat Stroke This serious, occasionally fatal, condition can occur if the body's heat-regulating mechanism breaks down and the body temperature rises to dangerous levels. Long, continuous periods of exposure to high temperatures and insufficient fluids can leave you vulnerable to heat stroke.

The symptoms are feeling unwell, not sweating very much (or at all) and a high body temperature (39°C to 41°C or 102°F to 106°F). Where sweating has ceased the skin becomes flushed and red. Severe, throbbing headaches and lack of coordination will also occur, and the sufferer may be confused or aggressive. Eventually the victim will become delirious or convulse. Hospitalisation is essential, but in the interim get victims out of the sun, remove their clothing, cover them with a wet sheet or towel and then fan continually. Give fluids if they are conscious.

Jet Lag Jet lag is experienced when a person travels by air across more than three time zones (each time zone usually represents a one-hour time difference). It occurs because many of the functions of the human body (such as temperature, pulse rate and emptying of the bladder and bowels) are regulated by internal 24-hour cycles. When we travel long distances rapidly, our bodies take time to adjust to the 'new time' of our destination, and we may experience fatigue, disorientation, insomnia, anxiety, impaired concentration and loss of appetite. These effects will usually be gone within three days of arrival, but to minimise the impact of jet lag:

- Rest for a couple of days prior to departure.
- Try to select flight schedules which minimise sleep deprivation; arriving late in the day means you can go to sleep soon after you arrive. For very long flights, try to organise a stopover.
- Avoid excessive eating (which bloats the stomach) and alcohol (which causes dehydration) during the flight. Instead, drink plenty of noncarbonated, nonalcoholic drinks such as fruit juice or water.
- Avoid smoking.
- Make yourself comfortable by wearing loose-fitting clothes and perhaps bringing an eye mask and ear plugs to help you sleep.
- Try to sleep at the appropriate time for the time zone you are travelling to.

Prickly Heat Prickly heat is an itchy rash caused by excessive perspiration trapped under the skin. It usually strikes people who have just arrived in a hot climate. Keeping cool, bathing often, drying the skin and using a mild talcum or prickly heat powder or even resorting to air-conditioning may help.

Sunburn In the tropics, the desert or at high altitude you can get sunburnt surprisingly quickly, even through cloud. Use a sunscreen, hat, and barrier cream for your nose and lips. Calamine lotion or Stingose are good for mild sunburn. Protect your eyes with good-quality sunglasses, particularly if you will be near water, sand or snow.

Infectious Diseases
Diarrhoea Simple things like a change of water, food or climate can all cause a mild bout of diarrhoea, but a few rushed toilet trips with no other symptoms is not indicative of a major problem.

Dehydration is the main danger with any diarrhoea, particularly in children or the elderly as dehydration can occur quite quickly. Under all circumstances *fluid replacement* (at least equal to the volume being lost) is the most important thing to remember. Weak black tea with a little sugar, soda water, or soft drinks allowed to go flat and diluted 50% with clean water are all good. With severe diarrhoea a rehydrating solution is preferable to replace minerals and salts lost. Commercially available oral rehydration salts (ORS) are very useful; add them to boiled or bottled water. In an emergency you can make up a solution of six teaspoons of sugar and a half teaspoon of salt to 1L of boiled or bottled water. Urine is the best guide to the adequacy of replacement – if you have small amounts of concentrated urine, you need to drink more. Keep drinking small amounts often, and stick to a bland diet as you recover.

Hepatitis Hepatitis is a general term for inflammation of the liver. It is a common disease worldwide. The symptoms are fever, chills, headache, fatigue, feelings of weakness and aches and pains, followed by loss of appetite, nausea, vomiting, abdominal pain, dark urine, light-coloured faeces, jaundiced (yellow) skin and the whites of the eyes may turn yellow. Hepatitis A is transmitted by contaminated food and drinking water. The disease poses a real threat to the western traveller. You should seek medical advice, but there is not much you can do apart from resting, drinking lots of fluids, eating lightly and avoiding fatty foods. People who have had hepatitis should avoid alcohol for some time after the illness, as the liver needs time to recover.

Hepatitis E is transmitted in the same way, it can be very serious in pregnant women.

There are almost 300 million chronic carriers of Hepatitis B in the world. It is spread through contact with infected blood, blood products or body fluids, eg through sexual contact, unsterilised needles and blood transfusions, or contact with blood via small breaks in the skin. Other risk situations include having a shave, tattoo, or having your body pierced with contaminated equipment. The symptoms of type B may be more severe and may lead to long-term problems. Hepatitis D is spread in the same way, but the risk is mainly in shared needles.

Hepatitis C can lead to chronic liver disease. The virus is spread by contact with blood usually via contaminated transfusions or shared needles. Avoiding these is the only means of prevention.

HIV & AIDS HIV, the Human Immunodeficiency Virus, develops into AIDS, Acquired Immune Deficiency Syndrome, which is a fatal disease. HIV is a major problem in many countries. Any exposure to blood, blood products or body fluids may put the individual at risk. The disease is often transmitted through sexual contact or dirty needles – vaccinations, acupuncture, tattooing and body piercing can be potentially as dangerous as intravenous drug use. HIV/AIDS can also be spread through infected blood transfusions; some developing countries cannot afford to screen blood used for transfusions.

If you do need an injection, ask to see the syringe unwrapped in front of you, or take a needle and syringe pack with you.

Fear of HIV infection should never preclude treatment for serious medical conditions.

Sexually Transmitted Diseases Gonorrhoea, herpes and syphilis are among these diseases; sores, blisters or rashes around the genitals, discharges or pain when urinating are common symptoms. In some sexually transmitted diseases (STDs), such as wart virus or chlamydia, symptoms may be less marked or not observed at all especially in women. Syphilis symptoms eventually disappear completely but the disease continues and can cause severe problems in later years. While abstinence from sexual contact is the only 100% effective prevention, using condoms is also effective. The treatment of gonorrhoea and syphilis is with antibiotics. The different sexually transmitted diseases each require specific antibiotics. There is no cure for herpes or AIDS.

Less Common Diseases
Rabies Rabies is a fatal viral infection found in many countries, although not much of an issue in the Canary Islands. Many animals can be infected (such as dogs, cats and bats) and it is their saliva which is infectious. Any bite, scratch or even lick from a warm-blooded, furry animal should be cleaned immediately and thoroughly. Scrub with soap and running water, and then apply alcohol or iodine solution. Medical help should be sought promptly to receive a course of injections to prevent the onset of symptoms and death.

Tetanus Tetanus occurs when a wound becomes infected by a germ that lives in soil and in the faeces of horses and other animals. It enters the body via breaks in the skin. All wounds should be cleaned promptly and adequately and an antiseptic cream or solution applied. Use antibiotics if the wound becomes hot, throbs or pus is seen. The first symptom may be discomfort in swallowing, or stiffening of the jaw and neck; this is followed by painful convulsions of the jaw and whole body. The disease can be fatal.

Insect Bites & Stings

Bee and wasp stings are usually painful rather than dangerous. However in people who are allergic to them severe breathing difficulties may occur and require urgent medical care. Calamine lotion or Stingose spray will give relief and ice packs will reduce the pain and swelling.

Cuts & Scratches

Wash well and treat any cut with an antiseptic such as povidone-iodine. Where possible avoid bandages and Band-aids, which can keep wounds wet.

Coral cuts are notoriously slow to heal and if they are not adequately cleaned small pieces of coral can become embedded in the wound. Clean any cut thoroughly with an antiseptic. Severe pain, throbbing, redness, fever or generally feeling unwell suggest infection and the need for antibiotics promptly as coral cuts may result in serious infections.

Women's Health

Gynaecological Problems Sexually transmitted diseases are a major cause of vaginal problems. Symptoms include a smelly discharge, painful intercourse and sometimes a burning sensation when urinating. Male sexual partners must also be treated. Medical attention should be sought and remember in addition to these diseases HIV or Hepatitis B may also be acquired during exposure. Besides abstinence, the best thing is to practise safe sex using condoms.

Antibiotic use, synthetic underwear, sweating and contraceptive pills can lead to fungal vaginal infections when travelling in hot climates. Maintaining good personal hygiene, and loose-fitting clothes and cotton underwear will help to prevent these infections.

Fungal infections, characterised by a rash, itch and discharge, can be treated with a vinegar or lemon-juice douche, or with yoghurt. Nystatin, miconazole or clotrimazole pessaries or vaginal cream are the usual treatment.

Pregnancy Most miscarriages occur during the first three months of pregnancy. Miscarriage is not uncommon, and can occasionally lead to severe bleeding. The last three months should also be spent within reasonable distance of good medical care. A baby born as early as 24 weeks stands a chance of survival, but only in a good modern hospital. Additional care should be taken to prevent illness and particular attention should be paid to diet and nutrition. Alcohol and nicotine, for example, should be avoided.

WOMEN TRAVELLERS

The best way for women travellers to approach the Canary Islands is simply to be ready to ignore stares, catcalls and unnecessary comments. Harassment is much less frequent than you might expect, and the advice here is really just the common sense stuff you need to keep in mind anywhere. Think twice about going alone to isolated stretches of beach or down dark city streets at night. Where there are crowds – as there often are very late into the night in towns and cities – you're safer. It's inadvisable for a woman to hitchhike alone – and not a great idea even for two women together.

Topless bathing and skimpy clothes are generally OK at the coastal resorts, but otherwise a little more modesty is the norm. Not a few local young women feel no compunction about dressing to kill, but equally feel absolutely no obligation to respond to any male interest this arouses.

Recommended reading is the *Handbook for Women Travellers* by M & G Moss.

GAY & LESBIAN TRAVELLERS

Gay and lesbian sex are both legal in Spain and hence in the Canary Islands, and the age of consent is 16 years, the same as for heterosexuals. The Playa del Inglés, on the southern end of Gran Canaria, is where the bulk of Europe's gay crowd heads when holidaying in the Canaries, and the night life here bumps and grinds all year round. *Guía Gay Visado* is a guide to gay and lesbian bars, discos and contacts throughout

Spain and can be found mostly in gay and lesbian bookshops. *Entiendes*, a gay magazine, is on sale at some newsstands for 500 ptas.

Before you leave home, check out the *Spartacus Guide for Gay Men* (the Spartacus list also includes the comprehensive *Spartacus National Edition España*, in English and German), published by Bruno Gmünder Verlag, Mail Order, PO Box 11 07 29, D-1000 Berlin 11. Ferrari Publications, Phoenix, AZ, USA, also does travel guides for gay men and *Places for Women*. Lesbians should look also at *Women Going Places*, published in London by Women Going Places.

There are a few Spanish queer sites on the World Wide Web, one of the best of which is *Gay Spain* (gayspain.com). It has city and regional listings of bars, clubs, accommodation and the like that include options in the Canary Islands. The information is in Spanish.

For information about gay groups in the islands, you might like to write in advance to the Colectivo de Gays y Lesbianas de Las Palmas, Apartado de Correos 707, 35080 Las Palmas de Gran Canaria.

DISABLED TRAVELLERS

The British-based Royal Association for Disability & Rehabilitation (RADAR) publishes a useful guide, *Holidays & Travel Abroad: A Guide for Disabled People*, with a section on Spain (including the Canary Islands) covering contact addresses, transport, services and accommodation. Contact RADAR (☎ 0171-250 3222) at 12 City Forum, 250 City Rd, London EC1 8AF. Mobility International (☎ 02-410 6274; fax 02-410 6297), Rue de Manchester 25, Brussels B1070, Belgium, has researched facilities for disabled tourists in Spain and the Canary Islands.

In the UK again, Holiday Care Service (☎ 01293-774535) can send you a fact sheet on hotels and other accommodation in the Canary Islands catering for the disabled, as well as travel agents who can help organise trips.

SENIOR TRAVELLERS

Senior citizens get reductions on the inter-island ferries and hydrofoils (see the Getting Around chapter for more information). Some of the luxurious *paradores* occasionally offer discounts for people over 60 (see Accommodation later in this chapter).

TRAVEL WITH CHILDREN

Canarios take quickly to children, who are welcome at all kinds of accommodation, and in virtually every café, bar and restaurant. In fact, having children with you can often open doors to contact with local people who you otherwise may not have the opportunity to meet.

The omnipresence of bars and cafés with outside tables allows drinking grown-ups to indulge in their favourite tipples while their little ones run around and play – a good sign of a comparatively child-friendly society. Local kids are quite used to staying up late and at fiestas it's commonplace to see even tiny ones toddling the streets at 2 or 3 am. Visiting kids like this idea too – but often can't cope with it quite so readily.

Travelling with kids obviously implies taking a different approach to your holiday. Constant moving around may be fascinating for adults, but children often fail to appreciate the joys of the road. Fortunately, the Canaries are in this sense an ideal location – only those determined to see all seven islands at lightning speed would be tempted to subject themselves, let alone their children, to day after day of tiring movement. As a rule, kids adapt quickly to new environments, but most would never budge if they had a choice. Hanging around the one spot for a few days at a time, or choosing a permanent base from which to make excursions, creates a sense of familiarity (quite nice for adults too!).

The kind of activities which take up most visitors' time in the islands, such as lounging around on beaches, are usually welcomed by kids, too. Children will be cheered by the knowledge that the Canaries are not overly laden with museums, monuments and other artificial wonders which so often are a source of incomprehensible fascination to grown-ups, and of desperate, yawn-inducing boredom to themselves.

Some of the stuff put on for tourists should appeal as much to kids as adults. Animal reserves (such as Tenerife's Loro Parque) and a plethora of theme parks on the main islands of Tenerife and Gran Canaria provide fun for all the family.

Bring along at least a couple of your kids' favourite toys and/or games to keep them occupied.

There are no particular health precautions you need to take with your children in the Canary Islands. That said, kids tend to be more affected than adults by unaccustomed heat, changes in diet and sleeping patterns, and just being in a strange place.

Nappies, creams, lotions, baby foods and so on are all as easily available in the Canary Islands as in any other western country, but if there's some particular brand you swear by it's best to bring it with you. Calpol, for instance, isn't easily found.

Infants generally travel free on ferries and other boats, and those from two to 12 go for half price.

Lonely Planet's *Travel with Children*, by Maureen Wheeler, has lots of practical advice on the subject, and first-hand stories from many Lonely Planet authors, and others, who have done it.

USEFUL ORGANISATIONS

The Instituto Cervantes, with branches in over 30 cities around the world, exists to promote Spanish language and culture in all Spanish-speaking countries. It's mainly involved in Spanish language teaching and library and information services. The library at the London branch – 102 Eaton Square, London SW1 W9AN (☎ 0171-486 4350) – has a wide range of material on Spain but little specifically on the Canary Islands. It includes reference books, literature, books on history and the arts, periodicals, over 1000 videos including

feature films, language-teaching material, electronic databases and music CDs.

TIVE, the Spanish youth and student travel organisation, is good for reduced-price youth and student travel tickets. It also issues various useful documents such as HI youth hostel cards, and FIYTO and ISIC cards (see Visas & Documents earlier in this chapter). TIVE has branches in Las Palmas de Gran Canaria and La Laguna (Tenerife).

DANGERS & ANNOYANCES

The Canary Islands are not exactly dangerous territory, and the vast majority of travellers to the islands risk little more than sunburn and the occasional hangover.

Petty theft (which may not seem so petty if your passport, cash, travellers cheques, credit card and camera all go missing), is a problem, but with a few simple precautions you can minimise the danger.

For some specific hints about looking after your luggage and money, and on safety for women, see the What to Bring, Money and Women Travellers sections earlier in this chapter.

Before you leave home, inscribe your name, address and telephone number inside your luggage, and take photocopies of the important pages of your passport, travel tickets and other important documents. Keep the copies separate from the originals and ideally leave one set of copies at home. These steps will make things easier if you do suffer loss or theft.

Travel insurance against theft and loss is another good idea; see the Health section in this chapter.

Theft & Loss

The risk of theft is highest in the resorts, the main towns and when you first arrive in the islands or a new town and may be off your guard, disoriented or unaware of danger signs. Pickpockets and bag snatchers are the main worry, along with theft from cars. Carry valuables under your clothes if possible – certainly not in a back pocket or in a day pack or anything that could be snatched away easily – and keep your eyes open for

In Case of Emergency

If you're seriously ill or injured, someone should let your embassy or consulate know. Otherwise, various emergency numbers are provided throughout this guide. Many numbers for the nearest police, Guardia Civil or ambulance are hard-to-remember nine-digit ones. There are, however, a few you can try in an emergency from (in most cases) anywhere in the archipelago:

☎ 091
Policía Nacional (National Police)
☎ 092
Policía Local (Local Police)
☎ 061
Urgencias Salud (Medical Emergencies)
☎ 062
Guardia Civil emergency – this only works in Gran Canaria, Lanzarote and Fuerteventura
☎ 080
Bomberos (Firefighters) – this only applies to Gran Canaria

La Policía Spanish police are on the whole more of a help than a threat to the average law-abiding traveller. Most of them are certainly friendly enough to be approachable for directions on the street. Unpleasant events such as random drug searches do occur, but not with great frequency. Spain has no real equivalent of 'bobby on the beat' street patrol police.

There are three main types of *policía*: the **Policía Nacional**, the **Guardia Civil** and the **Policía Local** (sometimes called the Policía Municipal). The words policía and guardia are used here to refer to the forces, but they also denote the individual members.

The **Policía Nacional** covers cities and bigger towns and is the main crime-fighting body because most crimes happen on its patch. Those in uniform wear blue, but there is also a large contingent in plain clothes, some of whom form special squads dealing with drugs, terrorism, etc. Most of them, though, are to be found in police stations called *comisarías*, shuffling masses of paper concerning things such as the issuing of passports, identity cards, and residence cards for foreigners who like Spain enough to opt for long-term entanglement with its bureaucracy.

More numerous are the green uniforms of the **Guardia Civil**, whose main responsibilities are villages, roads, the countryside, prisons, and some environmental protection.

The Guardia Civil was established in the 19th century to quell banditry, but soon came to be regarded as a politicised force repressing any challenge to the status quo. Though its image has softened since Franco and it has been moved out of the responsibility of the Defence Ministry into the Interior Ministry, it remains a military organisation in some ways: most officers have attended a military academy, and members qualify for military decorations.

The **Policía Local** is under the jurisdiction of city and town councils, and deals mainly with minor matters such as parking, traffic and bylaws. They wear a blue and white uniform.

If you need to go to the police, any of them will do, but you may find the Policía Local the most helpful.

people who get unnecessarily close to you. Never leave anything visible in cars – it is an open invitation to break in. If possible, don't even leave anything valuable in the boot (trunk). Hire cars in particular are targeted.

Take care with your belongings on the beach; anything lying on the sand could disappear in a flash when your back is turned – lone travellers should consider investing in a waterproof neck pouch so that they can keep money, passport and other (lightweight) valuables with them even while swimming.

Avoid dingy, empty city alleys and back streets, or anywhere that just doesn't feel 100% safe, at night.

Don't leave anything valuable lying around your room, and use a safe if one's available.

If anything valuable is stolen or lost, you must report it to the police, and get a copy of the report, if you want to make an insurance claim.

If your passport has gone, contact your embassy or consulate for help in issuing a replacement. Embassies and consulates can give help of various kinds in other emergencies, but as a rule cannot advance you money to get home. Where your country has no consulate in the islands, you may have to contact your embassy in Madrid.

Other Emergencies
Medical emergency numbers and locations of many hospitals and clinics are given in this book's city and town sections. See also the boxed aside on this page for general emergency numbers.

Annoyances
You would have to be in a bad mood to get all that annoyed in the Canaries, but several things can get on your nerves. In the bigger cities and, above all, in the resorts noise can be a problem. Of course, you can always leave cities and resorts behind in search of more tranquil locales.

While on the subject of resorts, party animals should be aware that some other party animals, when sufficiently tanked, can become quite unpredictable. In most cases, we are talking loud and drunken louts ferried in on charter flights from northern Europe and the UK, some of whom can't resist a good fight. It is sad but largely true that the bulk of those who end up in Canary Islands coolers are foreigners who just don't seem to know when enough is enough. The best thing you can probably do is walk away from trouble if you see it brewing, and if warranted try to contact the police – although locals will probably see to that before you can. See also Legal Matters below.

LEGAL MATTERS
If you're arrested you will be allotted the free services of a duty solicitor (*abogado de oficio*), who may speak only Spanish. You're also entitled to make a phone call. If you use this to contact your embassy or consulate, it will probably be able to do no more than refer you to a lawyer who speaks your language. If you end up in court, the authorities are obliged to provide a translator.

Drugs
Spain's liberal drug laws were tightened in 1992. The only legal drug is cannabis, and only in amounts for personal use – which means very small amounts.

Public consumption of any drug is apparently illegal, yet in some bars people still smoke joints openly. Other bars will ask you to step outside if you light up. The only sure moral of these stories is to be very discreet if you do use cannabis.

BUSINESS HOURS
Generally, people work Monday to Friday from about 9 am to 2 pm and then again from 4.30 or 5 pm for another three hours. Shops and travel agencies are usually open these hours on Saturday too, although some may skip the evening session. Big supermarkets and department stores such as the El Corte Inglés chain, often stay open all day Monday to Saturday, from about 9 am to 9 pm. A lot of government offices don't

bother with afternoon opening any day of the year. See earlier sections of this chapter for bank and post office hours.

PUBLIC HOLIDAYS & SPECIAL EVENTS
Public Holidays
There are at least 14 official holidays a year in the Canary Islands. When a holiday falls close to a weekend, locals like to make a *puente* (bridge) – meaning they take the intervening day off too. On occasion, when a couple of holidays fall close to the same weekend, the puente becomes an *acueducto* (acqueduct)!

The seven main national holidays, observed throughout the islands and the rest of Spain (the authorities seem to change their minds about some of these as the years go by), are:

1 January
  Anõ Nuevo (New Year's Day)
March/April
  Viernes Santo (Good Friday)
1 May
  Fiesta del Trabajo (Labour Day)
15 August
  La Asunción (Feast of the Assumption)
12 October
  Día de la Hispanidad (National Day)
1 November
  Todos Santos (All Saints' Day) – gets particular attention across the island of Tenerife
8 December
  La Inmaculada Concepción (Feast of the Immaculate Conception)
25 December
  Navidad (Christmas)

In addition, the Canary Islands regional government sets a further five holidays, while local councils allocate another two. Common dates include:

6 January
  Epifanía (Epiphany) or *Día de los Reyes Magos* (Three Kings' Day), when children receive presents
19 March
  Día de San Juan (St John's Day)

March/April
  Jueves Santo (Maundy Thursday, the day before Good Friday)
30 May
  Día de las Islas Canarias (Canary Islands Day)
June
  Corpus Christi (the Thursday after the eighth Sunday after Easter Sunday) – in Las Palmas de Gran Canaria, La Laguna and La Orotava (Tenerife), locals prepare extraordinary floral carpets to celebrate this feast day, and the celebration is also big in Mazo and El Paso, in La Palma
25 July
  Día de Santiago Apóstol (Feast of St James the Apostle, Spain's patron saint) – in Santa Cruz de Tenerife the day also marks the commemoration of the defence of the city against Horatio Nelson
6 December
  Día de la Constitución (Constitution Day)

Fiestas
Canarios, like many of their mainland cousins, have a penchant for letting it all hang out at numerous fiestas and local *ferias* (fairs) throughout the year. With little doubt *Carnaval* is the wildest time, but there are many others in the course of the year – indeed in August alone it is said there are more than 50.

Many of these fiestas have a religious background (saints' days are common) but in practice they are generally occasions for having fun. *Romerías* are particularly noteworthy. Processions of a more or less organised nature head from a town's churches to a hermitage or similar location dedicated to a saint or the Virgin Mary, located some way from the town.

Many local festivals are noted in city and town sections of this book and tourist offices can supply more detailed information. A few of the most outstanding include:

2 February
  Virgen de la Candelaria (festival of the patron of the archipelago) – an intense festival deriving from the supposed apparition before the Guanches of the Virgin Mary (the event is also celebrated on 15 August); the festival is celebrated in the town of the same name in Tenerife

February/March

Carnaval (Carnival) – several weeks of fancy-dress parades and merrymaking across the islands, ending on the Tuesday 47 days before Easter Sunday. This is at its wildest and most extravagant in Santa Cruz de Tenerife, where the locals put on a display rivalling that of Rio de Janeiro.

21-30 June

Bajada de Nuestra Señora de las Nieves – this fiesta is held only once every five years in Santa Cruz de Palma. The processions, dances and merrymaking constitute the island's premier religious festival.

July

Romería de San Benito Abad – held on the first Sunday of the month in La Laguna (Tenerife)

14 July

Día de San Buenaventura – patron saint of Betancuria, Fuerteventura

4 August

Fiesta de la Rama – held in Agaete (Gran Canaria)

August (dates vary)

Romería de San Roque – held in Garachico (Tenerife)

25 August

Día de San Ginés – held in Arrecife (Lanzarote)

6-8 September

Fiesta de la Virgen del Pino – held in Teror (Gran Canaria), it is the island's most important religious celebration. The festivities actually begin two weeks before these final key days.

7-15 September

Fiesta del Santísimo Cristo – held in La Laguna (Tenerife)

October

Romería de Nuestra Señora de la Luz – held in Las Palmas de Gran Canaria and marked by a boat procession

13 December

Día de Santa Lucía – celebrated all over Gran Canaria

Arts Festivals Las Palmas de Gran Canaria in particular plays host to several important arts festivals including the Festival Internacional de Música (January); the Festival de Opera (February-March); the Festival de Ballet y Danza (May); and the Muestra Internacional de Cine (an international film festival held every two years in October-November).

The Encuentro Teatral Tres Continentes (aka Festival Internacional de Teatro de los Tres Mundos) attracts theatre companies from Europe, Latin America and Africa to Agüimes (Gran Canaria) in September.

ACTIVITIES

There is no shortage of distractions in the Canaries, where everything from golf to water sports, trekking to diving are on offer.

Cycling

Mountain bikes can be rented from some resorts. They are a great way of escaping the crowds and heading for the hills and a less touristy experience. Some forest tracks are suitable for biking.

Trekking & Hiking

Not everyone who visits the islands wants simply to lounge around on the beaches and hang out in bars. Away from the coast there is plenty of surprising countryside to explore. The western islands in particular, not strong on beaches anyway, offer some great walking.

Surfing

The best islands to look for waves are Lanzarote and Gran Canaria, where you are likely to get a reliable combination of satisfying swell and wind that doesn't chop it all up.

Windsurfing

This must be one of the most popular sports in the islands. Wherever you are you can normally pick up a sufficient breeze to make it worth your while to head out with your board and sail. Hiring gear is generally no problem – you'll find outlets at the main resorts.

Gran Canaria is the windiest of the group and thus ideal for what locals call windsurfetas, who choose above all the beach of Bahía de Pozo Izquierdo to practise their sport. It is usually here that summertime world-class competitions are held. Pretty much all the island's beaches are fine for your average windsurfeta. Among other spots on this island, all situated between Las Palmas and Maspalomas, are: Playa del Ojo de Garza, Playa del Burrero, Vargas, Arinaga, Mosca Point (near Pozo Izquierdo), Juan Grande, Playa del Aguila, Bahía Feliz, and the Faro (lighthouse) de Maspalomas.

Playa de El Cabezo (near El Médano) in Tenerife, Playa de Sotavento in southern Fuerteventura, and Las Cucharas (near Costa Teguise) in Lanzarote all offer good windsurfing conditions too.

In general the conditions are so good that three rounds of the PWA World Tour are held in the islands every year (one each in Gran Canaria, Tenerife and Fuerteventura).

Warning The prevailing trade winds (*alisios*) are particularly strong in April and summer. Also, various spots, including some of those mentioned above, can be dangerous for the inexpert. If you are unsure, ask advice from a nearby windsurfing school or shop. It is illegal to head out to sea less than two hours before sunset. That's a hard law to enforce, but the idea is that you shouldn't be out there after dark – if you stuff up, you'll be hard to rescue.

Swimming

The Atlantic can get nasty in winter, with more powerful swells than in summer. This is particularly the case in the north, where swimming can be hazardous away from protected beaches and rockpools. Even strong swimmers should take care. Use common sense. A good rule of thumb is to stay out of the water unless you can see other people cavorting off your chosen beach.

Snorkelling & Scuba Diving

The clear waters of the Canaries offer good diving possibilities. Of course, we are not talking the spectacular reefs on offer in the Red Sea or Australia's Great Barrier Reef, but satisfying ocean diving with the chance to see a variety of rays, grouper, barracuda, turtles, a range of tropical fish and the occasional shark.

There are several marine parks where you can get into this, and many outfits offer diving safaris and wreck diving. Some of the better diving is around the islands of Tenerife and Lanzarote, where the sea life is rich and varied.

Off Tenerife you can dive and swim with dolphins or even feed rays, while around the islets and Famara coast of Lanzarote you can see coral covered rock walls, octopus colonies, big schools of various fish types and colourful marine flora. The walls and tunnels between Corralejo and Islote de Lobos, Fuerteventura, contrast with the shallow terraces off the south coast, teeming with sea life. The marine reserve off La Restinga in El Hierro is also a good spot.

The quality of the water means that you can generally rely on around 25-30m visibility, especially in summer and autumn.

You'll find about 40 dive centres (*centros de buceo*) scattered throughout the islands, and most hire out all the necessary gear. Some also offer diver-certification courses, including PADI, CMAS, NAUI and FEDAS courses. You would be looking at about 40,000 ptas for a beginners' course. You are advised to bring any submarine photographic equipment you are likely to want, as dive centres tend not to have it on hand.

Fishing

Deep-sea fishing is another popular activity for those with a little of Captain Ahab or Ernest Hemingway in them. You can get onto fully equipped fishing trips from the main resorts.

It is said that deep-sea fishing is especially good in the waters off Gran Canaria, where more than 30 world fishing records have been set.

Sailing

For those with looser purse strings, it is possible to charter yachts or catamarans for day excursions and longer trips. Several of the yacht clubs offer this possibility. The sailing conditions are good all year round, and

Considerations for Responsible Diving

The popularity of diving is placing immense pressure on many sites. Please consider the following tips when diving and help preserve the ecology and beauty of reefs:

Do not use anchors on the reef, and take care not to ground boats on coral. Encourage dive operators and regulatory bodies to establish permanent moorings at popular dive sites.

Avoid touching living marine organisms. Polyps can be damaged by even the gentlest contact. Never stand on corals, even if they look solid and robust. If you must secure yourself to the reef, only hold fast to exposed rock or dead coral.

Be conscious of your fins. Even without contact the surge from heavy fin strokes near the reef can damage delicate organisms. When treading water in shallow reef areas, take care not to kick up clouds of sand. Settling sand can easily smother the delicate organisms of the reef.

Practise and maintain proper buoyancy control. Major damage can be done by divers descending too fast and colliding with the reef. Make sure you are correctly weighted and that your weight belt is positioned so that you stay horizontal. If you have not dived for a while, have a practice dive in a pool before taking to the reef. Be aware that buoyancy can change over the period of an extended trip: initially you may breathe harder and need more weighting; a few days later you may breathe more easily and need less weight.

Take great care in underwater caves. Spend as little time within them as possible as your air bubbles may be caught within the roof and leave previously submerged organisms high and dry. Taking turns to inspect the interior of a small cave will lessen the chances of damaging contact.

Resist the temptation to collect or buy corals or shells. Aside from the ecological damage, taking home marine souvenirs depletes the beauty of a site and spoils the enjoyment for others.

The same goes for marine archaeological sites (mainly shipwrecks). Respect their integrity; they may even be protected from looting by law.

Ensure that you take home all your rubbish, and any litter you may find as well. Plastics in particular are a serious threat to marine life. Turtles will mistake plastic for jelly fish and eat it.

Resist the temptation to feed fish. You may disturb their normal eating habits, encourage aggressive behaviour or feed them food that is detrimental to their health.

Minimise your disturbance of marine animals. In particular, do not ride on the backs of turtles as this causes them great anxiety.

---

there are ports and facilities on all the islands.

Other Water Sports

All resorts offer the usual damp diversions, from water-skiing to banana-boats rides. Jet skis abound and you can try parascending (where you dangle beneath a parachute attached to a rocketing speedboat).

Golf

If bashing small white balls with sticks is your thing, you'll find six good courses in the Canaries. It was resident British businessmen who established the Real Club de Golf de Las Palmas on Gran Canaria back in 1891. It's still going strong, and the Spanish golf hero Severiano Ballesteros plays here often. There's another club at Maspalomas. On Lanzarote, the only course is at the northern edge of Costa Teguise, while on Tenerife there are three courses. The Real Club de Golf de Tenerife is just south of La Laguna and was established in 1932. The other two clubs are on the south coast near El Médano. All the courses host various national and international tournaments, and plans are afoot to see if yet more courses can't be laid out on the other islands!

LANGUAGE COURSES

A spot of study in the Canary Islands is a great way not only to learn something but also to meet people – locals as well as other travellers – and get more of an inside angle on life in the islands.

Branches of the Instituto Cervantes (see Useful Organisations in this chapter) can send you lists of places offering Spanish-language courses in the Canary Islands. Some Spanish embassies and consulates also have information on courses. In Spain contact the Servicio Central de Cursos de Español (☎ 91 593 19 49; fax 91 445 69 60), Calle de Trafalgar 32, 17MDSU7o D, 28010 Madrid.

The Universidad de la Laguna (☎/fax 922 60 33 45) on Tenerife island offers a variety of language and culture courses to foreigners. Write to: Secretaría de los Cursos para Extranjeros, Universidad de la Laguna, Avenida de Trinidad s/n, Edificio Becas 2°, 35015 La Laguna, Tenerife.

The Instituto Cervantes in your country can also supply a list of organisations that arrange study trips to Spain, although few such trips are directed to the Canaries.

Finally, several private language schools are dotted about the islands, above all in Las Palmas de Gran Canaria. Check the local Yellow Pages (Páginas Amarillas) under 'Academias de Idiomas'.

Language courses vary greatly in duration, cost and depth – your choice depends largely on your goals. Those with serious ambitions to learn Spanish will want to consider more intensive classes over an extended period.

It's worth asking whether your course will lead to any formal certificate of competence. The Diploma de Español como Lengua Extranjera (DELE) is a qualification recognised by Spain's Ministry of Education and Science.

Expect to pay around 2000 ptas per hour for individual private lessons.

WORK

Unemployment is as big a problem in the Canary Islands as in southern Spain, so there is no great demand for foreign labour. A couple of possibilities exist though, so you might have luck. If you have any contacts in the islands, locals or foreigners, sound them out, as word of mouth counts for a lot.

Nationals of EU countries, Norway and Iceland are allowed to work in Spain without a visa, but if they plan to stay more than three months, they are supposed to apply within the first month for a tarjeta de residencia (residence card); for information on this laborious process, see Visas & Documents earlier in this chapter. Virtually everyone else is supposed to obtain, from a Spanish consulate in their country of residence, a work permit and, if they plan to stay more than 90 days, a residence visa. These procedures are well-nigh impossible unless you have a job contract lined up before you begin them; in any case you should start the processes a long time before you aim to go to Spain. Quite a few people opt to work discreetly (less politely known as *trabajo negro* – black work) and skip the bureaucracy.

Language Teaching

The greatest employers of foreigners, particularly English speakers, in the Canary Islands are language schools. To get a job, some formal qualifications such as the RSA First Certificate for the Teaching of English as a Foreign Language (TEFL) make an enormous difference.

There are schools on all the islands, but only in any great number on Tenerife and Gran Canaria.

You can start your search with the Yellow Pages, looking under 'Academias de Idiomas'. Getting a job in one of them is harder if you're not an EU citizen. Some schools do employ people without work papers, although often at lower than normal rates. Giving private lessons is another avenue, although unlikely to bring you a living wage straight away.

Tourist Resorts

High season work in the islands' main resorts is another possibility, especially if you get in there early in the season and are prepared to stay a while. Many bars, restaurants and other businesses are run by foreigners, especially in the resort areas like Maspalomas and Playa de las Américas.

If you have relevant training, you may get lucky and snare work with one of the main dive companies.

Busking

A few travellers earn a crust (and not much more) busking in the resorts.

ACCOMMODATION
Seasons & Reservations

Prices at any type of accommodation may vary with the season. Some places have separate price structures for the high season (*temporada alta*), mid-season (*temporada media*) or the low season (*temporada baja*), all usually displayed on a notice in reception or close by. Hoteliers are not actually bound by these displayed prices. They are free to charge less, which they quite often do, or more, which happens fairly rarely.

High season in the Canary Islands runs from about December to March (including the Carnaval period), and this is when you are likely to find accommodation at its most costly – and elusive. Seaman Santa (Easter Week) is another busy time. Summer can also be busy, as this is when mainland Spaniards turn up.

Individual towns can fill up when a local fiesta is on, and the smaller islands can also fill quickly for important celebrations.

The overwhelming majority of visitors to the Canary Islands come with accommodation booked. This has certain advantages, especially in high season, when going it alone can be difficult.

The biggest problem for budget travellers is that there are often not many cheap-end accommodation options, ie pensiones, to choose from. Apartments sometimes fill this gap admirably, but not always. Independent travel is quite viable in the Canaries, but there can be moments when you wonder if you'll find a room you can afford.

For obvious reasons, the prices for accommodation in this book are intended as a guide only. Always check room charges before putting your bags down.

Camping

There are only three official camping grounds in the Canary Islands, and on some islands free camping is either forbidden (eg La Gomera) or strictly limited. On Tenerife for instance there are 17 grounds – but you need a special permit to use them. It is worth asking in the tourist offices about local camping possibilities. Do not assume that you will always be able to pitch a tent whenever you wish.

Note that Camping Gaz is the only common brand of camping gas: screw-on canisters are near-impossible to find.

Apartments

More common than hotels are apartments for rent. To give a random idea of just how much more common they are, the tourist office on La Gomera has an accommodation list for the island that counts 22 hotels, hostales and pensiones, compared with 154 apartment blocks. The quality of these can vary greatly, but they can be more comfortable than a simple pensión, especially if there are several of you. In an apartment you generally get a double bedroom, bathroom, lounge and kitchenette. In a few cases one-bed studios (*estudios*) are also available.

The down side for the independent traveller is that they can often all be booked ahead by package tourists. In the main resorts of Tenerife, Gran Canaria, Lanzarote and Fuerteventura, many apartments work only with tour operators and foreign travel agencies. They will simply not take in lone wanderers who just turn up.

In the case of many of the smaller ones, the owner doesn't live in or even near the building, so there's no point in just turning up – you need to call. This is particularly the case in the three westernmost islands, where small operators predominate. As a rule, the contact phone numbers will be posted at the entrance in these cases.

Solo travellers often find themselves being asked more than they would pay for a simple room in a pensión.

Apartments are officially categorised as one to three keys. At the bottom end of the scale they can cost as little as 3000 or 4000 ptas for a double. At the top you may be looking at anything up to 16,000 ptas.

If you arrive somewhere and money is limited, you have no luck finding a pensión and you don't see any of the usual signs for *apartamentos de alquiler* (apartments for rent – this applies above all to the western three islands), keep an eye peeled for the official white-on-red AT sign, which also denotes apartments.

Again, in the more touristed eastern four islands, you will often find no vacancy and little willingness to deal with independent travellers. In the western three islands, the usually small places more often than not have no-one in attendance. Rather a phone number will be posted and you will have to call to find out what the story is. This can sometimes be a trying business.

Because of the peculiar difficulties sometimes associated with apartments, and the need in most cases for a phone number, you should get a hold of each island's hotel/ apartment guide from the main tourist offices as soon as you can after arrival. They are often far from complete, but at least give you some information to work with. You can get provincial lists (which do not include the bottom-end, one-star options) at the main offices in Santa Cruz de Tenerife and Las Palmas de Gran Canaria.

Packages The overwhelming majority of people who end up in the apartments are package tourists who book their accommo-dation with flights at home. The problem here is that you can never really know what you are going to end up with. Make some enquiries about what services the apartment you have been offered has. Is there a pool? A bar? Children's facilities?

Youth Hostels
With only one official youth hostel, on Gran Canaria, it is hardly worth worrying about becoming a member just to travel in the Canary Islands.

Pensiones, Hostales, Hotels & Paradores
Officially, all these establishments are either *hoteles* (from one to five stars), *hostales* (one to three stars) or *pensiones* (one or two stars).

Compared with mainland Spain, there are precious few of any of these around. Since the bulk of the islands' visitors arrive with accommodation booked in advance – usually in villas or self-catering apartments – the demand for more standard hotels is low.

The one-star pensión is at the bottom of the rung and a double room without bathroom will generally start at around 2500/ 3000 ptas. Often no discount is made for single occupancy. These places are usually adequate, although some are more rundown than others. The second star usually means there is at least a wash basin in the room. Hostales are often little different from pensiones. Occasionally pensiones come with different names, eg *Casa de Huéspedes* (Guest House). In effect they are all the same thing.

Establishments calling themselves hotels range from simple places, where a single/ double room could cost around 4000/6000 ptas, up to wildly luxurious, five-star establishments where your imagination is often the limit on the price you pay. Even in the cheapest ones there'll probably be a restaurant and rooms are likely to have an attached bathroom.

In a special category are the *paradores* (officially *paradores de turismo*), a Spanish state-run chain of high-class hotels with six establishments in the Canary Islands. These can be wonderful places to splurge. They also offer discounts for staying more than one night, and for senior citizens. You can book a room at any parador through their Central de Reservas (Central Booking Service; ☎ 91 516 66 66; fax 91 516 66 57), Calle de Requena 3, 28013 Madrid.

Casas Rurales

Converted farmsteads or village houses sometimes form the only accommodation option in out-of-way places. They are often a highly agreeable option for those seeking to escape the noise and bustle of the resorts and head into the countryside. It is best to call ahead, as they usually offer limited places. Since they tend to be away from most public transport, you wouldn't want to just turn up at one only to be turned away. Prices start at around 6000 ptas for a double (single occupancy rarely attracts a reduction).

Timeshare

It is estimated that as many as three million people around the world buy their slice of holiday pleasure in advance this way. Timeshare involves purchasing a block of time in an apartment or resort that you elect to use regularly for your holidays. Of course nothing is to stop you lending or renting out your booked time to third parties if for whatever reason you decide not to use your annual allocation.

You may well come across timeshare touts if you hang around the main resorts in the Canary Islands. If you feel taken enough by the islands to consider wanting to return repeatedly for your holidays, timeshare may be worth considering – but you should be careful about how you choose. You want to be sure that the place you choose has the amenities you want. You need to see all your rights and obligations clearly in writing, especially where management companies promise to sell your timeshare for you if you decide to buy a new one. Remember that you are not buying property, but time in a property for your future holidays.

The cost variables are many. The type of accommodation (from a cottage through to a luxury resort apartment), its location and the season in which you want the time (high season will cost you more) will all affect the cost.

Find a reputable manager when buying a timeshare. In Europe, your first stop should be your country's member of the European Timeshare Federation. The Timeshare Council in the UK (☎ 0171-821 88 45), 23 Buckingham Gate London SW1E 6LB, is a founding member of the federation and can advise on timeshare purchases and managers. When you sign a timeshare deal, be sure you are granted a 'cooling off' period. This allows you to back out if you decide it's not such a hot idea. There is an EU-wide directive making such a period compulsory in all timeshare contracts in Europe, and Spain was due to ratify this clause in March 1998.

Tax

Virtually all accommodation prices are subject to IGIC, the Canary Islands' indirect tax, charged at a rate of 4.5%. This tax is often included in the quoted price at cheaper accommodation places, but less often at the more expensive ones. In some cases you will only be charged the tax if you ask for a receipt.

FOOD

The cuisine of the Canary Islands reflects a wide range of influences, from Spanish regional to global fast food. Travellers can, if they wish, stick to the resorts and eat English breakfasts, fish and chips and imitation pizzas, all washed down with your favourite northern European lager. But that would be a shame. The Canaries is not a seaside outpost of empire, but a fascinating archipelago whose culinary delights are too often overlooked for the easy, known options. If you have an even slightly adventurous approach to your travel, let your taste buds experiment too!

Meal Times

First adjustment – locals eat at times of day when most of us wouldn't dream of it! Breakfast (*desayuno*) is about the only meal of the day which takes place about the same time for everyone – that is, when you get up!

The serious eating starts with lunch (*la comida* or, less commonly, *el almuerzo*): the famous siesta time, the mid-afternoon, is actually reserved by many locals for this, the main meal of the day. While Canarios tend to eat at home with the family, there is plenty of action in the restaurants too, starting about 2 pm and continuing until 4 pm.

This late start sets the tone for the evening procedures too. If you turn up for dinner at 6 or 7 pm, you'll be eating alone – if the restaurant is even open. Of course, in the most heavily touristed areas the restaurants *will* be open to cater for the strange habits of foreigners, but you'll be unlikely to see a single Canario dining in them. Dinner (*cena*) is often a lighter meal for your average Canario, although this is not to say that they eschew restaurant outings. In any event, dinner begins, at the earliest, about 9 pm. The bulk of locals wouldn't seriously consider wandering in to their favourite eating house until 10 pm. As with lunch, the evening meal can easily last two or three hours – a leisurely and highly social affair.

Of course, this does not mean that outside these hours you can't eat in the Canaries! Snacks are an important part of the Spanish culinary heritage, particularly the bar snacks known as *tapas*, about which more later. You can usually pick up a quick bite to eat to tide you over until the main meal times swing around.

Where to Eat

Cafés & Bars Hanging around in bars and cafés, or simply dropping by for a quick caffeine or alcohol injection, is an integral part of life in the Canaries. Sometimes the distinction between cafés and bars is a little hard to pick, since coffee and alcohol are more often than not available in both. Bars take several different forms, including *cervecerías* (beer bars, a vague equivalent of the pub, although some bars take on the name 'pub' too, as seems to happen right across western Europe!). In *tabernas* (taverns) and *bodegas* (old-style wine bars) you can sometimes get a decent meal too.

You may begin to notice a lot of bars apparently called Piscolabis. No, this is not a chain. A *piscolabis* is simply a place where you can get sandwiches and other prepared snacks with your beer or coffee.

In most cases you can get a tapa with your alcoholic drink, although you may have to ask specifically. Standing at the bar rather than sitting down can often save you 10% to 20% of the bill, especially where the tables are outside on a picturesque terrace or in a posh attached dining room.

Restaurants *Restaurantes* generally open for lunch and dinner (see Meal Times above), unless they have an attached bar, in which case they may be open right through the day. Most of them close one day a week and advertise this fact with a sign in the window. It is common practice to display a menu (*carta*), usually with prices, out the front. Any taxes and service charges should also be advertised, but quite often are not. The scruffier places may not display any prices at all.

Variations on the theme include the *mesón* (traditionally a place for simple home cooking, although this is often no longer the case), *comedor* (literally a dining room, usually attached to a bar or hotel), *venta* (roadside inn) and *marisquería* (seafood specialist).

Staples

Nowadays, a good range of typical Spanish food is widely available in the islands, partly to satisfy the *godos* (Spaniards) who live here, partly to widen the choice on offer for locals and interlopers alike.

The basis of the local cuisine is, however, rather narrow, traditionally restricted to what the islands produced for themselves.

The staple product par excellence is

gofio, a uniquely Canario product. A roasted mixture of wheat, maize or barley, gofio takes the place of bread in the average Canario's diet. There is no shortage of bread (*pan*) these days, but gofio remains common. It is something of an acquired taste and, mixed in varying proportions is used as a breakfast food or combined with almonds and figs to make sweets. The Spanish author Antonio Muñoz Molina recalled in *Ardor Guerrero*, his recollections of conscript days in the Basque city of San Sebastián in northern Spain in the 80s:

Pepe Rifón had organised a kind of Leninist cell, a clandestine commune to which we all contributed what we could and where everything was shared, whether drugs or food packets sent by our families. The only thing we never managed to share was gofio, that passion of our chums from the Canaries ... who at our little food fests, when they had just received some package from their islands, would tear open the packets of gofio and shove fistfuls of the stuff into their mouths with the greed of exiles who, for the first time in years, savour a long lost flavour. 'You mainlanders are the dopes not liking gofio,' they'd say. 'It's God's own food'.

Other basic raw materials long common across the islands are bananas and tomatoes, but nowadays the markets are filled with a wide range of fruit and vegetables. Beef, pork, lamb and other meats are widely available (largely imported), but traditionally goat (*cabra*) and kid (*cabrito*) meat were, and remain, the go. Most local cheeses come from goats' milk too.

The Canary Islands owe a lot to Columbus; it was from South America that such elementary items like potatoes, tomatoes and corn, and some more exotic delights like avocados, mangoes and papayas, were introduced.

Breakfast
For those of us unaccustomed to Continental practices, breakfast is a flimsy affair, usually involving no more than white coffee and a pastry (*bollo*) taken at a bar. If you

prefer you can beef it up a little though by ordering some orange juice (*zumo de naranja*) and perhaps a *tostada*, a toasted sandwich or roll.

Locals would never do it, but you can order eggs in one form or another for breakfast if you need to, especially in the more touristed areas, where Canarios are quite unsurprised by foreign tastes. You can have your *huevos* (eggs) fried (*fritos*), scrambled (*revueltos* – definitely not normal breakfast fare for locals) and hard-boiled (*cocidos*). Some people have *churros con chocolate* – a kind of deep-fried doughnut dipped in thick dark chocolate – for brekkie

Snacks
Bar snacks, or tapas, are a mainland importation. They range from a tiny saucer with an olive or two and a thin slice of cheese through to quite substantial and delicious mouthfuls of anything from chips to seafood. These are provided at most bars as an accompaniment to your beer or wine. The idea is to stimulate your thirst, and generally it works. There was a time when they came free. Quite often now there is a small charge, and occasionally you actually have to ask the barman for the tapa. Generally they are on display – the barman will generally choose whatever he feels like and present you with it unless you make a specific request.

A larger version of the tapa is the ración. You always pay for this and three or four raciones makes a pretty decent meal. But you could even survive a night on beer and tapas, either propping up the one bar or doing the rounds – a popular and highly agreeable pastime.

The other standard snack (or *merienda*) is the *bocadillo*, or bread roll. Typically this will be a rather dry affair with a slice of ham (*jamón*) and/or cheese (*queso*), or a wedge of *tortilla española* (potato omelette).

All over the islands you'll notice little eateries known as *areperas*. This is where you can order yourself an *arepa*, basically a lightly deep-fried crispy pocket of cornmeal dough with a potatoey flavour and stuffed with chicken, cheese, ham, or whatever you want. It's a Venezuelan import and makes a really filling snack, usually costing not much more 300 ptas.

Main Meals

The traveller's friend in the Canary Islands, as in mainland Spain, is the *menú del día*, a set meal available at most restaurants for lunch, and occasionally in the evening too. Generally you get a starter or side dish, a main dish, a simple dessert and wine for a modest price – which hovers around the 900 ptas mark at budget establishments and can rise to 2000 ptas and even beyond at posh places.

Canarian cuisine is good and reasonably varied without being overly imaginative. Although much of it heavily reflects mainland Spanish tastes, particularly from the south, Latin American influences are also evident. The Muslim heritage in sweets and the use of certain spices like cumin and saffron remind us of the centuries of Arab control of southern Spain (right up until the time of the conquest of the islands).

As a result, you'll see plenty of classic mainland Spanish dishes, including *paella* (saffron-rice cooked with meats and/or seafood – though at its best with good seafood), *tortilla* (omelette), *gazpacho* (a cold, tomato-based soup usually available in summer only), various *sopas* (soups) and *pinchos morunos* (kebabs).

Main meals will generally consist of some form of *carne* (meat), including *ternera* (beef or veal), *cerdo* (pork), *cochinillo* (suckling pig), *cordero* (lamb), *pollo* (chicken), *cabrito* (kid meat) and *conejo* (rabbit), often accompanied by *papas fritas* (chips). Your meat may be done *a la parrilla* (grilled), *asado* (roasted) or come in an *estofado* or *puchero* (stew). *Chuletas* (chops) are popular, and if you are buying your own meat, the minced version is known as *carne picada*.

Otherwise you will have the choice of many kinds of *pescado* (fish) or *mariscos* (seafood).

Your main dish can be preceded by *entremeses*, or starters of various kinds. *Ensaladas* (salads) commonly figure as either starters or side dishes.

Canary Islands' Specialities

Away from the standard Spanish fare, and the many bland, tourist-oriented 'international' style restaurants in the resorts, there is a genuine local cuisine.

The most obvious Canarian contribution to the dinner table is the *mojo*. This sauce has many variants and is used to dip pretty much anything in – from chicken legs to gofio. See the boxed aside.

Papas arrugadas (wrinkly potatoes) are perhaps the next best known dish, although there is really not much to them. They are basically small new potatoes boiled and salted in their skin and only come to life when dipped in one of the mojos. Potatoes were introduced to the islands from Peru in the 1600s, and connoisseurs identify at least 23 varieties.

Of the many soups you'll find, one typically Canarian variant is *potaje de berros*, or watercress soup. Another is *rancho canario*, a kind of broth with thick noodles and the odd chunk of meat and potato – it's very hearty.

Conejo en salmorejo is rabbit in a marinade made of water, vinegar, olive oil, salt and pepper, sweet black pudding and avocado. Although now considered a pillar of local cuisine, the dish's origins lie in distant Aragón.

Sancocho canario is a salted-fish dish with mojo. On La Gomera you might get a chance to tuck into *buche gomero*, basically salted tuna stomach – it tastes a lot better than it sounds!

If you take the time to circulate around the islands, you'll find many variants on standard dishes and quite a few local specialities. Experiment and enjoy!

Vegetarians

The Canary Islands may seem like paradise to some, but they can be more like purgatory for vegetarians, and worse still for vegans. This is meat-eating country, so you will find your choices (unless you cater for yourself) a little limited. Salads are OK, and you will come across various side dishes such as *setas* (mushrooms, usually lightly fried in olive oil and garlic). Other possibilities include *berenjenas* (aubergines), *menestra* (a hearty vegetable stew), *espárragos* (asparagus) and other vegetables that are sometimes cooked as side dishes. There are a few vegetarian restaurants in the bigger centres.

Desserts & Sweets
On an ordinary day in a no-nonsense eatery, you may find your dessert options (*postres*) limited to timeless Spanish favourites such as *flan* (crème caramel), *helado* (ice cream) or a piece of fruit.

But the Canarios *do* have a sweet tooth. And if you are disappointed after your meal, the best thing you can do is head for the local *pastelería* (cake shop) and indulge yourself.

Some of the better known sticky sweets are *bienmesabes* (a kind of thick sticky goo made of almonds and honey – deadly sweet!), *frangollos*, *tirijalas*, *bizcochos lustrados* and *turrón de melaza* (molasses nougat).

La Palma's honey-and-sugar *rapaduras* are a favourite tooth-rotter, and you shouldn't miss the *quesadillas* of El Hierro – they've been making this cheesy-cinnamon pastry (sometimes also made with aniseed) since the Middle Ages. *Morcillas dulces* (sweet blood sausages), made with grapes, raisins and almonds are a rather odd concoction; perhaps the closest comparison is the Christmas mince pie consumed with such relish in the UK.

Cheese
Goat cheese is produced across several of the islands, but the best known cheese is probably the *queso de flor*. This is made of a mix of cow's and sheep's milk, then infused with the aroma of flowers from a type of thistle (the *cardo alcausi*). It is produced exclusively in the Guía area of northern Gran Canaria. Another prize-winning cow-sheep cheese mix is the *pastor*, from around Arucas.

Of the goat cheeses, Fuerteventura's *majorero*, a slightly acidic, creamy cheese, is probably the most highly sought after.

The cheese of El Hierro, *queso herreño*, is also much prized – and outside the island costs considerably more than at home.

Table Talk
Here are some basic words that can come in handy whatever kind of meal you're eating:

bill (check)	*cuenta*
bread	*pan*
breakfast	*desayuno*
butter	*mantequilla*
change	*cambio*
cold	*frío/a*
cup	*taza*
dining-room	*comedor*
dinner	*cena*
food, meal	*comida*
fork	*tenedor*
glass	*vaso* or *copa*
hot (temperature)	*caliente*
ice	*hielo*
jam	*mermelada*
knife	*cuchillo*
lunch	*almuerzo* or *comida*
menu	*carta*
milk	*leche*
olive oil	*aceite de oliva*
pastry (eg a croissant)	*bollo*
plate	*plato*
pepper	*pimienta*
salt	*sal*
sauce	*salsa*
spoon	*cuchara*
sugar	*azúcar*
table	*mesa*
vinegar	*vinagre*
waiter/waitress	*camerero/a*

Food Glossary
Deciphering a menu in the Canaries is always tricky. However much you already know, there will always be dishes and expressions with which you are not familiar.

Mojo Rising

Lying at the crossroads of the trade routes between imperial Spain and her vast possessions in Latin America, the Canary Islands were opened up to influences not only from the 'mother country', but also from the developing colonies in Latin America. Explorers and traders brought a wealth of new vegetables, fruit and herbs from the new territories to Spain, dropping samples off in the Canaries along the way. Among them was the humble capsicum (*pimiento*) and various kinds of chilli peppers, or *guindillas*.

Just where the original *mojo picón* came from is unknown. It is a spicy sauce made with red chilli peppers and used as a dip for a huge variety of foods – from papas arrugadas to chicken wings. There are at least 20 variants on this saucy theme, and good chefs often try to put their own particular spin on it.

Preparing your own mojo is not particularly difficult. For the standard mojo picón, try the following recipe:

Ingredients:
Half a cup of olive oil
Water
Eight small cloves of garlic, peeled
Quarter cup of wine vinegar
Four small, fresh red chilli peppers (more if you can take the heat)
Two ripe tomatoes
Half a teaspoon of cumin
One to two teaspoons of salt
Half a teaspoon of paprika

Method:
Pour all the olive oil into the blender and add the paprika, cumin, vinegar, garlic and salt.

Boil the chilli peppers in half a cup of water for about 15 minutes, then add to the mixture in the blender.

Put the tomatoes on a skewer and lightly roast them over a low flame until the skin is dry. Remove the skin, slice up the tomatoes and put them into the blender. Blend until you are left with a thick, smooth sauce.

You can vary the ingredients quite a lot, for instance by adjusting the number of chilli peppers you include. Some people like to add a dash of pepper and even oregano to the mix. If you find what you have made is too hot, add more olive oil and vinegar to dilute it.

If you don't like it so hot, you could try the *mojo verde*. This is very tasty with fish, and is sometimes served up with cheese as a starter. This is a mild version where you replace the red hot chilli with parsley and cilantro (coriander) or green capsicum.

The *mojo de cilantro* is particularly popular on Tenerife owing, it is said, to the one-time presence of a cilantro-loving Portuguese community. The trick with this mojo is to finely crush the fresh cilantro shortly before the mojo is eaten, because after a while the cilantro oxidises.

Mojo colorado leans more heavily on the tomatoes and less on the chillies than the mojo picón and adds a bit of zing to just about anything.

The following list should help you with the
basics at least.

aceite	oil
aceituna	olive
agua	water
aguacate	avocado
ajo	garlic
almejas	clams
almendra	almond
alubia	bean
anchoa	anchovy
arroz	rice
atún	tuna
bacalao	salted cod
bistek	beef steak
bonito	tuna
boquerones	a kind of anchovy, usually served in vinegar
brasa	char-grill
cacahuete	peanut
calabacín	zucchini, courgette
calabaza	pumpkin
caldo	broth, stock, consommé
calamares	squid
cangrejo	crab
caza	hunt, game
cazuela	casserole
cebolla	onion
cereza	cherry
champiñones	mushrooms
charcutería	cured pork meats, or a shop selling them
chipirón	small squid
chorizo	red sausage
cocido	cooked; also hotpot/stew
cocina	kitchen
crudo	raw
dorada	sea bass
dulce	sweet
empanada	pie
ensaimada	sweet bread (of lard)
espárragos	asparagus
espinacas	spinach
faba	type of dried bean
fideo	vermicelli noodle
filete	fillet
flan	crème caramel
frambuesa	raspberry
fresa	strawberry
frijol	dried bean
frito	fried
fruta	fruit
fuerte	strong
galleta	biscuit, cookie
gamba	prawn, shrimp
garbanzo	chickpea
guindilla	hot chilli pepper
guisante	pea
haba	broad bean
hamburguesa	hamburger
harina	flour
helado	ice cream
hierba buena	mint
hígado	liver
higo	fig
horno	oven
horneado	baked
hortalizas	vegetables
infusión	herbal tea
jabalí	wild boar
jamón	ham
judías blancas	butter beans
judías verdes	green beans
langosta	spiny lobster
langostino	large prawn
lechuga	lettuce
legumbre	pulse
lengua	tongue
lenguado	sole
lentejas	lentils
lima	lime
limón	lemon
lomo	pork loin
maíz	sweet corn
mandarina	tangerine

manzana	apple
mayonesa	mayonnaise
mejillones	mussels
melocotón	peach
menta	mint
merluza	hake
miel	honey
mojo	salsa/sauce
morcilla	blood sausage, ie black pudding
naranja	orange
nata	cream
nuez	nut, walnut; plural *nueces*
olla	pot
ostra	oyster
papas arrugadas	wrinkly potatoes, served with *mojo*
pasa	raisin
pastel	pastry, cake
pato	duck
pavo	turkey
pechuga	breast, of poultry
perdiz	partridge
peregrina	scallop
pez espada	swordfish
picadillo	minced meat
picante	hot, spicy, piquant
pimiento	pepper, capsicum
piña	pineapple
piñón	pine nut
plancha	grill, grilled, on the hot plate
plátano	banana
potaje	stew, potage
puerro	leek
pulpo	octopus
rape	monkfish
rebozado/a	battered and fried
riñón	kidney
relleno	stuffed
salado	salted, salty
salchicha	fresh pork sausage
salchichón	cured sausage
sandía	watermelon

sardina	sardine
seco	dry, dried
sepia	cuttlefish
serrano	mountain-cured ham
sesos	brains
seta	wild mushroom
soja	soy
solomillo	sirloin
tarta	cake
tomate	tomato
torta	round flat bun, cake
trucha	trout
turrón	almond nougat
uva	grape
vaca, carne de	beef
vegetal	vegetable
vegetariano/a	vegetarian
verdura	green vegetable
vieira	scallop
zanahoria	carrot
zarzuela	fish stew

DRINKS
Nonalcoholic Drinks
Coffee Coffee in the Canary Islands is strong and slightly bitter. Addicts should specify how they want their fix. A *café con leche* is about 50% coffee, 50% hot milk; ask for *grande* or *doble* if you want a large cup (usually a breakfast request), *en vaso* if you want a smaller shot in a glass, or *sombra* if you want lots of milk. A *café solo* is a short black; *café cortado* is a short black with a little milk (in the islands of Tenerife province known as *natural* to distinguish it from other versions, as will become clear). For those who like it hot, be sure to ask that any of the above is *caliente*. A café solo or cortado can cost as little as 60 ptas.

There are some local variations on the theme in the Canary Islands. *Cortado de condensado* is a short black with condensed milk; *cortado de leche y leche* is the same with a little standard milk thrown in. It sometimes comes in a larger cup and is then called a *barraquito*. You can also have your barraquito *con licor* or *con alcohol*, a shot of liquor usually accompanied by a shred of lemon and sometimes some cinnamon – this is the authentic *barraquito*, as any Canario will let you know. A good barraquito costs as much as 200 ptas. Strangely, these variations on the caffeine theme seem all but unknown in the province of Las Palmas, while in the western islands they are as common as muck. In the easternmost islands you will be asked if you want your milk *condensada* or *líquida*.

For iced coffee, ask for *café con hielo*: you'll get a glass of ice and a hot cup of coffee, to be poured over the ice – which, surprisingly, doesn't all melt straight away!

Tea Whilst coffee is generally preferred, tea is served in most cafés and bars. The brew (a tea bag) is invariably weak and locals drink it black. Ask for milk to be separate; otherwise, you'll end up with a cup of milky water with a tea bag thrown in. Most places also have camomile tea (*té de manzanilla*).

Chocolate Spaniards brought chocolate back from the New World and adopted it enthusiastically. At one time it was even a form of currency. The Spanish serve it thick; sometimes it even appears on the postres (desserts) section of menus. Generally it's a breakfast drink consumed with churros; see the Food section.

Soft Drinks *Refrescos* (cool drinks) include the usual international brands of soft drinks, local brands such as Kas, and expensive *granizado* (iced fruit crush).

Clear, cold water from a public fountain or tap is a Spanish favourite – but check that it's *potable*. For tap water in restaurants, ask for *agua de grifo*. Bottled water (*agua mineral*) comes in several brands, either fizzy (*con gas*) or still (*sin gas*). A 1.5L bottle of agua mineral sin gas costs 75 ptas in a supermarket, but out and about you may be charged as much as 175 ptas.

A *batido* is a flavoured milk drink or milk shake; the bottled variety is sickly. *Horcha-ta* is a Valencian drink of Islamic origin. Made from the juice of *chufa* (tiger nuts), sugar and water, it is sweet and tastes like soy milk with a hint of cinnamon. You'll come across it both fresh and bottled – Chufi is a delicious brand.

Fruit Juices Save the best until last. Fruit juices are popular with Canarios. Not just boring old *zumo de naranja* (orange juice, which is perfectly good, especially with sugar added!), but strawberry, papaya and a host of others too. They can be a little pricey at around 300 ptas, but are generally worth it. One thing you'll notice in many bars in the bigger and more affluent centres are the loads of mangoes, papaya and other fruit loaded up just waiting to be converted into liquid.

Alcoholic Drinks

Wine Spain is a great wine-drinking and producing country, and plenty of wine is consumed in the Canary Islands. The local wine-making industry is relatively modest, but you can come across the occasional good drop.

Vino comes in white (*blanco*), red (*tinto*) or rosé (*rosado*), and is generally pretty cheap, especially if you buy it at the supermarket. In restaurants, if you are not too particular about brands, you can simply order the house wine (*vino de la casa*), which also tends to be the cheapest option too.

One of the most common wines across the islands is the *malvasía* (malmsey wine, also produced in Madeira). It is generally sweet (*dulce*), although you can find the odd dry (*seco*) version. It is particularly common on La Palma.

Tenerife is the principal source of wine, and the red Tacoronte Acentejo was the first Canarian wine to earn the grade of DO (*denominación de orígen*). This term is one of many employed to regulate and judge wine and grape quality, and is one down from the coveted DOC label (*denominación de orígen calificada*). Other productive vineyards are in the Icod and Güímar areas of Tenerife. In Lanzarote, the vine has come back into vogue since the early 1980s, and in late 1993 the island's malvasías were awarded a DO. Wine is produced on the other islands too, but the quality is generally not as good.

Beer The most common way to order a beer (*cerveza*) is to ask for a *caña*, which is a small draught beer (*cerveza de barril* or *cerveza de presión*). A pint-sized version is called a *jarra*.

If you just ask for a cerveza you may get bottled beer, usually called a *botellín* and more expensive than the draught stuff. The Tenerife-brewed ale is Cerveza CCC Dorada, and it's fine. Cerveza Tropical, a little lighter than Dorada, is the most popular beer in Gran Canaria. Even in out of the way places you'll usually have the choice of at least one bottled import, such as Heineken. A *clara* is a shandy, a beer with a dash of lemonade.

Other Drinks Apart from the mainland Spanish imports, including brandy (*coñac*), the grape-based *aguardiente* (like schnapps or grappa) and a whole host of other *licores* (liqueurs), you could try some local firewater.

Although the sugar plantations have all but gone, what remains is put to good use in the production of rum (*ron*). The Ron de la Aldea of La Palma is considered the best of them. *Ron miel*, or honey rum, is more liqueur than rum, but interesting enough to taste. Quite a few liqueurs are produced in the islands, including the banana-based *cobana*. Both this and the honey rum are produced above all on Gran Canaria. Another one is *mistela*, from La Gomera – it is a mixture of wine, sugar, rum and sometimes honey. A potent taste!

Another import from the mainland is *sangría*, a wine and fruit punch sometimes laced with brandy. It's refreshing going down but can leave you with a sore head. *Tinto de verano* is a mix of wine and Casera, a brand of lemonade or sweet, bubbly water.

ENTERTAINMENT

Outside the main cities on Tenerife and

Have a Cigar

Smokers who have been dying to try a Havana cigar, but have not yet had the chance, could do worse than puff on the local *puro*, mostly hand rolled with tobacco on La Palma. The methods were brought back by reverse migrants from Cuba, and although not quite up to the standard of the real McCoy, are not a bad substitute – they are also cheap, and available across the islands.

Gran Canaria, and the discos and folklore shows put on for tourists in the main resorts, there is generally not an awful lot on in the line of urban entertainment.

Listings

Check out local papers such as *La Gaceta* or *Diario de Avisos* for entertainment listings. The national dailies *El País* and *El Mundo* also have a brief rundown – check under the heading *Cartelera*. Tourist offices can inform you about major upcoming events.

Cinemas

Cinemas are concentrated in Las Palmas de Gran Canaria and Santa Cruz de Tenerife. Otherwise a few are scattered across secondary towns on the main islands, as well as in Santa Cruz de la Palma. You will be lucky to find any foreign films which have not been dubbed into Spanish. On average, going to the flicks costs 700 ptas, unless you pick the cinema's chosen cheap day, or *día del espectador* (usually Wednesday), when it will cost about 400 ptas.

Bars, Discos & Nightclubs

Some holiday-makers come to the Canaries to do little more than party and then sleep off the results on the beach. But the outsiders are not the only ones: late nightlife is in the local blood.

Thursday to Saturday nights are always the wildest, and once you have found the part of town or your resort where all the bars are clustered (as tends to be the case) you won't need to move far to keep busy bar-hopping all night. Many locals don't think of going out until about midnight, although there is nothing to stop you making an earlier start.

Bars, which come in all shapes, sizes and themes, are the main attractions until around 2 or 3 am, after which you can move to the discos and various nightclubs until 5 or 6 am – or later! Discos can be expensive, and some won't let you in wearing jeans or trainers, but they aren't to be missed if you can manage to it.

All this is true of the main urban centres and resorts. In farther flung corners of the islands the tempo can be rather more slow, although you should be able to find the occasional bar open until about 2 am, and perhaps even the odd disco or nightclub. La

It's a Gay Old Life

The Canary Islands are gay Europe's winter escape playground. Or rather, the Playa del Inglés on the south side of Gran Canaria is. A seemingly endless string of bars, discos and clubs are crammed into the Centro Comercial Yumbo, right smack in the heart of the Playa del Inglés area. It is predominantly a gay men's scene, although of course this doesn't stop small numbers of lesbians and straights from wading in.

Little happens before 10 pm. From then until about 3 am the bars on the fourth level of the Yumbo centre bear the brunt of the fun, after which the clubs and discos on the second level take over.

At dawn, people stagger out for some rest. Some make for the beach at Maspalomas across the dunes, which are themselves a busy gay-cruising area.

Palma, La Gomera and El Hierro are all fairly quiet.

Live Rock, Pop & Jazz

Live music is alive and kicking in the islands, although the quality at times leaves something to be desired. Still, there are some fun local bands around, and occasionally good mainland and international acts come to town. Look out for music festivals.

Flamenco

Touristy performances of flamenco can be seen in some of the resorts and as a rule are to be avoided. Although some aspects of flamenco migrated to the islands from southern Spain, this is not its natural context, and most performances you are likely to see are something of a travesty.

Classical Music, Dance & Theatre

For the culturally inclined, the cities and some of the bigger towns are the places to look for classical music, dance and theatre. They often come in the form of festivals. Theatre is almost always in Spanish.

SPECTATOR SPORT
Football

Across Spain *fútbol* is a national preoccupation. This is as much the case in the Canaries as elsewhere, but only one local side, Club Deportivo Tenerife, is in the Primera División (first division) – and only just! In the Segunda División, the next rung down, the Canaries are represented by UD Las Palmas, which holds its own at the top of the ladder.

Three other island teams play in the even lower Segunda División B, which is divided into four regional sections.

Still, the locals take a pretty active interest in the big teams and the Copa del Rey, the Spanish version of the FA Cup, is as keenly followed in the Canaries as anywhere else in Spain. If you're wondering when there's an international clash, discretion is probably the better part of valour – if you are not backing Spain, then keep it to yourself!

To see a first-division game while in the islands, you'll have to wait until CD Tenerife is playing at home at the Estadio Heliodoro Rodríguez López, close to the centre of town. You can get tickets at least a week in advance at the stadium's *taquillas* (box offices). Ticket prices start at 2500 ptas.

Volleyball

This is a popular beachside game across the resorts of the Canary Islands, and it can sometimes get a little more serious. With an ideal climate, the islands often host competitions of world-championship level, which can attract thousands of spectators. If you like this game so much that you'd like to watch it, ask the tourist office if any major competitions are due to be held during your stay.

Bullfighting

Until a few years ago, the occasional bull fight used to be staged in the Canaries. But it is not a particularly popular spectator sport here and the cost of transporting bulls and bullfighters from the mainland was in any case prohibitive.

The Canaries' Weird World of Sports

Lucha Canaria The Guanches of Tenerife were a particularly robust and warlike crowd, who loved a trial of strength. Any island party was an excuse for indulging in tests of manhood, and apart from jumping over steep ravines and diving into the ocean from dizzying heights, one favourite pastime was wrestling. Rooted in this ancient diversion lies the essence of the modern *lucha canaria*, Canarian wrestling.

Bull fighting is not a notably popular activity in the Canary Islands, but sand rings (called *terreros*) still find their use for a little contact sport. Often, however, rings are to be found in modern buildings known as *luchaderos*. Lucha Canaria is practised throughout the islands. Teams of up to 12 face off for an afternoon of a kind of tag-team wrestling match that is, however, not the silly stuff some of you may have come to associate with TV spectacles like World Championship Wrestling.

A member of each team faces off in the ring and, after a formal greeting and other signs of goodwill, they set about trying to dump each other into the dust. The idea is that no part of the body but the soles of the feet may touch the ground, and whoever fails first in this department loses. Each pair fight it out in a best of three competition (each clash is known as a *brega*), and the team with the most winning wrestlers wins the whole show.

There is more skill to this than is perhaps at first apparent. Size and weight are not the determining factors (although these boys tend to be as beefy as rugby front-row forwards), but rather the skill with which the combatants grapple and manoeuvre their opponents into a position from which they can be toppled. This is not a violent sport, and kicking, punching, pinching etc are not permitted. Historically, the lucha was staged for fiestas but also often as a means of resolving disputes.

The Canarios, or at least some of them, take this all rather seriously, and there is a major league competition known as the Copa Presidente del Gobierno Canarias. Clashes at this level are often televised.

If you want to find out where matches are being held, call the Federación de Lucha Canaria (☎ 922 25 14 52), Callejón del Capitán Brotons 7, Santa Cruz de Tenerife.

Stick Fighting The *juego del palo* (literally, stick game) started off in preconquest days as anything but a game. Two combatants would arm themselves with heavy staves and

THINGS TO BUY

Shopping in the Canaries has one special attraction. It is virtually tax free (the local indirect tax, the IGIC, is a measly 4.5%, compared with VAT of 16% and more throughout the rest of the EU).

Electronics, watches, perfumes, tobacco, alcohol and the like are the first items that you should investigate, but even things like jeans can be a good buy. Levis can cost around 7000 ptas in the Canaries, more than in the USA, but better than the prices in London stores.

In any case, don't bother buying goods duty free in Canary Islands airports or on the flight back home. You will almost certainly find the same items for less in normal stores in the islands.

The prestigious Spanish stores, such as Corte Inglés and Cortefiel, have branches in the main centres in the Canary Islands.

Flea Markets

Some of the bigger towns have a weekly flea market, or *rastro*. A lot of the stuff on sale is junk, but occasionally you can find some interesting odds and ends.

---

stones and attempt to break as many bones in their opponents' bodies as possible. After the arrival of the Spaniards, the 'game' became increasingly marginalised to rural areas, and became more a trial of skill than a violent blood sport.

The sport, if such it can be called, is still practised throughout the islands, and there is even a federation devoted to it. The staff is of sturdy wood and about 2m long. The stick goes by various names, *banot* in Tenerife and *lata* in Fuerteventura. You are most likely to see a demonstration of the juego del palo at local fiestas.

Another sport involving poles is the *lucha al garrote*, involving still longer implements.

Vela Latina Canaria Since the end of the 19th century, the diminutive sail-cum-row boats, which once functioned as ferries between the great ocean-going vessels and docks of Las Palmas' port, have been sailed in a form of regatta unique to the Canary

Islands. For more on this see the boxed aside in the Las Palmas section of the Gran Canaria chapter.

Cockfighting Canarios may not be avid bullfighting fans, but the cockfighting business still has its aficionados. The sight of angry feathered beasties armed with spurs attempting to slice each other to shreds is an acquired taste. As with bullfighting, its supporters will beg to differ, taking pride in their cocks and assuring you that this is what they are bred to do – it's what they *like*. You'll need to be in the know to get to see this, and may not want to anyway.

Woodwork

The Canary Islands' pine, chestnut, mulberry and beech trees are all sources of timber for the carving of various household implements ranging from ladles and spoons, through bowls to a kind of tweezers for picking prickly pears.

The local version of castanets, known as *chácaras*, make a nice souvenir item.

Basketware

Baskets and other similar objects (*cestería*) fashioned of palm leaves, reeds, wicker and even banana leaves are popular (though not particularly sturdy) items.

On La Gomera, in particular, this is something of a fine art form. You'll also find such products on La Palma. The Lanzaroteños concentrate more on the straw version.

Embroidery, Lace & Silk

Women in certain parts of the islands, such as El Hierro, still make their own thread and weave bed spreads, rugs and bags on primitive wooden looms. Embroidered table cloths and napkins also make convenient and tasteful souvenirs. Embroidery is in fact one of the most widely available quality handicrafts in the Canary Islands, and only in La Gomera is there little or nothing to speak of.

Ingenio (Gran Canaria) is famous for its embroidery, and Vilaflor in Tenerife is known for its high-quality lace. For silk, keep your eyes peeled on the island of La Palma.

Ceramics

Even before the Europeans arrived, the Guanches were at their most artistically expressive in their pottery (*alfarería*). You can pick up some nice, simple pottery pieces at markets on the island of La Gomera. If you get to the village of Chipude, check out their wares.

On the island of Tenerife, the place to look first for ceramics is the unassuming hamlet of Arguayo, in the west. The more authentic stuff is generally not glazed.

Musical Instruments

If you have a hankering for a timple (a ukelele-style instrument), even in reduced size for display only, Fuerteventura is the place to look.

Liquor, Cigars & Honey

The rum of La Palma is reputed to be a fine drop, as are the strange concoctions made with it. Honey rum is one of them, along with such items as *mistela* on La Gomera, and nonalcoholic liqueurs made with bananas. These are all hard to find outside the islands and can make original gifts.

DAMIEN SIMONIS

Embroidery from Teror,
northern Isla de Gran Canaria

Cigar smokers should stock up on the cigars made in La Palma along much the same lines as the Cuban versions. They are cheap.

Honey, some of it made not by bees but with palm sap, is another product you are likely to come across in the western islands and Gran Canaria.

Getting There & Away

With an agreeable all-year-round climate, the Canary Islands are an especially popular holiday destination with Europeans, particularly those coming from the wintery northern reaches. As a result, there is no shortage of air links between many European cities and the islands. Sea links are fewer, and as yet it hasn't occurred to anyone to try digging some sort of sub-Atlantic tunnel between the islands and Europe or Africa.

Despite its proximity, Morocco does not represent a good-value launching pad for flights to the Canaries, and direct flights to the rest of Africa are close to nonexistent.

It is possible to book flights from North and South America, often routed through mainland Spain. These tend not to be super cheap, and often you are better off getting a cheap flight to London and booking a charter from there.

Those coming from Australasia will definitely want to consider getting a good-value ticket to a major European hub, such as London or Amsterdam, and then booking a charter flight to the Canaries.

Travel Insurance

A travel insurance policy to cover theft, loss and medical problems is a good idea. The policies handled by STA Travel and other student-travel organisations are usually good value. Some policies offer lower and higher medical-expense options; the higher ones are chiefly for countries such as the USA, which have extremely high medical costs. There is a wide variety of policies available so check the small print.

Some policies specifically exclude 'dangerous activities', which can include scuba diving, motorcycling, even trekking. A locally acquired motorcycle licence is not valid under some policies. Also, you often need to pay a surcharge for expensive camera equipment and the like. Standard insurance should at least cover luggage

theft and loss, cancellation of and delays in your travel arrangements.

You may prefer a policy which pays doctors or hospitals direct rather than you having to pay on the spot and claim later. If you have to claim later make sure you keep all documentation. Some policies ask you to call back (reverse charges) to a centre in your home country where an immediate assessment of your problem is made.

Check that the policy covers ambulances or an emergency flight home.

Paying for your ticket with a credit card often provides limited travel accident insurance, and you may be able to reclaim payment if the operator doesn't deliver. Ask your credit-card company what it will cover.

EU citizens should take their national health-care card or equivalent and any necessary forms (E111) with them to avail themselves of free Spanish health care in the Canary Islands (see also Health in the Facts for the Visitors chapter). Note that this cover simply entitles you to basic minimum state health care and may not always be adequate for your needs.

AIR

Although increasingly airlines do not require you to reconfirm your flights, particularly within Europe, it is probably safer to err on the side of caution and do so in any case. The rule of thumb is to reconfirm at least 72 hours before departure. Otherwise you risk turning up at the airport only to find you've missed your flight because it was rescheduled, or that you've been classified as a 'no show'.

Airports & Airlines

All the islands but La Gomera have airports, and one is being built there too. Tenerife, Gran Canaria and Lanzarote absorb the bulk of the direct international flights and those from mainland Spain,

DAMIEN SIMONIS

DAMIEN SIMONIS

DAMIEN SIMONIS

Isla de Gran Canaria
Top: Sunset at Playa de Maspalomas, southern Isla de Gran Canaria
Bottom: Casa de Colón (Columbus' House) in Plaza del Pilar Nuevo, old centre, Las Palmas

DAMIEN SIMONIS

DAMIEN SIMONIS

DAMIEN SIMONIS

Isla de Fuerteventura
Top Left: Old volcano behind Casa de los Coroneles, La Oliva
Top Right: Traditional mill near Tefía
Bottom: Farmer and goat at old mill, east of Betancuria

while the others are principally for interisland flights.

There are two main airports on Tenerife. Tenerife Norte (Los Rodeos) handles the interisland flights and some scheduled international flights. The remainder of the scheduled flights and virtually all charter flights to the island are channelled to the more modern Tenerife Sur (Reina Sofia). The bulk of international flights serving the islands directly are charters.

From Spain, Air Europa, Iberia and Spanair all fly to the Canary islands. They connect the islands with international destinations, but mostly such flights are routed via Madrid.

Buying Tickets

Depending on where you are coming from, the plane ticket could be the single most expensive item in your budget, and buying it can be intimidating. It is worth putting aside a few hours to check the many travel agents hoping to separate you from your money. Start early – some of the cheapest tickets have to be bought months in advance, and some popular flights sell out early. Talk to other recent travellers – they may be able to stop you making some of the same old mistakes. Look at the ads in newspapers and magazines, consult reference books and watch for special offers. Then phone round travel agents for bargains. (Airlines can supply information on routes and timetables; however, except at times of interairline war they do not supply the cheapest tickets.) Find out the fare, the route, the duration of the journey and any restrictions on the ticket (see the Air Travel Glossary). Then sit back and decide which is best for you.

You may discover that those impossibly cheap flights are 'fully booked, but we have another one that costs a bit more ... '. Or the flight is on an airline notorious for its poor safety standards. Or they claim only to have the last two seats available for your destination. Don't panic and keep ringing around.

If you are travelling from the UK or the USA, you will probably find that the cheapest flights are advertised by obscure bucket shops whose names haven't yet reached the telephone directory. They sell airline tickets at up to a 50% discount where places have not been filled, and although airlines may claim the contrary, many of them release tickets to selected bucket shops – it's better to sell tickets at a huge discount than not at all. Many such firms are honest and solvent, but there are a few rogues who will take your money and disappear, to reopen elsewhere a month or two later under a new name. If you feel suspicious about a firm, don't give them all the money at once – leave a deposit of 20% or so and pay the balance when you get the ticket. If they insist on cash in advance, go somewhere else. And once you have the ticket, ring the airline to confirm that you are actually booked on the flight.

You may decide to pay more than the rock-bottom fare by opting for the safety of a better known travel agent. Firms such as STA, who have offices worldwide, Council Travel in the USA and UK or Travel CUTS

Fare Surfing

Tomorrow's traveller may never even bother phoning a travel agent. Fare-booking services are expanding rapidly on the Internet. Still in its infancy (estimates of worldwide on-line travel sales were US$500 million in 1997), the Web looks set to become a major travel marketplace. Sabre, the US-based travel-reservations agency, which accounts for a third of all bookings worldwide (most of them through travel agents), launched its on-line Travelocity service in mid-1997. Another US site, Farefinder, trawls the airlines-reservations system four times a day looking for the latest flight deals. It concentrates on flights from the USA, but is bound to expand.

in Canada are not going to disappear overnight, leaving you clutching a receipt for a nonexistent ticket, but they do offer good prices to most destinations.

Once you have your ticket, write its number down, together with the flight number and other details, and keep the information somewhere separate. If the ticket is lost or stolen, this will help you get a replacement.

Air Travel Glossary

Apex Apex, or 'advance purchase excursion' is a discounted ticket which must be paid for in advance. There are penalties if you wish to change it.

Baggage Allowance This will be written on your ticket: usually one 20kg item to go in the hold, plus one item of hand luggage.

Bucket Shop An unbonded travel agency specialising in discounted airline tickets.

Budget Fare These can be booked at least three weeks in advance but the actual travel date is not confirmed until seven days prior to travel.

Bumped Just because you have a confirmed seat doesn't mean you're going to get on the plane – see Overbooking.

Cancellation Penalties If you have to cancel or change an Apex ticket there are often heavy penalties involved. Insurance can sometimes be taken out against these penalties. Some airlines impose penalties on regular tickets as well, particularly against 'no show' passengers.

Check-In Airlines ask you to check in a certain time ahead of the flight departure (usually one or two hours on international flights). If you fail to check in on time and the flight is overbooked, the airline can cancel your booking and give your seat to somebody else.

Confirmation Having a ticket written out with the flight and date you want doesn't mean you have a seat until the agent has checked with the airline that your status is 'OK' or confirmed. Meanwhile you could just be 'on request'.

Discounted Tickets There are two types of discounted fares – officially discounted (see Promotional Fares) and unofficially discounted. The lowest prices often impose drawbacks like flying with unpopular airlines, inconvenient schedules, or unpleasant routes and connections. A discounted ticket can save you other things than money – you may be able to pay Apex prices without the associated Apex advance booking and other requirements. Discounted tickets only exist where there is fierce competition.

Full Fares Airlines traditionally offer first-class (coded F), business-class (coded J) and economy-class (coded Y) tickets. These days there are so many promotional and discounted fares available from the regular economy class that few passengers pay the full economy fare.

Lost Tickets If you lose your airline ticket an airline will usually treat it like a travellers cheque and, after inquiries, issue you with another one. Legally, however, an airline is entitled to treat it like cash and if you lose it then it's gone forever. Take good care of your tickets.

No Shows No shows are passengers who fail to show up for their flight, sometimes due to unexpected delays or disasters, sometimes due to simply forgetting, sometimes because they made more than one booking and didn't bother to cancel the one they didn't want. Full-fare passengers who fail to turn up are sometimes entitled to travel on a later flight. The rest of us are penalised (see Cancellation Penalties).

On Request An unconfirmed booking for a flight, see Confirmation.

Open Jaws A return ticket where you fly out to one place but return from another. If avail-

You should use the fares quoted in this book as a guide only. They are approximate and based on the rates advertised by travel agents at the time of going to press. The quoted air fares in this book do not neces- sarily constitute a recommendation for the carrier.

Travellers with Special Needs
If you have special needs of any sort –

---

able, this can save you backtracking to your arrival point.

Overbooking Airlines hate to fly empty seats and since every flight has some passengers who fail to show up (see No Shows), airlines often book more passengers than they have seats. Usually the excess passengers balance those who fail to show up but occasionally somebody gets bumped. If this happens, guess who it is most likely to be? The passengers who check in late.

Promotional Fares Officially discounted fares like Apex fares, available from travel agents or direct from the airline.

Reconfirmation At least 72 hours prior to departure time of an onward or return flight, you must contact the airline and 'reconfirm' that you intend to be on the flight. If you don't do this the airline can delete your name from the passenger list and you could lose your seat. You don't have to reconfirm the first flight on your itinerary or if your stopover is less than 72 hours. It doesn't hurt to reconfirm more than once.

Restrictions Discounted tickets often have various restrictions on them – advance purchase is the most usual one (see Apex). Others are restrictions on the minimum and maximum period you must be away, such as a minimum of 14 days or a maximum of one year. See Cancellation Penalties.

Standby A discounted ticket where you only fly if there is a seat free at the last moment. Standby fares are usually only available on domestic routes.

Tickets Out An entry requirement for many countries is that you have an onward or return ticket, in other words, a ticket out of the country. If you're not sure what you intend to do next, the easiest solution is to buy the cheapest onward ticket to a neighbouring country or a ticket from a reliable airline which can later be refunded if you do not use it.

Transferred Tickets Airline tickets cannot be transferred from one person to another. Travellers sometimes try to sell the return half of their ticket, but officials can ask you to prove that you are the person named on the ticket. This is unlikely to happen on domestic flights, but on an international flight tickets may be compared with passports.

Travel Agencies Travel agencies vary widely and you should ensure you use one that suits your needs. Some simply handle tours while full-service agencies handle everything from tours and tickets to car rental and hotel bookings. A good one will do all these things and can save you a lot of money, but if all you want is a ticket at the lowest possible price, then you really need an agency specialising in discounted tickets. A discounted ticket agency, however, may not be useful for other things, like hotel bookings.

Travel Periods Some officially discounted fares, Apex fares in particular, vary with the time of year. There is often a low (off-peak) season and a high (peak) season. Sometimes there's an intermediate or shoulder season as well. At peak times, when everyone wants to fly, not only will the officially discounted fares be higher but so will unofficially discounted fares or there may simply be no discounted tickets available. Usually the fare depends on your outward flight – if you depart in the high season and return in the low season, you pay the high-season fare.

you've broken a leg, you're vegetarian, travelling in a wheelchair, taking the baby, terrified of flying – you should let the airline know as soon as possible so that they can make arrangements accordingly. You should remind them when you reconfirm your booking (at least 72 hours before departure) and again when you check in at the airport. It may also be worth ringing round the airlines before you make your booking to find out how they can handle your particular needs.

Airports and airlines can be surprisingly helpful, but they do need advance warning. Most international airports will provide escorts from check-in desk to plane where needed, and there should be ramps, lifts, accessible toilets and reachable phones. Aircraft toilets, on the other hand, are likely to present a problem; travellers should discuss this with the airline at an early stage and, if necessary, with their doctor.

Guide dogs for the blind will often have to travel in a specially pressurised baggage compartment with other animals, away from their owner; though smaller guide dogs may be admitted to the cabin. All guide dogs will be subject to the same quarantine laws (six months in isolation etc) as any other animal when entering or returning to countries currently free of rabies, such as Britain or Australia.

Deaf travellers can ask for airport and inflight announcements to be written down for them.

Children under two travel for 10% of the standard fare (or free, on some airlines), as long as they don't occupy a seat. They don't get a baggage allowance either. 'Skycots' should be provided by the airline if requested in advance; these will take a child weighing up to about 10kg. Children between two and 12 can usually occupy a seat for half to two-thirds of the full fare, and do get a baggage allowance. Push chairs (strollers) can often be taken as hand luggage.

The UK & Ireland

London is one of the best centres in the world for discounted air tickets, and the place abounds with bucket shops offering deals to the Canary Islands. These are often in the form of package holidays, but simple return charter flights are also plentiful.

For the latest fares, check out the travel page ads of the Sunday newspapers, *Time Out*, *TNT* and *Exchange & Mart*. All are available from most London newsstands. Another good source of information on cheap fares is the magazine *Business Traveller*. Those with access to Teletext on television will find a host of travel agents advertising just as in the publications already listed. As in North America (see below), the Internet is another possible source of information.

Most British travel agents are registered with ABTA (Association of British Travel Agents). If you have paid for your flight with an ABTA-registered agent who then goes bust, ABTA will guarantee a refund or an alternative. Unregistered bucket shops are riskier but sometimes cheaper.

One of the more reliable agencies, although not necessarily cheapest, is STA (☎ 0171-361 6161 for European flights). It has several offices in London, as well branches on many university campuses and in cities such as Bristol, Cambridge, Leeds, Manchester and Oxford. The main London branches are:

86 Old Brompton Rd, London SW7 3LH
117 Euston Rd, London NW1 2SX
38 Store St, London WC1E 7BZ
Priory House, 6 Wrights Lane, London W8 6TA
11 Goodge St, London, W1

A similar place is Trailfinders (☎ 0171-937 5400 for European flights). Its short-haul booking centre is at 215 Kensington High St. Other offices are at 42-50 Earls Court Rd, London W8 6FT (☎ 0171-938 3366) and 194 Kensington High St, London W8 7RG (☎ 0171-938 3939). The latter offers an inoculation service and a research library for customers. Trailfinders also has agencies in Bristol, Birmingham, Glasgow and Manchester.

Campus Travel is in much the same league and has the following branches in London:

52 Grosvenor Gardens, London SW1W 0AG (European flights on ☎ 0171-730 3402)
University College of London, 25 Gordon St, London WC1H 0AH (☎ 0171-383 5337)
YHA Adventure Shop, 174 Kensington High St, London W8 7RG (☎ 0171-938 2188)
YHA Adventure Shop, 14 Southampton St, London (☎ 0171-836 3343)
South Bank University, Keyworth St, London SE1 (☎ 0171-401 8666)

The two flag airlines that link the UK and the Canary Islands are British Airways (☎ 0171-434 4700; 24-hour line 0345-222111), 156 Regent St, London W1R, and Spain's Iberia (☎ 0171-830 0011), 11 Haymarket, London SW1Y 4BP. Of the two, BA is more likely to have special deals lower than the standard scheduled fares. Iberia flights all go via Madrid, and the standard shoulder-season return fare from London to Las Palmas, valid for six months, was UK£334 at the time of writing. Don't despair, the bucket shops can often get you across for much less, usually on charter flights. The Spanish airline Spanair has direct flights from Gatwick to Tenerife, Las Palmas and Arrecife (Lanzarote), but tickets are sold through travel agents.

Council Travel (☎ 0171-437 7767), 28a Poland St, London W1V 3DB, which specialises in student and under-26 fares, plus the occasional charter, had a student return fare with Transavia for UK£201. The ticket was valid for a year.

Spanish Travel Services (☎ 0171-387 5337), 138 Eversholt St, London NW1 1BL, has a good range of charter-flight options. If STS don't offer anything outstanding, look around other bucket shops. STS has charter flights from UK£119 return to Las Palmas and the other main islands. Another source of cheap flights to the Canaries is the Charter Flight Centre (☎ 0171-565 6755), 15 Gillingham St, London SW1 V1HN. It also does packages.

In low season, fares can fall as low as UK£99 return – keep your eyes on the bucket-shop ads! Otherwise, you could call the Air Travel Advisory Bureau (☎ 0171-636 5000). You tell the bureau your destination and it provides a list of relevant bucket shops that it has on its books.

The cheapest time to fly is midweek on a night flight. If you're looking to go in winter but wish to avoid the high-season crush and price rises, you'll need to fly out in late November or early December and return before Christmas. Always check the arrival and departure times on these flights, as inconvenience is usually part of the price you pay for a low fare. You should not be surprised, in peak times at any rate, to find your flight delayed. Remember too that, once booked, you cannot alter your flight details. If you miss a charter flight, you have lost your money. There is little rhyme or reason to the kinds of deals that can come up out of nowhere – the explanation is usually a last-minute attempt to fill empty seats with rock-bottom fares.

You needn't necessarily fly from London, as many good deals are as easily available from other major centres in the UK.

Flying as a courier (see also The USA below), is unlikely to be a possibility from the UK, but if you want to check try the BA Travel Shop (☎ 0181-564 7009), or trawl the Yellow Pages.

If you're coming from Ireland, it might be worth comparing what is available direct and from London – getting across to London first may save you a few quid.

In the Canaries Check around the budget travel agents for student fares, charters and other last-minute deals. In the main resorts and cities especially you can often dig up some extraordinary last-minute bargains. At the time of writing, one agent on Tenerife was virtually giving away one-way flights to London on certain days around Christmas and New Year for 5000 ptas!

Packages & Fly-Drive Most tourists to the islands book a package deal. This generally consists of flights, transfers and accommodation. This can work out well, and often more cheaply than going it alone, but it does limit you. See also Organised Tours below.

It can work out marginally cheaper to book a hire car before arriving in the islands, so you might consider a fly-drive package. Most reputable travel agents and tour operators can organise this. You do need to think about how long you will actually want a car though. Those staying on one island may find they can dispense with a car after a few days, and those island-hopping would find it expensive to hall their hire car around from island to island (in those few instances where that is even permitted). In that case you are better off hiring a car in each island as you go, for just the amount of time you require.

Spain

One might have thought Spain was the obvious place to get a plane for the Canary Islands, since in effect it represents an internal flight. Appearances can be deceptive, however. Aside from charters, Air Europa and Spanair both operate regular scheduled flights between the Canaries and a host of mainland Spanish cities, including Madrid, Barcelona, Alicante and Málaga.

The Mallorca-based Spanair has flights to Tenerife Norte, Las Palmas de Gran Canaria and Lanzarote (Arrecife) from Madrid, Barcelona, Santiago de Compostela and Palma de Mallorca.

Air Europa flies to Tenerife (Sur and Norte), Gran Canaria, Lanzarote and Fuerteventura from numerous mainland airports.

Iberia serves eight mainland destinations from Tenerife (both airports), and connects Madrid with Santa Cruz de la Palma four times a week.

Return flights between either Madrid or Barcelona and Tenerife can cost 27,900 ptas, but much depends on the season. A return charter fare from Madrid to Tenerife can be as low as 18,900 ptas.

Scheduled airline fares tend to be much higher. A one-year open return ticket with Air Europa to Tenerife would cost 51,700 ptas from Madrid and 64,500 ptas from Barcelona.

The Rest of Europe

Given the popularity of the Canary Islands with sun-starved Europeans across the continent (or at least its northern half), plenty of charter options present themselves from a series of cities across Europe, not unlike the offers available in the UK.

Germany Munich is a haven of bucket shops and more mainstream budget-travel outlets. Council Travel office (☎ 089-39 50 22), Adalbertstr 32, near the university, is one of the best. STA Travel (☎ 089-39 90 96), Königstr 49, is also good.

In Berlin, Kilroy Travel-ARTU Reisen (☎ 030-310 00 40), at Hardenbergstr 9, near Berlin Zoo (with five branches around the city) is a good travel agent. In Frankfurt, you could try STA Travel (☎ 069-70 30 35), Bockenheimer Landstr 133 and another branch in Bornheim (☎ 069-43 01 91), Bergerstr 118. Connections (☎ 069-70 50 60), Adalbertstr 8, in Bockenheim, is another consolidator.

Lufthansa's subsidiary, Condor, has frequent flights from a dozen locations in Germany to Tenerife Sur, Las Palmas de Gran Canaria, Santa Cruz de la Palma, Arrecife (Lanzarote) and Fuerteventura.

Other airlines with frequent direct flights to various of the Canary Islands include Hapag-Lloyd Flug and LTU.

The Netherlands Amsterdam is a popular departure point. The student travel agency NBBS Reiswinkels, Rokin 38 (☎ 020-624 09 89), offers reliable and reasonably low fares. Compare with the pickings in the bucket shops along Rokin before deciding. NBBS has several branches throughout the city, as well as in Brussels, Belgium.

Transavia Airlines has direct flights between Amsterdam and Tenerife Sur twice a week.

Italy A reliable place to look for cheap flights is CTS (Centro Turistico Studentesco). It has branches all over the country. In Rome (☎ 06-46791), it's at Via Genova 16.

France In Paris, Voyages et Découvertes (☎ 1-42 61 00 01), 21 Rue Cambon, is a good place to start hunting down the best air fares.

Portugal Portugalia Airlines connects Lisbon with Tenerife Sur at least four days a week. A couple of these fly via Las Palmas de Gran Canaria. The return fare is 62,000 ptas.

Morocco
Although barely 100km away, the shores of Morocco are expensive to reach. A straightforward return trip to Agadir from Las Palmas with Royal Air Maroc (☎ 928-26 84 64) costs 64,510 ptas. To Marrakesh the fare is 83,710 ptas and involves a three-hour layover in Casablanca. In terms of cost, the Agadir flight is the best bet, as the buses from there to Marrakesh and other points are good and a damned sight cheaper than the extra money you would pay for the flight. If you're feeling particularly adventurous, RAM also has flights twice a week to Laayoune, in the Moroccan-occupied Sahara. There's not an awful lot there, although you could undertake the rough overland ride south to Mauritania (check the latest situation on visas and whether the frontier is open or not).

If you are thinking about making a brief excursion into Morocco while in the Canaries, you should look into the package offers, as these represent comparatively good value. At the time of writing, one-week packages comprising flights, hotel and half board to Marrakesh with excursions to Fés, Meknés, Casablanca and Rabat were going for 75,900 ptas.

The Rest of Africa
There are few direct links between the Canary Islands and the rest of Africa. At the time of writing one option was an Iberia service from Las Palmas to Dakar (Sene-

gal), which cost 93,000 ptas return for a maximum stay of two months. Sometimes there are flights to Banjul, Ghana, with Ghana Airways (☎ 928-27 21 08), and to Mauritania with Air Mauritanie (☎ 928-47 00 50), both from Las Palmas.

The USA
The North Atlantic is the world's busiest long-haul air corridor and the flight options are bewildering. That said, the options to the Canary Islands are rather limited.

Several airlines fly direct to mainland Spain, landing in Madrid, from where you can get connecting flights to the Canaries. Using the information above on flights between mainland Spain and the islands, compare the cost of a ticket right through to the Canaries from the USA with a ticket to Madrid plus a round-trip flight from Madrid. In general there will be little difference, but it's worth checking. The other option is a package trip with a charter airline (see Organised Tours below).

Otherwise, consider getting a cheap flight to London and a charter from there.

If your European trip is not going to be confined to the islands, consult your travel agent about how best to incorporate them into your vacation.

The *New York Times*, the *LA Times*, the *Chicago Tribune* and the *San Francisco Examiner* produce weekly travel sections in which you'll find any number of travel agents' ads. Council Travel and STA Travel have offices in major cities nationwide. The magazine *Travel Unlimited* (PO Box 1058, Allston, Mass 02134) publishes details of cheap air fares.

Standard fares on commercial airlines are expensive and probably best avoided. However, travelling on a normal, scheduled flight can be more secure and reliable, particularly for more elderly travellers and families, who might prefer to avoid the potential inconveniences of the budget alternatives.

Discount and rock-bottom options from the USA include charter flights, stand-by and courier flights. Stand-by fares are often sold at 60% of the normal price for one-way tickets. Airhitch (☎ 212-864 2000; airhitch @netcom.com), 2641 Broadway, New York, NY 10025, specialises in this sort of thing. You will need to give a general idea of where and when you need to go, and a few days before your departure you will be presented with a choice of two or three flights. Airhitch has several other offices in the USA, including Los Angeles (☎ 310-726 5000), as well as others in London, Paris, Amsterdam, Prague, Rome, Bonn and Madrid. Such a flight will get you to Europe, but for the Canary Islands you'll need to then look for a cheap charter.

Charter flights tend to be significantly cheaper than scheduled flights. They are usually tied in with accommodation packages, tend not to be very comfortable and preclude changing return-flight dates.

Reliable travel agents specialising in budget travel (especially for students) include STA (sta-travel.com) and Council Travel (ciee.org/travel.htm), both of which have offices in major cities:

STA
　　10 Downing Street (corner of 6th Ave and Bleeker St), New York, NY 10014 (☎ 212-627 3111)
　　920 Westwood Blvd, Los Angeles, CA 90024 (☎ 310-824 1574)
　　51 Grant Ave, San Francisco, CA 94108 (☎ 415-391 8407)
Council Travel
　　254 Green St, New York, NY 10003 (☎ 212-254 2525)
　　205 East 42nd St, New York, NY 10017 (☎ 212-822 2600)
　　1094 Lindbrook Drive, Los Angeles, CA 90024 (☎ 310-208 3551)
　　530 Bush St, San Francisco, CA 94108 (☎ 415-421 3473)

Another travel agent specialising in budget air fares is Discount Tickets in New York (☎ 212-391 2313).

Courier flights are where you accompany a parcel to its destination. Again, you'd be highly unlikely to get anything directly to the islands, but a New York-Madrid return

on a courier flight can cost under US$300 in the low season (more expensive from the west coast). You could also get one to London and take a charter flight on to the islands from there, although you'll probably end up spending much the same amount either way. Generally courier flights require that you return within a specified period (sometimes within one or two weeks, but on occasion up to three months). You may find your luggage allowance being restricted, although increasingly couriers are asked simply to deliver documents to a company representative at the destination. You may have to be a US resident and apply for an interview before they take you on. Most flights depart from New York.

A good source of information on courier flights is Now Voyager (☎ 212-431 1616), Suite 307, 74 Varrick St, New York, NY 10013. This company specialises in courier flights, but you must pay an annual membership fee (around US$50), which entitles you to take as many courier flights as you like. Phone for a recorded message detailing all available flights and prices. The Denver-based Air Courier Association (☎ 303-278 8810) also does this kind of thing. You join the association, which is used by international air-freight companies to provide the escorts. You may be able to organise such flights direct with courier companies – try the Yellow Pages.

Courier prices can be 10-40% below scheduled fares and are also seasonal. They also tend to drop if you are prepared to fly at short notice. Always check conditions and details with the company.

For the hi-tech navigator, information and flights can be had in the travel forums open to users of the Internet and assorted computer information-and-communication services. They are a step further down the travellers' superhighway from television Teletext services – another source of fares and other information.

At the time of writing, Iberia flew to Tenerife via Madrid from New York in low season for US$750 return. STA offers tickets for as low as US$550, while Discount Tickets had a fare of US$650, also via Madrid. All fares include taxes. From Tenerife there was a weekly direct charter to New York on Saturday for 89,900 ptas return plus taxes. The return flight was also on Saturday. Always look for low-season deals though – around the time of writing, return flights to New York via Madrid were going for 66,000 ptas.

At these rates, it really is worth looking at the option of a cheap flight to London and a charter from there.

Canada

Iberia has direct flights to the Canaries via Madrid from Toronto and Montreal. As with the USA, the thing to do is work out the best possible route/fare combination, and again a direct flight to London combined with a charter from there can often work out the cheapest and simplest method for reaching the Canaries.

Travel CUTS (☎ 1-800-777 0112; travelcuts.com), which specialises in discount fares for students, has offices in all major cities. Otherwise scan the budget travel agents' ads in the *Toronto Star*, the *Globe & Mail*, and the *Vancouver Province*. The magazine *Great Expeditions* (PO Box 8000-411, Abbotsford BC V2S 6H1) is sometimes useful.

See the previous section for information on courier flights. For courier flights originating in Canada, contact FB on Board Courier Services (☎ 514-633 0740 in Toronto or Montreal, or 604-338 1366 in Vancouver). Airhitch (see the USA section) has stand-by fares to and from Toronto, Montreal and Vancouver.

South America

There is little in the way of scheduled direct flights between the Canaries and South America. One exception is an Iberia run to Caracas (Venezuela) from Las Palmas or Tenerife. A return ticket in low season, valid for up to two months, costs 122,000 ptas.

Air Europa also has a weekly flight to Salvador de Bahía in Brazil.

Otherwise flights are generally routed through Madrid. Look for deals to places such as the Dominican Republic and Mexican resorts. At the time of writing, some of these were going for around 80,000 ptas.

Australia

There are no direct flights from Australia to the Canaries, so you'll have to book connecting flights via Madrid or another European capital.

STA and Flight Centres International are major dealers in cheap air fares, although heavily discounted fares can often be found at the travel agent in your local shopping centre. The Saturday travel sections of the Melbourne *Age* and the *Sydney Morning Herald* have many advertisements offering cheap fares to Europe, but don't be surprised if they happen to be 'sold out' when you contact the agents – they are usually low-season fares on obscure airlines with conditions attached.

Discounted return air fares to European destinations on mainstream airlines through reputable agents can be surprisingly cheap, with low-season fares around A$1600 to A$1800 return and high-season fares up to A$2500. You'd then have to tack on the difference for the return flights between Europe and the islands.

For courier flights you could try Jupiter (☎ 02-9317 2230), Unit 3, 55 Kent Rd, Mascot in Sydney.

The following are some addresses for agencies offering good-value fares:

STA Travel
224 Faraday St, Carlton, Vic 3053
(☎ 03-9347 6911)
Shop 3, 702-730 Harris St, Ultimo, NSW 2007 (☎ 02-9281 1530)
1st Floor, New Guild Building, University of Western Australia, Crawley, WA 6009
(☎ 08-9380 2302)
Flight Centres International
Bourke Street Flight Centre, 19 Bourke St, Melbourne, Vic 3000 (☎ 03-9650 2899)
Martin Place Flight Centre, Shop 5, State Bank Centre, 52 Martin Place, Sydney, NSW 2000 (☎ 02-9235 0166)
City Flight Centre, Shop 25, Cinema City Arcade, Perth, WA 6000 (☎ 08-9325 9222)

New Zealand

As with Australia, STA and Flight Centres International are popular travel agents in New Zealand. The cheapest fares to Europe are generally routed through the USA, although in the case of the Canary Islands you may well get a deal via Latin America. An RTW ticket may be cheaper than a normal return. Otherwise, you can fly from Auckland to pick up a connecting flight in Melbourne or Sydney.

Useful addresses include:

Flight Centres International
    Auckland Flight Centre, Shop 3A, National Bank Towers, 205-225 Queen St, Auckland (☎ 09-309 6171)
STA Travel & International Travellers Centre
    10 High St, Auckland (☎ 09-309 0458)
Campus Travel
    Gate 1, Knighton Rd, Waikato University, Hamilton (☎ 07-856 9139)

Asia

Hong Kong is the discount-ticket capital of the region. Its bucket shops are at least as unreliable as those of other cities. Ask the advice of other travellers before buying a ticket.

STA has branches in Hong Kong, Tokyo, Singapore, Bangkok and Kuala Lumpur.

LAND

For reasons that will become apparent after a brief glance at the atlas, there are no bus or rail routes to the Canary Islands. However, there is nothing to stop you from making your way across Spain to the southern port of Cádiz, from where you can get a weekly ferry to the islands (provided you have booked well ahead – refer to Sea below).

The ferry ride throws up the option of taking your own car or motorbike, but of course first you have to make it to Cádiz. From there it is a long and expensive haul, and probably only worth contemplating if you are planning an extended sojourn in the islands. See the Getting Around chapter for information on car and motorcycle travel within the Canaries.

Car & Motorcycle

Paperwork & Preparations Proof of ownership of a private vehicle should always be carried (Vehicle Registration Document for UK-registered cars) when driving through Europe, and that includes the Canary Islands. All EU-member states' driving licences are fully recognised in the Canary Islands, although if you stay for more than a year (that is, virtually become resident) you are supposed to apply for a local licence. In practice many residents don't bother. The old-style UK green licence is not accepted, and you'd be wise to get an International Driving Permit for non-EU licences (see Documents in the Facts for the Visitor chapter).

Third-party motor insurance is a minimum requirement in the Canary Islands, Spain and throughout Europe, as is a Green Card, an internationally recognised proof of insurance that can be obtained from your insurer. Also ask your insurer for a European Accident Statement form, which can simplify matters in the event of an accident. Never sign statements you can't read or understand – insist on a translation and sign that only if it's acceptable.

A European breakdown-assistance policy is a good investment, such as the AA Five Star Service or the RAC Eurocover Motoring Assistance. In the Canary Islands and Spain in general, assistance can be obtained through the RACE. See the Getting Around chapter for details.

Every vehicle travelling across an international border should display a nationality plate of its country of registration. A warning triangle (to be used in the event of a breakdown) is compulsory throughout Europe. Recommended accessories are a first-aid kit, a spare bulb kit and a fire extinguisher.

In the UK, further information can be obtained from the RAC (☎ 0990-722722) or the AA (☎ 0990-500600).

Rental There is a mind-boggling variety of special deals, terms and conditions attached to car rental. However, there are a few pointers to help you through. Multinational agencies – Hertz, Avis and Europe's largest rental agency, Europcar – will provide a reliable service and good standard of vehicle.

If you walk into an office for such a multinational and request a car on the spot, you will generally pay a slightly higher rate than you would if you had arranged it in advance, even allowing for special weekend deals. Local firms can sometimes undercut the multinationals, but examine the rental agreement carefully (difficult if it is in Spanish only!).

Booking a rental car through a multinational agency before leaving home will generally enable you to find the best deals. Prepaid rates are sometimes cheaper, and it may be worth your while looking into fly/drive combinations and other programs. You will simply pick up the vehicle on arrival and return it to a nominated point at the end of the rental period. Ask your travel agent for information, or contact one of the major rental agencies.

Another possibility if you don't know when you want to rent is to call back (or perhaps even email!) home and reserve through an agent there. This way you get the benefits of booking from home. One US reader suggested taking out American Automobile Association membership before leaving home – companies such as Hertz often have discounts for AAA members booking a car through a US office.

Before going to all this trouble, however, do look around to see what local rates are. Car rental in the Canaries is much cheaper than in mainland Spain, so the savings on pre-booked cars are likely to be less spectacular.

No matter where you rent, make sure you understand what is included in the price (unlimited kilometres, tax, insurance, collision damage waiver etc) and what your liabilities are. The minimum rental age in Spain, and hence the Canary Islands, is 21 years. A credit card is usually required.

For more details of rental rates and options, see Car & Motorcycle in the Getting Around chapter.

Purchase Only residents in Spain can buy a car there, and only those who can prove residence in the Canary Islands may avail themselves of the local tax breaks to buy a car cheaply.

Otherwise, the UK is probably the best place to buy, as second-hand prices are good and, whether buying privately or from a dealer, the absence of language difficulties will help you to establish exactly what you are getting for your money. Bear in mind that you will be getting a left-hand drive car (ie steering wheel on the right) if you buy in the UK. If you want a right-hand drive car and can afford to buy new, prices are relatively low in Belgium, the Netherlands and Luxembourg.

Motorcycling If you get your own bike to the islands, or hire one on the spot, remember that wearing crash helmets is obligatory. A bike will be easier and cheaper than a car to get on to the interisland ferries and the boat from Cádiz too.

Anyone considering joining a motorcycle tour from the UK might want to join the International Motorcyclists Tour Club (UK£19 per annum plus UK£3 joining fee). The club counts 400 members, and in addition to holidays on the Continent, they also have social weekends! The present secretary, James Clegg, can be contacted on ☎ 1484-66 48 68.

SEA
Spain
Most people choose to fly to the islands, but a Trasmediterránea car ferry (which can carry up to 135 cars) leaves from Cádiz for Santa Cruz de Tenerife and Las Palmas de Gran Canaria every Saturday at 6 pm. It's a long and often bumpy ride, arriving in Santa Cruz de Tenerife on Monday at 9 am (where it stops for six hours) and 7 pm in Las Palmas de Gran Canaria. The boat back to Spain leaves Santa Cruz at 8 am on Wednesday, calling in at Las Palmas (noon) and Arrecife (Lanzarote; 9 pm) on the way. However, unless you especially like ocean voyages or you have a car that you need to

transport, you are probably better off travelling by air.

Fares per person range from 28,975 ptas to 54,915 ptas depending on the type of cabin. The fares include all meals. Return fares are double, and children under 13 pay half the adult fare. Senior citizens should ask for a 20% reduction on adult fares. All prices rise marginally from July to the end of December. A car up to 6m long and 1.8m high costs from 23,950 ptas one way. Motorcycles cost 8980 ptas one way.

You generally need to book at least a month in advance if you want to get your car on, and can do so through selected representatives for Trasmediterránea outside Spain. These include:

Belgium
  Voyages Wasteels – Chaussée de Boondael 6, 1050 Brussels (☎ 02-645 0611)
Denmark
  Ferry Cruising Center – Strandvejen 6, 2100 Copenhagen (☎ 39 27 78 00)
France
  Iberrail France – Blvd Poissonnière 8, 75009 Paris (☎ 1-48 01 97 97)
Italy
  Alpitour Italia – Via Roccavione 14, 12100 Cuneo (☎ 0171-3131)
Germany
  Deutsches Reisebüro (DER), 60439 Frankfurt/ Main 50 (☎ 069-95 88 17 17)
Netherlands
  VCK Zeereizen – Scandia Termina, PO Box 1418, 1000 BK Amsterdam (☎ 020-587 7877)
Portugal
  Iberrail Portugal Viagens – Rua Latino Coelho 50 3°D, 1000 Lisbon (☎ 01-353 9475)
Sweden
  Ferry Center – Botildenborgs 21, box 15017, 20032 Malmö (☎ 040-210050)
Switzerland
  Voyages Cristal – Rue Chantepoulet 1-3, Geneva 1201 (☎ 022-738 0466)
UK
  Southern Ferries – First Floor, 179 Piccadilly, London W1V 9DB (☎ 0171-491 4968)

DEPARTURE TAXES

There are departure taxes when leaving the Canary islands by air (fluctuating around 1000 ptas for European flights; rising to as much as 5000 ptas beyond Europe) but these are included in the price of the ticket at purchase. For European flights they are generally only charged if you are taking a *return* flight.

ORGANISED TOURS

There is no shortage of companies providing travel services to the Canary Islands from anywhere in Europe and North America. Spanish tourist offices can provide you with extensive lists of companies offering all kinds of holidays, although the emphasis is on flight and accommodation packages. Ask in particular for the Holidays of Special Interest list, which categorises companies thematically (eg coach tours, birdwatching, golf and fishing).

It is worth shopping around and comparing what's on offer. Remember that, while packages take a lot of the hassle out of travelling, they also remove much of the adventure and liberty of movement. Once you've paid up your apartment for two weeks, you're stuck with it. If you plan to travel the islands more extensively, independent travel is really the way to go. The only proviso being that in high season, especially on the smaller islands, it is possible to be left out on a limb.

Package Tours In the UK, Key to the Canaries (☎ 0161-834 1187), 16 Lloyd St, Manchester M2 5WA, specialises in all-inclusive packages to the Canary Islands.

Lanzarote Leisure (☎ 0181-449 74 41), 4 Lytton Rd, New Barnet, Herts EN5 5BY, has an extensive list of apartments and villas in Lanzarote, Fuerteventura and Tenerife. Prices vary greatly depending on the season, kind of accommodation, how many people occupy the villa/apartment and so on. As a rule of thumb, a week's accommodation and airfare start at about UK£200 per person.

In the USA, you could have a look at Spanish Heritage Tours (☎ 1-800-221 2250), 47 Queens Blvd, Forest Hills, NY 11375. From New York you would be looking at from US$710 per person for a week, including flights, transfers, accommodation and sometimes breakfast. There are many other tour operators specialising in Spain and most can help with packages to the Canary Islands. Another worth investigating in New York is Spain Tours & Beyond (☎ 212-595 24 00).

Cruises & Freighters If travelling is more important to you than arriving, and money is no object, you could take a leisurely cruise out to the Canary Islands.

Fred Olsen Cruise Lines (☎ 01473-29 22 22), White House Rd, Ipswich, Suffolk IP1 5LL, offers a series of two-week cruises aboard the *Black Watch* and *Black Prince*. The routes usually take in intermediate stops (like Lisbon and Madeira) and, say, a couple of days along the Moroccan coast. Hold on to your wallet – the cheapest fares hover around UK£1200 per person. A little more economical is Cruise International (☎ 0171-436 0827), Suite 304, Albany House, 324-326 Regent St, London W1R 5AA, offering 12-day cruises starting at UK£625 per person in four-berth cabins. Cruises start in Genova (Italy – return flights from Gatwick included) and cruise along the Spanish coast, out to the islands and back along the Moroccan coast.

With both companies, inquire about extra charges for on-shore activities and discounts for early booking.

The Cruise People Ltd can organise you on to still more expensive cruise ships doing the Canaries, as well as anything from an expedition ship to the Antarctic to a West Indies banana boat. Its London office (☎ 0800-56 23 13), 88 York St, London W1 1DP, can get you passage on a German container ship departing Hamburg on two and three-week trips to the Canaries. You can opt for a one-way trip. You'll be looking at roughly UK£1000 for the full three weeks. Again, make sure you know exactly what is included in the price. The Cruise People Ltd has a Canadian office too (☎ 416-444 2410), at 1252 Lawrence Ave, East, Suite 202, Don Mills, Ontario, Canada M3A 1C3.

WARNING
The information in this chapter is particularly vulnerable to change: prices for international travel are volatile, routes are introduced and cancelled, schedules change, special deals come and go, and rules and visa requirements are amended. Airlines and governments seem to take a perverse pleasure in making price structures and regulations as complicated as possible. You should check directly with the airline or a travel agent to make sure you understand how a fare (and ticket you may buy) works. In addition, the travel industry is highly competitive and there are many lurks and perks.

The upshot of this is that you should get opinions, quotes and advice from as many airlines and travel agents as possible before you part with your hard-earned cash. The details given in this chapter should be regarded as indicators and are not a substitute for your own careful, up-to-date research.

Getting Around

AIR

Binter (☎ 902 40 05 00), the former subsidiary of Spain's national airline, Iberia, connects six of the seven islands (La Gomera still has no airport) with fairly regular flights. It's not a cheap way to get around, but infinitely quicker than the ferry.

In business since 1988, it operates nine ATR-72 prop aircraft and was hived off and fully privatised in April 1998. Iberia too, was heading for privatisation in 1998.

See the table at the bottom of this page for a a rundown of available flights. Frequency and fares are the same in reverse and there is no reduction for getting round-trip tickets (residents of the islands are entitled to a 10% discount).

Putting up a little competition is Canarias Regional Air (☎ 902 24 00 42), with daily flights between Tenerife Norte and Gran Canaria, Lanzarote and Fuerteventura. Air Atlantic has two direct flights a week between Gran Canaria and El Hierro.

Some of the islands are also connected by two other airlines serving the Spanish mainland. They are Air Europa (Tenerife, Gran Canaria, Lanzarote and Fuerteventura) and Spanair (Tenerife, Gran Canaria and Lanzarote).

The regional government is looking at ways to increase flights and competition; the idea is to reduce prices and increase passenger volume (as many people still elect to go by sea).

BUS

The first thing you need to know about buses in the Canary Islands is that they are generally known as *guaguas*. Anyone who has travelled around in Latin America will be familiar with the term. Still, if you ask about *autobuses*, you'll have no trouble being understood.

Basically each island has its own interurban service. One way or another, they can get you to most main locations, but in many cases the number of runs is hardly impressive. This is especially so on the smaller islands where the population is low and most people have their own wheels anyway. Even on major runs in the bigger islands, a frequent weekday service can trickle off to just a few departures on Saturday and one, or none, on Sunday.

In the larger towns and cities, buses leave from a bus station (*estación de guaguas*). Otherwise, they terminate at a particular street or plaza.

You pay for tickets on the bus. Alternatively, on some islands, you can buy a Bonobus card (called a Tarjeta Dinero on Gran Canaria), usually for 2000 ptas, at bus

Domestic Flights

Departure point	Destination	Frequency	Flight time	One-way fare
Tenerife Norte	Gran Canaria	Up to 11 daily	30 minutes	5800 ptas
Tenerife Sur	Gran Canaria	1 daily but Sunday	30 minutes	5800 ptas
Tenerife Norte	Lanzarote	3 daily	50 minutes	10,550 ptas
Tenerife Norte	Fuerteventura	2 daily	50 minutes	9800 ptas
Tenerife Norte	La Palma	8 daily	30 minutes	6530 ptas
Tenerife Norte	El Hierro	2-3 daily	40 minutes	7230 ptas
Gran Canaria	La Palma	2 daily	50 minutes	9950 ptas
Gran Canaria	Lanzarote	6 daily	40 minutes	8550 ptas
Gran Canaria	Fuerteventura	6 daily	35 minutes	7610 ptas

Bus Routes

Island	Departure point	Destination	Fare
Gran Canaria	Las Palmas de Gran Canaria	Mogán	910 ptas
Lanzarote	Arrecife	Playa Blanca	375 ptas
Fuerteventura	Puerto del Rosario	Morro Jable	1000 ptas
Tenerife	Santa Cruz de Tenerife	Playa de las Américas	875 ptas
La Palma	Santa Cruz de la Palma	Los Llanos de Aridane	570 ptas
La Gomera	San Sebastián de la Gomera	Valle de Gran Rey	675 ptas
El Hierro	Valverde	La Restinga	300 ptas

stations and shops such as newsagents. Insert the card into the machine on the bus, tell the driver where you are going and he will deduct the fare from the card. You get about 25-30% off standard fares if you use these cards, so they are a good investment if you intend to use the buses a lot on islands like Tenerife and La Palma.

The table at the top of this page gives some sample standard one-way fares, which should give you an idea of the most you are likely to pay for any one ticket on all the islands.

CAR & MOTORCYCLE
Road Rules
If bringing your own car, remember to have your insurance and other papers in order (see the Getting There & Away chapter). If the car is from the UK or Ireland, remember to have the headlights adjusted for driving in Continental Europe. If fitted, rear seatbelts must be worn – fines for failure to comply range from 50,000 to 100,000 ptas. The minimum driving age is 18.

Motorcyclists note that headlights must be used at all times. Crash helmets are obligatory on bikes of 125cc or more. The minimum age for riding bikes and scooters under 75cc is 16 (no licence is required).

In built up areas the speed limit is generally 40km/h, rising to 100km/h on major roads and 120km/h on *autovías* (motorways). Cars towing caravans are restricted to a maximum speed of 80km/h.

The blood-alcohol limit is 0.08% and breath testing is carried out on occasion.

Fines ranging up to 100,000 ptas are imposed if you are caught driving under the influence or alcohol. Fines for many traffic offences range from 50,000 up to 100,000 ptas.

Nonresident foreigners can be fined on the spot – the minor compensation being that with immediate settlement they get 20% deducted from normal fines.

Road Atlases & Maps
There are no real road atlases for the Canary Islands collectively, so you are better off buying maps for the islands you need. Firestone's Islas Canarias map of all the islands, at a scale of 1:150,000 is not bad for drivers. See also Maps in the Facts for the Visitor chapter and in the introduction to destination chapters for more information about maps.

Road Assistance
The Real Automóvil Club de España's head office (☎ 91 447 32 00) is at Calle de José Abascal 10 in Madrid, but operates in the Canary Islands too. It has an office (☎ 922 27 07 16) at Avenida de Anaga s/n in Santa Cruz de Tenerife.

For RACE's 24-hour emergency breakdown assistance, call the free number ☎ 900-11 81 18. This service is available to members of foreign motoring organisations such as the RAC and AA.

City Driving & Parking
Driving in the biggest cities, Las Palmas de Gran Canarias and Santa Cruz de Tenerife,

doesn't present particular difficulties, although the traffic can be a little intense.

Parking, however, is more problematic. Most of the city centres (and this goes for smaller towns too) operate restricted meter parking. On average you get up to two hours for 200 ptas. Otherwise, there are several parking stations in the two capitals.

If you double park or leave your vehicle in a designated no-parking zone, you risk being towed – recovering the vehicle costs 6000 ptas.

Don't leave anything in the car if you can avoid it. Theft from cars, and hire cars in particular, is always a threat.

Petrol

Gasolina is much cheaper in the Canary Islands than elsewhere on Spanish territory, as it is free of normal consumer taxes.

You'll not find regular petrol anywhere nowadays, but lead-free (*sin plomo*) is available pretty much everywhere. Prices vary slightly between service stations and fluctuate with oil tariffs and tax policy, so what follows serves as a guide only. Super costs 81.2 ptas per litre and the increasingly popular diesel (or *gasóleo*) 65 ptas per litre. Lead-free (95 octane) costs 79.1 ptas and 98 octane super, sometimes known as *Súper Star*, comes in at 83.3 ptas. You can pay with major credit cards at many service stations.

Rental

All the big international car rental companies are represented in the Canary Islands, and there are also some local operators. If you intend to stay on the one island for any length of time, it might be worth booking a car in advance, for example in a fly/drive deal (see Car & Motorbike in the Getting There & Away chapter). Companies operating in all or most of the islands include Hertz (☎ 901 101 001), Avis, Europcar/BC Betacar, Euro Dollar/Atesa (☎ 902 100 101) and Cicar (☎ 928 59 70 19).

If you do decide to hire a car after arriving, shop around. You need to be at least 21 years old and have held a driver's licence for a minimum of two years. It is easier, and with some companies obligatory, to pay with a credit card.

You'll find no shortage of local companies competing with the big international crowds. With some of these you can get quite reasonable deals. A Seat Marbella might cost you as little as 16,000 ptas for a week including insurance and unlimited kilometres. No matter where you rent, the daily rate comes down the longer you hire the car for.

More standard rates with the bigger firms hover around 3000 ptas to 4000 ptas per day for a week for a small car. Europcar, for instance, will give you an Opel Corsa 1.2 for 3475 ptas per day with unlimited mileage. On top of this you need to calculate 1400 ptas a day in collision damage waiver, as well as 550 ptas a day in theft and third-party insurance. Hertz, on the other hand, has the same car for 3925 ptas a day all up. Remember to ask if the 4.5% IGIC tax is included in the price offered. You may also want to take out extra personal insurance, which generally costs around 2000 ptas a day.

Note that, in general, you may *not* take a hire car from one island to another without the firm's explicit permission. Some companies, such as Hertz, offer a special rate which allows you to island-hop. An exception to the above rule for most companies is the Fuerteventura-Lanzarote crossing. Major companies at least have no problem with you taking your car from one to the other, and in some cases you can hire in one and drop the car off in the other.

Renting motorbikes and mopeds can be expensive. A sample rate is 6500 ptas a day for a Honda Enduro X250. You have to leave a refundable deposit of at least 20,000 ptas (or a credit card). An 80cc scooter will cost from at least 3000 ptas a day.

See also Car & Motorbike in the Getting There & Away chapter for more general rental information.

Purchase

You can only purchase a vehicle in the

Canary Islands if you are a permanent resident. If that is the case, you can get good deals as vehicles, like everything else, are exempt from the standard taxes.

TAXI

You can tour around the islands by taxi if you want, but this is definitely the expensive way to go. Also, taxi drivers operating between towns tend to be sharkish, and meters are noticeable by their absence – always confirm the fare before taking (or being taken for) a ride.

The Tenerife Taxi Drivers Union puts out a brochure publishing return fares between Santa Cruz and destinations all over the island. Their suggested *return* fare to Puerto de la Cruz is around 4500 ptas. Ask a taxi driver at the Tenerife Norte airport how much the one-way fare is to the same spot (and the airport is 12km closer to Puerto de la Cruz than Santa Cruz) and you will probably be told 3000 ptas! Go figure.

BICYCLE

You can rent mountain bikes in various resorts and the more touristed areas of the islands. Expect to pay at least 1000 ptas a day.

If you plan to bring your own bike, check with the airline about any hidden costs. It will have to be disassembled and packed for the journey.

You should travel light on a cycle tour, but bring tools and some spare parts, including a puncture-repair kit and a spare inner tube. Panniers are essential to balance your possessions on either side of the bike frame. A bike helmet is a good idea, as is a solid bike lock and chain to prevent your bike from being stolen.

One organisation that can help you plan your bike tour is the Cyclists' Touring Club (☎ 01483-417217), Cotterell House, 69 Meadrow, Godalming, Surrey GU7 3HS, Britain. It can supply information to members on cycling conditions, itineraries and cheap insurance. Membership costs UK£25 per annum or UK£12.50 for people aged under 18.

HITCHING

Hitching is never entirely safe and we don't recommend it. Travellers who decide to hitch should understand that they are taking a small but potentially serious risk. You'll also need plenty of patience and common sense. Women should avoid hitching alone, and even men should consider the safer alternative of hitching in pairs.

Hitching is illegal on the islands' few autovías (motorways) and difficult on major highways.

You really need to choose a spot where cars can safely stop before the highway slipways, or use minor roads.

There is little point in trying to hitch from city centres. Take local transport to town exits and carry a sign with your destination in Spanish.

In all, hitching is a bit hit and miss in the islands. With so many tourists getting around in hire vehicles it can often seem a breeze. At other times the lack of traffic on back roads can be frustrating, and locals are not always so keen on giving strangers a lift.

BOAT

All the islands are connected by a series of ferries, hydrofoils and jetfoils. The main company, Trasmediterránea, gets some competition on selected routes from a few other outfits. You should get a hold of all the relevant timetables from a travel agent as early in your trip as possible to better plan ahead your island hopping. Below is a quick summary of routes operated by the various companies. For more detailed information, refer to the Getting There & Away sections under the appropriate destinations.

Ferry

Trasmediterránea operates roll-on roll-off car ferries to major ports around the islands. Between Las Palmas de Gran Canaria and Santa Cruz de Tenerife there are one or two departures three or four days a week (the lack of ferries is explained by the frequency of jetfoil services).

Interisland Boat Travel
Ferries

Departure point	Destination	Duration	One-way fare
Las Palmas de Gran Canaria	Santa Cruz de Tenerife	3½ hours	2700 ptas
Las Palmas de Gran Canaria	Puerto del Rosario	8 hours	3500 ptas
Las Palmas de Gran Canaria	Arrecife	7 hours (direct) or 14 hours (via Fuerteventura)	3500 ptas
Las Palmas de Gran Canaria	Morro Jable	3 hours	3100 ptas
Las Palmas de Gran Canaria	Santa Cruz de la Palma	13½ hours	3500 ptas
Santa Cruz de Tenerife	Puerto del Rosario	8 hours	4600 ptas
Santa Cruz de Tenerife	Arrecife	20 hours (via Las Palmas & Fuerteventura)	4600 ptas
Los Cristianos (Tenerife)	Santa Cruz de la Palma	5 hours (via San Sebastián de la Gomera)	2690 ptas
Puerto del Rosario	Arrecife	3 hours	1050 ptas
El Hierro	Los Cristianos (Tenerife)	5 hours	2350 ptas
El Hierro	San Sebastián de la Gomera	3¼ hours	2350 ptas
Los Cristianos (Tenerife)	San Sebastián de la Gomera	1½ hours	1920 ptas
Playa Blanca (Lanzarote)	Corralejo (Fuerteventura)	1 hour	1700-1800 ptas

Jetfoils

Departure point	Destination	Duration	One-way off-peak/tourist/ premier-class fare
Las Palmas de Gran Canaria	Santa Cruz de Tenerife	80 minutes	3200/5600/7200 ptas
Las Palmas de Gran Canaria	Morro Jable	80 minutes	NA/5600/7200 ptas
Santa Cruz de Tenerife	Morro Jable (via Las Palmas)	3¼ hours	NA/8000/10,500 ptas

Hydrofoils

Departure point	Destination	Duration	One-way fare
San Sebastián de la Gomera	Los Cristianos (Tenerife)	45 minutes	1920 ptas
San Sebastián de la Gomera	Valle de Gran Rey	30 minutes	1000 ptas
Los Cristianos (Tenerife)	Valle de Gran Rey (via San Sebastián de la Gomera)	1½ hours	2350 ptas

About three times a week, ferries depart from both Las Palmas and Santa Cruz de Tenerife for Arrecife (Lanzarote), Puerto del Rosario (Fuerteventura) and Santa Cruz de la Palma (La Palma). Similarly, there are three weekly ferries between Arrecife and Puerto del Rosario.

Several daily ferries operate from Los Cristianos (south-west Tenerife) to San Sebastián de la Gomera (La Gomera). A daily ferry plies the Los Cristianos-El Hierro route. Every other day they call at San Sebastián de la Gomera en route.

Other ferry companies also operate limited services. Líneas Fred Olsen has ferries between Los Cristianos (Tenerife), San Sebastián de la Gomera and Santa Cruz de la Palma. The same company also runs four ferries a day between Santa Cruz de Tenerife and Agaete in Gran Canaria, and four a day between Lanzarote (Playa Blanca) and Fuerteventura (Corralejo).

Naviera Armas runs ferries from Santa Cruz de Tenerife to Las Palmas de Gran Canaria (at least once daily).

The same company operates ferries between Las Palmas and Morro Jable in Fuerteventura (daily), Arrecife (three times a week) and Puerto del Rosario (twice a week). It also has four runs a day between Corralejo and Playa Blanca.

Jetfoil
High-speed jetfoils make the crossing between Las Palmas de Gran Canaria and Santa Cruz de Tenerife in 80 minutes. There are from three to five departures daily, depending on the day and season. Jetfoils also link Las Palmas with Morro Jable (Fuerteventura). There is generally one departure a day except Sunday, although in low season (such as November), services can drop as low as twice a week.

Hydrofoil
A hydrofoil service links Los Cristianos (Tenerife) to San Sebastián and Valle de Gran Rey, both on La Gomera. Boats leave up to four times a day.

Fares & Travel Times
The table on the preceding page sets out sample fares and travel times for the main ferry, jetfoil and hydrofoil services between the islands. As a rule, fares between rival companies do not vary substantially (but it is always worth comparing).

You'll notice that in some cases the same fare is charged for trips of varying length (eg the Los Cristianos-El Hierro fare is the same as the San Sebastián de la Gomera-El Hierro fare, although the latter trip is shorter). Timetables are subject to change, so you should check out the latest information on the spot.

Infants travel free and children from two to 12 years pay half price. EU nationals over 60 years old should always ask about 20% reductions. Holders of the Carnet Joven (Euro26) get 35% off.

The ferry companies sometimes offer discounts for group travel. For instance Trasmediterránea has a *paquete ahorro* (savings package) for groups of four with one car. Also, groups of 20 or more are entitled to 20% off. Normal cars cost from 2000 ptas to 10,500 ptas to transport, depending on the destination. Motorbikes cost from 950 ptas to 2600 ptas and bicycles go for free with Trasmediterránea (this is *not* the case on the other lines).

LOCAL TRANSPORT
In the handful of cities throughout the islands large enough to need a public-transport system, the average visitor won't need to use it much anyway. Accommodation, restaurants, bars and attractions are in most cases concentrated in a small area.

Bus
Bus companies operate fairly extensive services in the two capitals, allowing you to get from the centre to bus stations and airports cheaply and with little fuss.

City Taxi
Taxis in the cities use meters. The flagfall is 150 ptas in Tenerife and 165 ptas in Gran Canaria. After that you pay 52 ptas per kilometre. Surcharges of 50 ptas (55 ptas in Tenerife) are imposed for: travel between 10 pm and 6 am; travel on Sunday and holidays; fares to airports; fares to the docks in Las Palmas de Gran Canaria and Santa Cruz de Tenerife; and for each piece of luggage carried (Tenerife only). By European standards, city taxis in the Canaries are cheap.

You may notice on the roof of taxis a green light and the numbers 1, 2 and 3.

When the green light is on the cab is free. The numbers refer to the kind of fare. No 1 is what you should expect, as this is the standard city zone. Fare types 2 and 3 apply to trips which take the cabs out of their city zone (Las Palmas to the airport falls into this category). In these cases, the passenger doesn't pay a flagfall or any surcharge.

ORGANISED TOURS

You'll stumble into a forest of tour possibilities in the main tourist resorts. They range from bog standard tours of whichever island you happen to be on, to whale-spotting and deep-sea fishing excursions. Various options are mentioned throughout the destination chapters.

Isla de Gran Canaria

The Canariones, as the islanders tend to refer to themselves, like to think of Gran Canaria as a 'continent in miniature'. And although the startling range of terrain, from the fertile north to the arid interior and desert south, largely justifies the claim, it has to be said that this is no more the case than, say, on Tenerife.

The island, covering 1560 sq km, is the third largest of the group but, with 714,200 residents, accounts for almost half the archipelago's population.

In many respects this is perhaps the least attractive of the Canary Islands. But it all depends on your tastes. If you're after a ball-breaking beachside nightlife with the one-week charter-flight crowd, then the Playa del Inglés scene is marginally preferable to Tenerife's equivalent, Playa de las Américas – if only because of the pretty dunes of Maspalomas.

Otherwise, the capital Las Palmas is a busy, happening city and worth a visit for its historic old quarter, nightlife and the golden sands of Playa de las Canteras. Surfers can pick up some waves there and off Maspalomas, and windsurfers are in heaven on the south-east coast.

The interior is a world away from both the capital and the southern resorts, and worth exploring. It is nevertheless a somewhat arid affair and frankly less captivating than the volcanic splendours of Tenerife or the mountainous western islands.

History

Gran Canaria was known to its original inhabitants as Tamarán, which scholars have linked with the Arabic name for date palms (*tamar*). This sounds feasible, but could not go back much beyond the 8th century, when the Muslim Arabs invaded Morocco.

Later, it appears the island was known to the Romans as Canaria. Speculation as to why is discussed in the History section of the Facts About the Islands chapter. How

HIGHLIGHTS

- Strolling through the Vegueta quarter of Las Palmas
- Enjoying a seafood lunch on the waterfront in Puerto de las Nieves
- Wandering over the expansive sand dunes of Maspalomas
- Exploring the fishing port town of Puerto de Mogán
- Cruising the bars of Las Palmas, followed by a lazy day on Playa de las Canteras
- Driving along the scenic route from Agaete to Aldea de San Nicolás on the island's west coast

Canaria came to be considered Gran (big) is also open to question. Some say it was because the Spaniards thought the locals put up a big fight while resisting the *conquista*, and others simply say that the island was at one point thought the biggest in the archipelago.

Conquest began in earnest with Juan Rejón's landing in 1478. Rejón beat off a counterattack by Doramas but was soon succeeded by Pedro de Vera, who pressed home the campaign in the following five years.

The turning point was the conversion of the Guanche chief Tenesor Semidan to Christianity. In April 1483 he convinced his

ISLA DE GRAN CANARIA

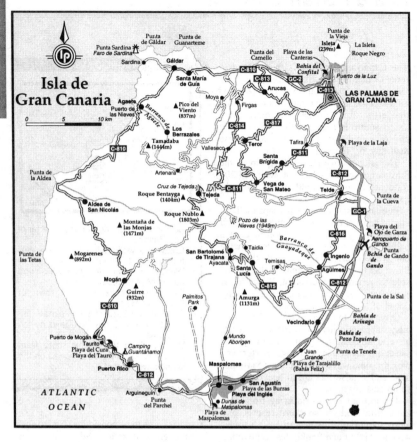

Isla de Gran Canaria

countrymen to lay down their arms and submit.

The island was soon colonised by a ragtag assortment of adventurers and landless hopefuls from as far away as Galicia, Andalucía, Portugal, Italy, France, the Low Countries and even Britain and Ireland.

Initially, the island boomed on the back of sugar exports and trans-Atlantic trade between Spain and the Americas. But as the demand for Canary Islands sugar fell and the fortunes of wine grew, so the island de-

clined before its main rival and superior wine-grower, Tenerife. It was not until the late 19th century that Gran Canaria recovered its position. To this day the two islands remain rivals and, between them, are home to most of the islands' permanent populace.

Maps

The single best map of the island is *Gran Canaria*, published by Distrimapas Telstar (500 ptas). It comes with accurate city maps of Las Palmas, Maspalomas and Playa del Inglés, and various other towns.

Accommodation

Away from Las Palmas and the south coast resorts, accommodation is remarkably thin on the ground. As a rule you should not have too much trouble in the capital, but the resorts can be full to overflowing in high season.

There is also a growing network of *casas rurales* (there are 18 so far) on the island. You can organise trips involving stays in such country houses, combined with hiking and other healthy activities, by calling ☎ 928 66 64 45.

Getting There & Away

Air The Aeropuerto de Gando on Gran Canaria is, along with the two on Tenerife, the main hub in the islands. There are connections to all the other islands except La Gomera, as well as regular flights to mainland Spain, and a raft of international scheduled and charter flights. For more details, see the Las Palmas Getting There & Away section below.

Sea Ferries and jetfoils link Gran Canaria with Tenerife, Lanzarote and Fuerteventura, using Las Palmas and Agaete ports. See the Getting There & Away sections under these destinations for more details.

Getting Around

Bus Two bus companies provide the island with a pretty good transport network. The green Salcai (☎ 928 38 11 10) buses cover the south (including the airport), while the orange and blue buses of Utinsa (☎ 928 36 83 35) ferry passengers to the north and centre of the island.

If you plan to move around a lot on the buses it makes sense to get a Tarjeta Dinero for 2000 ptas (available at the Estación de Guaguas in Las Palmas and bus stations around the island, as well as many newsagents). You use it instead of buying normal tickets, and save about 30% over the standard ticket prices – insert the card in the machine on the bus, tell the driver where you are going and the amount is deducted from the card.

The problem is that each company requires you to buy a separate card for their services. The two companies and Guaguas Municipales (the Las Palmas urban service) are considering pooling resources and coming up with a card valid on all services, urban or intercity. This would be handy (and bring the island into line with Tenerife and La Palma, where the one 2000-ptas ticket can be used on any bus service).

Las Palmas de Gran Canaria

• *population 356,000*

This is the big smoke, the only place in the Canary Islands with that unmistakeable big-city feel. OK, it oozes the kind of sunny languor you'd associate with the Mediterranean or North Africa, but the snarled traffic, bustling shopping districts and thriving port all give off the energy of *the* city.

The historic centre is rich in interest (if small), and the restaurant and bar-lined Playa de las Canteras could keep the average hedonist busy for days. The flavour is Spanish, with a heavy international overlay. Unlike in the southern resorts, however, the foreign crowd in Las Palmas is a more eclectic mix of straggling tourists, container-ship crews and all sorts of other unlikely misfits that inevitably seem to turn up in port cities.

For most tourists in search of either peace and quiet or an uncomplicated beach-bar scene with English breakfasts thrown in, Las Palmas will probably seem like too much of a headache. Perhaps that's a good thing, but if you like a little city activity, the place rewards at least a couple of days' attention.

History

Although Jean de Béthencourt's partner in mischief, Gadifer de la Salle, sailed past here in 1403, it wasn't until 1478 that Europeans made a determined landing in the

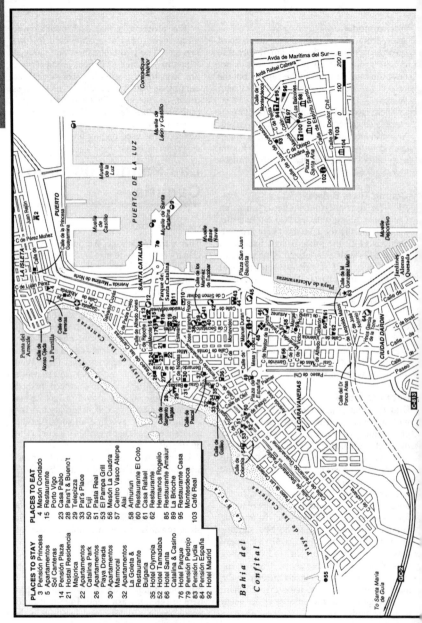

PLACES TO STAY

3   Pensión Princesa
5   Apartamentos
    Sol Canteras
14 Pensión Perez
21 Hostal Residencia
    Majorica
22 Apartamentos
    Catalina Park
26 Apartamentos
    Playa Dorada
30 Apartamentos
    Marmoral
32 Apartamentos
    La Goleta &
    Restaurante
    Bulgaria
35 Hotel Olympia
52 Hotel Tamadaba
66 Hotel Santa
    Catalina & Casino
76 Hotel Parque
79 Pensión Pedrojo
83 Pensión Lydia
84 Pensión España
92 Hotel Madrid

PLACES TO EAT

4   Mesón Condado
15 Restaurante
    Porto Vigo
23 Casa Pablo
28 Pans'i & Bueno't
29 Telepizza
33 Pat's Place
50 Fuji
51 Pasta Real
53 El Pampa Grill
56 Mesón La Cuadra
57 Centro Vasco Aterpe
    Alai
58 Arthurium
60 Restaurante El Coto
61 Casa Rafael
62 Restaurante
    Hermanos Rogelio
85 Restaurante Amaiur
89 La Brioche
95 Restaurante Casa
    Montesdeoca
103 Café Real

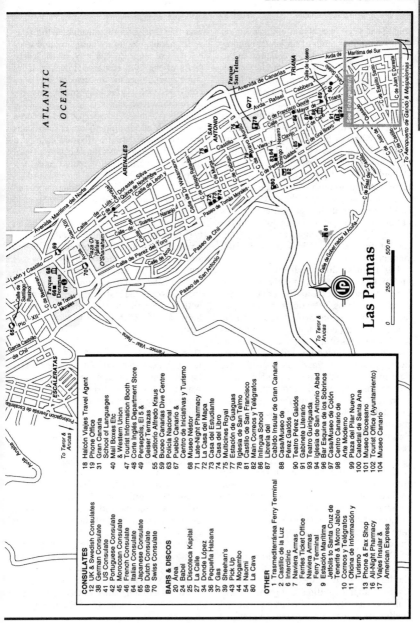

ATLANTIC OCEAN

ARENALES

SAN ANTONIO

TRIANA

Parque San Telmo

Avenida de Canarias

Las Palmas

0   250   500 m

To Terror & Arucas

To Terror & Arucas

To Aeropuerto de Gando & Maspalomas

See Enlargement

CONSULATES
12 UK & Swedish Consulates
38 German Consulate
41 US Consulate
42 Portuguese Consulate
45 Moroccan Consulate
46 French Consulate
64 Italian Consulate
65 Japanese Consulate
69 Dutch Consulate
70 Swiss Consulate

BARS & DISCOS
20 Area
24 Babel
25 Discoteca Kapital
27 La Calle
34 Donde López
36 Pequeña Habana
37 Gas
39 Sheehan's
43 Pick Up
44 Mogambo
54 Naomi
80 La Cava

OTHER
1 Trasmediterránea Ferry Terminal
2 Castillo de la Luz
6 Interclinic
7 Naviera Armas Ferries Ticket Office
8 Naviera Armas Ferry Terminal
9 Estación Marítima Jetfoils to Santa Cruz de Tenerife & Morro Jable
10 Correos y Telégrafos
11 Oficina de Información y Turismo
13 Phone & Fax Shop
16 All-Night Pharmacy
17 Viajes Insular & American Express
18 Halcón Viajes Travel Agent
19 Phone Office
31 Gran Canaria School of Languages
40 Mail Boxes Etc & Western Union
47 Tourist Information Booth
48 Corte Inglés Department Store
49 Persépolis, El 5 & Geiser Terrazas
55 Auditorio Alfredo Kraus
59 Buceo Canarias Dive Centre
63 Policia Nacional
67 Pueblo Canario & Centro de Iniciativas y Turismo
68 Museo Néstor
71 Late-Night Pharmacy
72 La Casa del Mapa
73 Casa del Estudiante
74 Casa del Libro
75 Multicines Royal
77 Estación de Guaguas
78 Iglesia de San Telmo
81 Castillo de San Francisco
82 Main Correos y Telégrafos
86 Inlingua School
87 Librería del Cabildo Insular de Gran Canaria
88 Casa/Museo de Pérez Galdós
90 Teatro Pérez Galdós
91 Gabinete Literario
93 Teatro Guiniguada
94 Iglesia de San Antonio Abad
96 Bar Esquina de los Sobrinos
97 Casa/Museo de Colón
98 Centro Canario de Arte Moderno
99 Plaza del Pilar Nuevo
100 Catedral de Santa Ana
101 Museo Diocesano
102 Tourist Office (Ayuntamiento)
104 Museo Canario

area. That year Juan Rejón and his troops set up camp just south of La Isleta, naming it Real de las Palmas. As the conquest of the island proceeded, the original military camp began to take on a more permanent look, and so the barrio of San Antonio Abad, later known as Vegueta, began to expand.

By the time Christopher Columbus sailed by on his way to the Americas in 1492, the busy little hub of the old town had already been traced out. Everybody likes to claim a hero for their very own, but it appears Columbus did not put in to port here, preferring instead to push on to La Gomera.

Las Palmas grew quickly as a commercial centre, and in recognition of its importance the seat of the bishopric of the Canary Islands was transferred here from Lanzarote halfway through the 16th century.

Las Palmas, along with the rest of the archipelago, benefited greatly from the Spanish conquest of Latin America and the subsequent trans-Atlantic trade. But you have to take the good with the bad, and the islands were a favourite target for pirates and buccaneers of all nations. In 1595, Sir Francis Drake raided Las Palmas with particular gusto. Four years later a still more determined Dutch band of adventurers reduced much of the town to ruins.

In 1821, Santa Cruz de Tenerife was declared the capital of the single new Spanish province of Las Islas Canarias. Those in Las Palmas were not overly impressed, but redress was some time in coming.

The fortunes of the port city fluctuated with those of the rest of the islands as boom followed bust in a chain of cash-crop cycles. However, Las Palmas began to go its own way towards the end of the 19th century, and this was due in no small measure to the growing British presence in the city.

The trading families of the Millers and Swanstons were already well established by the time Sir Alfred Lewis Jones set up the Grand Canary Coaling Company in Las Palmas. The city flourished as a crucial refuelling stop for trans-Atlantic shipping. It was the British who introduced the first water mains, electricity company and telephone exchange to the city in the early years of the 20th century. However, it all came apart before the outbreak of WWII, as coal-fired ships gradually made way for more modern vessels.

Still, the city's prosperity had become such that Madrid could no longer resist calls for the islands to be divided into two provinces. Las Palmas thus became capital of Gran Canaria, Fuerteventura and Lanzarote in 1927.

Las Palmas was where Franco launched the coup in July 1936 that led to the Spanish Civil War in 1936-39.

Since the 1960s, when the tourism boom was first felt in the islands, Las Palmas has grown from a middling port city of 70,000 souls to a bustling metropolis of up to half a million (if the floating element of the population is taken into account). And while it shares evenly the status of regional capital with Santa Cruz de Tenerife, there is no doubt about which of the two is the main centre.

Orientation

Las Palmas is the only city in the Canary Islands where you might feel a little overwhelmed. It stretches from the old historical centre in the south, centred on the Vegueta and Triana districts, up a series of long boulevards towards the bustling Santa Catalina and Puerto de la Luz – a good 3km. From there it continues up to what was once a islet off the island, still called La Isleta.

Most of what will be of interest to sightseers is concentrated in Vegueta. There is a small tourist office here, but the main one is in Santa Catalina, close to the 3km-long golden sands of Playa de las Canteras, bars and shops.

The bulk of the hotels are concentrated in Santa Catalina, near Playa de las Canteras and the port. You'll find plenty of restaurants in Vegueta and Triana, but again the action is around Santa Catalina, which is also where the majority of the discos and nightclubs are.

Born to be a Republican

It must have been one of the most thankless tasks with which a Spaniard has been entrusted this century. Appointment as head of the fractious Republican government in Madrid nevertheless galvanised Juan Negrín into a frenzy of action – all of which would prove futile in spite of his efforts until the last.

Negrín was born in Las Palmas de Gran Canaria on 3 February 1894. As he grew up far from the hurly-burly of the continent he could have little suspected what would be his fate – the poisoned chalice of power in a government doomed by its own infighting to fall, and thereafter an ignominious exile in France, where he died on 14 November 1956.

Like so many Canarios, Negrín moved to the Peninsula to study, and by the 1920s had become an eminent physiologist holding a chair at the university in Madrid. He entered politics in 1929 as a democratic socialist. As the Republican finance minister in the first year of the Civil War, he was largely responsible for shipping the country's gold reserves to the Soviet Union in return for arms. He became Prime Minister in May 1937 and set about unifying the disparate leftist groups into a determined resistance against Franco's nationalists. But he was on a hiding to nothing. The growing power of the communists and his increasing dependence on Moscow for aid, while probably unavoidable, alienated the west still further from Madrid and deepened the rifts among the Republicans. The communists were as intent on fighting 'unorthodox' leftists among the Republican ranks as opposing Franco.

Even after the fall of Cataluña in 1939, Negrín insisted on continuing the fight, but by then the Republicans were hopelessly divided. Madrid held out until the end, but the rest of Red Spain quickly collapsed. Negrín, virtually abandoned in his grimmest hour, fled to France and then, after the German invasion in 1940, to the UK and the USA. He remained Prime Minister of the republican government in exile until 1945.

This is the only city in the Canaries where you will probably need to use the local bus service (see Getting Around below).

Maps The local public-transport map is the best city plan – it has a yellow cover and is called *La Ciudad, En Guagua*. You can get it at tourist offices and the Estación de Guaguas near the Parque de San Telmo.

Information
Tourist Offices The main Oficina de Información y Turismo (☎ 928 26 46 23) is in the Parque de Santa Catalina, in the north of the city. It is open only Monday to Friday from 9 am to 2 pm, and the information available leaves something to be desired.

There is a Centro de Iniciativas y Turismo (☎ 928 24 35 93) just inside the entrance to the Pueblo Canario complex. This is not too well equipped either. It opens Monday to Friday from 10 am to 1 pm and 5 to 8 pm.

Yet another tourist information office is open Monday to Saturday from 10 am to 5.30 pm in the Ayuntamiento (town hall) on Plaza de Santa Ana. It has even less in the line of brochures and the like, but can help out with local information and does keep a hand-written list of pensiones – more than the others manage!

Finally, tourist information is also available at a booth on Avenida de Mesa y López by the Corte Inglés department store.

Foreign Consulates For a list of foreign consulates in Las Palmas, see the Embassies section in the Facts for the Visitor chapter.

Money Las Palmas has plenty of banks and in most you can change cash or cheques, get a cash advance or use the ATMs. Calle de Triana has several.

American Express is represented by Viajes Insular (☎ 928 22 79 50/4), at Calle de Luis Morote 9. It is also the only agent in the island for receiving money transfers through MoneyGram.

Western Union, for emergency money transfers, has an office at the airport. It is also represented by Mail Boxes Etc, Calle de los Martínez de Escobar 5.

Post The main Correos y Telégrafos is at Avenida del Primero de Mayo 62. Another big post office is located on Parque de Santa Catalina. The postcode for Las Palmas is 35080.

Telephone & Fax Several small public phone offices are dotted about Santa Catalina. One is at Calle de Luis Morote 12; another on Calle de Ripoche even has a few tattered phone books.

Email You can send email from the Casa del Estudiante, Paseo de Tomás Morales 48.

Travel Agencies Viajes Insular (see Money above) is reliable, as is Halcón. The latter has several offices across town, including one (☎ 928 27 94 06) at Calle del General Vives 77.

Student & Youth Information The TIVE student travel organisation (☎ 928 36 91 96) is at Paseo de Tomás Morales 48, in the Casa del Estudiante.

Gay & Lesbian Information For information about gay groups in the islands, write in advance to the Colectivo de Gays y Lesbianas de Las Palmas, Apartado de Correos 707, 35080 Las Palmas.

Bookshops Probably the best bookstore in town is the Casa del Libro, Paseo de Tomás Morales 46. For all you ever wanted to know about the Canary Islands, and then

some, try the Librería del Cabildo Insular de Gran Canaria, Calle del Travieso 15.

If you need to stock up on maps, La Casa del Mapa, Paseo de Tomás Morales 58, is the place to go.

Cultural Centres The British Council (☎/fax 928 35 52 56) is no longer in Las Palmas itself. It is at the Antiguo Edificio de Ciencias Económicas y Empresariales, Campus Universitario de Tafira, Calle de Saulo Torón 4. Utinsa bus No 327 goes there.

Laundry Strange as it may seem in a big port city, the only coin-operated laundrette ever opened in Las Palmas went bust within a year. There are plenty of traditional *lavanderías* and dry cleaners around if you don't want to do your own washing.

Medical Services The Hospital Insular (☎ 928 44 40 00) is at Plaza del Doctor Pasteur s/n, several kilometres south of the city along the Avenida Marítima del Sur (which becomes the main motorway south to Maspalomas).

There are several walk-in clinics dotted about the Santa Catalina and beach area. One, called Interclinic, is at Paseo de las Canteras 62.

A 24-hour pharmacy is open at Calle de Luis Morote 5. Another, open until midnight, is at Calle de León y Castillo 162. However, they only fill urgent prescriptions after normal shopping hours.

Emergency For an ambulance call the Cruz Roja on ☎ 928 22 22 22. For police emergency numbers, see the boxed aside called In Case of Emergency in the Facts for the Visitor chapter. The national police HQ (☎ 928 36 11 36) is just by Playa de las Alcaravaneras.

Dangers & Annoyances Las Palmas is not only the largest city in the islands, but palpably the dodgiest. Drug abusers loiter about much of the city and, as a major port, a lot of shady characters are inevitably on the move in and out of the place.

All this means is that you should take the standard city streetwise precautions. Carry as little money and as few valuables on you as possible. Leave *nothing* of value (preferably nothing at all) in cars, especially the hired variety.

At night, avoid dark quiet streets and parks. The Parque de San Telmo, for instance, is crawling with down-and-outs even during the day (although they are pretty harmless in daylight).

If unhealthy hookers with attitude hanging around in doorways are your scene, head for Calle del Molino de Viento, a block west of Calle de León y Castillo. Otherwise, this louche zone is also best avoided.

Vegueta & Triana

Casa/Museo de Colón This is a beautiful example of Canarian architecture, built around two patios overlooked by the fine wooden balconies of the upper level. The exterior of the building is itself something of a work of art, with some showy plateresque elements mixing in original fashion with the brown-stained balconies typical of the islands – a unique combination of styles.

Although it's called Columbus' house (it is possible he stayed here, although it is uncertain on just how many, if any, of his voyages he actually set foot in Las Palmas), most of what you see was the residence of Las Palmas' early governors.

The collection inside is a rag-bag ranging from old sea charts to pre-Columbian artefacts brought back from South America, with a few portraits of the Hispanic-Flemish school thrown in, some model ships and displays recounting the history of emigration from the Canaries to South America

It is open Monday to Friday from 9 am to 6 pm; weekends from 9 am to 3 pm. Entry is free.

Catedral de Santa Ana The city's main place of worship was begun in the 15th century, but took 350 years to complete. The exterior is neoclassical, but inside the dominant style, plateresque in a gothic key, betrays the earlier beginnings of construction. The gothic retablo above the high altar comes from Cataluña in mainland Spain, while the exquisite lamp hanging before the altar was made in Genova (Italy).

Restoration work, begun in 1995, is nearly complete. At the time of writing entry to the cathedral was via the **Museo Diocesano**, whose entrance is at Calle del Espíritu Santo 20. The museum is set on two levels around the Patio de los Naranjos (Orange Tree Courtyard), once home to the Inquisition. It contains a fairly standard collection of religious art and memorabilia, including centuries-old manuscripts, a good deal of wooden sculptures and other ornaments.

The museum and cathedral are open Monday to Friday from 9 am to 1.30 pm

DAMIEN SIMONIS

Detail, Casa de Colón (Columbus' House) in Plaza del Pilar Nuevo, old centre, Las Palmas de Gran Canaria

and 4 to 6.30 pm. The price of admission is 300 ptas.

Iglesia de San Antonio Abad Just behind the Casa de Colón (heading towards the waterfront), this little church of modest Romanesque-Canarian design is supposedly where Columbus used to pray for divine help on his missions.

Museo Canario The island's main museum is dedicated to chronicling Gran Canaria's preconquest history. It claims to be home to the biggest collection of Cro-Magnon skulls in the world, which one has to suppose is quite a boast. Some heads come attached to other body parts in the form of mummies. Predictably enough, there is also a fair collection of pottery and other Guanche implements too. The material comes from across the island, and a mock-up of the Cueva Pintada of Gáldar has been set up to compensate for the fact that the real thing is closed.

The museum, at Calle del Doctor Chil 25, is open Monday to Friday from 10 am to 5 pm; Saturday from 10 am to 1 pm and Sunday from 10 am to 2 pm. Admission costs 400 ptas.

Centro Canario de Arte Moderno The city's main museum of modern art is basically a holding centre for temporary exhibits. There's usually something interesting on show. The centre opens Tuesday to Saturday from 10 am to 9 pm (Sunday from 10 am to 2 pm) and admission is free.

Gabinete Literario This sumptuous one-time theatre has been declared a national monument. It is an old-world display of faded elegance, illumined by chandeliers and lined with bookcases crammed with learned-looking volumes. The place functions now as a kind of well-to-do club, but lesser mortals can eat outside on Plazoleta de Cairasco.

Calle Mayor de Triana Traditionally, Calle Mayor de Triana was the main shopping street in Las Palmas and it's now a pedestrianised mall. You need to keep your head up and eyes peeled to enjoy the little architectural gems, among them some nice examples of modernism, that line this busy thoroughfare.

Casa/Museo de Pérez Galdós The Canary Islands' greatest writer, Benito Pérez Galdós, was born in this house in the heart of old Las Palmas in 1843. He lived the first 19 years of his life here before moving on to Madrid and literary greatness.

The house contains the sorts of things you'd expect: various personal effects and other objects in some way related to the author's life, including drawings done to accompany his *Episodios Nacionales* and photos of actors who performed his stage pieces. The house is at Calle de Cano 6, and opens Monday to Friday from 9 am to 1 pm and 4 to 8 pm. Admission is free.

Parque de San Telmo The chapel of the same name was one of the first churches in the nascent town. Apart from the bums, the other noteworthy feature is the restored modernist kiosk in the north-western corner.

Pueblo Canario & Museo Néstor
Designed by the artist Néstor Martín Fernández de la Torre and built by his brother Miguel, the Pueblo Canario forms a focal point in the gardens of the Parque Doramas. With a restaurant, terraces, shops and a kiddies' play area, it is designed as a pleasant bit of escapism in a clearly Canarian architectural style.

The museo is an art gallery dedicated to the works of Néstor, who died in 1938. It was inaugurated in 1956 and expanded in 1987 to accommodate a broader collection of works – the Gallery of Contemporary Canarian Art (rooms 11 to 13). It also houses period furniture and other memorabilia. The gallery opens Tuesday to Friday from 10 am to 1 pm and 4 to 8 pm; Sunday from 11 am to 2 pm. Admission costs 150 ptas.

Casino & Ciudad Jardín

If you remembered to bring along your black tie evening wear and want to have a flutter in style, head for the **Casino de Las Palmas**, housed in the city's prestige Hotel Santa Catalina, which was built in 1904 in the heart of the Parque Doramas. The casino opens nightly at 8 pm and closes between 4 and 5 am.

The park is the focus of an area of the city laid out by the British towards the end of the 19th century and known as **Ciudad Jardín**. British businessmen at the time dominated the economic life of Las Palmas, and it appears that you can take the British out of Britain, but not Britain out of the British – this is not the only 'Garden City' they managed to map out in a foreign city (in Egypt, Cairo's Garden City is now a posh embassy district). That said, this leafy upper-class 'suburb' is a rather odd mix of architectural styles, ranging from British colonial to Andalucían.

Santa Catalina

Playa de las Canteras The 3km stretch of golden sandy beach here is the main attraction, and has made of the Santa Catalina part of town the city's main tourist drawcard. The area fairly hums with the activity of bars, restaurants, nightclubs and shops.

This is by far the nicest beach, so there is little need to use the little **Playa de las Alcaravaneras**, in the port area, or **Playa de la Laja**, south of the city in a pretty grim, barren and partly industrial setting.

Castillo de la Luz

Built in the 16th century (like most other such fortresses around the Canary Islands) to ward off pirate attacks, the *castillo* is now used for occasional art exhibitions. It is otherwise closed.

Other forts around town include the dilapidated hulk of the Castillo de San Francisco high up above Vegueta, and Castillo de San Cristóbal to the south of the city.

Jardín Botánico Canario Viera y Clavijo

About 6km south-west of the city (take the C-811 road or an Utinsa bus for Tafira), the botanical garden is in the protected park area of Monte Lentiscal, and contains a broad range of Macronesian flora, many examples of which are on the verge of extinction. Among the exhibits is a surprising variety of cacti. It opens daily except public holidays from 9 am to 6 pm. Admission is free.

Activities

Surfing Playa de las Canteras is not the world's greatest surf beach, but you can pick up some good waves and plenty of local lads are out there on the weekend. It is one of the better beaches on the island.

Diving Buceo Canarias (☎ 928 29 05 05), Calle de Victor Hugo 24, organises courses at most levels and sells diving gear.

Language Courses

There are a dozen or so language schools in Las Palmas, where you could try for work teaching or enrol for Spanish classes – check the Yellow Pages.

Inlingua (☎ 928 37 27 07) is at Calle de Francisco Gourié 67. Another one is the Gran Canaria School of Languages (☎ 928 26 79 71; fax 928 27 89 80), at Calle del Doctor Grau Bassans 27.

Special Events

Fiestas Although overshadowed by its more famous version in Santa Cruz de Tenerife, Carnaval is nevertheless a big event in Las Palmas. Two weeks of madness and fancy dress mark the first rupture with winter in February (the dates move depending on when Lent falls) – not that winter out here is any great trial! The bulk of the action takes place around Parque de Santa Catalina.

June is dedicated to celebrating the Fiesta de San Juan, patron saint of the city. Cultural activities are staged across the city, and big fireworks displays and concerts take place on Playa de las Canteras.

Corpus Christi, another feast with moveable dates that takes place around June, is

Plain Sailing

In the 1880s, when Puerto de la Luz was developing as a port, the passenger and merchant ships which used it were obliged, for various reasons, to moor some way from the docks. As a result of this, a local variety of shuttle boat, equipped with oars and sails up to 13m high, was developed. From poop to prow these boats measured no more than 7m, and they were soon doing a brisk trade ferrying people and goods from ship to shore.

Like any business, these little *botes* knew both busy and slack times: during the latter their captains and crews organised regattas in the port area. An idea born to ease the boredom of empty days sitting on the docks slowly transformed itself into a regular competition whose tradition has been maintained to the present day.

Eighteen of these curious craft remain today, and they regularly gather for an afternoon's racing on Saturday (usually from 5 pm) and Sunday (noon) from April to October. They are crewed by eight to 12 people, and each boat represents a barrio of Las Palmas.

Apart from the odd appearance of the participating vessels, the race itself is a little peculiar in that the competitors race only *en bolina*, against the wind, but in such a way as to get the maximum power from it. The fact that the prevailing wind is pretty much the same in the competition months off the east coast of Gran Canaria makes it the ideal spot for these races – they are never held anywhere else in the islands. The botes start at Playa de la Laja, a few kilometres south of the southern suburbs of Las Palmas, and finish off Playa de Alcaravaneras.

marked in particular by the laying out of extraordinary floral 'carpets' in some of the central streets of the old city.

Among the oldest religious festivals in Las Palmas is the *romería* or pilgrimage/procession in honour of the Virgen de la Luz, held in October. Most of the action takes place around Playa de las Canteras and in La Isleta. The battle with the pirate Sir Francis Drake is commemorated at the same time.

Festivals Las Palmas hosts a range of international festivals including: the Festival Internacional de Música (January); Festival de Opera (February-March); Festival de Ballet y Danza (May); and the Muestra Internacional de Cine (an international film festival held every two years in October-November).

Places to Stay – budget

The bulk of the accommodation of all classes is up in the area around Santa Catalina beach and the port.

Vegueta & Triana The pick of the crop, in a ramshackle sort of way, has to be *Hotel Madrid* (☎ 928 36 06 64), Plazoleta de Cairasco 4, right by the Gabinete Literario. Singles/doubles with only a basin start at 3500/5500 ptas. Those with shower are 4500/6500 ptas and full bathroom 5500/7500 ptas. Some of those without bath or shower are in one respect better – they are likely to have a balcony looking over the square.

A less appetising but perfectly acceptable alternative is the *Pensión Pedrojo* (☎ 928 37 13 87), Calle de Pedrojo 1, which has simple rooms without bath for 2000/3000 ptas.

In *Pensión España* and *Pensión Lydia*, along Calle de Domingo J Navarro, you'll probably wake up feeling life has vomited on you. They charge 2000/3000 ptas but should be a last resort.

Santa Catalina The bulk of the clientele at *Pensión Plaza* (☎ 928 26 52 12) seems to have lobbed on the latest container ship. Still, it's OK and there's usually a room

Isla de Lanzarote
Top: Sailing boat, Playa Blanca
Bottom Left: Playa del Papagayo
Bottom Right: At Islote de Hilario the volcanic heat is 100ºC just centimetres below the surface

Cactus in the garden of Fundación César Manrique, Taho de Tahiche, Isla de Lanzarote

going. Singles/doubles go for 2600/3200 ptas and have their own bathroom.

Pensión Princesa (☎ 928 46 77 04), Calle de la Princesa Guayarmina 2, offers basic rooms with loo for 2000/3000 ptas.

Hostal Residencia Majorica (☎ 928 26 28 78), Calle de Ripoche 22, is right in the heart of Santa Catalina, but perhaps a little too much so for some as it can be pretty noisy. Singles/doubles/triples go for 2500/3500/5000 ptas. The rooms are spartan but at least they're cheap.

Hotel Tamadaba (☎ 928 22 07 92) has double rooms with own shower and toilet for 3500 ptas. There is no reduction for single occupancy.

Apartamentos La Goleta (☎ 928 38 09 78), Paseo de las Canteras 58, is nothing flash but right on the beach and fairly cheap. Apartments for two cost 5000 ptas.

Places to Stay – middle
Vegueta & Triana There really is not a lot in this area, so if you are adamant on staying near the old centre and want a little luxury, about your only option is *Hotel Parque* (☎ 928 36 80 00), Parque de San Telmo s/n, where you will be charged 7200/10,400 ptas.

Santa Catalina & Puerto Moving up the line a tad from the cheapies is the *Hotel Olympia* (☎ 928 26 17 20), Calle del Doctor Grau Bassas 1, which offers perfectly reasonable if dull singles/doubles with own bath and loo for 4600/5500 ptas.

At this level, you may prefer to consider an apartment. *Apartamentos Marmoral* (☎ 928 27 12 08), Calle del Doctor Grau Bassas 38, has functional ones at 5500 ptas for two. Better are the *Apartamentos Catalina Park* (☎ 928 26 41 20), Calle de Tomás Miller 67, which cost 6200 ptas for two

Apartamentos Sol Canteras (☎ 928 26 65 58), Calle de Sagasta 76, is another step up in quality and costs 6000 ptas or 7000 ptas with ocean views. The 1000 ptas extra is a worthwhile investment. Also right on the beach are *Apartamentos Playa Dorada*

(☎ 928 26 51 00), Calle de Luis Morote 69, where two people are charged 7500 ptas for an apartment with lounge, minibar, bathroom and balcony.

Places to Stay – top end
Hotel Santa Catalina (☎ 928 24 30 40), Parque Doramas 3, is *the* address in Las Palmas. It exudes the class of another era, and if the 17,400/21,750 ptas price tag for singles/doubles doesn't sufficiently dent your life savings, you can always throw away more at the casino.

Places to Eat
Vegueta & Triana A good little place for breakfast is *La Brioche*, on the corner of Calle Mayor de Triana and Calle de Losero. A ham-and-cheese croissant, orange juice and coffee will cost about 700 ptas.

Restaurante Casa Montesdeoca, Calle de Montesdeoca 10, is set in an exquisitely maintained 16th-century house in Canarian colonial style. The patio (internal courtyard) is cool and relaxing. Mains cost between 1500 ptas and 2000 ptas (the fish is deliciously fresh).

Another good but expensive establishment is the popular *Restaurante Amaiur*, Calle de Pérez Galdós 2, where mains start at about 2000 ptas.

If you just want a simple, wholesome but unexciting set menu, you could do a lot worse than sit on Plazoleta de Cairasco and eat at the *Café Madrid*. The set price meal comes to 950 ptas.

Santa Catalina & Puerto For quick food, *Pans't & Bueno't* and *Telepizza* at Paseo de las Cantera 38 are fine for bocadillos and pizza. *Restaurante Porto Vigo*, Calle del General Vives 90 (the main entrance is on Parque de Santa Catalina) puts on very good cuisine from Galicia, in Spain's northwest. It specialises in octopus and other seafood, washed down with a crisp Gallego Ribeiro white.

Restaurante El Coto, Calle de Alfredo Calderón 21, is a promising little Lebanese joint. Not far away, *Casa Rafael*, Calle de

Luis Antunez 25, represents a return to more traditional local cooking, and is popular with Canariones. Mains start at around 1000 ptas.

Mesón La Cuadra, Calle del General Mas de Gaminde 32, has an excellent set menu for 1400 ptas.

For good Basque cooking you can't go past the *Centro Vasco Aterpe Alai*, Calle de Menéndez y Pelayo 10. This prized cuisine rarely comes cheap, so you'll be looking at up to 3000 ptas a head.

Another expensive place with a fine reputation is *Arthuriun*, Calle de Pi y Margall 10, where mains come in at about 2000 ptas.

More modest is the *Restaurante Hermanos Rogelio*, Calle de Valencia 4, where you can dine on hearty mainstream Spanish and Canarian food for about 1500 ptas a person.

Those with a hankering for the British Isles can gather at *Pat's Place*, Calle de Galileo 9. At least there isn't a big sign out saying 'Real English Breakfast'.

Pasta Real, Calle del Secretario Padilla 28, is not so much an Italian eatery as a haven for vegetarians. The food is good and inventive, and mains cost around 1000 ptas.

For Japanese food you could do worse than the unassuming *Fuji*, Calle de Fernando Guanarteme 56. Tempura and other mains cost 900 to 1000 ptas.

Mesón Condado, Calle de Ferreras 22, serves up a mix of Gallego food (concentrating on shellfish), Canarian and more mainstream Spanish dishes. Count on spending the best part of 2000 ptas.

If it's a fat steak you're after, head for the Argentinian *El Pampa Grill*, Calle de Colombia 6.

Casa Pablo, Calle de Tomás Miller 73, has Spanish mains for about 1000 ptas. It is a highly popular little spot oozing atmosphere.

For a walk on the eastern European side, head for the beachside *Restaurante Bulgaria*, Paseo de las Canteras 48. Here you can wash down the simple food with some Sliwowitz!

Cafés In Vegueta, the *Café Real*, Calle del Doctor Chil 21, is an elegant place for a cup of coffee, apéritif or even a bocadillo.

Entertainment
For all the latest information on what's on where, and everything from bars to restaurants and bus timetables, pick up a copy of the weekly *La Guía* (100 ptas).

Theatre The Teatro Pérez Galdós (☎ 928 36 15 09), Calle de Lentini 1, is the scene of some dramatic art but as often as not is used for music recitals.

The other mainstream theatre, Teatro Guiniguada (☎ 928 38 09 86), is at Calle de la Mesa de León s/n, and gets the lion's share of the better quality productions, be they classics or more modern pieces. If you are into more alternative or avant garde stuff, several small theatres cater to this – watch the local press.

Classical Music & Opera The brand new Auditorio Alfredo Kraus, designed by the Catalan architect Óscar Tusquets, is what one French expert described as 'a boat of air, sea and light'. Constructed partly of volcanic rock and with a huge window affording the spectators (up to 1700) broad ocean views, it is the dominant feature of the southern end of Playa de las Canteras.

Concerts are also sometimes performed in the Teatro Pérez Galdós.

Cinema There are three *multicines* complexes in Las Palmas. The chances of seeing undubbed versions of foreign movies are slight. Multicines Royal, Calle de León y Castillo 85, is central and as good as any of them.

The only real chance of seeing classics in the original language is at the Tuesday night session (9 pm; 300 ptas) of the Filmoteca, held at the Teatro Guiniguada.

Folk Music You can be almost guaranteed of seeing performances of Canarian folk music in the Pueblo Canario on Thursday afternoon and Sunday morning. On occasion, folk groups stage concerts in the Parque Doramas. The tourist offices should be able to tell you of any upcoming events.

Other Live Music The Auditorio Alfredo Kraus is used for quite a few big-name concerts. Otherwise, in summer lots of events are staged on Playa de las Canteras. Tickets are often available at the Corte Inglés department store.

Bars, Pubs & Terrazas There is no shortage of watering holes in Las Palmas, especially in Santa Catalina and around Playa de las Canteras. Using Plaza de España as a reference point, you'll find plenty of activity from 1 am on.

The Vegueta area also gets busy at this time, although for some tastes it's a little too rowdy to be fun. A more sedate and posey area are the bars around the Muelle Deportivo (this is yachtie territory after all).

Vegueta & Triana Bar Esquina de los Sobrinos, Calle de Montesdeoca 3, is a great old place with huge hams dangling from the ceiling.

La Cava, Calle del Primero de Mayo 57, is easy to miss, and has a rather conspiratorial air about it. It stays open until about 3 am.

Santa Catalina & Puerto Persepolis, El 5 and Geiser are three popular terrazas (sidewalk café/bars) at Plaza de España 5. They are a good place to kick the evening's fun off.

If you're in need of a Guinness or just feel like being in a spot of almost Irish territory, Sheehan's is the place for you. It's at Calle de los Martínez de Escobar 8.

Late-Night Bars & Discos The late-night bars and discos are found mostly in the Santa Catalina-beach-Puerto de la Luz area. Don't expect to pay less than 500 ptas a drink, whatever it is.

La Calle, Calle del Sargento Llagas 35, is a hip place that opens its doors at midnight. Gas, Calle de Pascal 1, is another late-night

hangout, although it starts up at the uncommonly early hour of 10.30 pm.

Pequeña Habana, Calle de Fernando Guanarteme 45, is a cool salsa bar open until 3.30 am. Drinks are an equally cool 800 ptas – no wonder the locals need the dancing to loosen up!

Naomi, Calle de Portugal 79, opens at 11 pm and thumps on well into the wee hours with a good mix of Spanish and international music.

Donde López, Calle de Galileo 9, doesn't get going until after midnight. It's a slightly louche little place but has a great atmosphere if it doesn't fill up too much.

Discoteca Kapital, Calle de Luis Morote 51, is a pretty standard disco and attracts a varied crowd, some of it definitely off the boats. Babel, Calle de Luis Morote 49, falls into much the same category.

Mogambo, Calle de Montevideo 5 and Pick Up, next door at No 3, are both good dance places that don't bother opening before midnight. The former attracts a younger, marginally wilder set, while the music in the latter is fairly mainstream stuff.

Área, Calle del Secretario Artiles 48, is a disco that plays mainly Spanish pop music and opens Thursday to Saturday only.

Spectator Sport
Football You'll see no First Division football (soccer) in Las Palmas, but if you want to the see the local sides play, head for the Estadio Insular on Calle de Pio XII.

Things to Buy
Before buying handicrafts and other souvenirs, head first to the Fedac (Fundación para la Etnografía y el Desarollo de la Artesanía Canaria) shop at Calle de Domingo J Navarro 7. This is a government-controlled store where prices and quality are a good standard by which to measure those of products sold elsewhere.

For more conventional acquisitions, the traditional shopper's street has for centuries been Calle Mayor de Triana. The street is nowadays more interesting for its jumble of modernist architecture than its stores.

Las Palmas' self-promoted chic shoppers' hangout is Avenida de Mesa y López. Here you'll find a gigantic Corte Inglés and a host of other shops and boutiques. Nearby, Indians have moved in to many of the shops around Parque de Santa Catalina to sell cheap electronic goods (or sell electronic goods cheaply, depending on how you view these things).

Diehard shoppers may want to take a look around the Centro Comercial Las Arenas, out by the Auditorio Alfredo Kraus at Calle de Pavía 18. It's got everything from fashion stores to a cinema complex. One better still is the 120,000 sq m Centro Comercial La Ballena, built in the shape of a whale! It's north of town at Carretera del Norte 113.

Getting There & Away
Air The Aeropuerto de Gando (☎ 928 57 90 00) is 16km south of Las Palmas. Binter connects the island with Tenerife 12 times daily (all but once to the Norte airport). It has two flights to La Palma and regular connections to Lanzarote and Fuerteventura.

Air Europa has several scheduled flights a day to Tenerife Norte, Fuerteventura and Lanzarote, and Spanair has a flight a day on weekdays to Lanzarote. Air Atlantic has two a week to El Hierro.

Air Europa has regular direct flights (at least one on weekdays) to Madrid, Barcelona, Seville and Santiago de Compostela. Connections from Madrid include Vigo, Bilbao, Málaga and Palma de Mallorca. Spanair has two daily flights from Gran Canaria to Madrid, from where you can make several connections, including to Barcelona.

Although Tenerife is a busier international destination, there are plenty of charters and many scheduled international flights to Gran Canaria.

At the airport you'll find a tourist information office on the ground floor (it doesn't have much information though), car-rental outlets, a post office and money-changing facilities (including a Western Union representative).

Bus The Estación de Guaguas (☎ 928 38 11 30) is handily located just off the waterfront near the Parque de San Telmo, itself on the north end of the Triana district.

The green Salcai buses leave from here to all destinations south, while the orange and blue Utinsa company runs buses across the north and centre of the island. The yellow buses are local city buses only. Standard one-way tickets to Maspalomas cost 615 ptas; to Mogán 910 ptas; 175 ptas to Telde and 305 ptas to Gáldar (the last is with Utinsa; all the others with Salcai).

Car & Motorcycle The GC-1 autovía leads south past the airport to Playa del Inglés, while the GC-2 heads west towards Gáldar. If you want to contact the RACE (☎ 928 23 09 88 for assistance), it is at Calle de León y Castillo 281.

Rental There are rental firms at the airport, jetfoil terminal and scattered across the Santa Catalina district of the city.

Sea The weekly ferry to Cádiz (mainland Spain) calls in here en route from Tenerife, leaving at 2 pm.

Trasmediterránea (☎ 928 26 00 70) ferries leave a few times a week for Santa Cruz de Tenerife. Crossing time is four hours and the ticket costs 2700 ptas. Most people use the jetfoils, which leave five times a day (thrice on Sunday) and take one hour and 20 minutes – the standard fare is 5600 ptas (3200 ptas off-peak). Coming *from* Santa Cruz, some of the jetfoils proceed to Morro Jable in Fuerteventura, another 1½ hours. From Las Palmas the fare is 5600 ptas.

If you prefer the ferry, Naviera Armas (☎ 928 47 40 80) has two ferries Monday to Friday and one each on Saturday and Sunday to Santa Cruz. Tickets cost 2700 ptas.

Three Trasmediterránea ferries serve Puerto del Rosario (Fuerteventura) each week (eight hours; 3500 ptas) and then Arrecife in Lanzarote (10 hours; 3500 ptas). A direct ferry to Arrecife on Wednesday takes seven hours and costs the same.

Naviera Armas has two ferries a week to Puerto del Rosario (Fuerteventura; 3500 ptas) and three to Arrecife (Lanzarote; 3500 ptas). A daily ferry also plies the Morro Jable route (Fuerteventura) in three hours. Tickets cost 3100 ptas and the departure time is 7.15 am.

Getting Around

To/From the Airport Salcai buses run from the airport to Las Palmas every half hour from 6.30 am to 9 pm, and then hourly until 2 am. From Las Palmas the first departure is at 6 am. The fare is 230 ptas. A taxi between the airport and central Las Palmas is likely to cost you about 3000 ptas.

Bus Guaguas Municipales runs the yellow buses around Las Palmas and its suburbs. You buy single tickets (125 ptas) on the bus. If you plan to hang around Las Palmas for any length of time, you should consider either the Bono-Guagua ticket (10 trips for 745 ptas) or the Tarjeta Mensual de Bono-Facil, good for a month's unlimited travel. These can be bought at the Guaguas Municipales desk at the Estación de Guaguas.

A useful service is the red line No 1, which runs from the Teatro Pérez Galdós and along Calle de Rafael Cabrera in the Triana district on Calle de León y Castillo to Puerto de la Luz and on to Castillo de la Luz. The same bus will also drop you at the northern end of Playa de las Canteras. The red line No 17 starts from the same spot and will get you out to the Auditorio Alfredo Kraus (although return services dry up too soon to make it back from most performances).

Car & Motorcycle Driving (and parking) in Las Palmas is a pain. It's not really any worse than many mainland Spanish cities, but rush hour traffic jams are frustrating, as is the sometimes misleading one-way street system. Most of the centre operates meter-parking (205 ptas for two hours maximum). Otherwise there are several private car parks, where you pay up to 200 ptas an hour. If you get towed, call the Depósito

Municipal (☎ 928 27 76 45). It's open 24 hours a day and it costs 6000 ptas to get your chariot out of the pound.

Taxi If you need to call a taxi try ☎ 928 46 00 00, 928 46 56 66 or 928 46 22 12. You can flag them down or pick one up at one of 34 taxi stands across the city.

Around the Island

With your own transport, you could get a reasonable look at the entire island in two days (you can drive around it in one day, but you would be hard pressed to do this and explore the centre of the island as well). Buses connect most towns and villages, but you will use up more time this way. Cyclists not averse to some tough inclines can get around too.

CENTRAL CIRCUIT

Starting from Las Palmas, a fairly obvious circuit presents itself, heading first south and then cutting inland to take in the mountainous Tejeda region before swinging north-eastwards back towards the capital.

Telde

• *population 77,400*

The island's second city, Telde offers the visitor precious little joy and may easily be skipped with no loss. The 12km trip south from Las Palmas passes through a disheartening scene of arid and semi-industrialised landscape that does little to evoke the images of subtropical island paradise.

If you do take the trouble to stop in Telde, head for the San Juan area, which constitutes the heart of the old town. Telde was founded *before* the Spanish conquest by monks from Mallorca seeking to set up a bishopric in the Fortunate Isles.

The city is known for its production of string instruments, above all the timple, the islands' musical emblem.

The tourist office (☎ 928 68 31 44), is on Calle de Juan Carlos I, just off Plaza de San

Juan. Among the well-aged noble houses of the area, the 15th-century **Iglesia de San Juan** stands well out. You enter by a gothic-mudéjar doorway, which was finished in the 16th century. Inside, the oddest of the artistic jewels is a 5kg figure of Christ made in Mexico of a corn-based plaster.

A short walk away is the **Museo León y Castillo**, devoted to the family of the same name and in particular a late 19th-century politician – you'll want to be a serious Spanish history buff to get much out of this.

Salcai buses from Las Palmas run every 20 minutes from 7 am (175 ptas), so there's no need to stay, and precious few places to stay in.

Ingenio & Agüimes

A short bus ride south of Telde brings you to the towns of Ingenio and Agüimes, separated from one another by the Barranco de Guayadeque and in themselves of little interest. Of the two the latter boasts a marginally more attractive town centre, the centrepiece of which is the shady Plaza del Rosario, sealed off at one end by the **Iglesia de San Sebastián**, considered one of the best examples of Canarian neoclassicism. If you're here in the evening, you may want to visit one of the three bars on the same square.

What does make Agüimes special is the Encuentro Teatral Tres Continentes, an annual (September) attempt to bring together theatre companies from Europe, South America and Africa. This theatre bonanza has grown from strength to strength, turning an otherwise fairly dull place into a temporary hotbed of international creativity.

There's nowhere much to stay here and little enticement to do so anyway – plenty of buses connect the two towns with Telde and Las Palmas. From Agüimes, another Salcai bus heads east to the coast and **Arinaga** – it's a popular local spot for swimming, but there's no beach.

Barranco de Guayadeque

The real reason for drifting about this part of the island lies *between* Ingenio and Agüimes. The Barranco de Guayadeque rises up into central Gran Canaria in a majestic sweep of crumpled ridges, its close-cropped vegetation softening the otherwise arid terrain with a little green. Most curiously, about halfway along the 9km road from Agüimes (there is another road from Ingenio too), you'll find an odd relic of bygone ages – a troglodyte hamlet. Some of the handful of inhabitants here live in cleverly decked-out caves.

Another 4km and the road peters out in an impassable (for vehicles) track and a couple of restaurants. Of these, *Restaurante Tagoror* is recommended and modestly priced.

Temisas

If you have a vehicle, you can take a back road from Agüimes heading for Santa Lucía de Tirajana. The C-815 highway also heads this way (and Salcai buses travel this route), but the back road takes you through more rugged country and the sleepy village of Temisas. It's not that the place is full of riveting monuments, but the setting is impressive, with a backdrop of impenetrable cliffs. And the village itself has preserved a good deal of its older stone houses.

Very occasional buses connect Temisas with San Bartolomé de Tirajana and El Doctoral (the latter on the GC-1 autovía).

Santa Lucía de Tirajana

This place, although very prettily set around the upper reaches of a palm-studded valley, is something of a tourist travesty. Someone has seen fit to build a very cheap-looking Disney castle and shoved several hundred Guanche artefacts inside it any which way. Entry costs 300 ptas, but you need a healthy sense of the silly to be able to wander around inside this 'Castillo de la Fortaleza'. Just behind it is the *Restaurante Hao*, a well advertised and patronised tour-bus eating stopover.

If you want to eat but not contribute to this particular venture, you could try the more humble *Restaurante Casa Antonio* or *Restaurante Mirador Santa Lucía*, at the western exit of the village.

San Bartolomé de Tirajana
• *population 24,000*
This is a comparatively substantial town, although with no notable sights. The views out over the Tirajana valley are pleasing and you could choose a worse spot to get stuck for the night. *Hostal Santana* (☎ 928 12 71 32), on the main street, has simple singles/doubles without own bath for 2000/3200 ptas. Along the same street are several eateries and bars.

The road south leads straight into the heart of the Playa del Inglés beach resort (Salcai bus No 18).

Tejeda & Around
• *population 2300*
Tejeda is 33km of winding road away from San Bartolomé. It is a quiet, unprepossessing hill village whose main attraction is its marvellous setting. A good place for lunch is the *Restaurante Cueva de la Tea*, Calle de Domingo Hernández Guerra (near the southern exit from town).

Cruz de Tejeda The cross in greenish stone from which this spot, 8km north of Tejeda, takes its name marks the centre of Gran Canaria and its old *caminos reales* (king's roads), along which it is still possible to cross the entire island.

From the **lookouts** here you can contemplate the island's greatest natural wonders: to the west the Roque Bentayga (and in clear weather the great cone of Teide on Tenerife); to the south Pozo de las Nieves (the island's highest point) and the odd-looking Roque Nublo (which as often as not truly is enveloped in a wad of cloud); and dropping away to the north-east the plains of San Mateo.

You can also buy souvenirs and ride donkeys if you feel the urge.

Hotel El Refugio (☎ 928 66 65 13; fax 928 66 65 20) has singles/doubles for 8000/10,000 ptas in high season (6800/8800 ptas

in low season). You can dine here too, or at the former *Parador* across the road (no rooms).

One Salcai bus (No 18) comes up from Playa del Inglés at 8 am on Sunday *only*, returning at 12.30 pm. There are five Utinsa buses a day from Las Palmas (via Santa Brígida and San Mateo) to Tejeda, which stop at Cruz de Tejeda on the way.

Parque Arqueológico del Bentayga
About 10km south of Tejeda village rises up the **Roque Bentayga** (1404m), a natural landmark on the island (signposted – you need your own transport). The archaeological park has been established to provide information about the area's ancient history. Around the Roque are various reminders of the Guanche presence here, from rock inscriptions to granaries and a sacred ritual site. Further reminders of the

DAMIEN SIMONIS

Cruz de Tejeda

Guanches are scattered about the park area, and staff at the Centro de Interpretación can help with hiking suggestions (although a serious guidebook on walking on the island might be more reliable). The centre itself has a display explaining something of the preconquest history of the area (entry is 250 ptas, if the centre is open that is!).

Pozo de las Nieves Those with their own wheels can drive the 15km east to this, the highest peak on the island (1949m). Follow the signs for Los Pechos and keep an eye on the military communications post, which sits atop the rise. The views are breathtaking on a clear day. Directly west is the distinctive **Roque Nublo** (1803m).

Vega de San Mateo

Descending from the barren, chilly heights of Tejeda, the scene around you quickly transforms itself. The plain (*vega*) of San Mateo is a sea of green. As with most of the northern strip of the island (but especially the northeast), the area is busily cultivated and receives enough rain to keep local farmers well occupied. You'll notice too that the area is much more densely populated – most of the island's population lives in the north. There's not an awful lot to San Mateo, but it makes a pleasant stop. If you happen to be around in September, try to make it up for the *romería* (pilgrimage) and celebrations of the patron saint, St Matthew, on 21 September.

Santa Brígida

About 9km further east on the road to Las Palmas, the next town of any note is Santa Brígida, whose centre repays a wander. The narrow streets are tree-lined and attractive, and from the parish church you have nice views inland over fields and palm groves to the central mountains.

Back on the road to Las Palmas, there is a turn-off south after 4km for the **Caldera de Bandama**, one of the biggest extinct craters on the island. There are superb views. Utinsa bus 311 from Las Palmas takes you close – ask for Bandama.

Should you want to stay (although there's hardly any need, with Las Palmas just a 15km bus ride away), there is a small nameless pensión (☎ 928 35 63 37) at Calle Real de Coello 34. Simple doubles cost 2500 ptas.

If you have your own transport, the best restaurants in the area are all out of town. *Restaurante Monte Verde*, on the road to Vega de San Mateo, is in a nice location. Mains here cost from 1300 ptas. Loads of Utinsa buses ply this route to Las Palmas.

THE NORTH

As is the case on most of the islands, the rain-blessed fertile north of Gran Canaria presents a radically different picture from the largely grim interior and south of the island. Rolling hills, intensively tilled fields and terraces, and myriad villages and hamlets make up a busy and interesting picture as you wind along twisting roads, negotiating *barrancos* (ravines) and an ever-changing terrain. Only as you reach the west does the green give way to a more austere, although no less captivating landscape – the west coast is the most dramatic on the island.

Teror

• *population 10,300*

In spite of the name, this place, 22km southwest of Las Palmas, does anything but inspire fear. The central Plaza de Nuestra Señora del Pino and Calle Real have survived the modern age more or less intact, the latter lined with fine old houses.

Among them is the **Casa de los Patronos**, now serving as a museum full of all sorts of intriguing odds and ends, mostly from the families who once lived here. The ancestors of Simón Bolívar's wife, the Venezuelan María Teresa Rodríguez del Toro, lived here at one point.

Dominating the square is the **Basílica de la Virgen del Pino**, a neoclassical edifice built in the 18th century. Inside, the most compelling detail is the 15th-century carving of the enthroned Virgen de la Nieve, illuminated in her place of honour above the altar.

The Virgen is the patron of the island and Teror, hence, is the religious capital. The Fiesta de la Virgen del Pino, on 6 to 8 September, is not only a big event in Teror – it is the most important religious feast day on the island's calendar.

If you need to stay, there is a little pensión (☎ 928 63 07 24) at Paseo de González Díaz s/n. Doubles cost 3000 ptas. The *Mesón Los Parranderos*, Calle de la Diputación 6, has a filling set menu with steak as its centrepiece for 1375 ptas. It's just off the central square. Utinsa bus 216 connects every half hour or so with Arucas and Las Palmas.

Arucas
• *population 26,974*
The extraordinary neogothic **Catedral de San Juan** stands sullen watch over the bright white houses of Arucas in a striking display of disproportion. Inside, the retablo above the main altar and the *Cristo Yacente* (*Reclining Christ*) by Manuel Ramos are the most noteworthy artworks.

Heading into the centre from the cathedral, you soon walk into Plaza de la Constitución, whose most interesting building is the restrained modernist town hall (Ayuntamiento). Opposite are the somewhat ragged municipal gardens, also known as the **Jardín de las Hespérides**. Calle de la Heredad flanks the gardens and is dominated by one of the town's oldest edifices, the **Heredad de Aguas de Arucas y Firgas**, completed in 1502. The clock was added in the 19th century.

Signs point north away from the town centre to the Mirador, a lookout from where you can see Las Palmas to the north-east and the northern coast of the island. It's a long walk, so if you have wheels, use them. *Mesón de la Montaña de Arucas*, up at the lookout of the same name, is the best restaurant in town and seems to be aware of it. The set menu is a little pricey at 1475 ptas, but you can be pretty sure of the quality.

Utinsa bus 216 connects every half hour or so with Teror and Las Palmas.

Moya
There's precious little to hold you up here, unless you feel like having a look at the **Casa/Museo de Morales**, where the Canarian modernist poet, Tomás Morales, lived. It is across the road from the 16th-century church on the main road through town. As you head out along Calle de Alejandro Hidalgo, you can get a hearty set meal for 725 ptas at the *Mesón Casa Plácido*, at No 6.

Occasional buses link Moya with Arucas and Las Palmas.

Santa María de Guía
• *population 12,383*
Lying on the main C-810 highway 25km west of Las Palmas, Santa María de Guía was for a while home to the French composer Camille Saint-Saêns (1835-1921), who occasionally tickled the ivories in the town's 17th-century neoclassical church.

In the 18th century the town and surrounding area was devastated by a plague of locusts. To rid themselves of this blight, town and country people got together to implore the Virgin Mary for help. This has remained a tradition and on the third Sunday of September the locals celebrate La Rama de las Marías, in which they dance their way to the doors of the church to make offerings of fruits of the earth to Mary. The town is also known for its *queso de flor* (flower cheese).

The Canary Islands' only *youth hostel* (☎ 928 88 27 28) is well out of town and has little to recommend it. Otherwise you could stay at the equally out of the way *Hotel Hacienda de Anzo* (☎ 928 55 16 55), Vega de Anzo. Rooms cost from 6000 ptas per person and they have a respectable restaurant – but it is a pain to find. You'll need your own wheels or a taxi.

The town is on the Las Palmas-Gáldar No 105 Utinsa bus route.

Gáldar
• *population 20,500*
The reasons for coming to Gáldar are all closed and unlikely to open in the near

future. Possibly the most important archaeological find in the islands was the so-called **Cueva Pintada**, near the Agaete exit of town. Its walls bear deteriorating designs in red, black and white left behind by the Guanches. The area around it, which has yielded some remains of a Guanche settlement, has been declared an archaeological park – work continues at a snail's pace on its development. A copy can be seen at the Museo Canario in Las Palmas.

A couple of kilometres out of town at Playa del Agujero are the **Necrópolis de Gáldar**. Mummies, objects used in Guanche funeral rites and other bits and bobs have been discovered in among the tombs here. The area has however been fenced off and a lack of funds to do anything with it means it may well stay that way.

There's nowhere much to stay here. Utinsa bus No 105 heads east for Las Palmas. No 103 heads south for Agaete and Puerto de las Nieves.

Agaete & Puerto de las Nieves
• *population 53,270*
There is virtually nothing to attract visitors in the main town of Agaete, just 10km south of Gáldar, but the nearby Puerto de las Nieves is a different story. Apart from the ferry to Santa Cruz de Tenerife and a limited pebbly beach, the cheery waterfront of what until the 19th century was the island's principal port is blessed with a series of modest little seafood restaurants.

Just in from the beach is the striking **Iglesia de Nuestra Señora de la Concepción**. Built in 1874, it is quite unique in the islands for its pronounced Mediterranean style. For a moment it feels like you've landed in Greece! Inside are two parts of a 16th-century Flemish triptych. The middle panel is preserved in the nearby **Ermita de las Nieves**, a small chapel.

Around Agaete the coast begins to take on a sterner countenance than further north. Right behind the beach rises up the Roque Partido, known to locals as the **Dedo de Diós** (God's Finger). This basalt monolith has weathered the elements for 100,000 years.

Special Event If you manage to be in Agaete around 4 August, you'll witness the Fiesta de la Rama, whose origins lie in an obscure Guanche rain dance. Nowadays locals accompanied by marching bands parade into town brandishing tree branches and then get down to the serious business of having a good time.

Places to Stay & Eat You can stay at *Apartamentos El Angosto* (☎ 928 55 41 92), Paseo del Obispo Pildaín 11. The apartments have a small kitchenette and lounge room, and cost 6000 ptas for two. The only other option in the area is the two-star *Hotel Princesa Guayarmina* (☎ 928 89 80 09; fax 928 89 85 25), 8km east of Agaete along the back road to Los Berrazales, whose mineral waters are reputed to have curative qualities.

You have a choice of seafood restaurants along the waterfront of Puerto de las Nieves.

Getting There & Away Utinsa bus No 103 links the town and port with Las Palmas via Gáldar. Bus No 101 heads south for Aldea de San Nicolás.

Líneas Fred Olsen operates four ferries a day to Santa Cruz de Tenerife from Puerto de las Nieves. Tickets cost 2700 ptas. There is a free bus connection to Las Palmas (Calle de Eduardo Benot 1). Going the other way, the bus leaves Las Palmas 1½ hours before the ferry is due to depart.

Aldea de San Nicolás
Also known as San Nicolás de Tolentino, this is one of those places where you might well arrive in the evening and need to stop and recharge batteries before heading on round the island.

The treat here is travelling, not arriving. The road between Agaete and San Nicolás takes you on a magnificent cliff-side journey. If you head south-west in the late afternoon, the setting sun before you delights the eyes with a soft light display, marking out each successive ridge in an ever-darker shadowy mantle. Those in their own vehicles can stop at numerous points along the way to take in the rugged views.

The rather scruffy town has little to excite the senses, but if you arrive late in the day you may be relieved to discover the *Hotel Los Cascajos* (☎ 928 89 11 65), Calle de los Cascajos 9, where decent enough singles/doubles with own shower and toilet cost 3000/4500 ptas, including breakfast. The same guy owns a small pensión nearby on the main square, where simple rooms come in at 2000/3000 ptas without breakfast.

Salcai has four buses (No 38) a day to Playa del Inglés via Puerto de Mogán. Two of these go all the way around to Las Palmas. Utinsa bus No 101 goes to Las Palmas via Puerto de las Nieves and Santa María de Guía.

Artenara

A back road climbs westward up the barranco from Aldea de San Nicolás to the hilltop village of Artenara, from where you are a short distance to Tejeda. The sparsely populated country, made up of bare ridges and rugged hills, is dotted with troglodyte caves, some of them still inhabited. When you consider that only 50km separates you from Las Palmas, the closeness of two such utterly different worlds (let alone that of Playa del Inglés!) gives plenty of food for thought – at least for the thoughtful.

Infrequent Utinsa buses link Artenara with Las Palmas via Teror. No buses run from Aldea de San Nicolás.

PLAYA DEL INGLÉS & MASPALOMAS

This is the international party end of the island. It appeals to many, but it won't appeal to all. A good chunk of the coast has basically been converted into a giant holiday home, with drinks. You come here for sun (especially if escaping the European winter) and nocturnal fun. Of course there is nothing to stop you exploring the rest of the island from here, but do not come to Playa del Inglés (not an Englishman at all, but a French fellow who was one of the first foreigners to live in the area early this century) and Maspalomas for

the history and impressive monuments – there aren't any.

The heart of the resort is Playa del Inglés, and the heart of the heart is the Yumbo Centrum, a big four-level shopping jungle. You could spend your entire holiday in here. By day it is akin to an Arab bazaar, bursting with all sorts of goods from rags to radios. In between them innumerable restaurants compete for your attention with 'international' food, traditional breakfasts from half a dozen countries and anything else they can come up with. Here you will also find banks, doctors, telephone and fax offices, a laundrette and supermarkets. Oh, and the tourist office is just outside the centre, on the same block.

As day gives way to night the scene transforms itself, so that by the wee small hours the leather handbags and wallets in the stores have been replaced by leather underpants in steamy gay bars. The vaguely wholesome bustly family atmosphere evaporates as the discos swing until dawn, and the drag shows, saunas and sex shops all do a roaring trade.

Beyond Yumbo is the rest, which in many respects is not unlike Yumbo. This is of course an artificial settlement, and you feel it immediately – all the nice boulevards and roundabouts betraying all the spontaneity in town design of a Five Year Plan. It's all hotels, apartments, restaurants and bars, and then some.

In Maspalomas especially the street names are revealing – Avenida del Touroperador Saga Tours, Avenida del Touroperador Alpitours, Neckerman, Tui, and so on and so on. No plain old streets (*calles*) either – all avenues, no matter how small.

To the south are the beaches, and the only item of genuine interest – the dunes of Maspalomas. Maspalomas itself is the quieter, you might say more exclusive, western perimeter of the resort. East of Playa del Inglés the resort continues but thins out in the areas known as Veril and San Agustín.

There are bus stops all over the resorts, a couple of them right by Yumbo (which, given the tourist office is here, is not a bad first stop for those who have not booked a room ahead).

Information

Tourist Offices The Oficina de Información Turística (☎ 928 77 15 50) is on the corner of Avenida de España and Avenida de los Estados Unidos. It opens Monday to Friday from 9 am to 9 pm; Saturday from 9 am to 2 pm.

Foreign Consulate Austria maintains a consulate (☎ 928 76 25 00) at Avenida de Gran Canaria 26 (in Hotel Eugenia Victoria).

Money Playa del Inglés is crawling with banks and exchange booths, Maspalomas less so. American Express is represented by Viajes Insular (☎ 928 76 05 00), at Avenida de Moya 14.

Email Mike's Bistro, next to Viajes Poseidón in San Fernando de Maspalomas, offers drinkers free Internet access.

Playa del Inglés & Maspalomas

OTHER
3   Guardia Civil
4   Mike's Bistro
5   Centro de Salud
6   Policía Local
8   Correos y Telégrafos
10 Austrian Consulate
12 Viajes Insular &
    American Express
13 Hotel Buenaventura
16 Joy Disco
18 International Cinema
19 24-Hour Clinic
20 Oficina de
    Información Turística
21 Salcai Bus
22 Happy Biking
    Information Office
23 Coin Laundrette

PLACES TO STAY
7   Apartamentos Liberty y Sol
14 Hotel Escorial
15 Caserío Azul
17 Apartamentos
    Royal Plaza
27 Hotel Palm Beach
28 Hotel Maspalomas Oasis

PLACES TO EAT
1   La Tasca Gallega
2   Casa Vieja
9   Mesón la
    Viuda de Franco
11 Casa Antonio
24 Restauranta Rías Bajas
25 Restaurante La Liguria
26 Restaurante La Toja

Medical Services It's probably because of all the drunken brawls and ecstasy overdoses, but the resort is swarming with clinics. The public clinic (Centro de Salud) is rather awkwardly located just inside the GC-1 *autopista* at the northern end of Maspalomas.

Across the road from the tourist office on the corner of Avenida de España and Avenida de los Estados Unidos is a 24-hour clinic (☎ 928 76 12 92).

Emergency The local police (☎ 928 14 15 72) are near the Ayuntamiento on the Barranco de Maspalomas. The Guardia Civil barracks (emergency ☎ 062) are on Avenida de Tunte.

The main emergency numbers for the rest of the island are valid here: local police (☎ 092); national police (☎ 091) and medical emergency (☎ 061).

Things to See & Do
Theme Parks Bored adults and ankle biters alike can be distracted by any number of theme parks especially developed in the south of the island for their benefit. You'll soon know all about them, as brochures are everywhere to be found along with touts to promote them.

Palmitos Park, a few kilometres north of the resort area, is a subtropical oasis crammed with exotic flora and 230 species of birds, along with an aquarium and 15 performing parrots. It opens daily from 9 am to 6 pm and buses run there regularly from various stops in Playa del Inglés (see also Getting Around below for more information on buses to these attractions).

Mundo Aborigen, on the road north to Fataga, is where 100 or so model Guanches stand in various ancient poses designed to give you an idea of what life was like here before the *conquistadores* lobbed up to build theme parks about how they once lived.

Aqua Sur and **Ocean Park** are basically pools with slides and rides.

For those who need a vacation from their vacation, **Holiday World** might do the trick. It's basically an old-fashioned amusement park, with the kind of gut-wrenching rides you'd expect.

Want to see a showdown (maybe even a hoe-down?). Then it's off to **Sioux City** for you, where good guys and bad guys shoot 'em up, round 'em up and generally get (mildly) wild for your entertainment.

After the west, a trip to the Orient? Try **Camel Safari Park**, on the road to Fataga. According to the brochure you can come and enjoy the oasis of palms and 'relax listening to the singing of the birds and the murmur of the camels'. Murmur?!

The list goes on, but you probably get the general idea by now. Entry to these sorts of things generally ranges from 1000 ptas up, so keep your wallets topped up!

Swimming For many, the only energy available after partying at night will be just enough to get down to the beach and collapse for the day. From east to west, the beaches are known as Playa de las Burras, Playa del Inglés and Playa de Maspalomas. Basically they all link up to form the one beach.

The best part about Maspalomas is the dunes, which fold back from the beach and have been declared a protected park.

There is a nudist area about where the dunes begin if you are approaching from Playa del Inglés. At the end of a hard day's baking, some nudists seem to think it is OK to wander around the rest of the dunes in the altogether too. Oh well.

Diving The Centro Turístico de Actividades Subcuaticas Sun-Sub (☎ 928 76 88 64), in the Hotel Buenaventura, Plaza de Ansite, in Playa del Inglés, organises diving trips and other water activities. You'll find a couple of other diving outfits scattered around the resort too.

Surfing & Windsurfing Although surfing is possible here (the best waves tend to break off the west end of Maspalomas by the lighthouse, or *faro*), this is not mind-blowing surfing territory. Windsurfers hang around in the same spot, but are better off heading east beyond the resorts to Bahía Feliz, Juan Grande and, best of all, Pozo Izquierdo. Pozo Izquierdo is for experienced windsurfers.

Other Water Sports Everything from deep-sea fishing to yacht trips or excursions in old schooners can be organised here through travel agents and many of the hotels and apartments.

Mountain Biking Happy Biking (☎ 928 76 82 98), in the Yumbo Centrum, rents out a range of mountain bikes for up to 3000 ptas a day. They also organise cycle tours of up to 50km starting at 3900 ptas. The price includes bike hire and a picnic. The tourist office also produces a little brochure suggesting several cycling routes.

Places to Stay

When you consider that there are at least 500 hotels, apartment blocks and bungalows in Playa del Inglés and Maspalomas, and that in peak periods these places are often full to bursting, you can begin to measure just what sort of phenomenon we are dealing with here. It is quite impossible to even begin to assess where you should head. At the end of the day you get, in reasonable measure, what you pay for. In moderate to high season you are unlikely to find anything for less than 5000 ptas for two people – these are usually apartments, which can mean bedroom, bathroom, kitchen and balcony.

Most people come here on a package. This is not to say you can't do it alone. But in high season especially you should get here early in the day, pick up a list of places to stay if you don't already have one and start letting your fingers do the walking. If you don't have your own wheels, get a good map (like the one mentioned at the beginning of this chapter) and concentrate your efforts in an area within reasonable walking distance. Remember that many apartments don't have anyone in permanent attendance – it is often useless to simply turn up at the address if you have not called ahead. The following places are fine in their category – large and impersonal, but perhaps for this reason they'll have a chance of something being spare when you call. But remember the other 500 places.

Apartamentos Royal Playa (☎ 928 76 04 50), Avenida de los Alfereces Provisionales 5, is not far from the beach in Playa del Inglés and offers functional apartments for two with bathroom and kitchen for 5000 ptas.

For the same price you can get a similar deal at *Apartamentos Liberty y Sol* (☎ 928 76 74 54), Avenida de Tirajana 32, but it's further away from the beach.

The apartments in *Caserío Azul* (☎ 928 77 40 60), Avenida de Italia 5, are better, cost 6000 ptas for two and are close to the beach. Across the road at No 6, *Hotel Escorial* has comfortable doubles for 8700 ptas.

Just so you know how the other half live, the premier establishments are out by the dunes in Maspalomas. Starting at 16,000 ptas and rising to 22,700 ptas per person, you can share a double and get half board at *Hotel Palm Beach* (☎ 928 14 08 06), Avenida del Oasis s/n. Or you could try *Hotel Maspalomas Oasis* (☎ 928 14 14 48; fax 928 14 11 92), on the same avenue. A double with ocean views and breakfast thrown in will cost a cool 21,300 ptas per person.

Places to Eat

The place is predictably swarming with eateries. The bulk of them serve up a pretty bland array of 'international' dishes designed to keep any stomach filled, without upsetting any palates.

Casa Antonio, Calle del Alcalde Marcial Franco 3, is a good place for grills, and it has a decent set lunch menu for just 750 ptas

Restauranta Rías Bajas, on the corner of Avenida de Tirajana and Avenida de los Estados Unidos, is a solid seafood place. Expect to pay about 1800 ptas for a full meal with wine.

The *Mesón la Viuda de Franco*, on the roundabout where the C-812 highway intersects with Avenida de Tirajana, has been serving up tapas and solid meals since WWII. You have to ask yourself what sort of trade they did back in those days. Still, the food makes no concession to non-Canary palates and is not too pricey.

Casa Vieja is just north of the GC-1 motorway along the road to Fataga. You could get a bus out here but a taxi or your own wheels make life easier. The 'old house' is indeed a low-roofed and charmingly bucolic affair, where a hearty meal will cost you around 1500 ptas.

La Tasca Gallega, Avenida de las Américas 40, in the outer dormitory satellite suburb of El Tablero, is a lively local place with great seafood and tapas – it really takes you away from the tourist crowd. You can eat well for around 1500 ptas.

Of the Italian places around, *Restaurante La Liguria*, Avenida de Tirajana 24, is not bad. Not fantastic (if you are Italian, do not eat Italian food outside Italy!), but not bad, and you can get away with a little over 1000 ptas.

Restaurante La Toja, Avenida de Tirajana (Edificio Barbados II) is a quality establishment blending the best of cuisines from France and Galicia. You shell out for it though – don't be surprised to see 3000 ptas or more slip effortlessly out of the pocket.

Entertainment
Trying to name particular bars and discos here is as utterly pointless within the scope of this guide as listing hotels. You could hang around in Yumbo Centrum for weeks and not try all the various bars and discos. Of course, since many of them are gay, they might not cater to all tastes – but there are plenty of straight places in there too.

If you ever break out beyond Yumbo Centrum, all the big shopping centres (*centros comerciales*) have at least some bars and discos in them. And beyond there are still more bars and discos.

Things to Buy
About the only interruption to the stream of apartments, hotels, restaurants and bars comes in the form of the above-mentioned centros comerciales. In them you can buy anything from children's wear to electronics. There's a lot of junk in there, so take care. There is a Fedac store in the same building as the tourist office in Playa del Inglés. It opens Monday to Friday from 9 am to 2 pm and 4 to 7 pm, and is worth a look before heading out to stock up on souvenirs.

Getting There & Around
Bus Bus 66 goes to the airport eight times a day, leaving every two hours (first one from the airport is at 7.15 am). The fare is 350 ptas.

Buses also link regularly with other points along the south coast as far as Puerto de Mogán, and Las Palmas. You should pick up a Salcai bus-route map from the information office in the Yumbo Centrum in Playa del Inglés. It shows in detail where all the bus stops are throughout Maspalomas and Playa del Inglés (there are plenty). Salcai puts on not only regular intercity services, but also has buses to many of the theme parks listed above.

AROUND PLAYA DEL INGLÉS & MASPALOMAS
Puerto Rico & Resort Coast
If Maspalomas has redeeming features in the shape of its great dunes and nightlife, little good can be said of the chain of its resort cousins further west along the coast.

The original fishing towns of **Arguineguín** and **Puerto Rico** must be in there somewhere, but they have been submerged below the serried ranks of apartment blocks scaling the barren cliffs and hills of what must once have been a spectacular (if harsh) coastline. Not even the beaches are particularly good at either of these massive, characterless resorts (nor are those further west still, such as Playa del Cura and the resorts of Tauro and Taurito), which leaves you wondering just what all the fuss is about. In Puerto Rico you can eat McDonalds, head to the pub for a pint of bitter and feel as though you'd never left

Britain (which is all very well if you are *from* Britain).

It would take months and be quite pointless trying to single out specific apartments, three-star hotels and the like here. If this is your thing, you are advised to book it ahead from home.

One of the few official camping grounds on the island is located off the C-812 highway just east of Playa del Cura – it's the *Camping Guantanamo* (☎ 928 56 02 07) and is nothing much to write home about.

If you are dying for British food, you could do a lot worse than the *Winston Churchill*, which is buried inside the Puerto Rico Shopping Center. It is pretty good value for money. On the 2nd floor of the same complex, *Restaurant Oliver* puts an imaginative French spin on international cuisine. You'll be lucky to get any change from 2000 ptas, but the food is good and makes a nice change from both Spanish and British fare!

In Arguineguín, good seafood can be had at modest prices from *Cofradía de Pescadores*, the fishing cooperative. It's at Avenida del Muelle s/n. It even does *gofio*, which you do not tend to see in big city restaurants or the resorts.

Regular buses connect the two places with Maspalomas and Playa del Inglés (275 ptas), and less frequently with Puerto de Mogán and Las Palmas (755 ptas).

Puerto de Mogán

After Taurito, a couple of kilometres of rugged and pretty much unspoiled coastline give you an impression of what this whole southern stretch of the island must have been like 40 years ago before anyone much had thought of tourism in the Canaries.

Finally you round a bend and below you is a smallish crescent of sandy beach and next to it a busy little yacht harbour and fishing port. Puerto de Mogán, although now largely given over to the tourist trade, is light years from its garish counterparts to the east.

The waterfront is a purpose built holiday zone, but tastefully done, with low two and three-storey apartments, covered in bougainvillea and other exotic flora and exuding an air of quiet charm despite the artificiality of the place. And here at least, there really is a fishing port and its small town clustered in behind the tourist façade. You have to wonder how the locals will be able to hang on to this fairly admirable balance – when will the developers move in? As it is, you can see the eyesore of Taurito from the quays.

If you need medical help, try the European Medical Centre (☎ 928 56 50 90).

Activities The kinds of activities you would expect from such a place are on offer here – from trips in a yellow submarine to diving and fishing trips (fishing trips cost 6500 ptas per person from 3 to 8 pm – hangers-on can come too for 4500 ptas).

If you want a taste of the horrors of Puerto Rico alluded to above, you can get a sea-borne ride with Líneas Salmon – there are seven daily boats each way and the return fare is 1000 ptas.

If parasailing rings your bell, call Watersports Mogán on mobile ☎ 970 81 28 00.

Places to Stay The apartments along the waterfront are generally let by local people, and if you simply turn up in the town, start asking around the shops below the apartments – if the ones you try don't let apartments themselves, they'll soon point you in the right direction. Prices vary according to the kind of apartment, views and season, but a basic rule of thumb is about 6000 ptas for two.

In the town itself you can also hunt down apartments. Otherwise, try *Pensión Salvador* (☎ 928 56 53 74), Calle de la Corriente 13, where small but clean rooms in a ramshackle house will cost around 2500 ptas a double (no singles).

If you have no luck at all on the waterfront or simply want a dirt cheap room, you can try a couple of places about 2km inland on the main road out of Puerto de Mogán. *Pensión Lucrecia* (☎ 928 56 56 43), Calle de Lomo Quiebre 16, and *Pensión Eva* (☎ 928 56 52 35), at No 35, both offer simple double rooms without own bath for 2000 ptas (no singles).

Comfort-seekers could try the *Hotel Club de Mar* (☎ 928 56 50 66; fax 928 56 54 38), right on the yacht harbourside. Rooms and apartments range from about 8000 ptas to 14,000 ptas for doubles, depending on season and views.

Places to Eat For seafood, head for *Restaurante Cofradía*, the fishing cooperative restaurant on the quay – if *they* can't deliver good fish, who can? The yacht harbour is lined with the usual international resort-style restaurants and cafés. Inland, *Restaurante Calipso*, Calle del Pasaje de los Pescadores, is another local seafood place with a slightly more authentic air than the average tourist eatery. *Restaurante El Barranco*, just over the bridge from the Calipso and on the main road out of town, sometimes puts on a cold buffet for 700 ptas.

Getting There & Away There is no shortage of Salcai buses heading east to Puerto Rico and Playa del Inglés (415 ptas). You also have regular departures for Las Palmas (910 ptas).

North of Puerto de Mogán

Just as Puerto de Mogán is a heavenly relief from the relentless armies of apartments, bungalows and 'true British pubs' that have occupied most of the coast to the east, so the C-811 road north out of here represents another extraordinary leap away from the maddening tourist crowds.

The road starts a gradual ascent to the town of **Mogán**, the municipal capital. It's a pleasant place with a handful of restaurants and bars, but nothing in particular to see or do. From here the C-811 winds off to the north-west, leading 24km to the Aldea de San Nicolás (see The North above).

Alternatively, you could head north-east up the barranco for **Ayacata**. About 5km of this road, which climbs tortuously up the barren and lonely ravine, is dirt track – quite driveable but a pain. From Ayacata you can hang a left and head for Tejeda and the highest points of the island (see Central Circuit above).

Isla de Fuerteventura

If you were to close your eyes and fly in from Laayoune, little more than 100km east in Moroccan-occupied western Sahara, you could be forgiven for thinking you hadn't gone anywhere. Lapped (and sometimes lashed) by the Atlantic, the dunes, shrub-studded plains and arid, knife-edged mountain ridges of Fuerteventura present an extremely parched picture. Its villages and towns, with their bundles of white-washed, flat-roofed houses, largely modern and unimaginatively fashioned of poured concrete, would be right at home cast across the semi-desert wastes of North Africa.

Fuerteventura's 1660 sq km make it the second largest island in the archipelago but, with only 41,629 inhabitants (known as Majoreros, from the Guanche name for the northern kingdom of the island – Maxorata), it is one of the least populous. It is also rather flat – the highest peak, known variously as the Orejas del Asno and the Pico de la Zarza, in the southern Jandía hills, reaches 807m.

The empty interior, where for centuries tough-living herdsmen have scratched out a living with their flocks of equally hardy goats, holds a definite fascination, although for most visitors the coast is the main attraction. And the miles of white sandy beaches are not only a sun-seeker's delight. Serious surfers and windsurfers will find near ideal conditions year round.

The ocean is not just for frolicking in – it is the islanders' life blood. Rainfall here is negligible, so virtually all the water consumed on the island is desalinated Atlantic. Diving and big game fishing are also hooks to hang your holiday on. Blue and white marlin, various kinds of tuna, wahoo and skipjack all ply the ocean waters off the island. If you support tag and release, there is nothing to stop you catching fish and letting the poor blighters go.

Tourism is here to stay, but Fuerteventura is still a long way from the resort horrors

HIGHLIGHTS

- Relaxing on the endless strands of the Jandía peninsula's Playa de Sotavento
- The rolling dunes of Corralejo
- Surfing and windsurfing around Corralejo and El Cotillo
- Exploring the old town of Betancuria
- Lunch on Isla de Lobos

of southern Gran Canaria and Tenerife. Perhaps it's just a question of time, but for the moment, the official line seems to be to keep development under control.

History

The island was known (at least in theory) to the Romans as Planaria, but the Guanches called it Maxorata – or most of it at any rate. What the Europeans came to dub Fuerteventura ('strong winds') was in fact divided into two tribal kingdoms: Jandía, which took up the southern peninsula as far north as La Pared, and Maxorata, which occupied the rest of the island.

Fuerteventura was the second island to fall to the first wave of conquerors under Jean de Béthencourt in January 1405. He had already established a fort there in 1402, but had been obliged to seek aid for his ambitions from the Castilian crown in Spain before proceeding. Although the islanders resisted the Spaniards they could not hold out for long.

De Béthencourt chose to set up a permanent base in the mountainous zone of what came to be known as Betancuria (funny about that). He had a chapel built and the village that grew up around it, Santa María de Betancuria, became the island's capital. The choice of location was determined not by aesthetics but by hard reasoning. The area provided one of the island's few limited water supplies and the terrain formed a natural if imperfect defence against counter-attack from Guanches and, later, raids by pirates.

New settlements spread slowly across the island, but not until the 17th century did the Europeans occupy El Cotillo, once the seat of the Guanche Maxorata kingdom. At this time the Arias and Saavedra families took control of the *señorío*, the island government deputising for the Spanish crown. By the following century, however, officers of the island militia had established themselves as a rival power base in La Oliva. Los Coroneles (the Colonels) gradually took virtual control of the island's affairs, their main aim apparently being to enrich themselves at the expense of both the *señores* and the hard-pressed peasantry.

The militia was disbanded in 1834 and in 1912 the island was granted a degree of self-administration with the installation of the Cabildo, as in the remainder of the archipelago.

Accommodation

Finding a place to stay among the apartments and occasional hotel, *hostal* and *pensión* in the coastal resorts can be problematic. In the case of many apartments you can't even book ahead, as they work exclusively with tour operators and their clientele.

This is not to say it's impossible, but you definitely need some luck on your side. If things look grim, head for Puerto del Rosario where you should encounter few problems getting a room. With a roof over your head you can work out your next strategy (hiring a vehicle of some sort will simplify life greatly!).

Camping is not permitted on the island, although there is one ground on the Isla de Lobos (for which you need a special permit).

Getting There & Away

Air The airport (☎ 928 85 12 50) is 6km south of Puerto del Rosario. Binter has six flights a day to Gran Canaria (35 minutes; 7610 ptas) and two a day to Tenerife Norte (50 minutes; 9800 ptas). Air Europa has several daily scheduled flights to Gran Canaria, Tenerife Norte and also Lanzarote (Arrecife).

Otherwise, charter flights connect the island with mainland Spanish cities and several European centres (including London, Manchester, Amsterdam, Munich and Frankfurt). The charters generally operate only two or three days a week.

At the airport you'll find a tourist information office (☎ 928 85 12 50; open 9 am to 8 pm seven days a week), car rental representatives, money exchange services and an ATM good for most international cards.

Sea Three weekly ferries link Arrecife (Lanzarote) and Las Palmas de Gran Canaria with Puerto del Rosario, while jetfoils go to Las Palmas from Morro Jable.

Regular ferries make the one-hour crossing between Corralejo in the north and Playa Blanca in Lanzarote's south.

Getting Around

Given the less than comprehensive public transport cover, having your own wheels will greatly enhance your capacity to get around the island.

To/From the Airport You can get buses or taxis to Puerto del Rosario (see the Getting Around entry under Puerto del Rosario below) and from there buses to other parts of the island. Taxis direct from the airport to Corralejo cost 4300 ptas, to El Cotillo 4900 ptas and to the Jandía beaches around 9500 ptas.

Isla de Fuerteventura

Bus Tiadhe provides a limited service, with 13 lines operating around the island. The most frequent runs link Puerto del Rosario with Corralejo in the north (No 6) and with Caleta de Fuste (via the airport) to the south (No 3). Line No 5 from Morro Jable to the Costa Calma is also fairly regular, but otherwise the frequency drops off radically to as few as one bus a day. Some lines don't operate at all on Sunday.

If you intend to use the buses a lot (even one return trip between Morro Jable and Corralejo, changing at Puerto del Rosario),

it is worth investing in a Tarjeta Dinero, a discount card for 2000 ptas. Instead of buying individual tickets on the bus for each trip, you tell the driver where you are going and stamp it in a machine on the bus – it represents about a 30% saving on each trip.

Taxi You can belt around in taxis, but it soon becomes an expensive habit. The trip from Puerto del Rosario to Corralejo costs about 3200 ptas; to Morro Jable you'd pay 9500 ptas.

Puerto del Rosario

• *population 16,500*

With almost half the island's population, Puerto del Rosario is a relatively modern little port town that only really took off in the 19th century. If you fly in to the island or use the buses you may well find yourself passing through. It's a scruffy sort of place, giving the impression of having been spread like a thick clump of white peanut butter over the dusty earth. Pedestrian concrete housing developments seep slowly and higgledy-piggledy into the surrounding dry country.

When Spain pulled out of the Sahara in 1975, it sent about 5000 Legión Extranjera (Foreign Legion) troops to Fuerteventura to keep a watch on North Africa. Their huge quarters – a cross between a prison and a Beau Geste fort – are still in use, although the remaining Regimiento de Soria only numbers about 1000.

History

Although it was founded in 1797 and was for a long time little more than an insignificant cluster of houses, Puerto del Rosario became the island's capital in 1860, due to its growing importance as a harbour.

Until 1956 it was known as Puerto de las Cabras, named after the goats for which it had long been a watering hole before becoming the main departure point for their export in the form of chops to the rest of the archipelago.

Orientation

The centre of town backs away from the port, and anything you might need is within easy strolling distance.

Information

Tourist Office You can get information at the Oficina de Turismo (☎ 928 53 08 44), Avenida de la Constitución 5. It opens Monday to Friday from 8 am to 2 pm. Otherwise, the office at the airport (see Getting

There & Away above) is open daily from 9 am to 8 pm.

Money You'll find plenty of banks with ATMs along and around Avenida del Uno de Mayo. Banco de Santander, at No 31, is just one of half a dozen.

Post & Communications The central Correos y Telégrafos is at Avenida del Uno de Mayo 58. You'll find plenty of telephone boxes around the centre. The postcode for Puerto del Rosario is 35600.

Medical Services & Emergency The island's Hospital General (☎ 928 53 17 99) is on the highway towards the airport. For an ambulance call 061 or the Cruz Roja (Red Cross; ☎ 928 85 13 76), Avenida de la Constitución 19. There's a Centro de Salud (health clinic) on Calle del Uno de Mayo.

The main Policiá Nacional (police station; ☎ 928 85 09 09) is on Avenida de Juan de Béthencourt.

Things to See

About the only specific sight is the **Casa Museo de Unamuno**, Calle del Rosario 11. The Basque-born philosopher Miguel de Unamuno, exiled for his opposition to the dictatorship of Primo de Rivera, ended up in this house, then the Hotel Fuerteventura, from March to July 1924. He later escaped to France and returned to his position at Salamanca University when the Republican government came to power in 1931.

Part of the house has been turned into a period piece, with furnishings and other odds and ends from Unamuno's day, including his desk. It opens Monday to Friday from 9 am to 1 pm and 5 to 7 pm; Saturday from 10 am to 1.30 pm. Admission is free.

During his exile, Unamuno used to seek solace on the **Playa Blanca**, about a 45 minute walk south of the town centre.

Special Events

The town puts on its party clothes on the first Sunday of October to celebrate the

Fiesta de la Virgen del Rosario, the capital's patron.

Places to Stay

There are few good reasons for staying, but if you have a hard time getting a room elsewhere on the island you can be pretty sure that something will be available here.

Hostal Tamasite (☎ 928 85 02 80), Calle de León y Castillo 9, is a well situated pensión with charmless but good, clean singles/doubles for 3500/4500 ptas. Rooms have a bath, phone and TV. It's one of the better choices in town, but not if you are a light sleeper; the noise from the bar in the same building can be a bit much on weekends.

Cheaper is *Pensión Macario* (☎ 928 85 11 97), Calle de Juan de Austria 24, where doubles (no singles) cost 2625 ptas. The rooms are fine but the area is, to put it mildly, forlorn. At No 27 the same people also run some apartments (unavailable at the time of writing).

Pensión Ruben Tinguaro (☎ 928 85 10 88), Calle de Juan XXIII 48, has basic rooms for 2500/3500 ptas.

Hotel Valerón (☎ 928 85 06 18), Calle de la Candelaria del Castillo 10, has singles/doubles for 2090/3750 ptas. It's OK, but nothing spectacular.

The *Parador Nacional de Turismo* (☎ 928 85 11 50; fax 928 85 11 58), Calle de la Playa Blanca 45, overlooks Playa Blanca, 3km south of the town centre. You will have to overlook the fact that it sits right under the flight path for the nearby airport. Rooms are nice enough, but not worth the 9200/11,500 ptas given the location.

Places to Eat

Restaurante El Granero, Calle del Alcalde Alonso Patallo 8, is hardly the last word on ambience, but it has a solid menu and the set lunch (menú del día) costs 950 ptas. Otherwise main dishes start at around 1000 ptas.

A rung up in the décor department, but with much the same quality food at similar prices, is the *Restaurante Casino El Porvenir* on Calle de la Cruz.

For pizza, or a reasonable approximation thereof, you could do worse than *Pizzeria El Patio*, Plazoleta de Lazaro Rugama Nieves 3.

If you end up staying at the Pensión Ruben Tinguaro, *Mesón Las Brasas,* Calle de Juan XXIII 68, is a good place nearby, serving a fair range of fish and meat dishes starting at around 1200 ptas, and you can order a side dish of papas arrugadas con mojo picón.

For churros and chocolate, you should stop by at the *Cafetería Tinguaro V*, Plaza de España 7.

Entertainment

You can enjoy a pleasant drink at the terraza on the waterside Avenida de los Reyes. For grungier, blue-lit boozing, stop by Pub Milena, in the lane next to Hostal Tamasite. Paco's Bar, Calle del Doctor Mena 8, is another popular hangout.

For later in the evening, on weekends at any rate, head for Pub Evening, Calle del Profesor Juan Tadeo Cabrera 17, and Disco Pub Mambo, located at No 4 on the same street.

Getting There & Away

Air See the beginning of this chapter for flight information.

Bus Tiadhe (☎ 928 85 21 66) buses leave from the main bus stop on the corner of Avenida de León y Castillo and Avenida de la Constitución. The following services operate from Puerto del Rosario:

Line No 1
    To Morro Jable via Tuineje (eight times a day; two hours; 1000 ptas)
Line No 2
    To Vega del Río de Palmas via Betancuria (twice a day, 50 minutes, 400 ptas)
Line No 3
    To Caleta de Fuste via the airport (26 times a day; 20 minutes; 200 ptas)
Line No 6
    To Corralejo (26 times a day; 40 minutes; 350 ptas)

Line No 7

To El Cotillo via La Oliva (three times a day; 1½ hours; 500 ptas)

Line No 10

To Morro Jable via the airport (three times a day except on Sunday; 1½ hours; 1000 ptas)

Car & Motorcycle Four main roads fan out from the town. The northern coast route to Corralejo is the FV-1. Heading in the opposite direction to the airport and ultimately the Jandía peninsula is the FV-2. The FV-10 strikes north-west for El Cotillo and Cor-

ralejo via La Oliva, while the FV-20 takes you to Betancuria and on to Pájara and the south-west coast.

Sea Trasmediterránea ferries leave from the Estación Marítima at midnight on Tuesday, Thursday and Saturday for Las Palmas de Gran Canaria (eight hours; 3500 ptas). At 11 am on the same days a ferry departs for Arrecife (Lanzarote). The trip takes three hours and costs 1050 ptas. You can get tickets at their office (☎ 928 85 08 77) at Calle de León y Castillo 58. Naviera

PLACES TO STAY
2 Pensión Ruben Tinguaro
3 Apartamentos Macario
4 Pensión Macario
11 Hotel Valerón
14 Hostal Tamasite

PLACES TO EAT
1 Mesón Las Brasas
12 Restaurante Casino El Porvenir
16 Cafetería Tinguaro V
17 Pizzeria El Patio
27 Restaurante El Granero

OTHER
5 Centro de Salud
6 Policía Nacional
7 Oficina de Turismo
8 Cruz Roja
9 Intercity Bus Stop
10 Trasmediterránea Office
13 Paco's Bar
15 Pub Milena
18 Correos y Telégrafos
19 Iglesia de Nuestra Señora del Rosario
20 Cabildo
21 Taxi Rank
22 Casa Museo de Unamuno
23 Pub Evening
24 Oficina de Medio Ambiente
25 Banco de Santander
26 Disco Pub Mambo
28 Terraza
29 Taxi Rank
30 Estación Marítima
31 Hospital General

Puerto del Rosario

ISLA DE FUERTEVENTURA

Armas also has a ferry for Las Palmas on Tuesday and Thursday. Tickets are available at the same office.

Getting Around

To/From the Airport The No 3 bus to Caleta de Fuste runs 26 times a day from Monday to Saturday (6.30 am to 9 pm), stopping at the airport about 10 minutes before reaching Caleta de Fuste. Going the other way, the bus leaves pretty much every half hour from 6.30 am to 9.30 pm. The No 10 direct bus between Puerto del Rosario and Morro Jable also calls in at the airport. The trip between Puerto and the airport takes 10 to 15 minutes and costs 125 ptas. A taxi will cost about 700 ptas.

Bus One municipal bus does the rounds of the town every hour, but you are unlikely to need it.

Taxi If you need a cab, call ☎ 928 85 00 59 or 928 85 02 16.

The North

ROAD TO LA OLIVA

The FV-10 highway shoots westwards away from Puerto del Rosario into the barren interior of the island. Before it crosses the ridgeback that forms the island's backbone, the road passes through the sleepy hamlets of **Tetir** and **La Matilla**. The demure chapel in the latter is a good example of the simple, bucolic buildings of the Canaries.

About 4km south of La Matilla, **Tefía** lies on the FV-207 to Betancuria (see Betancuria later in this chapter). What makes this place interesting is the handful of partly restored rural houses. You can wander about it any time of day, but if you want to get a peek inside the houses, you should turn up between 10.30 am and 6.30 pm. The displays tell you something of how islanders used to live and explain the process of restoration. It's a shame that this was the only way to preserve something of 'old

Fuerteventura', as it has that unmistakably fake air about it.

You can follow the road out of Tefía and swing right (west) on the FV-211 for **Casa de los Molinos**. On the way you can't miss the old mill, sited on the property of what is now a handicrafts school. Casa de los Molinos itself is little more than a few simple houses overlooking a small black pebble beach. You can eat seafood at the *Restaurante Los Molinos* while gazing over Atlantic breakers.

Turning on your tracks and heading north again for La Oliva, you pass on your left a monument to Miguel de Unamuno; the statue, created by sculptor Juan Borges Lineres in 1970, lies just south of **Tindaya**, a sprawling centre where some of the island's goat cheese, *queso majorero*, is produced.

The Basque sculptor, Eduardo Chillida, has caused considerable controversy with his plan to bore a hole into Montaña de Tindaya, just to the north of the town. The 50 cubic metre space, a kind of internal esplanade, is supposed to make its visitors 'feel small in their physical dimension, and brotherhood with all other people'. Ecological groups perceive all sorts of dark capitalist interests behind the project, although Chillida claims to have explicit promises from the Canary Islands government that no hotels or other money-spinning operations will be built in the area. Anonymous threatening phone calls and letters notwithstanding, Chillida is undeterred.

The No 7 bus from Puerto del Rosario to El Cotillo passes through all but Tefía and Casa de los Molinos three times a day. Bus No 2 between Puerto del Rosario and Vega del Río de Palmas passes by Tefía twice a day. There are no buses to Casa de los Molinos.

LA OLIVA

• *population 2300*

One-time capital, in fact if not in name, of the island, La Oliva still bears a few traces of grander days. The weighty bell tower of the 18th-century **Iglesia de Nuestra Señora de la Candelaria** is the focal point of this now unprepossessing town. To the south, the 18th-century **Casa de los Coroneles** stands in decrepit isolation, overrun by goats. The officers who once presided here certainly led the high life. Virtually controlling the affairs of the island from the early 1700s, the only kind of law and order these guys were interested in was that which helped increase their own power and wealth. They appropriated land and threw the peasant class into such a state of abject feudal subjugation that in 1834 Madrid, faced with repeated bloody mutinies on the island, saw itself compelled to disband the militia. Problem was, the now ex-colonels still held onto the appropriated wealth.

There is nowhere to stay here. The No 7 bus between Puerto del Rosario and El Cotillo passes through three times a day.

CORRALEJO
* *population 4000*

Tourism is what makes this place tick, but, surprisingly, it has been kept to manageable levels. The bulk of the holiday apartments and resorts are resolutely low rise and the town centre still retains some resonance of what was once a simple fishing village.

You can but wonder what goes through the minds of the weather-beaten fishermen sitting down to a beer and cards in their portside club, the Cofradía de los Pescadores. Just what do they really think about

DAMIEN SIMONIS
Sand sculpture on Playa de Corralejo

the lobster-red foreigners wandering naked around the dunes to the south of town?

In fact, what makes Corralejo are the blinding white sands of the dunes which sweep back in gentle sugarloaf rolls from the crystal blue ocean. Set aside as a park, no one can build on or near them.

Information
Tourist Office The Oficina de Turismo (☎ 928 86 62 35), Plaza Grande de Corralejo, opens Monday to Friday from 9 am to 1 pm and 4.30 to 7.30 pm; Saturday from 9 am to noon.

Money There are plenty of banks with ATMs. The BBV bank on the corner of Avenida del General Franco and Calle de Lepanto is a handy one.

Post & Communications The main Correos y Telégrafos is on Calle de Lepanto. For phone calls, go to the special cabin set up outside the Centro Comercial Atlántico on Avenida del General Franco. It opens seven days from 9.30 am to 1 pm and 5.30 to 10 pm. The postcode for Corralejo is 35660.

Medical Services You can choose from several private clinics set up here, as in other resorts, for tourists. Clínica Médica Brisamar (☎ 928 53 64 02), on Avenida del General Franco, is open 24 hours a day.

Emergency For an ambulance, call the Cruz Roja on ☎ 928 86 00 00. The Policía Local (☎ 928 86 61 07) have a station on Paseo del Atlántico.

Things to See & Do
Parque Natural de Corralejo y Lobos
The beach dunes of this park stretch along the east coast for about 10km from Corralejo.

It can get breezy here, and your predecessors have already applied their ingenuity to the problem – the little fortresses of loose stones, most commonly erected atop shrub-covered sandy knolls, are designed to protect sun-worshippers from the wind. You

ISLA DE FUERTEVENTURA

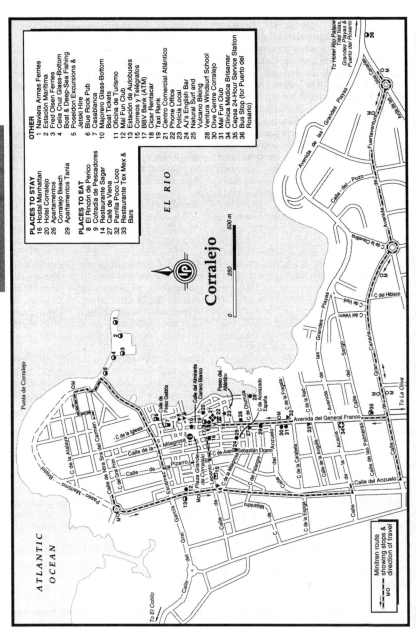

PLACES TO STAY
16 Hostal Manhattan
20 Hotel Corralejo
26 Apartamentos
   Corralejo Beach
29 Apartamentos Tania

PLACES TO EAT
8 El Rincón de Perico
9 Cofradía de Pescadores
14 Restaurante Sagar
27 Café de Viena
32 Parrilla Poco Loco
33 Restaurante Tex Mex &
   Bars

OTHER
1 Naviera Armas Ferries
2 Estación Marítima
3 Fred Olsen Ferries
4 Celia Cruz Glass-Bottom
   Boat & Deep-Sea Fishing
5 Poseidon Excursions &
   Jetski Hire
6 Blue Rock Pub
7 Casablanca
10 Majorero Glass-Bottom
   Boat Tickets
11 Oficina de Turismo
12 Mal Fun Club
13 Estación de Autobuses
15 Correos y Telégrafos
17 BBV Bank (ATM)
18 Cicar Rentacar
19 Taxi Rank
21 Centro Comercial Atlántico
22 Phone Office
23 Policía Local
24 AJ's English Bar
25 Natural Surf and
   Vulcano Biking
28 Ventura Windsurf School
30 Dive Centre Corralejo
31 Mal Fun Club
34 Clínica Médica Brisamar
35 Cepsa 24-Hour Service Station
36 Bus Stop (for Puerto del
   Rosario)

Corralejo

may have to search around a while to find one that isn't already occupied – more often than not by nudists who, when they meander about the dunes in all their glory, seem utterly impervious to the elements. Nudity on these beaches is not, by the way, obligatory, so you should not feel embarrassed to keep one or two items of clothing on if you so choose.

Diving Dive Centre Corralejo (☎ 928 86 62 43), just back from the waterfront, organises two-dive day trips. They leave at 8.30 am and return at 1.30 pm. You can also learn to dive here and hire all the necessary equipment. Information is available at the booth at Avenida del General Franco 50.

Windsurfing Conditions along much of the coast and in the strait between Corralejo and Lanzarote, the Estrecho de la Bocaina, are ideal for windsurfing. The Ventura Windsor school (☎ 928 86 62 95) is one of several in the area if you are a beginner – or you can just hire the gear. It is on the beach behind the Apartamentos Hopalco.

Surfing Corralejo is a popular base for surfers. If you need equipment, lessons or advice on where to get the best breaks, you could try Natural Surf (☎ 928 53 57 06), one of three surf schools in the town, at Calle del Acorazado España 10.

Glass-Bottom Boats You can muck around in the *El Majorero*, a glass-bottom boat. Day cruises to and around the Isla de Lobos with lunch thrown in cost 4500 ptas (from 11 am to 5.30 pm). One-hour tours cost 1700 ptas, or you can simply use the boat to get across to the islet for 1300 ptas return. For this latter operation, departure is at 10 am and the return trip at 4 pm. You can get tickets from the booth at Calle del Almirante Carrero Blanco or at the port.

At the port you will find alternative vessels. The *Poseidon* does a simple return trip to Isla de Lobos for 1000 ptas, and the glass-bottom catamaran *Celia Cruz* does

cruises to Isla de Lobos for 1700 ptas per person.

Fishing & Jetskiing At the port, you can also organise deep sea fishing trips with Barvik (☎ 928 53 57 10), with departures at 8.30 am, or Pez Velero (☎ 86 61 73). They cook your catch.

Jetskis (4000 ptas for 20 minutes) are available for rent at the port, from Lobos Jets (☎ 928 53 52 10).

Places to Stay
It can be a real hassle finding somewhere to stay here. If you don't have wheels it can be worse, because a lot of the apartments are strung out along the beach south of the town. Still more of a pain, many deal only with tour operators (although if you arrive during a quiet patch they will happily take your money). Even ringing ahead can be a waste of time. So, if you don't come with a package, come prepared to move on to, say, Puerto del Rosario until you can organise something.

Hotel Corralejo (☎ 928 53 52 46), Calle de Colón 12, is right in the heart of the town and has spacious singles/doubles/triples for 2500/3500/5000 ptas. Most rooms overlook the little town beach. If you want to go cheaper, try *Hostal Manhattan* (☎ 928 86 66 43), Calle de Gravina 32, which has basic (and noisy) digs for 2000/3500 ptas. Both are often full.

Apartamentos Tania (☎ 928 53 50 20), Avenida del General Franco 58, has basic apartments for 5000 ptas. The main problem is noise coming from the bars downstairs.

Apartamentos Corralejo Beach (☎ 928 86 63 15), Avenida del General Franco s/n, has apartments for two from 6000 ptas to 7000 ptas. The position is handy for accessing the town centre, but far enough away not to be disturbed by the whoops of the partying.

Hotel Riu Palace Tres Islas (☎ 928 53 57 00; fax 928 53 58 58), Avenida de las Grandes Playas, is a luxury seaside fortress on the edge of the dunes. Singles cost

16,100 ptas including half board, while doubles with ocean views and half board come in at 19,720 ptas per person.

Places to Eat

Among the waterside eateries and bars in the town centre, the least prepossessing is potentially the best. The *Cofradía de Pescadores*, the local fishermen's hangout, prepares good fish mains for up to 1300 ptas.

If you want to try gofio followed by a plate of cabrito (kid meat), head for *El Rincón de Perico*, where Calle de la Iglesia runs into Plaza Chica. These items and a beer will set you back 1800 ptas.

The *Parrilla Poco Loco*, Avenida del General Franco 16, is great for grills – a healthy T-bone (no mad cow disease here) costs 1800 ptas.

For a change, the Indian food at *Restaurante Sagar*, Calle de Lepanto 25, isn't bad. *Restaurante Tex Mex*, in the gaudy yellow shopping centre on the corner of Avenida del General Franco and Calle de la Anguila, is another option.

For a civilised cup of coffee or breakfast, *Café de Viena*, Calle de Juan de Austria 27, hits the spot.

Entertainment

Finding a drink shouldn't pose too much of a problem. Bars, like the popular Oink, take up much of the Centro Comercial Atlántico, on Avenida del General Franco, as well as the bright yellow centre further down the road, on the corner of Calle de la Anguila.

For a relaxed cocktail just out of earshot of the main hurly-burly, Casablanca, Calle de Pérez Galdós, is perfect. For a late night tipple (until about 3 am), the Blue Rock Pub, at the northern end of the pedestrianised part of Calle de la Iglesia makes a refreshing alternative to the rowdier 'real British pubs'.

Still, if you want one of the latter, you could do worse than AJ's English Bar, on the corner of Calle del Acorazado España and Calle de Juan Sebastián Elcano.

Getting There & Away

Bus The No 6 bus runs regularly from Corralejo's bus station to Puerto del Rosario. The trip takes 45 minutes and costs 350 ptas. You can also pick up the bus by the last Minitren stop and at the Hotel Riu Palace Tres Islas.

The No 8 bus heads west to El Cotillo (via La Oliva) six times a day (40 minutes; 320 ptas).

Car & Motorbike The FV-1 leads past the Grandes Playas and Corralejo's dunes to Puerto del Rosario, from where the FV-2 proceeds right down the coast to Morro Jable.

The coast road west to El Cotillo is unsealed but generally passable for normal cars. The only other direction you can head is directly south for La Oliva.

Rental There are oceans of car rental companies here. Cicar (☎ 928 86 64 13), in the Centro Comercial Atlántico on Avenida del General Franco, is perfectly reliable.

If you want only two motorised wheels, one option is Mal Fun Club (☎ 928 53 51 52), Avenida de Juan Carlos I, opposite the bus station. Scooters start at 2900 ptas a day, while a Kawasaki KLR 650 costs 8400 ptas. The price includes third party insurance and a helmet. They have another office (☎ 928 86 75 41) at Avenida del General Franco 50; also on the same road is a Cespa 24-hour service station.

Sea Líneas Fred Olsen ferries leave four times a day for Playa Blanca in Lanzarote. The trip takes about an hour and tickets cost 1800 ptas. Otherwise, hop onto one of Naviera Armas' five boats, for which tickets cost 1700 ptas.

At the Lanzarote end, Fred Olsen puts on a free connecting bus as far as Puerto del Carmen and Lanzarote's airport for its 9 am and 5 pm services. Naviera Armas has one stopping at Puerto del Carmen, Arrecife and Costa Teguise, but only if you are on the 6 pm ferry. The free buses operate in the other direction too.

Getting Around

Minitren You know those irritating little trains which often transport sheepishly grinning tourists around resorts and theme parks? Well there's one in Corralejo and, if you can swallow your pride, it might even come in handy.

It runs every half hour from 9 am to 11.30 pm from Avenida del General Franco – taking in the port, bus station and most of the apartments at the north end of the dunes – in its circuit of the town. A ride costs 150 ptas.

Taxi A taxi from the town centre to the beaches will cost about 500 ptas.

Bicycle You can rent bikes from several places. Mountain bikes are available at Vulcano Biking (☎ 928 53 57 06), Calle del Acorazado España 10.

ISLA DE LOBOS

The bare 4.4 sq km of this islet take their name from the seawolves (*lobos marinos*) which long called it home. They were in fact monk seals (*focas monje*), which have long since disappeared. Plans to reintroduce them from Mauretania have been put on ice because seal numbers there are also on the decline.

You can go on an excursion to Isla de Lobos from Corralejo, and once you have arrived there's little to do but go for a quick walk, put in an order for lunch at the quayside *chiringuito* (kiosk; you must let them know when you arrive if you intend to lunch there) and head for the pleasant little beach.

It is possible to camp here, but first you need a permit from the Oficina de Medio Ambiente (☎ 928 85 20 38), Calle del Professor Juan Tadeo Cabrera 10, in Puerto del Rosario.

For details on how to get here, see the Corralejo section above.

EL COTILLO

Once the seat of power of the tribal chiefs of Maxorata, the northern kingdom of Guanche Fuerteventura, El Cotillo has been largely ignored since the conquest. The exceptions to the rule were cut-throat pirates who occasionally sought to land here, and the slowly growing invasion of less violently-minded sun-seekers who prize the area's unaffected peacefulness. The developers have so far largely left this small fishing village on Fuerteventura's north-western coast alone, but for how long? Fingers crossed.

Apart from the delights of the sea (the better beaches stretch out south of town), the only object of note is the tubby little **Fortaleza del Tostón**. Built in 1797 to ward off pirates of all persuasions, it now seems oddly out of place, sitting isolated above the modest cliffs south of the port. The beaches between El Cotillo and Corralejo are generally small and pebbly. Experienced surfers will want to make for a spot known as Bubbles. Waves break over reef and rocks, and plenty of casualties can be seen walking the streets of El Cotillo and Corralejo.

Places to Stay

El Cotillo remains a laid-back and comparatively undeveloped haven. There are several groups of apartments to choose from, and more are being built. Hopefully they won't go overboard.

Apartamentos Bar Playa (☎ 928 53 85 22), in the centre of the town at Calle de San Pedro 12, is pretty basic but perfectly acceptable. Doubles cost 5500 ptas.

Closer to the castillo and to the southern beaches are the *Apartamentos Juan Benítez* (☎ 928 53 85 03), at Calle del Caletón 10. They stand out like a sore thumb, but the apartments are spotlessly clean and have TV and phone. They start at 6500 ptas.

More resorty is the comparatively large *Apartamentos Cotillo Lagos* complex (☎ 928 908-64 96 86; fax 928 85 20 99). It is a low-level development about 2km north of the town in the satellite Urbanización Los Lagos. The area is still a bit of a mess, with dirt tracks for roads; there's certainly an air of hasty town planning with an eye to the quick tourist buck. For all that, the apartments are comfortable and not a bad choice at 6000 ptas.

Places to Eat
The most pleasant spot to eat and drink is the *Restaurante La Vaca Loca*, presided over by a surreal, model cow, floodlit in lurid blue at night, right on the little harbour in the middle of town. They serve up decent food all day from noon to 10 pm, including pizzas.

A couple of good little places at the southern end of the village (within sight of the castillo), are *Restaurante Los Chacones* and *Casa Chano*, the latter at Calle de Fuerteventura 1. They both serve up standard fish and meat dishes which will set you back about 2000 ptas a head (including a side dish and wine).

Getting There & Away
Bus No 7 for Puerto del Rosario (500 ptas) leaves at 6.45 am, noon and 5 pm. No 8 leaves for Corralejo (320 ptas) seven times a day. The dirt road around the coast to Corralejo is normally passable for ordinary cars.

The Centre

The central chunk of Fuerteventura offers some of the most varied countryside a desert island can manage. The mountains of the Parque Natural de Betancuria are sliced in their southern reaches by a palm-studded ravine starting at Vega del Río de Palmas. While the west and east coasts are largely rocky cliffs interspersed with small black-sand beaches and fishing hamlets, the central, copper-coloured plains around Antigua are dotted by old windmills in various states of repair and dating back a couple of centuries.

BETANCURIA
Jean de Béthencourt thought this the ideal spot to set up house in 1405, so he had

living quarters and a chapel built. To this nascent settlement he gave his own name, which with time was corrupted to Betancuria (or the Villa de Santa María de Betancuria in the unexpurgated version). In the course of the century Franciscan friars moved in and expanded the town, which remained the island capital until 1834. The island's proximity to the North African coast made it easy prey for Moroccan and European pirates who, on numerous occasions, managed to defy Betancuria's natural mountain defences and sack it. Tucked prettily into the protective folds of the basalt hills, the town is now home to fewer than 600 people.

Things to See
If you approach from the north, your gaze will be drawn down to the left, where ruins of the island's first **monastery**, built by the Franciscans, stand empty but proud. The centre of the settlement is watched over by the 17th-century **Iglesia de Santa María**. Pirates had destroyed its Gothic predecessor in 1593. A short walk away is the **Museo de Arte Sacro**. This contains a mixed bag of valuable religious art, including paintings, gold and silverware. Entry to both is covered by one 100 ptas ticket; the custodian races back and forth to open the church and museo alternately every half hour from 10 am to 5 pm, daily except Sunday. Of vague interest also is the **Casa Museo de Betancuria**, just on the east bank of what would be the village stream if any water ran in it. It houses a modest collection of Guanche artefacts, and is open Tuesday to Saturday from 10 am to 5 pm and Sunday from 10 am to 2 pm. Entry is 100 ptas.

If you have 800 ptas to burn, you can enter the Restaurante Casa de Santa María's theme show, in which pottery and weaving workshops have been set up; the price includes a bit of wine and cheese tasting.

Special Event
On 14 July, townspeople celebrate the Día de San Buenaventura, patron saint of the town, a fiesta dating to 1456.

DAMIEN SIMONIS

Old mill east of Betancuria

Places to Eat
There is no doubt that the *Restaurante Casa de Santa María*, part of the tourist complex opposite the main portal of the church, wins hands down on atmosphere. Mains cost up to 1900 ptas.

The food at the inconspicuous *Restaurante Valtarajal*, Calle del Presidente Hormiga s/n (at the southern exit of town), leaves little to be envied by its classier competitor, and will do half the damage to your purse.

Getting There & Away
Bus No 2 passes through here twice a day on its way between Puerto del Rosario (400 ptas) and Vega del Río de Palmas (a short distance south).

The FV-30 road leads north to Los Llanos de la Concepción, after which it forks east for Puerto del Rosario and north for Corralejo via La Oliva.

AROUND BETANCURIA
A couple of kilometres north of Betancuria, the **Mirador de Morro Velosa** offers mesmerising views across the island's weird and disconsolate moonscape. The FV-30 highway twists its way north through the barely perceptible settlements of Valle de Santa Inés and Los Llanos de la Concepción before running into the FV-20, just short of the village of **Casillas del Ángel**. Here, the petite **Iglesia de Santa Ana** contains an 18th-century wooden carving of St Anne. For a hearty meal of *cabrito* (goat meat, an island speciality for reasons which have probably become apparent by now), try *Casa Felo*, along the main road at the west end of the town.

Heading south for Pájara, you soon hit **Vega del Río de Palmas**. As you proceed, the reason for the name becomes clear, as the road follows the course of a near dry watercourse, still wet enough below the surface to keep a stand of palms alive.

ANTIGUA
This is one of the bigger inland villages, but there is not much to do except make a quick visit to the 18th-century church.

About 2km north of town is the **Antiguo Molino,** a fully restored windmill open to the public daily from 10 am to 6 pm.

The pizzeria across the road from the church is handy for a snack, or you could try the restaurant next door to the Antiguo Molino for a classier meal.

The No 1 bus passes through here en route between Puerto del Rosario and Morro Jable.

AROUND ANTIGUA
La Ampuyenta
The 17th-century **Ermita de San Pedro de Alcántara** makes a quick stop here worthwhile if you have your own wheels and can move on freely. The ermita (chapel) is surrounded by a stout, protective wall built by French from the Normandy area.

Tiscamanita
Nine km south of Antigua on the road to

ISLA DE FUERTEVENTURA

Tuineje, the windmill-obsessed might like to call in at this tiny hamlet where you can visit a working restored mill (and see what a hard grind it all was) at the Windmill Interpretation Centre. The centre opens daily from 10 am to 6 pm.

TUINEJE
Although something of a crossroads in the interior, Tuineje has no particular attractions. The No 1 bus calls in here. The No 11 bus to La Lajita on the coast takes about half an hour, travelling inland via El Cardón; it runs only twice daily, Monday to Saturday. The No 13 from Pájara calls in here on its way to Gran Tarajal and La Lajita.

PÁJARA
What makes the 17th-century **Iglesia de Nuestra Señora de la Regla** unique in the islands are the *retablos* behind the altar (stick 100 ptas in the machine on the right shortly after you enter the church to light them up). They are an example of influences flowing back from Latin America – in this case Mexico. Outside, the decoration above the main portal is said to be of Aztec inspiration.

Right next to the church you can eat well at the *Centro Cultural*. Across the Tuineje road is the *Restaurante La Fonda*, a more pleasant establishment, although the food and prices are much of a muchness.

Two buses a day connect Pájara with Morro Jable (Nos 4 & 9); and another two run to Gran Tarajal and on to La Lajita (No 13). The Morro Jable services stop all over the place and can take up to 1½ hours. The trip to Gran Tarajal takes about 30 minutes. The bus calls in at Tuineje and the beach villages between Gran Tarajal and La Lajita.

AROUND PÁJARA
The drive directly north towards Betancuria is one of the most spectacular routes on the island. While it is fair to say that Fuerteventura is quite flat when compared to the other islands to the west, you would never think

so as you wend your way through this spectacularly harsh terrain.

Ajuy & Puerto de la Peña
A 9km side trip from Pájara (there are no buses) will see you heading north-west to Ajuy and the virtually contiguous Puerto de la Peña. A dishevelled fishing settlement, its black-sand beach makes a change from its illustrious golden neighbours to the south in the Jandía peninsula. The strand is fronted by a couple of simple eateries serving up the day's catch.

CALETA DE FUSTE
Of the main resorts on the island, this is the most convenient for the airport but the least attractive. The squat little round tower (hyperbolically known as El Castillo) has been turned into an appendage of the Barceló Club El Castillo bungalow complex and the beach, while perfectly pleasant, is a poor relation compared with what's on offer at Corralejo, Jandía and even El Cotillo.

Activities
Diving Apart from lying on the beach and splashing about in the calm waters of the inlet, you could go diving with Dressel Divers Club (☎ 928 16 35 54), based at the little port. A single dive costs 3825 ptas, plus 850 ptas for full equipment hire. They also do beginners courses for PADI certification.

Windsurfing You can learn to windsurf here. Ask at the reception of the Barceló Club El Castillo complex, by the port.

Mountain Biking Also at the port, you can enquire about mountain bike hire at the Oficina del Puerto. Hire costs 1000 ptas a day or 4500 ptas for a week.

Places to Stay & Eat
As with all the resorts, the problem here is that most places fill with package guests and some deal only with tour operators.

Bungalows Beach Sol (☎ 928 16 30 01), in the El Castillo area across the FV-1

Isla de Tenerife
Top: Playa de las Teresitas, San Andrés
Bottom left: Catching the rays at Lago Martiánez, Puerto de la Cruz
Bottom right: Fisherman, Puerto de la Cruz

Isla de Tenerife
Top Left: Iglesia de la Concepción, La Orotava
Top Right: Roque Cinchado, remains of an eroded volcanic dyke, at the base of Pico del Teide
Bottom: Balconies on two modern houses built in Canaries style, Puerto de la Cruz

(about a 15-minute walk from the beach) has bungalows for two at 5500 ptas.

The *Hotel El Majay* (☎ 928 16 33 53), Tercera Avenida, Urbanización Tindaya, is a comfortable option, although the area (about a 10-minute walk to the beach) looks like a half-finished construction site – that may change of course! Rooms cost 5500/ 8300 ptas. The restaurant is mid-priced, but offers a good range of Spanish and international cuisine, including lobster thermidor and paella (2400 ptas for two).

If only because it is right on the beach, *Barceló Club El Castillo* (☎ 928 16 31 00) is top value here with bungalows for two starting at 7300 ptas.

AROUND CALETA DE FUSTE
Pozo Negro
At less than 10km south of Caleta de Fuste, this tiny fishing backwater is light years away from the resort. A couple of ramshackle restaurants front the black-sand beach (hence the name).

GRAN TARAJAL & SOUTH-EAST BEACHES
The grey-maroon beach gives locals in this surprisingly big town their own place to enjoy the ocean, but for the outsider the only attraction is being in a real Canaries town and getting away from the rarefied atmosphere of the resorts – an interesting distraction but no match for the beaches of the Jandía peninsula to the south. There are two daily buses (No 13) inland to Pájara from Monday to Saturday. The trip takes about 30 minutes.

Giniginamar & Tarajalejo
South of Gran Tarajal, these two quiet fishing hamlets go about their business largely undisturbed by tourists. The brief, grey beaches make a poor show compared with their brilliant white cousins further south – but at least they're not crowded. The No 1 bus between Puerto del Rosario and Morro Jable stops at Tarajalejo, but not in Giniginamar. The same goes for the No 4 from Pájara.

La Lajita
This unimpressive little fishing village presents yet another faintly grubby looking black-sand and pebble beach. At the southern exit of the town is one of those theme park arrangements which have so utterly overrun Fuerteventura's big sister island, Gran Canaria.

At **Zoo Parque de los Camellos** you can wander around the little zoo (900 ptas), populated by monkeys, exotic birds and other unfortunates and/or join a half hour camel trek for 1000 ptas. The zoo is open daily from 9 am to 5 pm. Bus Nos 1 and 4 stop only at the highway exit to town, from where it's a short walk south to the camels.

Península de Jandía

Most of the peninsula is protected by its status as the Parque Natural de Jandía. The south-west is a canvas of craggy hills and bald plains leading to cliffs west of Morro Jable. Much of the rest is made up of dunes, scrub and beaches.

Somewhere along this peninsula, they say, German submarine crews used to hole up occasionally during WWII. You think these beaches are paradise now – just imagine them with not a single tourist, not one little apartment block, only you and your mates from the U-boat!

According to other stories, Nazi officials passed through here after the war to pick up false papers before heading on to South America. One version has hordes of Nazi gold buried here too!

LA PARED
If on occasion you've had the feeling that you've been dropped into North Africa, it probably won't come much stronger than when you clatter into this town-planner's nightmare.

Here once began a crude stone wall (*la pared*) which marked off the boundary between the rival Guanche fiefdoms of

Maxorata and Jandía. Nothing of the wall remains, and late 20th-century civilisation has arrived with a distinct lack of style. A dirt track leads off the highway to a boulevard lined with trees, a roundabout of exaggerated proportions and then a narrower road leading into what seems like an utterly deserted Third World resort. There's nothing here but an expensive hotel and a growing scab of resort bungalows.

Rooms at the *Hotel Rey Guize* (☎ 928 54 90 04; fax 928 54 91 04) cost from 6150 ptas to 7350 ptas per person with half board, although you will probably be quoted prices in deutschmarks.

Coming back down to earth a little, *Restaurante Bahía la Pared* (signposted), down by a rocky beach, is not a bad place for fish – a meal will cost about 1700 ptas a head.

The No 9 bus between Pájara and Morro Jable passes through here.

COSTA CALMA

This is a 'Tidy Town' version of Caleta de Fuste. The beach is truly desirable and the developments are in general more tasteful. In all, it's a superior resort, but, once again, lacks a soul; its whole existence is due to tourism.

You'll find a CEM 24-hour clinic (☎ 928 87 53 00) at the south end of the resort in the Centro Comercial Botánico, Local 17, Avenida de Jahn Reisen s/n.

Places to Stay & Eat

Apartamentos Maryvent (☎ 928 54 70 92) has self-contained apartments for two to three people from 8000 ptas to 16,000 ptas. They cater above all, like many places here, to German package tourists.

Bungalows Bahía Calma (☎ 928 54 71 58) has a series of pretty bungalows located within a spit of the beach. They start at 8000 ptas for up to three occupants.

Restaurante Canario, in the Centro Comercial Costa Calma, does Canarian specialities. Another decent restaurant in the same complex is *Restaurante Arena*. You'll also find a couple of bars there.

PLAYA DE SOTAVENTO DE JANDÍA

The name refers to the line of beaches that stretch along the south coast of the peninsula. This is not surfing territory, but for swimming and sun-bathing this strand is the most beautiful in the islands (the dunes of Corralejo run a close second). There's not a lot more to be said about this coastal paradise – miles and miles of fine white sand which creeps its way almost imperceptibly into the turquoise expanse of the Atlantic.

Various driveable trails lead down off the FV-2 highway to vantage points off the beach – its generous expanses mean you should have little trouble finding a nice tranquil plot for yourself.

MORRO JABLE

• *population 6000*

Morro Jable is the southernmost town on Fuerteventura, on the eastern side of the Peninsula de Jandía.

Information

Tourist Office The Oficina de Turismo (☎ 928 54 07 76) is in the Centro Comercial de Jandía (look for the big Shopping Centre sign) on Avenida del Saladar.

Money There are several banks with ATMs on and near Calle de Nuestra Señora del Carmen. Banco de Santander, on the corner of Avenida de Jandía is just one. Bank Inter, Calle de Nuestra Señora del Carmen 9, represents the Western Union money transfer crowd for those moments of fiscal failure.

Post & Communications The central Correos y Telégrafos is on Avenida de Jandía. There's also a small phone office at Calle de Nuestra Señora del Carmen 12. The postcode for Morro Jable is 35625.

Travel Agents Several agents operate in Morro Jable, where you can book flights as well as ferry and jetfoil tickets. Halcón Viajes, Calle de Nuestra Señora del Carmen 29, is reliable.

Medical Services There are several inter-

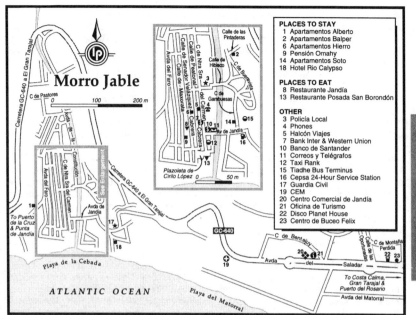

Morro Jable

PLACES TO STAY
1 Apartamentos Alberto
2 Apartamentos Balper
6 Apartamentos Hierro
9 Pensión Omahy
14 Apartamentos Soto
18 Hotel Rio Calypso

PLACES TO EAT
8 Restaurante Jandía
13 Restaurante Posada San Borondón

OTHER
3 Policía Local
4 Phones
5 Halcón Viajes
7 Bank Inter & Western Union
10 Banco de Santander
11 Correos y Telégrafos
12 Taxi Rank
15 Tiadhe Bus Terminus
16 Cepsa 24-Hour Service Station
17 Guardia Civil
19 CEM
20 Centro Comercial de Jandía
21 Oficina de Turismo
22 Disco Planet House
23 Centro de Buceo Felix

ISLA DE FUERTEVENTURA

national clinics around Morro Jable, especially along Avenida del Saladar. CEM (☎ 928 54 03 33), on Playa del Matorral, is open 24 hours.

Emergency The Policía Local (☎ 928 54 10 22) are at Calle del Hibisco 1, and the Guardia Civil (☎ 062) are just off Avenida de Jandía.

Things to See & Do
Beaches The beaches which stretch around to the east from Morro Jable are fine, and you can rent pedalos and other water-borne vehicles. As noted above, however, the pick of the beaches lie between Morro Jable and Costa Calma, and are really only accessible with some kind of transport (from car to bicycle).

Diving You can organise dives with the Centro de Buceo Felix (☎ 928 54 14 18),

Avenida del Saladar. A single dive will cost you 4000 ptas, but you get better value if you take a package (10 dives cost 33,200 ptas). These prices rise respectively to 5000 ptas and 41,500 ptas if you have to hire all the gear. They also do CMAS and FEDAS courses for beginners.

Off-Road Driving You can hire quads, which are basically four-wheeled motorbikes with fat tyres capable of tooling around on the sand, from Canaria Drive (☎ 928 54 15 84), a couple of doors west of Centro de Buceo Felix. The problem with these things, and 4WDs, is that a lot of people belt around the beaches and dunes of Playa de Barlovento de Jandía – not a very environmentally friendly activity.

Places to Stay
In the centre of the town there are a couple of what might be cheap options – there was

no sign of any life in either of them at the time of researching, but given that it ain't always easy to find budget accommodation, it's worth bearing them in mind. *Pensión Omahy* (☎ 928 54 12 54) is at Calle de Maxorata 6, and bears no sign. Also in the centre are *Apartamentos Hierro* (☎ 928 54 11 13), Calle del Senador Velázquez Cabrera 16.

Not far away, *Apartamentos Balper* (☎ 928 54 06 70), Calle de las Pintaderas s/n, has straightforward apartments with cooker and phone. Apartments for two cost 5000 ptas. *Apartamentos Soto* (☎ 928 54 14 19), Calle de Gambuesas s/n, is pretty similar.

A slight move up the ladder, *Apartamentos Alberto* (☎ 928 54 15 22), Avenida del Faro, offers apartments with kitchenette, lounge room and phone for 6000 ptas.

Heading into the interstellar range, *Hotel Riu Calypso* (☎ 928 54 00 26; fax 928 54 07 30), Carretera General de Morro Jable s/n, has rooms for 12,500 ptas per person including breakfast and all the mod cons you are likely to need.

Places to Eat
The usual resort 'international cuisine' and fast food can be had at innumerable places spread among the apartments, condos and shopping centres along Avenida del Saladar.

Something a little more interesting and with solid Spanish food is *Restaurante Posada San Borondón*, Plazoleta de Cirilo López. A full meal with wine will cost you about 2500 ptas. The main problem about this place (if you haven't noticed yet), is that it is trying to look like a steamship.

A couple of restaurants on the waterfront behind San Borondón restaurant serve average food in seaside surroundings. For earthier ambience and large serves of good Castilian cooking, try *Restaurante Jandía*, Calle del Senador Velázquez Cabrera 7.

Entertainment
For drinking, and related activities, the main scene of the action is along the beachfront part of the resort. A cluster of pubs is concentrated in the Centro Comercial de Jandía. Some of them cater to all types and age groups, but others, such as Surf Inn and Alex Café aim at a younger and later arriving crowd. When they start closing, you could head for Disco Planet House, a block east along Avenida del Saladar.

Getting There & Away
Bus The Tiadhe bus terminus is just off Calle de Gambuesas in the town centre (look for the Supermercado Padilla sign). The first bus (line No 1) for Puerto del Rosario leaves at 6 am and the last at 7 pm. The trip takes about two hours (unless you get the fast No 10 bus via the airport). The No 5 service to Costa Calma runs frequently. The No 9 to Pájara runs twice a day, and the No 4 to the same destination just once.

Sea Trasmediterránea jetfoils leave most days for Las Palmas de Gran Canaria. They take 1½ hours and cost 5600 ptas. Otherwise, take the Naviera Armas ferry for 3100 ptas. It leaves at 7 pm and takes three hours. You can get tickets at the port (1km west of the town centre) or at travel agents.

Getting Around
Taxi There is a rank in the town centre just off Avenida de Jandía.

AROUND MORRO JABLE
Punta de Jandía
Sixteen kilometres of graded but unsealed road winds out along the southern reaches of the peninsula to a lone lighthouse.

The tiny, bedraggled fishing settlement of Puerto de la Cruz, a couple of kilometres short (east) of the lighthouse, seems truly abandoned. Two little restaurants, the *Tenderete* and *Punta de Jandía*, serve up the local catch to passing tourists unable to contain their curiosity about what the island's westernmost point looks like.

Cofete
About 10km along the same road from Morro Jable, a turn-off leads north-east to this, another tiny peninsula village at the southern extreme of the Playa de Barloven-

to de Jandía. Dirt tracks lead to this wind-whipped strand which are negotiable by foot or 4WD. Food and drinks are available at the *Restaurante Cofete*.

PLAYA DE BARLOVENTO DE JANDÍA

Much wilder than their leeward counterparts, the long stretch of beaches on the windward side of the peninsula are also harder to get to. You basically need a 4WD to safely negotiate the various tracks leading into the area – but once you've found a spot you like, refrain from chopping up the dunes with your vehicle.

This stretch of the coast can get very windy – though the flying sand doesn't seem to deter the nude bathers, who are as common as the partly clothed variety. Care must be taken when swimming here: the waves and currents are altogether a different experience from the usually becalmed waters on the other side of the island.

ISLA DE FUERTEVENTURA

Isla de Lanzarote

Covering 846 sq km, Lanzarote is the fourth largest and most north-easterly of the Canary Islands. It measures only about 60km north to south and a mere 21km at its widest point east to west. It is known as the Isla de los Volcanes, with 300 cones peppered about it. The island's name is assumed to be a corruption of Lanzarotto (or Lancelotto) Malocello, the Genoese seafarer who landed on the island in the late 13th or early 14th century.

It hardly ever rains here, so all the water you use is desalinated sea water – not the tastiest stuff around, but better than cleaning your teeth with beer.

The immediate reaction of many who come to the island is that there is nothing here. True, it's a largely arid place, but bizarrely so and UNESCO has declared the entire island a Biosphere Reserve. Its largely volcanic terrain is quite unique, and those who take the time to move around the island, away from the three main resorts, will be pleasantly surprised by its stark, weird but very real beauty.

The island's approach to tourism has in no small measure been shaped by the inspiration of artist César Manrique, who died in 1992. Not only has he left his personal stamp on many of the attractions around the island, but his ideas continue to inform policy on tourism development. The near absence of high rises even in the three main resort areas, and careful adherence to traditional building styles in the interior, is largely due to Manrique's vigilance, and to that of his successors. Locals and visitors alike should be grateful such care has been maintained.

History

Lanzarote was the first of the Canary Islands to fall to Jean de Béthencourt in 1402, marking the beginning of the Spanish conquest. Along with Fuerteventura, Lanzarote was particularly exposed to frequent

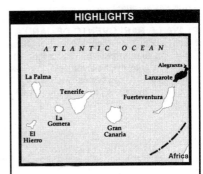

HIGHLIGHTS

- Taking a tour of the lava landscape of Las Montañas del Fuego
- Enjoying a volcanic BBQ lunch at the Restaurante del Diablo
- The beaches and coves of Punta del Papagayo
- The old town of Teguise, once the island's capital
- Visiting the bizarre and wonderful landmarks created by César Manrique
- Exploring the spectacular Cueva de los Verdes

raids by Moroccan pirates operating from ports along the north-west African coast, barely 100km away. The then-capital, Teguise, was frequently sacked and many inhabitants hauled into captivity, later to be sold as slaves. The problem was especially grave during the 16th century, and the Moroccans weren't the only source of grief. British buccaneers, like Sir Walter Raleigh, Sir John Hawkins and John Poole, also visited the island, as did French bearers of the skull and crossbones like Jean Florin and Pegleg le Clerc.

By the middle of the 17th century, misery, piracy and emigration had reduced the number of Conejeros (as the islanders are sometimes called) to just 300.

ISLA DE LANZAROTE

The massive and disastrous eruptions of the 1730s destroyed some of the island's most fertile land. Beyond the heartland of the great upheaval, though, islanders were to discover a rather ironic fact. The volcanic mix in the soil eventually proved a highly fertile bedrock for farming (particularly for wine grapes), bringing relative prosperity to the descendants of those who had fled to Gran Canaria in terror of the lava flows. Today, with tourism flourishing alongside the healthy if small agricultural sector, the island is home to 77,200, plus of course all the holiday blow-ins who at any given time can double the population.

Accommodation

There are no camping grounds or youth hostels on the island.

Most of the accommodation is made up of apartments and bungalows, and the majority of these are concentrated in the resorts of Puerto del Carmen, Playa Blanca and Costa Teguise. The problem, as in neighbouring Fuerteventura, is that the bulk of these deal with tour operators and are often full.

Arrecife is not the most fascinating capital in the world, but lone travellers with no bookings might consider it as a temporary solution if nothing else turns up.

Otherwise, there is a small spattering of alternatives at other points around the coast, and a handful of inland options.

Getting There & Away

Air After Tenerife and Gran Canaria, Lanzarote probably absorbs the third greatest intake of tourists arriving in the Canaries by air. There are some inter-island flights too.

From Guasimeta airport (☎ 928 81 14 50), 6km south-west of Arrecife, Binter has six daily flights to Las Palmas de Gran Canaria (40 minutes; 8550 ptas) and three to Tenerife Norte (50 minutes; 10,550 ptas). Air Europa also flies occasionally to Tenerife. Otherwise the traffic is made up of some regular flights (Air Europa and Spanair) from the mainland and charters from all over Europe.

Sea Ferries connect the island regularly with neighbouring Fuerteventura, and less regularly with Las Palmas de Gran Canaria.

Getting Around

Bus Arrecife Bus (☎ 928 81 14 56) provides the public transport. The service is frequent around Arrecife, especially to Puerto del Carmen and Costa Teguise. Fairly regular runs also connect with Playa Blanca in the south and such inland towns as Teguise. Otherwise services are minimal or nonexistent.

Taxi As elsewhere, you have the option of moving around the island by taxi, but it is an expensive way of doing things. The fare from Arrecife south to Playa Blanca is 4300 ptas. An excursion of the island is supposed to cost 18,000 ptas plus 1460 ptas for each hour of waiting time.

Arrecife

• *population 33,900*

The island's capital is not its best advertisement. Aside from a couple of forts, one converted into a stylish art gallery and restaurant, and a fairly decent beach, it offers little of real interest. Its handful of hotels and apartments may come in handy for those without reservations in the resorts – and to the mildly perverse among you it may even appeal simply because it's *not* in the resorts.

History

The single biggest factor behind Arrecife's blandness is probably that it only became capital in 1852. Until then Teguise ruled supreme – and the architectural heritage of that town shows what Arrecife missed out on by simply being a port for the capital.

In 1574, the Castillo de San Gabriel first went up (it was subsequently attacked and rebuilt) to protect the port. Its sister further up the coast, the Castillo de San José, was raised in 1771. A semblance of a town had only taken uncertain shape around the harbour by the close of the 18th century. As its commerce grew and the threat of sea raids dropped off in the 19th century, Arrecife thrived. The defensive imperatives for keeping the capital inland having melted away, the move to Arrecife of the island's administration was a foregone conclusion.

Orientation

The sun-blanched capital of the island presents no great navigational problems. With the notable exceptions of the Castillo de San José and port, everything of interest is located in a tight area around the centre. If you arrive by bus, you'll find yourself on the north-east flank of central Arrecife. Head right (west) along Vía Medular to the big roundabout, from where you follow Avenida de León y Castillo into the middle of town.

A series of apartments and hotels is on or near Calle del Doctor Rafael González Negrín. A trio of cheap places is clustered around Avenida de León y Castillo.

Maps The map distributed by the tourist office is quite adequate, which is a good thing, since there appear to be no alternatives.

Information

Tourist Office The Oficina de Información Turística (☎ 928 81 18 60) is in the Parque Municipal. It opens Monday to Friday from 9 am to 1 pm and 4.30 to 7.30 pm (in summer from 9.30 am to 1.30 pm and 5.30 to 7.30 pm); Saturday from 9 am to 1 pm.

Money There is no shortage of banks with ATMs near the waterfront, such as the Caja Rural de Canarias at Calle del Doctor Rafael González Negrín 2. American Express is represented by Viajes Insular (☎ 928 81 31 13), at No 13 on the same street.

Post & Communications The main Correos y Telégrafos is at Avenida del Generalísimo Franco 8. There are a few telephone offices scattered about the town. One is at Avenida de León y Castillo 53. Faxes can be sent from the post office. The postcode for Arrecife is 35500.

If you need to send or receive email, pop into Internet Lanzarote, Avenida de Fred Olsen 6 (the big building with the Opel dealership).

Medical Services The Hospital General (☎ 928 80 16 36) is north-west of the town centre on the highway to San Bartolomé. Near the beach is the Centro Medico Lansalud (☎ 928 81 58 54), Calle del Coronel I. Valls de la Torre 6.

Emergency The police (☎ 928 81 23 50) can be found at Avenida de Coll 5. For an ambulance, call the Cruz Roja (Red Cross) on ☎ 81 22 22. Otherwise, in case of medical emergency, try ☎ 928 80 30 60.

Things to See

Castillo de San Gabriel The first building of any note in what was little more than a landing point for the odd caravel from Spain, the doughty fort was sorely tested on several occasions by Moroccan corsairs and European pirates in the years after its construction in 1574.

Today it houses the **Museo Arqueológico**, a somewhat grandiloquent name for a modest collection of artefacts found on the

DAMIEN SIMONIS

Cannons at Castillo de San Gabriel, one of Arrecife's most striking landmarks

ISLA DE LANZAROTE

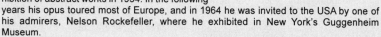

The Life & Art of César Manrique

Some Lanzaroteños will tell you César Manrique 'made Lanzarote'. Perhaps an overstatement, but the internationally renowned artist's love of his island home no doubt left many marks across its length and breadth.

Born in Arrecife on 24 April 1919, he grew up in relative tranquillity by the sea. His ancestors were of Castilian and Andalucían origin. After a stint as a volunteer with Franco's forces during the 1936-39 Civil War, he eventually followed his heart's desire and enrolled in Madrid's Academia de Bellas Artes de San Fernando in 1945. His first exhibition was actually held five years earlier in Arrecife.

Influenced but not stylistically dominated by Picasso and Matisse, he held his first major exhibition of abstract works in 1954. In the following years his opus toured most of Europe, and in 1964 he was invited to the USA by one of his admirers, Nelson Rockefeller, where he exhibited in New York's Guggenheim Museum.

But Manrique never forgot his birthplace, and after his successful US tour returned home in 1968 brimming with ideas for enhancing what he already felt to be the incomparable beauty of Lanzarote.

He started out with a campaign to preserve traditional building methods, especially in rural architecture, and another to ban the blight of advertising billboards on roadsides and across the countryside.

A multifaceted artist, Manrique subsequently turned his flair and vision to a broad range of projects across the island. In a sense Lanzarote became his canvas, living his own artistic ethos: 'To be absolutely free to create without fear or formula heartens the soul

---

island, including in the Cueva de los Verdes (see below).

To reach the promontory where the fort stands, you can cross a rather quaint drawbridge, the Puente de las Bolas.

Museo Internacional de Arte Contemporáneo Converted in 1994 by the Fundación César Manrique into an attractive home for modern art, the Castillo de San José was originally raised in the 18th century to deal with pirates and provide unemployed locals with a public-works job scheme.

The gallery is the most important collection of modern art in the Canaries. Aside from works by Manrique himself, artists such as Miró, Millares, Mompó, Oscar Domínguez, Gerardo Rueda, Sempere and Cárdena are on show. It will come as no great shock to know that Manrique designed the restaurant (which itself is well worth a visit).

The gallery is open daily from 8 am to 9 pm, and the restaurant until 1 am. Admission is free.

Playa del Reducto Arrecife has quite a respectable beach of its own, a spit away from Calle del Doctor Rafael González Negrín.

and opens a path to the joy of living'. In all, he carried out seven major projects on the island, numerous others elsewhere in the archipelago and beyond, and at the time of his death had several others on the boil.

In the north-east, he directed the works to make the grotto of the Jameos del Agua accessible to visitors without ruining the natural beauty of the spot. In the same place he directed the construction of a music auditorium in a cavern of volcanic rock.

He chose also to live, not just in harmony with, but directly amid the blue-black hardened lava flows that so characterise the island, building his house in a flow in Taro de Tahiche, about 6km north of Arrecife. Since his death in a car accident on 25 September 1992, the unusual house has served as the home to the Fundación César Manrique. Further north, the bizarre Jardín de Cactus is another of his ideas, containing 10,000 cacti of more than 1000 species. In the Montañas del Fuego he thought to turn the volcanic energy to good account. He installed the Restaurante del Diablo in this hostile terrain, where the meat is grilled using the subterranean heat.

Manrique's unstinting efforts to promote the maintenance of traditional architecture and protect the natural environment prompted the Cabildo to pass laws restricting urban development.

The growing wave of tourist development since the early 1980s has, however, threatened to sweep all before it. Manrique's untiring opposition to such unchecked urban sprawl touched a nerve with many Lanzaroteños, and led to the creation of an environmental group known as El Guincho, which has had some success in revealing and at times even reversing abuses by developers. Manrique was posthumously made its honorary president.

There is no doubting the artist's lasting influence. As you pass through villages across the island, the almost rigid adherence to certain stylistic norms in housing will hardly escape your attention. The standard whitewashed houses are adorned with green painted doors, window shutters and strange onion-shaped chimney pots. Hotels beyond the resorts are sparse and the island seems to deal with the waves of tourism in a dignified and thoughtful way, weighing up the dollars with the quality of island life (and trying not to cook the goose). In that respect, Manrique's spirit lives on.

ISLA DE LANZAROTE

Activities

Diving About 3km south of the centre of town at Playa Honda, the Club de Actividades Subacuaticas Pastinaca (☎ 928 80 52 99), Calle de Tinecheide 6 (bajo), does diving trips.

Special Events

Carnaval is celebrated here, as in the rest of the Canary Islands, with plenty of enthusiasm if not the same style as in Las Palmas de Gran Canaria and Santa Cruz de Tenerife.

The other big event of the year is the Día de San Ginés, on 25 August.

Places to Stay – budget

Pensión Arrocha 2 (☎ 928 80 24 21), Avenida de León y Castillo 98, has small singles/doubles for 2000/3000 ptas.

The cheapest deal in town, if not the entire Canary Islands, is the basic but cheerful *Hostal España* (☎ 928 81 11 90), Calle de Gran Canaria 4, where spartan rooms cost just 1400/2000 ptas. It is often full, if only because of the prices.

Hotel Residencia San Ginés (☎ 928 81 18 63), around the corner at Calle del Molino 9, is another cheap choice, with little to distinguish it from the others. Rooms come in at 2000/2500 ptas with own bath.

Better is *Hostal Residencia Cardona* (☎ 928 81 10 08), Calle del 18 de Julio 11. Rooms with bath are quite spacious and cost 3000/4500 ptas. Don't take a front room though, as they look straight across the narrow street to a noisy disco.

Places to Stay – middle

The Soviet-style *Apartamentos Arrecife Playa* (☎ 928 81 03 00), Calle del Doctor Rafael González Negrín 4, has big but somewhat depressing apartments for 5000 ptas.

Apartamentos Islamar (☎ 928 81 15 04), Calle del Doctor Rafael González Negrín 15, has spacious apartments with kitchen, TV and balcony for 6000 ptas.

The waterfront *Hotel Miramar* (☎ 928 80 15 22; fax 928 80 33 66), Avenida de Coll 2, is a slightly shabby mid-range place – it's comfortable enough though and singles/doubles go for 5017/6378 ptas.

Places to Stay – top end

Top of the line in Arrecife is *Hotel Lancelot* (☎ 928 80 50 99; fax 928 80 50 39), Aveni-

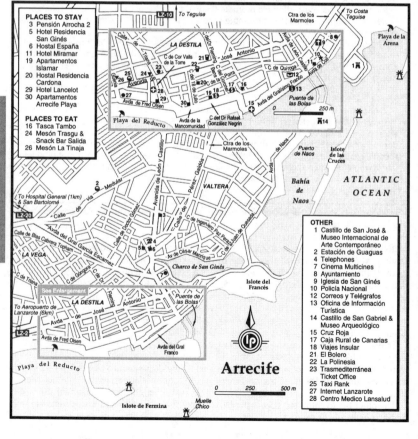

ISLA DE LANZAROTE

PLACES TO STAY
3 Pensión Arrocha 2
5 Hotel Residencia San Ginés
6 Hostal España
11 Hotel Miramar
19 Apartamentos Islamar
20 Hostal Residencia Cardona
29 Hotel Lancelot
30 Apartamentos Arrecife Playa

PLACES TO EAT
16 Tasca Tambo
24 Mesón Trasgu & Snack Bar Salida
26 Mesón La Tinaja

OTHER
1 Castillo de San José & Museo Internacional de Arte Contemporáneo
2 Estación de Guaguas
4 Telephones
7 Cinema Multicines
8 Ayuntamiento
9 Iglesia de San Ginés
10 Policía Nacional
12 Correos y Telégrafos
13 Oficina de Información Turística
14 Castillo de San Gabriel & Museo Arqueológico
15 Cruz Roja
17 Caja Rural de Canarias
18 Viajes Insular
21 El Bolero
22 La Polinesia
23 Trasmediterránea Ticket Office
25 Taxi Rank
27 Internet Lanzarote
28 Centro Medico Lansalud

Arrecife

da de la Mancomunidad s/n. Rooms here cost 7000/8800 ptas including obligatory breakfast.

Places to Eat

Arrecife appears to have a limitless appetite for pizza. If you would like something else, try the *Mesón La Tinaja*, Calle de Guenia 2, a pleasant little Castilian eating house with partly tiled walls and moderately priced food.

Tasca Tambo, Calle de Luis Morote 28, does reasonable tapas and is a popular spot.

If you feel like a culinary excursion to northern Spain, the Asturian and Basque dishes prepared by *Mesón Trasgu*, Calle de José Antonio 98, could be for you. Mains cost about 1500 ptas. If that's a little steep, you can pig out for lunch next door at *Snack Bar Salida*, where the set *menú del día* costs 900 ptas.

Calle del Doctor Ruperto González Negrín is lined with sidewalk cafés, and makes a relaxing coffee stop or breakfast destination.

Last but by no means least, the restaurant at the Castillo de San José, mentioned above, is a treat. It looks out over the water and deserves time for a relaxing tipple, if not a meal.

Entertainment

Bars For your night-time entertainment you are probably better off heading to Puerto del Carmen. If you want to mix with local young hormones and don't mind having your hearing damaged, Disco Pub No Name, Calle del 18 de Julio 10, might be the place for you. If it's not to your taste, there's a good half dozen other places nearby on Calle de José Antonio, including El Bolero at No 62 and La Polinesia on the corner of Calle del 18 de Julio.

Getting There & Away

Air For details on flights to the island, see the Getting There & Away section in the introduction to this chapter.

Bus Arrecife Bus runs services from the Estación de Guaguas on Vía Medular, near the sports stadium. Many of these also stop at Playa del Reducto. Buses run to Puerto del Carmen (40 minutes; 180 ptas) Costa Teguise (20 minutes; 130 ptas) about every half hour. Up to six a day go to Playa Blanca (1½ hours; 375 ptas), and up to seven to Teguise via Tahiche (30 minutes; 110 ptas). Two buses head north for Orzola (1½ hours; 375 ptas), from where you can get a boat to the islet of Graciosa.

Car & Motorcycle The LZ-2 is the main road leading west and eventually south of the capital, passing the airport, Puerto del Carmen and Yaiza en route to Playa Blanca. The LZ-1 leads north to Tahiche and then on to Orzola via Arrieta and Jameos del Agua. From Tahiche, the LZ-10 pushes further inland to Teguise.

If you didn't rent a car at the airport or in Playa Blanca on arrival, you have plenty of choices in Arrecife – especially around Avenida de la Mancomunidad and Calle del Doctor Rafael González Negrín.

Sea The Trasmediterránea ferry to Cádiz (mainland Spain) stops here on the way from Las Palmas. It leaves at 10 pm on Wednesday and arrives two days later.

Otherwise there are three ferries a week to Puerto del Rosario, in Fuerteventura (three hours; 1050 ptas). It proceeds thence to Las Palmas de Gran Canaria (another 10 hours; 3500 ptas from Arrecife). Naviera Armas also puts a few ferries on this run.

Puerto de los Mármoles is about 4km north-east from central Arrecife. You can get tickets at the Estación Marítima or at the Trasmediterránea office (☎ 928 81 10 19), Calle de José Antonio 90.

Getting Around

To/From the Airport Seventeen Arrecife Bus services run between the airport and Playa del Reducto (20 minutes; 100 ptas). A taxi will set you back 750 ptas.

To/From the Port The Arrecife-Costa Teguise bus calls in at the port. A taxi will cost about 400 ptas.

ISLA DE LANZAROTE

Bus A couple of local buses (*guaguas municipales*) describe circuits around town, but you are unlikely to need them.

Taxi There's a taxi rank on Calle de José Antonio. Otherwise you can call ☎ 928 80 31 04 or 928 81 27 10.

AROUND ARRECIFE
Costa Teguise

Only about 8km north-east of Arrecife, Costa Teguise is a low-rise resort next to a series of small but happy little beaches. With a few exceptions, the holiday houses, apartments and bungalows are not in overly bad taste, but the place is, like most resorts of its ilk, utterly devoid of character. There's not even a fishing village at its core to create the impression that it's anything other than a big holiday camp.

The main and most pleasant beach is Playa de las Cucharas. Those further south are blessed with unfortunate views of the ports and industry near Arrecife. The Centro Comercial Las Cucharas is a focal point for the resort.

Information There is a post office in the Centro Comercial Las Maretas. You can surf the net at Café Meral, Las Coronas, Avenida del Mar 24.

In the Lanzarote Gardens complex along Avenida de las Islas Canarias is a 24-hour medical service, Salus (☎ 900 10 01 44).

Activities You can sign up for diving at Calipso Diving (☎ 928 59 08 79), Avenida de las Islas Canarias, or Diving Lanzarote (☎ 928 59 04 07), on Playa de las Cucharas.

At Surf Club Celeste, Calle del Marajo (in the Centro Comercial Las Maretas) you can organise windsurfing lessons. A 3½-day course for beginners costs 12,000 ptas. For mountain bikes, try Trax, in the same shopping complex.

Places to Stay The *Hotel Meliá Salinas* (☎ 928 59 00 40; fax 928 59 03 11), Avenida de las Islas Canarias, stands out above all for its gardens and pools, designed by

César Manrique. You pay for these aesthetic pleasures, to the tune of 21,600/30,800 ptas. The prices include breakfast but not the IGIC tax.

If you want to be on the seaside but protect the bank account a little more, try *Apartamentos Las Cucharas* (☎ 928 59 07 00), Avenida de las Islas 14. Apartments start at 6000 ptas.

Places to Eat There is no shortage of places to eat serving whatever sort of cuisine you may want (although Spanish seems to be hard to find!). In the Centro Comercial Las Cucharas you have at your service *Texas* for Tex-Mex; *Kovklaki* for Greek and *Robinson Grill* for steaks.

Entertainment There are quite a few bars in the shopping complexes. Carabico, on the top floor of the Centro Comercial Las Maretas, is not bad for dancing and drinking later in the night.

Getting There & Away Arrecife Bus No 1 connects with Arrecife (via Los Mármoles port) regularly from 7.15 am to midnight (130 ptas).

Tahiche

Only 6km north of Arrecife, the only reason to make a halt here is to visit the Fundación César Manrique, the one-time home of the artist who on the island is seen as something of a mystical hero. He built his home, **Taro de Tahiche**, into the lava fields just outside the town. The subterranean rooms are in fact huge air bubbles left behind by flowing lava.

It is hard to imagine what it was like living here now that the place functions as an art gallery and centre for the island's cultural life.

The house is definitely worth the once over, and you can see a fair mix of works by Manrique and other modern artists, including Picasso, Chillida, Miró and Tàpies.

The Fundación opens Monday to Saturday from 10 am to 6 pm; Sunday from 10 am to 3 pm. From 1 July to 31 October it opens daily from 10 am to 7 pm. Admission costs 1000 ptas.

At least seven buses stop here on their way from Arrecife to Teguise and beyond. Get off at the Cruce Manrique (the 'Manrique Intersection') and walk 200m down the San Bartolomé road.

Teguise

This town is quite a surprise packet, an unexpected little treasure trove amid the bare plains of central Lanzarote. The island's capital until Arrecife took the baton in 1852, Teguise has preserved a fistful of monuments testifying to its leading roll in the island over the centuries.

Jean de Béthencourt's son, Maciot, moved in to what was a Guanche settlement, Acatife, and ended up living with Teguise, daughter of the one-time local chieftain. Various convents were founded and the town prospered. But with prosperity came other problems: pirates of various nationalities descended on the place several times – the only reminder of these attacks today is the ominously named Calle de la Sangre (Blood Street).

Sunday morning is market day in Teguise, which, although rather touristy, is worth a look.

Palacio Spínola Built between 1730 and 1780, this sprawling mansion only passed to the Spínolas, a prominent family on the island, in 1895. It now serves a double role as a museum and the official residence of the Canary Islands government. On the occasions when any government members do come to stay, it would appear they live very nicely, thank you. The house deserves a leisurely inspection, although much of the furnishings are clearly not precious period pieces from some long forgotten era.

It is open Monday to Friday from 9 am to 3 pm (but closed Wednesday); weekends 9.30 am to 2 pm. The price of admission is 300 ptas.

Around the Town Across the square is the rather eclectic **Iglesia de la Virgen de Guadelupe**, which has suffered numerous remodellings (leaving it in a rather confusing state) since it was first built in the 16th century.

Several monasteries dot the town, and since wandering Teguise's pedestrianised lanes is a pleasure in itself, take a stroll and keep your eyes peeled for the Franciscan **Convento de Miraflores**, the **Convento de Santo Domingo** and the **Palacio de Herrera y Rojas**.

Castillo de Santa Bárbara It is not only the oldest fort in the islands, but about the only castle worthy of the name. Perched up on Guanapay peak, 1.5km east of Teguise and with commanding views across the plains, it was erected in the 16th century by Sancho de Herrera; it was expanded in later years and then fell into disuse. Since restored, it is now the **Museo del Emigrante Canario**, housing a collection relating to the long history of migration from the islands to Spain's American colonies. The people of the Canary Islands did not always go voluntarily in search of a new life. The imperial government, under pressure in the Americas from the growing French and British incursions, felt the need to populate its occupied territories: the government organised the transfer of families to Cuba, Florida, Texas, Mexico and other colonies, where they were expected to establish new settlements.

The material is interesting, but the castle is worth a visit in its own right, if only for the great views. It is open Tuesday to Friday from 10 am to 4 pm, and weekends from 11 am to 3 pm. Admission costs 300 ptas.

Places to Eat *Restaurante Acatife*, Plaza de la Constitución, is one of several enticing places to eat here. The interior is all deep, dark timber and whitewash, and meals start at around 1000 ptas.

Restaurante La Cantina, on the corner of Calle de León and Calle de José Betancourt, is housed in the same block as the Palacio de Herrera y Rojas. A full meal will cost about 2000 ptas per person.

ISLA DE LANZAROTE

Getting There & Away Up to seven buses from Arrecife stop in Teguise en route to destinations such as Orzola and Haría.

San Bartolomé
Starting life as the Guanche settlement of Ajei, San Bartolomé ended up in the 18th century as the de facto private fiefdom of a militia leader, Francisco Guerra Clavijo y Perdomo, and his descendants. In the main church, which itself is unremarkable, are stored a number of Romanesque wooden statues.

A couple of kilometres further west of the town on the Tinajo road (just before the town of Mozaga), rises up the weird, white **Monumento al Campesino** (Peasants' Monument), erected in 1968 by (surprise, surprise) César Manrique to honour the unending and thankless labour that most of the islanders had endured for generations. In the surrounding buildings an attempt has been made to reconstruct the bucolic lifestyle; though the kind of meal you'll get at the restaurant is not a reflection of what would have been the average peasant's daily diet.

The monument and adjacent buildings are open daily from 10 am to 6 pm and admission is free. The restaurant does lunch only.

The **El Grifo Museo del Vino** is 3km south along the road to Yaiza. Here you can see wine-making instruments dating back 200 years, stroll around the 40-hectare vineyard and indulge in some wine-tasting. The museum and vineyard open daily from 10.30 am to 6 pm, and entry is free.

The North

One principal highway, the LZ-1, leads north out of Arrecife. It passes through Tahiche and then (converting to the LZ-10) Teguise (see the preceding Around Arrecife section). From Teguise the LZ-10 swings north towards Haría, while the LZ-1 forks right at Tahiche and takes you up to the north-east coast of the island.

Many of the towns are pretty, but the principal attractions are the combined work of nature and César Manrique, from lava caves to a stunning lookout point and cactus gardens.

GUATIZA
Guatiza is a fairly stock standard Conejero town 9km north of Tahiche along the LZ-1. Just outside it (east of the highway) is the **Jardín de los Cactus**, for those interested in inspecting thousands of varieties of this prickly customer. The garden is open daily from 10 am to 6 pm. Admission costs 500 ptas.

ARRIETA & PLAYA DE LA GARITA
Next up along the road is the fishing village of Arrieta. Its only attraction is the modest Playa de la Garita.

It's a quiet, unassuming little redoubt, and you can stay in one of a few little pensiones and apartments. *Casitas del Mar* (☎ 928 83 51 99), on the coast road between Arrieta and Punta Mujeres, is a discreet collection of bungalows that cost 6000 ptas for two.

Restaurante El Ancla, on the corner of Calle de Garita and Calle de la Marina, will charge you about 1200 ptas for enticing main courses of fresh fish.

The No 9 bus from Arrecife to Orzola, which only runs twice a day, calls in here.

MALPAÍS DE LA CORONA
The 'bad lands of the crown' are the living (or dead) testimony to the volcanic upsurges that shook the north of the island thousands of years ago. Flora is quietly, patiently winning its way back, and it is here that you can visit two of the island's better known volcanic caverns.

Cueva de los Verdes & Jameos del Agua
Perhaps more obviously than on any of the other islands, lava seems the hallmark of Lanzarote. So it should come as little surprise that, after the lunar wonders of the Parque Nacional de Timanfaya (see later on

in this chapter), the flow of visitors should be strongest here, at the site of an ancient lava slide into the ocean. The cavernous Cueva de los Verdes and the hollows of the Jameos del Agua (adapted by César Manrique into a kind of New Age retreat), part of the same phenomenon, are only 1km apart from one another.

Cueva de los Verdes This yawning, 1km-long chasm is the most spectacular segment of an almost 8km lava tube left behind by an eruption that occured 5000 years ago. As the lava ploughed down towards the sea (a little more than 6km of tunnel are above sea level today, and another 1.5km extend below the water's surface), the top layers cooled and formed a roof, beneath which the liquid stone continued to shift until the eruption exhausted itself.

You will be guided through two chambers, one below the other. The ceiling is largely covered with what look like mini-stalactites. In fact, no water penetrates the cave. The odd pointy extrusions are where bubbles of air and lava were thrown up onto the ceiling by gases released while the boiling lava flowed; as they hit the ceiling and air, they 'froze' in the process of dripping back into the lava stream.

In spite of the name, there is nothing green about the cave. Some 200 years ago it was considered property of a shepherd family – the Verdes! Hundreds of years before it had served as a refuge for locals during pirate assaults on the island. All sorts of evidence of their presence – from bones to tools and ceramics – have been found and assembled on display in the Museo Arqueológico in Arrecife.

Anyone with severe back problems who thinks they might not enjoy having to bend over a lot should think twice about entering the cave – there are a few passages that require you to bend over almost double to get through. The New Age music is a rather gratuitous backdrop that could probably be dispensed with.

The Cueva is open daily from 10 am to 6 pm, and entry costs 1000 ptas.

Jameos del Agua The piped New Age music continues here, where it is perhaps a little more appropriate. Great wedges of molten lava plunged through here on their way to the sea, but in this case the ocean leaked in a bit, forming the azure lake at the heart of the Jameos. Manrique's idea of installing bars and a restaurant around the lake, adding a pool, a concert hall seating 500 (with wonderful acoustics) and the didactic Casa de los Volcanes, was quite a brainwave.

Have a closer look into the lake's waters. The tiny white flecks at the bottom are crabs. Small ones yes, and the only examples known of *Munidopsis polymorpha* – blind crabs. Please take notice of the signs and do *not* throw coins into the water – the corrosion caused could kill off this unique species.

The complex is open daily from 9.30 am to 7 pm, and entry costs 1000 ptas. On Tuesday, Friday and Saturday, the bars' function becomes paramount and the place opens until 3 am. Admission after 7 pm costs 1100 ptas.

The No 9 bus between Arrecife and Orzola, which only runs twice a day, stops at the turn-off for Jameos del Agua. The Cueva de los Verdes is a further 1km walk inland. The problem is, you'd have to get the 7.40 am bus from Arrecife and wait until the 4.30 pm bus from Orzola passing back the other way (or the 3.30 pm from Arrecife on to Orzola).

Orzola

Most people just pass through this northern fishing town on their way to the Isla Graciosa. Some stop for a food break in one of the many little restaurants flanking the port, but relatively few get wind of the beach a couple of kilometres west of the town – about the only one in this part of the island, otherwise dominated by steep uncompromising cliffs. For details of the boat to the Isla Graciosa, see below.

THE MINOR CANARIES
The string of tiny islets flung out north of

ISLA DE LANZAROTE

Lanzarote are known as the Minor Canaries, and minor they certainly are. The only one you can visit is the Isla Graciosa (aka La Graciosa).

Isla Graciosa
About 500 people live on the island, virtually all of them in the village of Caleta del Sebo, which is where you alight from the Orzola boat. Behind it stretches 27.5 sq km of largely barren scrub land, interrupted by five minor volcanic peaks ranged from north to south. About a half hour walk south of Caleta del Sebo is a pleasant little beach, and there's another at the northern end of the islet.

On a windy day, Caleta del Sebo can seem a cross between a bare Moroccan village and sand-swept Wild West outpost – without anything particularly wild about it. This place is worlds away from the tourist mainstream.

There are three places to stay. *Pensión Enriqueta* (☎ 928 84 20 51), Calle de la Mar del Barlovento 6, has simple but clean doubles for 2500 ptas with private bath, or 2000 ptas without. It is a few blocks in from the port.

Near the church, *Apartamentos El Pescador* (☎ 928 84 20 36), has apartments for two people at 4000 ptas. There's no sign, so you'll have to ask which house it is. *Pensión Girasol* (☎ 928 84 21 01), about 100m left along the waterfront after you get off the boat, has rooms for 2500/3000 ptas. The two pensiones have restaurants, and on Calle de Tegala (near Pensión Enriqueta) is the Disco Pub Las Arenas for your weekend entertainment.

Líneas Marítimas Romero (☎ 928 84 20 70) runs three boats a day from Orzola in the north of Lanzarote around to the islet. The number rises to four from July to September. Tickets cost 1700 ptas return and the trip takes 20 minutes.

Other Islets
The other islets are all uninhabited. The tiniest of them, the **Roque del Este** and **Roque del Oeste**, are little more than pimples, measuring respectively 64 sq m and 15.7 sq m.

In comparison, **Isla de Montaña Clara**, the tip of a volcano poking its nose above the Atlantic waves, is a giant at 1.3 sq km.

The northernmost land mass of the Canaries is **Isla de Alegranza**, but its 10.2 sq km are uninhabited. A key landfall lighthouse operates on the island, but that's about it.

Since these islets all form part of a nature reserve, people are not supposed to set foot on them, which is one reason why no regular boats go out from Orzola. It may be you could pay a fisherman to take you, but you'd want to ask yourself why and if your desire to stamp around on them is sufficient grounds for actually doing so.

THE NORTH-WEST
Mirador del Río
About 2km north of Yé, the Spanish armed forces set up gun batteries at the end of the 19th century at a strategic site overlooking El Río, the straits separating Lanzarote from the Isla Graciosa. Spain had gone to war with the USA over control of Cuba, and you couldn't be too careful! Here the artist César Manrique left his imprimatur, converting the gun emplacement into a lookout point for tourists in 1973.

It now has a bar and souvenir stand to accompany the views. The lookout is open daily from 10 am to 6 pm, and entry costs 400 ptas.

Guinate
The village of Guinate, about 5km south of the Mirador del Río, is nothing special, but if you are a bird lover you'd better stop here for the 45,000 sq m **Tropical Park**, home to some 1300 exotic birds. Many of them are really beautiful, but the bird show – parrots on scooters etc – is a little silly. It's open daily from 10 am to 5 pm. Admission costs 1200 ptas.

Behind the park there is a fine *mirador* (lookout) overlooking El Río and the islets. The main difference between this one and the Mirador del Río is the absence of a bar and admission charge.

Haría

The shady centre of this village makes a delightful resting spot and, if the time is right, lunch or a mid-afternoon drink.

César Manrique moved into a farmhouse outside Haría after his house, Taro de Tahiche, had become untenable because of all the visitors who liked to drop by and see how he was getting on.

Restaurante Papa Loca, on Plaza de León y Castillo, has a set lunch menu for 850 ptas. *Restaurante Casa Kura*, Calle de la Encarnación Rodríguez Lasso, is another option on the road heading out of town to the north. Mains cost 1500 ptas. Several buses connect Haría to Arrecife via Teguise and Tahiche.

Famara

As a young boy, before he hit the big time, Manrique whiled away many a childhood summer on the wild beach of Famara. The scrappy seaside hamlet of La Caleta de Famara doesn't seem to have changed much in many years, and makes few concessions to tourists, apart from a couple of restaurants.

A couple of kilometres north, however, the Urbanización Famara is an inconspicuous, step-terraced arrangement of holiday homes and little else. There you can stay at *Bungalows Famara* (☎ 928 84 51 32) for 5500 ptas a night.

One bus a day connects Arrecife with La Caleta. It leaves the capital Monday to Friday at 2 pm.

Tiagua

About 10km south of La Caleta and 8km north-west of San Bartolomé, Tiagua is nothing special. But if you have an abiding interest in farm life, you may just want to call in at the **Museo Agrícola El Patio**, where people dressed in traditional peasant garb pretend the clock has stood completely still and toil away (but not too hard) on the farm. It is open Monday to Friday from 10 am to 5.30 pm, and Saturday from 10 am to 2.30 pm. Admission costs 600 ptas.

Tiagua is on the bus route from Arrecife to Tinajo. Buses to La Caleta de Famara also call in here.

La Santa

Although little more than 10km west of Famara as the crow flies, you need to detour inland via Tinajo to reach La Santa. And if you do, you may well wonder why you bothered. When you enter the village, it looks quite promising. Several spiffy little eateries line the main road, along with the odd surf shop. It's plain there is no beach here, but perhaps further on …

Well, further on (a little way north in what is known as La Isleta) is a needlessly complex warren of roads weaving through the bare volcanic soil and scrub to the rocky coast. The giant concrete mess is *Club La Santa* (☎ 928 59 99 95). It's mainly a time-share place for people seeking unlimited options for physical exertion. Indeed it claims to be the world's most famous fitness holiday centre, where Olympic athletes get themselves into shape. Doesn't sound like much fun, and anyway it is really quite an ugly place.

Four buses run here from Arrecife via Tinajo, but only Monday to Friday.

The South

PARQUE NACIONAL DE TIMANFAYA

The eruption that began on 1 September 1730 and convulsed the southern end of the island was among the greatest volcanic cataclysms in recorded history. Not only on account of the considerable amounts of molten rock which were angrily rocketed out over the countryside and into the ocean through an infernal number of craters, but because it did not let up until April 1736!

The Montañas del Fuego, which lie at the heart of this eerie 52 sq km national park, are not inappropriately named. When you reach the Manrique-designed lookout and Restaurante del Diablo at a rise known as the Islote de Hilario, try scrabbling around in the pebbles – it'll be interesting to see just how long you can hold them in your hands. At a depth of a few centimetres, the temperature is already 100°C. By the time you hit 10m, the mercury shows 600°C (that would have to be quite a thermometer!). The cause of this phenomenon is a broiling magma chamber 5km below the surface.

Some feeble (or under the circumstances perhaps rather robust) scraps of vegetation, including 200 species of lichen, are reclaiming the earth in a few stretches of an otherwise fascinatingly moribund landscape of fantastic forms and shades of black, grey, maroon and red. Fine, copper-hued soil slithers down volcano cones, arrested then by twisted, swirling and folded mounds of solidified lava – looking in parts like a licorice-addict's idea of heaven. From the Islote de Hilario the view across the lava sea punctured by volcanic cones is like a scene from a sci-fi film.

The people running the show at Islote de Hilario have a series of endearing tricks for you. In one, a clump of brushwood is shoved into a hole in the ground and within seconds is converted by the subterranean furnace into a burning bush. A pot of water poured down another hole is promptly shot back up in explosive geyser fashion.

And the restaurant is, of course, a gag in itself – whatever meat you order comes off the all-natural, volcano-powered BBQ out the back (which you may observe). The final product tastes very good.

The flesh-coloured buses with the Lanzarote tourist logo take you along the 14km Ruta de los Volcanes, an excursion through some of the most spectacular volcanic country you are ever likely to see. The trilingual taped commentary can be a bit painful at times, but it is informative. More frustrating perhaps is one's inability to abandon the bus to simply experience the awesome silence and majesty of this stony waste. The buses leave every hour or so and the trip takes about 40 minutes.

A few kilometres south along the road that traverses the eastern edge of the park is a geological museum, the Museo de las

Doubling up on a dromedary

Rocas (about 5km north of Yaiza). From here you can also go on camel rides from about 9 am to 4 pm. The museum was closed at the time of writing.

North of the park on the same road (near Mancha Blanca) is the Centro de Visitantes e Interpretación, a didactic display on the ins and outs of volcanic activity. It opens daily from 9 am to 5 pm and is free.

The main park installations are open daily from 9 am to 6 pm. The last bus trip along the Ruta de los Volcanes departs at 5 pm. Entrance, which includes the excursion and the courtesy heat displays at the Islote de Hilario, costs 1000 ptas.

You can only get into the park under your own steam or on a tour bus – which you can organise through most travel agents and the larger hotels.

INLAND & WEST COAST
La Geria
From San Bartolomé (see the preceding Around Arrecife section), the LZ-30 highway proceeds south-west through what has to be one of the oddest-looking wine-growing regions around. The vignerons of Lanzarote have found the deep, black lava-soil, enriched by the island's shaky seismic history, perfect for the grape. The further south you proceed, the more common are these unique vineyards consisting of little dugouts nurtured behind crescent shaped

stone walls, known as *zocos*, implanted in the dark earth.

The *malvasía* (Malmsey wine) produced here is a good drop and along the road you pass a good half dozen *bodegas* where you can buy the local produce at wholesale prices.

Uga Nothing much will keep you up in this little hamlet, but it may be of interest to know that the camels used for tourist rides in the Parque Nacional de Timanfaya (see above) call Uga home.

Yaiza

Yaiza is something of a southern cross-roads, so you'll probably pass through on your travels. There's no specific reason for hanging about, but if you arrive at lunch time and are feeling peckish, you'll be able to find a few pleasant enough eateries.

El Golfo & Around

The tour buses pile past this half-forgotten fishing village, which can make a pleasant alternative retreat for those uninterested in the hurly-burly of the international beach set.

Just south of the settlement begins a string of small and largely unvisited black-sand (or lava, if you prefer) beaches. The one near the Charco de los Clicos is particularly pleasant (although a little too pebbly) and protected. The Charco (pond) itself is a modest lake known for its uncanny emerald green hues. It's just in from the beach, over-shadowed by a rocky cliff. This is what the tour buses (and their occupants) are after!

If you have wheels, take the time to skittle down the coast road which eventually leads to La Hoya. On the way you will pass **Los Hervideros**, lava formations even more bizarre than the bog standard lava coastline here. After about 6km you reach the long Playa de Janubio, behind which are **Las Salinas de Janubio**, or salt pans, from which is extracted sea salt by evaporation.

There is just one little place to stay in El Golfo, and it's the charming *Hotelito del*

DAMIEN SIMONIS

La Geria wine-growing region, where *malvasía* (Malmsey wine) is produced

Golfo (☎ 928 17 32 72; 928 51 16 28). It has half a dozen doubles going for 6600 ptas. You'll find no shortage of eating options beyond the hotel, which is just at the entrance to the hamlet. On the waterfront, three eateries compete for your attention: the *Casa Torado*, *Lago Verde* and *Mar Azul*.

THE EAST COAST TO PLAYA BLANCA
Puerto del Carmen

Only about 6km south of the airport sprawls Lanzarote's premier resort, facing 3km of golden beach. It is doubtless the best beach on the island (those on Fuerteventura are, however, miles better), so it is hardly surprising that this is the biggest development on the island.

What else can you say? Walk the esplanade and you'll soon get a feel for the place from the signs: Ye Olde Spanish Inn, Pie In The Sky – For the Best in British

ISLA DE LANZAROTE

Home Cooking, Tonight! Miss Sexy Bum Elections! Says it all really.

Information The white kiosk that houses the tourist office (☎ 928 81 17 62), Avenida de las Playas, opens Monday to Friday from 9 am to 1 pm and 4.30 to 7.30 pm; Saturday from 9 am to 1 pm.

The post office is at Calle de Juan Carlos I s/n, at the western end of town.

The Bookshop, Calle de Timanfaya 4, is the best source of English-language books on the island.

If you have medical trouble, there is no shortage of private clinics. Salus (☎ 900 10 01 44), Avenida de las Playas, operates 24 hours a day. For an ambulance you could call the Cruz Roja on ☎ 928 81 22 22. The local police station (☎ 928 83 41 01) is just behind the post office.

Activities The main activity seems to be flaking out on the beach after a night's drinking. That said, you will soon notice advertisements around for excursions and courses in the usual watery activities, predominantly windsurfing, diving and deep-sea fishing. For diving, try R&C Diving Delfin Club (☎ 928 51 42 90), Centro Comercial Aquarium. For deep-sea fishing contact MA Ana Segundo (☎ 928 51 37 36). You are probably best off booking through the reception of one of the larger hotels.

Places to Stay At last count there were more than 170 hotels, apartment blocks and bungalow complexes in Puerto del Carmen. Many deal only with tour operators, but if they have a spare room going will often oblige the independent blow-in. The problem, of course, especially if you don't have transport, is finding the ones that will and that you can afford. The tourist office in Arrecife has a full list of all the establishments (the one in Puerto del Carmen can be less relied upon to have this list), which gives you the phone numbers but no indication of what category the places fall into.

There is just one standard pensión in

Puerto del Carmen. Doubles with own bath at *Pensión Magec* (☎ 928 51 38 74), Calle del Hierro 8, cost 3300 ptas, while singles are 2500 ptas.

Apartamentos Barranquillo (☎ 928 51 02 88), Calle del Ancla 1, is a short walk off Avenida de las Playas – far enough away to be insulated from the rowdiness but close enough to stumble home at the end of a long night. Apartments for one/two people start at 5000/6000 ptas. The complex has a bar and several swimming pools (for those without the strength to make it to the beach).

For a little luxury that is close to the old nucleus of town and the main happening scene along Avenida de las Playas, you could indulge yourself at *Hotel Los Fariones* (☎ 928 51 01 75; fax 928 51 02 02), Calle del Roque del Este 1. Single/double rooms cost a cool 10,250/14,600 ptas plus IGIC.

Places to Eat Among all the sauerkraut, fish and chips and other delights on offer, you'll occasionally stumble across a place offering some local cuisine. *Restaurante La Cañada*, Calle de César Manrique 3, just off Avenida de las Playas, is one such rarity.

It might be worth your while getting a taxi to *Restaurante La Finca* (☎ 928 51 35 50), on the main road from Puerto del Carmen to Mácher. It's only open for dinner and the chef often comes up with a few surprise dishes not listed on the excellent menu. Count on spending about 2500 ptas a head.

Entertainment The bulk of the bars, discos and nightclubs are lined up along the waterfront Avenida de las Playas. If you're not interested in the Miss Sexy Bum Elections, you could try Waikiki, in the Centro Comercial Atlántico, Avenida de las Playas (a little way east of the tourist office). It's popular with local ex-pats, mixing it with the tourists.

Half a dozen other bars and discos are crammed into the same complex, and there's plenty of choice up and down the street.

Getting There & Away Buses run from stops along the waterfront Avenida de las Playas to Arrecife (and some on to Costa Teguise) regularly from 7 am to midnight. The fare to Arrecife is 180 ptas.

If you intend to get a ferry to Corralejo (Fuerteventura) from Playa Blanca (see below), you might want to hop onto one of the free bus services which connect with Playa Blanca. Buses for two of the Fred Olsen ferries leave from the Varadero (the western end of Puerto del Carmen at the port). At the time of writing Naviera Armas only put on a bus (coming from Costa Teguise and Arrecife) for its first morning ferry. Pick it up from Hotel San Antonio and Apartamentos La Perla.

Puerto Calero

A few kilometres west of Puerto del Carmen, Puerto Calero is little more than a yacht harbour with a few restaurants. About the only thing that might attract you here is the chance to join a submarine safari.

The yellow submarine takes 44 passengers and generally makes three one-hour tours a day, reaching a depth of 27m. You can book through a travel agent or call direct (☎ 928 51 28 98).

Playa Blanca

Not a bad little beach and a resort that has not gotten out of control yet, but frankly you are much better off crossing the ocean to Corralejo in Fuerteventura, where the beaches and dunes put the effort here to shame. That said, the beaches at Punta del Papagayo to the east (see below) are pretty.

If it's thumping nightlife you're after, then you should push on up the coast to Puerto del Carmen.

Information The tourist office in the port is of precious little use.

Activities Again, the main activity here is to loll about on the sand or go for a soothing splash in the briny.

The main beach is about a 1km stroll along the waterfront east from the port. Do not stop at the tiny rock-and-sand beach you first encounter. About the only building of note is the Supermercado Papagayo.

Places to Stay & Eat One of the cheapest places to stay is *Apartamentos Gutiérrez* (☎ 928 51 70 89), Calle de la Plaza 8. It's just by the church in the town and is nothing flash, but apartments start at 4000 ptas.

For something more stylish, *Apartamentos Bahía Blanca Rock* (☎ 928 51 70 37; fax 928 51 70 55), Calle de Janubio s/n, has comfortable apartments for two in a complex just off Avenida del Papagayo and a 100m stroll from the main beach. They cost 8500 ptas.

Restaurante El Almacen de la Sal, Paseo Marítimo 12, is an excellent waterfront restaurant. The fish dishes are the pick and, although they can set you back up to 2000 ptas, are worth every peseta. It's about halfway between the port and the main beach.

Getting There & Away Up to six buses (three on Sunday) depart daily for Arrecife via Puerto del Carmen. The ticket to Arrecife costs 375 ptas.

Líneas Fred Olsen ferries connect with Corralejo, in Fuerteventura, four times a day. The tickets cost 1800 ptas and the crossing takes about an hour. The competition comes from Naviera Armas, which has five daily ferry departures at 1700 ptas a head.

Free buses from Puerto del Carmen (9 am and 5 pm) take you to meet the 10 am and 6 pm Fred Olsen ferry departures. Similarly, a free bus operates from Costa Teguise (Aparthotel Albatros), Arrecife (Hotel Lancelot) and Puerto del Carmen (Hotel San Antonio and Apartamentos La Perla) for the 9 am Naviera Armas ferry.

Punta del Papagayo

The south-east coast leading up to Punta del Papagayo is peppered with a series of pretty golden-sand coves, Playa de las Mujeres, Playa del Pozo, Playa del Papagayo and Caleta del Congrio.

They can be reached by a dirt trail heading east of Playa Blanca, or on a boat organised by Atoxa Excursiones (☎ 989 74 30 43) from the port. The boat does the run up to four times a day and the return trip costs 1300 ptas. At least one other boat company runs competition excursions there for the same price.

Isla de Tenerife

The largest island in the archipelago (2034 sq km), Tenerife is also the highest. The Pico del Teide, at 3718m, is in fact Spain's tallest peak. The barren east coast contrasts starkly with the rich green north-west, and the vertigo-inducing cliffs of the north seem worlds away from the international holiday beach playgrounds of Playa de las Américas and the south-west.

The bulk of the population of 655,652, known in the local slang as los Chicharreros after the *chicharros* (horse mackerel) once favoured by the islands' fishermen, is concentrated in the north. Half of them occupy the adjacent cities of Santa Cruz (the island and provincial capital) and the university city of La Laguna, 10km away. The latter is a pearl of urban elegance, and there is something for everyone on the island – from whale-spotting to hiking, from nightclubbing to bird-watching.

The main drawback with the place is the sheer volume of tourists pouring through. Luckily, most of them stick to the southern resorts and Puerto de la Cruz, making it possible elsewhere to feel you really are in Spanish territory and not a sunny version of Millwall or Munich. And if it does all get a bit much, you can easily escape westwards to the province's other islands, as yet not nearly as saturated.

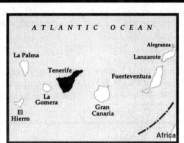

HIGHLIGHTS

- Climbing the volcanic peak of the Parque Nacional de las Cañadas del Teide for breathtaking vistas
- Letting your hair down for Carnaval, second only to Rio de Janeiro's
- The charming old mansions of La Laguna
- Journeying through La Laguna's student bars, late into the night
- Walking or driving through the Anaga mountains, winding up with the surf and a meal on the Playa de San Roque
- Watching the sun set from Masca, a village with a stunning location
- Roaming the streets of La Orotava's atmospheric old town

History

Tenerife was the last island to fall to the Spanish, and the Guanches did not give up without a fight (see History in the Facts about the Islands chapter). The island's name appears to have been coined by the people of La Palma, who knew it as Tinerife – White Mountain (from *tiner*, mountain, and *ife*, white) – since all they could usually see was the snow-capped peak of Teide.

Tenerife, like its neighbour and competitor Gran Canaria, soon attracted a big chunk of the settlers coming from Spain, Portugal, Italy, France and even Britain.

As elsewhere in the islands, sugar became the main export crop, then followed by wine as South American sugar undercut the market. A lot of the wine was produced on Tenerife, giving it an enviable edge over the other islands. So much so that, even when the importance of the wine trade diminished, the island's overall dominance remained intact until well into the 19th century. This prompted Madrid to declare Santa Cruz, by then the island's main port, the capital of the Canaries in 1821. The good and the great of Las Palmas remained incensed about this for a century, until Madrid finally decided to split the archipelago into two provinces, with Santa Cruz the provincial capital of Tenerife, La Palma, La Gomera and El Hierro. Today, Santa Cruz shares the duties of regional capital of all seven islands with its eternal rival, Las Palmas.

Maps

The Editorial Everest map (green cover) of the island (1:150,000) with street plans of Puerto de la Cruz, La Laguna, La Orotava,

Playa de las Américas and other spots is not a bad investment.

Activities

The whole gamut of sports, from diving to sailing, fishing to windsurfing, is available on the island. Most of the activity is concentrated in and around the resort area of Playa de las Américas.

Hiking is another possibility. There are 21 marked trails through the Parque Nacional de las Cañadas del Teide, and ICONA publishes simple hiking maps for

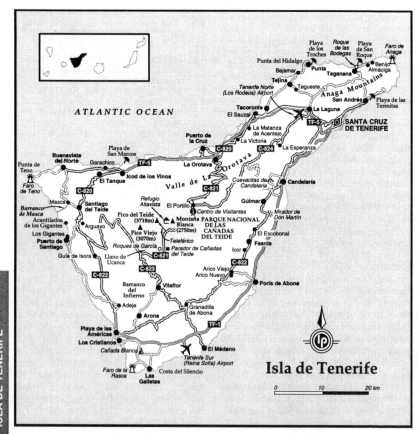

other areas, such as the Anaga mountain area in the north-east and around the Valle de la Orotava – the tourist office in Santa Cruz stocks some of these.

Accommodation

While finding a room is generally not such a problem in Santa Cruz and the northern half of the island, the same cannot be said for the resort areas of the south, particularly around Los Cristianos and Playa de las Américas. Arriving here at night without a reservation can be a dodgy business, even in low season. It can be a trial finding an expensive room, let alone something modest!

Cañada Blanca has the only established camping ground on the island (near Las Galletas in the south). However, there are 17 other sites around the island where camping is possible if you have official permission. Ask at the tourist office in Santa Cruz de Tenerife or call ☎ 922 27 81 00 or ☎ 922 63 04 88.

If you are interested in staying in farmhouses either on Tenerife or the other islands of the province (La Palma, La Gomera and El Hierro), you might like to contact *Alojamientos Rurales* (☎ 922 24 08 16), Calle de Villalba Hervás 4. They have a Web site at cip.es/aecan.

Getting There & Away

Air There are two airports on the island, with flights to all the other islands (except La Gomera, where the airport is still under construction), the Spanish mainland and a host of international destinations.

Tenerife Sur All international charter flights use the modern Reina Sofia airport (☎ 922 77 00 50), about 20km east of Playa de las Américas. Most scheduled direct international flights and some flights to mainland Spain also use this airport.

Here you will find: a half dozen car rental offices; a post office; several banks, ATMs and exchange booths; and a modest tourist information office. TITSA Bus No 487 departs more or less hourly for Los Cristianos (225 ptas) and Playa de las Américas

(250 ptas) from 8.10 am to 10 pm. It's about a 20-minute ride. Bus No 341 departs hourly from 6.50 for Santa Cruz (about 1½ hours; 700 ptas). Taxis to Los Cristianos and Santa Cruz respectively cost about 2000 ptas and 6000 to 7000 ptas. They do multihire, but charge per person in this case.

Tenerife Norte The remainder of scheduled international and mainland flights use the older and smaller Los Rodeos airport (☎ 922 25 79 40). This is also where practically all inter-island flights arrive. There is an exchange booth, some car rental reps, a bar and an information desk where you can get a map of Santa Cruz but little else.

TITSA bus Nos 063, 102, 107 and 108 all head into Santa Cruz (20 minutes; 150 ptas). No 062 goes to La Laguna, only 3km away. Heading west of the airport, they connect with La Orotava (Nos 062 & 063), Puerto de la Cruz (Nos 102 & 103) and Icod de los Vinos (Nos 107 & 108). Bus No 340 stops at the airport on its way between Puerto de la Cruz and Reina Sofia, the Tenerife Sur airport.

A taxi into Santa Cruz from Tenerife Norte costs around 1500 ptas. The fare to Puerto de la Cruz is around 3000 ptas.

Sea For details of the weekly ship from Cádiz in mainland Spain, see the Getting There & Away section.

There are regular ferry, hydrofoil and jetfoil services from Tenerife to all the other islands. Details appear in the Getting There & Away sections of the appropriate destinations throughout the chapter.

Getting Around

Bus TITSA (Transportes Interurbanos de Tenerife SA) buses run all over the island, as well as providing the local bus service in the capital, and other major centres. If you intend to use the buses a lot, get a Bonobus card. These cost 2000 ptas and are used instead of buying normal tickets. You actually pay about 30% less per trip this way; insert the card in the machine on the bus, tell the driver where you are going and the amount is subtracted from the card. The card is good for any trip, intercity or local, throughout the island. It also gives you half price entry into some of the island's museums.

If you stick with normal tickets, these are always bought on the bus itself.

Taxi Taxis will take you anywhere you want on the island – but it is an expensive way to get around. You are better off hiring a car.

Santa Cruz de Tenerife

• *population 200,100*

Capital of the island and the province of the same name (taking in La Palma, La Gomera and El Hierro), Santa Cruz de Tenerife is a bustling port city – one of the busiest in all Spain. The long harbour gives protection to countless container ships, cruise liners and a host of inter-island ferries and jetfoils. It is interesting enough for a day or so, although somewhat short on sights. With good bus transport it makes a sensible base for exploring the north-east of the island, and at least here you feel you are truly in Canario territory, not the land of full English breakfasts and sauerkraut.

History

Alonso Fernández de Lugo landed here in 1494 to embark on the conquest of the toughest and last remaining island in the archipelago. But Santa Cruz de Santiago, as it was then known, got off to a slow start. La Laguna, a few kilometres inland, blossomed as the island's capital, and Santa Cruz remained a backwater until its port flourished in the 18th and 19th centuries. Only in 1803 was Santa Cruz 'liberated' by royal decree from the municipal control of La Laguna, and in 1859 it was declared a city. From then on Santa Cruz never looked back, its port giving it an advantage La Laguna could never match.

Orientation

Taking Plaza de España as a centre point, everything of interest lies within a kilometre or less. At the western extreme is the Estación de Guaguas, where you'll arrive by bus, and to the north-east the terminal for jetfoils from Las Palmas. With the exception of the Museo Militar (near the jetfoil terminal), most of the handful of sights and good shopping lie within the central grid of streets which lead inland from Plaza de España. The tourist and post offices are

Father of Gestalt

In 1913, at the age of 26, the German psychologist Wolfgang Köhler left the hothouse of the European academic world and migrated to the Canary Islands, where he took up a post at the Prussian Academy of Sciences in Tenerife.

Born in Tallinn, Estonia, and educated in Berlin and Frankfurt, Köhler launched the Gestalt theory of psychology, which attempts to understand learning, perception and other mental processes in terms of structured wholes.

When in 1913 he elected to leave behind his colleagues (including Kurt Koffka and Max Wertheimer) for sunnier climes, did he have an inkling of the madness that was about to befall the European continent, or was he just plain lucky? In any event, he pursued his studies in Tenerife for the next seven years, investigating among other things chimpanzees' capacity for problem solving and constructing simple tools.

His findings were eventually brought together in his ground-breaking *Intelligenzprüfungen an Menschenaffen* (*The Mentality of Apes*), published in 1917, as well as other books. In 1921 he returned to Berlin but, no great fan of a rather different and unpleasant kind of chimp – Adolf Hitler – he migrated to the USA in 1935.

right on Plaza de España. Mid-level hotels are here too, but cheapies and luxury jobs are more widely scattered.

The city is divided by the Barranco de los Santos, a dry ravine. Apart from the bus station, stadium and produce market, little of interest is to be found south-west of the divide.

Maps The small city centre map handed out by the tourist office is refreshingly accurate.

Information

Tourist Office The Oficina de Información Turística (☎ 922 60 55 92) is in the Cabildo Insular de Tenerife, Plaza de España s/n. It opens from 8 am to 6 pm Monday to Friday, and from 9 am to 1 pm Saturday. They have quite a lot of information and most staff speak English and one or two other languages besides Spanish. The postcode for Santa Cruz de Tenerife is 38080.

Foreign Consulates For a list of foreign consulates in Santa Cruz, see the Embassies section in the Facts for the Visitor chapter.

Money There are banks all over the centre of town, most with user-friendly ATMs. A few are located on the map.

Post & Communications The main post office is on Plaza de España. For phones, try the *locutorio* at Paseo de las Milícias de Garachico 3. It opens from 9 am to 2 pm and 4 to 10 pm Monday to Friday, from 9 am to 2 pm and 4 to 8 pm weekends and holidays. You can send faxes from the post office.

Email You can get onto the Net at Bar Ciber El Navegante, Callejón del Combate 12.

Travel Agencies The city is fairly swarming with travel agencies. A reliable firm is Halcón Viajes (☎ 922 24 93 71) – they have a branch at Plaza del General Weyler 9.

Viajes del Rosal (☎ 922 22 24 45), Avenida de Bélgica 3, specialise in travel to

Cuba and also organise tours around Tenerife.

Newspaper The *Weekly Canarian* is a useful little paper that you can pick up free at the tourist office (or pay 150 ptas for at newsstands).

Bookshops Canary Books Librería, Calle del General Porlier 79, is about as good as you'll find for novels in English, French and German in Santa Cruz.

One of the best bookshops throughout the islands for books on the Canary Islands must be Librería Goytec, Calle de Pérez Galdós 15. The whole upstairs floor is devoted to every possible word written in, and, or about the islands. Of course nearly all of it is in Spanish, but if you intend to become an authority on the islands, this is where to buy your book collection – they have everything from the most obscure historical treatises to cook books, studies of flora, geography and Canarian literature.

Laundry The Lavandería Autoservicio at Calle de San Antonio 59 is the only self-service laundrette in Santa Cruz. It opens from 9 am to 1 pm and 5 to 7 pm Monday to Friday, 8 am to noon Saturday. A 4kg load will cost 1500 ptas to wash and dry in an hour.

Medical Services The best hospital is the Hospital de Nuestra Señora de la Candelaria (☎ 922 60 20 00), off the TF-5 highway towards La Laguna. A 24-hour doctor's service operates at Hospiten Rambla (free phone ☎ 902 20 01 44), Rambla del General Franco 115.

Emergency For an ambulance you can call the Cruz Roja (Red Cross) on ☎ 922 28 18 00. The Policía Nacional is at Avenida del Tres de Mayo 32.

Museums

There are three museums you may want to have a look at while in Santa Cruz. The **Museo de la Naturaleza y El Hombre**, re-opened in late 1997 and easily the most

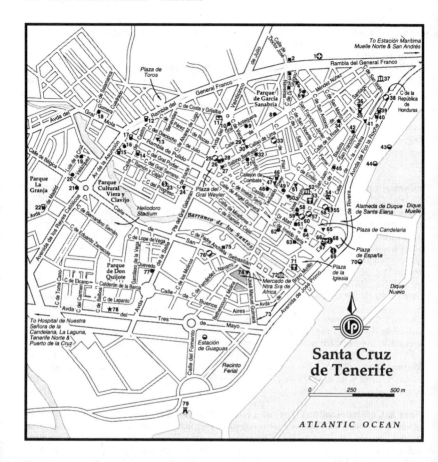

Santa Cruz
de Tenerife

ATLANTIC OCEAN

interesting, houses several Guanche mummies and skulls, a handful of artefacts including pottery, and a nicely arranged natural sciences section. The museum is in a former hospital on the corner of Calle de San Sebastián and Avenida de Bravo Murillo. It is open from 10 am to 8 pm daily except Monday. Admission costs 400 ptas (200 ptas for bearers of TITSA Bonobus cards; 100 ptas for students), but is free on Sunday.

The **Museo de Bellas Artes**, on Plaza del Príncipe de Asturias, is home to an eclectic mix of paintings by Canarian and Flemish artists (including Bruegel), as well as sculpture, a weapons collection and old coins. It is open from 10 am to 7.30 pm (in summer it closes for an hour at 1.30 pm), Monday to Friday. Entry is free.

Finally, war buffs might want to check out the **Museo Militar de Almeyda**, on Calle de San Isidro. The most famous item here is El Tigre (The Tiger), the cannon which blew off Nelson's arm when he attacked Santa Cruz. It opens from 10 am to 2 pm daily except Monday, and admission is free.

PLACES TO STAY
2 Hotel Mencey
3 Hotel
   Contemporáneo
7 Hotel Taburiente
31 Casa de Huéspedes
   Casablanca
32 Pensión Valverde
34 Pensión Mova
42 Pensión Rivera
45 Pensión Cejas
59 Hotel Atlántico
61 Pensión Oviedo
63 Hotel Anaga
64 Hotel El Dorado
75 Hotel Tanausú

PLACES TO EAT
4 Mesón El Portón
6 Sidrería Mariano
13 La Latería
24 Bar/Restaurant
27 Mesón
   Castellano
28 Platillo Volante
29 Restaurante Vu-Do
30 Mesón Treinta
   y Ocho
36 Bar Cristóbal
41 Bar 3 de Mayo
47 Mesón del Duque
50 Cafeteria El Aguila
51 Café del Príncipe
65 Plaza de Candelaria;
   Terrazas
74 Bar Mercado

OTHER
1 Hospiten Rambla
5 Lavandería
   Autoservicio
8 Kids' Swings and
   Terrazas
9 Ayuntamiento
10 Gobierno de
   Canarias
11 Correos y Telégrafos
12 Terrazas
14 Bar Sucre
15 Cervecería Rhin
16 Canary Books
   Librería
17 Metro
18 Multicines Price
19 Multicines Greco
20 Multicines Oscar's
21 Viajes del Rosal
22 Discoteca Ku
23 Deutsche Bank
25 UK Consulate &
   Barclays Bank
26 Halcón Viajes
33 Italian Consulate
35 Cueva de
   Tinguaro
37 Museo Militar de
   Almeyda
38 Norwegian, Swedish &
   Danish Consulates
39 Tam Tam
40 Nooctua
43 Trasmediterránea
   Ferry Departures

44 Estación Marítima
   Muelle Ribera &
   Líneas Fred Olsen
   Ferry Departures
46 Bar Ciber El
   Navegante
48 Librería Goytec
49 ICONA
52 Museo de Bellas Artes
53 Iglesia de
   San Francisco
54 Locutorio
55 Barclays Bank
56 Belgian Consulate &
   Alojamientos Rurales
57 Austrian Consulate
58 Discos Manzana
60 Irish Consulate
62 Teatro Guimer
66 Correos y Telégrafos
67 015 Bus to La Laguna
68 Centro de Iniciativas y
   Turismo
69 Tourist Office
70 Naviera Armas Ferry
   Departures
71 Iglesia de la
   Concepción
72 Museo de la Natu-
   raleza y El Hombre
73 Rastro (Sunday Flea
   Market)
76 French Consulate
77 Canarias Trekking
78 Policía Nacional
79 Castillo de San Juan

Around the Centre

Apart from the museums, there is really not an awful lot to see in Santa Cruz. It is a busy port city (and one of Spain's most important in terms of tonnage) and simply meandering around the place is a pleasant way to while away the day. Starting a wander from the waterfront Plaza de España, whose centrepiece is a somewhat controversial memorial to the fallen of the 1936-39 Civil War, you could head inland along Plaza de la Candelaria and the pedestrianised shopping strip of Calle del Castillo. A right turn along Calle de José Murphy will, after a couple of blocks, bring you to the Museo de Bellas Artes and, next door, the **Iglesia de San Francisco**, a baroque church built in the 17th and 18th centuries.

Three small blocks south-west of Calle del Castillo is the city's 19th-century **Teatro Guimerá**, whose austere façade belies a rather sumptuous interior. Back towards the waterfront, on Plaza de la Iglesia, rises the striking bell tower of the city's oldest church, the **Iglesia de la Concepción**. The present church dates to about the same era as the Iglesia de San Francisco, but the original building went up in

ISLA DE TENERIFE

DAMIEN SIMONIS

Construction of the Iglesia de la
Concepción began in 1498

1498. Dominating the altar is the silver
Santa Cruz de la Conquista (Holy Cross of
the Conquest), which gave the city its name.
Check out the anteroom to the sacristy (to
the right of the altar).

The retablo in the side chapel was carved
from cedar on the orders of Don Matías
Carta, a prominent personage who died
before it was completed – he lies buried
here and the pallid portrait on the wall was
done *after* his death (hence the closed eyes
and crossed arms).

About another 10-minute walk south-
west along the waterfront brings you to the
17th-century **Castillo de San Juan**. In the
shadow of this protective fort there used to
be a lively trade in African slaves.

When you've had enough of all that,
make for the pretty **Parque de García
Sanabria**, where kids will be delighted
with slides and rides and you can sit down
for coffee at a shady terraza table.

Language Courses
If the university at La Laguna doesn't
appeal, enquire at the Escuela Oficial de
Idiomas (☎ 922 28 37 12), Calle de Rubens
Marichal López 12.

Organised Tours
Viajes del Rosal (see Travel Agents above),
is one of several agents which organise

tours of the island and to Tenerife's smaller
cousins, La Gomera and El Hierro.

Canarias Trekking (☎/fax 922 20 10 51),
Calle de Quevedo 1, organises hikes all
over the island. Their Web site is at: canari-
astrekking.com.

Special Events
Carnaval is *the* event in Santa Cruz,
throughout the island, and, for that matter,
the Canarian fiesta par excellence, in most
people's eyes. Only Rio de Janeiro does it
better, and even that famous party doesn't
overshadow Santa Cruz's efforts by a great
deal. The fun begins in early February and
lasts about three weeks. Many of the gala
performances and fancy dress competitions
take place in the Recinto Ferial (fair
grounds), but the streets, especially around
Plaza de España, burst into a frenzy of out-
landish activity as the whole island seems to
participate in masked balls and an almost
permanent state of good-natured frivolity.
Needless to say, finding a place to stay anywhere in Tenerife at this time without an
advance booking is a rather tall order.

The founding of the city is celebrated on
3 May, but this a sober affair in comparison
to the Carnaval.

Places to Stay – budget
For a city its size, there are not too many
budget places to get a bed. If you arrive by
air, call from the airport and try to secure a
room before coming into the centre and
simply wandering around. The problem
with most of the dirt cheap places is that
they are none too inviting.

Casa de Huéspedes Casablanca (☎ 922
27 85 99), Calle de Viera y Clavijo 15, has
tiny, cell-like singles/doubles for 2500/3800
ptas. The communal bathrooms can be a
little on the nose, the beds are more like
hammocks and the place is noisy. Still, it's
bearable. The nearby *Pensión Valverde*
(☎ 922 27 40 63), Calle de Sabino Berthelot
46, is a rather unfriendly locale and often
full. They charge 2500/3500 ptas.

Pensión Cejas (☎ 922 28 18 72), at Calle
de San Francisco 47, is a fairly gloomy

Vegetation of Isla de la Palma

DAMIEN SIMONIS

Playa de la Rajita, La Dama, southern Isla de la Gomera

The Luck of the Irish

On 12 January 1809, Leopoldo O'Donnell saw the light of day in Santa Cruz de Tenerife. Strange name for a Spaniard, let alone a Canario? Well, yes. Little Leopoldo was a descendant of the O'Donnell family, one of many Irish clans which fled the Emerald Isle after the disaster of the Battle of the Boyne back in 1690 (the street name José Murphy is a little hard to swallow, and O'Shanahan is another good Canario name!).

Perhaps it was a bit of the Blarney and some fighting Irish spirit which set Leopoldo on the road of the soldier-politician. He, like just about anyone else hoping to make a mark in the Spanish world in those days, headed for the mainland just as soon as he could. A staunch conservative and partisan of Queen Isabel II, he played a distinguished role in the First Carlist War (1833-39), after which he ended up exiled in France. However, O'Donnell was destined to have more comebacks than Lazarus, and in 1843 he helped stage a coup to oust the government of General Baldomero Espartero. O'Donnell's prize was the captaincy-general of Cuba, which he held from 1844 to 1848.

He was soon back in Madrid, and in 1854 staged yet another revolt – from which he emerged as minister for war. Heading the government again was Espartero, but O'Donnell eased him out two years later and became prime minister. He lasted only for few months, but returned to power in 1858, and remained there for five years. During that time Spain remained uncharacteristically stable and O'Donnell made a name for himself in the war in Morocco, eventually receiving the title Duque de Tetuán.

After a break from leadership, he returned to head the government in 1865-66, but Queen Isabel was displeased by his comparatively conciliatory approach towards the opposition. She may well have regretted her decision to replace him, one of her most faithful supporters; O'Donnell saw fit to leave the country, and died the following year in Biarritz in the French Basque Country. Isabel lost her throne a year later.

place, and only offers double rooms at 4000 ptas.

Pensión Rivera (☎ 922 24 99 32), Calle de San Martín 6, has slightly better rooms for 3500 ptas. A further improvement is *Pensión Mova* (☎ 922 28 32 61), up the road at No 33. Just for a change, they have singles too. Rooms cost 1700/3200 ptas.

Hotel Anaga (☎ 922 24 50 90), Calle de Imeldo Serís 19, is a little ragged around the edges, but the rooms with private bath and shower are big and have a phone. They cost 3200/5400 ptas (plus 4.5% IGIC) for singles/doubles in low season, or 4200/6900 ptas in high season. If you have the few extra pesetas, this is the hotel of choice in its range.

If all else fails, *Pensión Oviedo* (☎ 922 24 36 43) at Calle del Doctor Allart 24 has doubles for 3000 ptas.

Places to Stay – middle

Hotel Tanausú (☎ 922 21 70 00), Calle de Padre Ancieta 8, is OK but a little pricey for what you get at 4000/6000 ptas. Much better is *Hotel Taburiente* (☎ 922 27 60 00), Calle de José Naveirs 24A. The rooms have TV, phone and private bath, are nicely maintained and start at 7800/8500 ptas.

More central is *Hotel Atlántico* (☎ 922 24 63 75), Calle del Castillo 12, where singles/doubles cost 6000/8000 ptas.

Places to Stay – top end

Hotel El Dorado (☎ 922 24 31 84), Calle de la Cruz Verde 24, is also central, but charges a hefty 10,500 ptas for doubles.

A much better deal is *Hotel Contemporáneo* (☎ 922 27 15 71; fax 922 27 12 23), Rambla del General Franco 116, where singles/doubles start at 6500/8500 ptas.

If it's class you want and money is no object, head for *Hotel Mencey* (☎ 922 27 67 00; fax 922 28 00 17), Calle del Doctor José Naveiras 38. Here you can pay up to 24,500 ptas for a double.

Places to Eat

Breakfast You probably wouldn't go out of your way for it, but *Bar 3 de Mayo*, Calle de la Marina 93, is not bad for breakfast, especially with all the great juices on offer (papaya, strawberry etc).

Better still for the juices and fruit shakes is *Platillo Volante*, Calle de Callao de Lima 3. Actually, they are great at any time of day!

Restaurants If cheap is the main requirement, you need to search out bars with a comedor attached. The sign 'comidas caseras' (home-cooked meals) is a good lead. *Bar Cristóbal*, Calle de la Rosa 75 is one such place. The food is filling and won't set you back more than 1000 ptas.

The *Mesón del Duque*, Calle de Teobaldo Power 15, has wine barrels for tables and a fine old wooden bar – a perfect spot for a glass of red and a ración of tortilla con chorizo – or head to the restaurant out the back and try a plate of gambas al Duque con champiñones y jamón (prawns with mushrooms and ham) for 1250 ptas.

Restaurante Vu-Do, Calle de Viera y Clavijo 44, is a so-called Vietnamese spot, although a lot of the food looks like your average international Chinese fare. It's a pleasant enough place to eat though, and makes a change.

Down the road at No 38, *Mesón Treinta y Ocho* is an elegant place where fine Canarian food is prepared – do not expect to get away for much less than 2000 ptas.

A little more down-to-earth is *La Latería*, an attractively decorated old Canarian house, with lots of exposed wood beams, at Calle de Benavides 32. This place gets pretty lively at lunch time.

The unnamed bar/restaurant right on Plaza de Pedro Schwartz is popular. The food is average but the shady location a big plus.

Sidrería Mariano, Calle de Méndez Núñez 33, is the place to go if you're hankering for an Asturian (northern Spanish) style cider to wash down your meal.

Mesón El Portón, Calle del Doctor Guigou 18, is a swanky sort of eatery with fine food at fine prices – mains start at around 1400 ptas. Also a little pricey but highly regarded is *Mesón Castellano*, Calle de Callao de Lima 4.

Cafés & Terrazas Cafés are strewn all about the city. Because of the pleasant climate, many have tables set up outside and make great places to sip and watch.

Café del Príncipe, right on the leafy Plaza del Príncipe de Asturias, is a lovely setting for a coffee or cocktail. *Cafetería El Aguila*, on Plaza del Alférez Provisional, is another lively spot.

Among the terrazas, pleasant places to while away your time include those on Plaza de la Candelaria and Rambla del General Franco (near the Plaza de Toros); the shady one on the edge of the Parque de García Sanabria.

On Sundays, a great place to hang out is *Bar Mercado*, right amid the flea market on Calle de José Manuel Guimerá.

Entertainment

Cinema Three cinema complexes keep the locals happy. Your only hope of seeing undubbed (*versión original – VO*) movies is at Multicines Price (☎ 922 28 94 59), Calle de Salamanca 16. Otherwise, mainstream Hollywood movies, dubbed into Spanish, can be seen at Multicines Oscar's, Avenida de Bélgica 8-10; and Multicines Greco, Calle de Luis de la Cruz 1. Occasionally the Caja Canarias bank sponsors art house film cycles – keep your eyes on the local papers for details.

Bars, Pubs & Discos Bar Sucre, Calle de Castro 15, is a busy little hangout, and usually packed with locals and serving up good arepas should you need food with your beer.

If you like the rough, spit-and-sawdust

edge of neighbourhood bars, the Cueva de Tinguaro, Calle de la Rosa 72, is a personal favourite. There is not really anything to recommend this place – unless you feel like a bit of local grit, beer swilling and mixing with loud patrons.

Otherwise, there are two or three concentrated areas of *marcha*. There's a bunch of bars at Plaza de Isabel II (also signposted as the continuation of Calle de San Vicente Ferrer), and more along Calle de Ramón y Cajal. If you are dying for a Guinness then head for Cervecería Rhin at No 74.

However, the peak of the nightlife takes off from about 2 am along Avenida de Francisco La Roche, around Calle de la República de Honduras. Tam Tam at No 39 and Nooctua next door at No 37 are both good.

Of the four discos around town, the only vaguely handy (and more popular) one is Discoteca Ku, Avenida de Madrid s/n (it's actually in the Parque La Granja).

Theatre & Classical Music The city's main centre for the presentation of high brow entertainment, whether music or theatre, is the Teatro Guimerá (☎ 922 29 08 38), on Calle de Imeldo Serís. The biggest event on the serious music calendar is the Festival de Música de Canarias, held annually in January-February.

Live Music Big name acts tend to perform at the Plaza de Toros or the Recinto Ferial. Ask at the tourist office if anything is on and how to get tickets, as often a bank such as La Caixa becomes the temporary box office for such events. Discos Manzana, a record store at Calle de José Murphy 2, often sells tickets to the big gigs.

Spectator Sport
Football Santa Cruz is home to the only Canaries team in the first division, CD Tenerife. You need to buy tickets at least a week in advance at the *taquillas* (box office) of the Estadio Heliodoro Rodríguez López, which open from 10 am to 1 pm and

5 to 8 pm on weekdays. For more information call the club on ☎ 922 29 16 99 or ☎ 922 24 06 13.

Things to Buy
A lot of tourists come to Santa Cruz for the shopping, largely because of the Canary Islands' status as a tax haven. The main shopping strip is the pedestrianised Calle del Castillo and surrounding streets. Calle del Pilar is for more snooty shoppers (there's a Corte Inglés and Marks & Spencer). The most promising deals are on electronics, watches etc, but even items such as jeans are worth considering.

On a more souvenir-oriented level, the embroidery work in the shops along Calle del Castillo is attractive, and you can even buy traditional Canarian dress.

On Sundays there is a *rastro*, or flea market, along Calle de José Manuel Guimerá and Avenida de Bravo Murillo, just by the produce market – the Mercado de Nuestra Señora de África.

Getting There & Away
Air Because Tenerife is served by two airports at either end of the island, see the Getting There & Away section at the beginning of this chapter.

Bus TITSA buses leave from the Estación de Guaguas (☎ 922 21 81 22), on the corner of Avenida del Tres de Mayo and Calle del Fomento. They go to pretty much all destinations that are of interest around the island, including: Playa de las Américas (875 ptas); Puerto de la Cruz (500 ptas); Icod de los Vinos (700 ptas); and La Laguna (150 ptas).

Car & Motorcycle To head out of town for the west or south, take the Avenida del Tres de Mayo and follow the signs for the TF-5 (the autovía for La Laguna, Tenerife Norte airport and Puerto de la Cruz) or the TF-1 (the autovía for Tenerife Sur airport, Los Cristianos and Playa de las Américas). To head north, follow the waterfront road north and signs for Playa de las Teresitas.

ISLA DE TENERIFE

Rental Car-rental companies are scattered all over the city centre, as well as several at the Estación Marítima.

Ferry The ferry to Cádiz (see under Sea in the Getting There & Away chapter earlier in this book) leaves once a week from Tenerife at 8 am on Wednesday, stopping in Las Palmas de Gran Canaria and Arrecife (Lanzarote) en route. The trip takes a couple of days.

Trasmediterránea has occasional ferries to Las Palmas de Gran Canaria and five jet-foils a day (three on Sundays). (For more details see the Las Palmas Getting There & Away section. See the same section for details on the Naviera Armas ferries.)

Líneas Fred Olsen has four ferries a day to Agaete, in the north-west of Gran Canaria. Tickets cost 2700 ptas.

Tickets for Trasmediterránea and Fred Olsen are available at the Estación Marítima Muelle de Ribera (which is where the Fred Olsen boats leave from), or from travel agents. Trasmediterránea's ferries leave from further north-east along the quays, and Naviera Armas boats depart further along to the south-west, where they have a separate ticket office.

Jetfoil Trasmediterránea's Las Palmas jetfoils leave from the Estación Marítima Muelle Norte. You can get tickets here or at travel agents. The standard fare is 5600 ptas (3200 ptas off-peak).

Getting Around

Bus TITSA buses provide the city service in Santa Cruz, as well as the intercity buses. No 914 goes from the Estación de Guaguas to the centre (Plaza del General Weyler and Plaza de España).

Car & Motorcycle As in any Spanish city, the traffic can get a little much in Santa Cruz. Otherwise it is not terribly difficult to navigate, but parking is tough. Most of the centre has metered parking (up to two hours for 200 ptas). You must use the meters from 9 am to 1.30 pm and 4.30 to 8 pm Monday to Friday, and from 9 am to 1.30 pm Saturday.

Taxi The city taxis use their meters (or should do). The flagfall is 150 ptas. After that, you pay 50 ptas per kilometre. Surcharges of 55 ptas are imposed for: travel between 10 pm and 6 am; travel on Sunday and holidays; fares to the docks area; and for each piece of luggage carried. A ride from the Estación de Guaguas into the centre on a weekday (without luggage) should cost around 300 ptas.

Around the Island

LA LAGUNA
• *population 110,000*

One of the two urban jewels in Tenerife's crown (La Orotava is the other), the former capital and lively student town of San Cristóbal de la Laguna (to give it its full name) deserves a visit. It is an easy day trip from Santa Cruz or Puerto de la Cruz and should not be missed.

History
Alonso Fernández de Lugo's merry band of troopers ended up making a permanent camp in what is now known as La Laguna (the lagoon from which the name comes was only drained in 1837).

By the end of the 15th century, the old town as it is today was pretty much complete, and the Muy Noble, Ilustre, Leal y Fiel Ciudad de San Cristóbal de la Laguna (The Very Noble, Illustrious, Loyal & Faithful City of Saint Christopher of the Lagoon) was a bustling city of merchants, soldiers, bureaucrats and the pious. In 1701 the university was established, and still flourishes today.

Orientation
The Estación de Guaguas is about a 10-minute walk to the south-west of the old centre (*casco histórico*). The university lies to the south of the casco, and that's where

you'll find the bulk of the bars and plenty of simple eateries. What little accommodation is available is in the casco, as are some nice restaurants, banks, the post office and tourist office.

Information
Tourist Office The information kiosk is right on Plaza del Adelantado, and opens from 8.30 am to 7 pm daily except Sunday. Be sure to get a copy of *Arquitectura en el Casco Histórico de La Laguna*, a brochure explaining the evolution of style in house building over the centuries.

The TIVE student travel organisation (☎ 922 25 96 30) is at Calle de Heraclio Sánchez 40.

Money There is no shortage of banks all over the centre of town.

Post & Communications The main post office is next to the Iglesia de Santo Domingo, on the street of the same name. The postcode for La Laguna is 38200.

Medical & Emergency There is a Centro de Salud (clinic) at Calle de San Agustín 54. For ambulances, the Cruz Roja (Red Cross; ☎ 922 25 96 26) is at Calle de los Hermanos Marrero 1. The Policía Nacional are at Calle de Nava y Grimón 66.

Canarian Mansions
Apart from the fine-balconied houses of La Orotava, La Laguna is where you will most fully appreciate the beauty and eccentricity of Canarian urban architecture – bright façades graced with ponderous wooden double doors and pretty balconies. Broad, elegant, wood-shuttered windows hide behind them cool and shady *patios*, in the best cases surrounded by first-storey verandas propped up by slender timber columns. Wherever you see an open door, look inside – with luck the inner sanctum will also be open and you can see what lies behind the exterior walls.

The best place to start your wanderings is at **Casa Lercaro**, on Calle de San Agustín.

Built in 1593 and carefully restored since, it houses the **Museo de la Historia de Tenerife**. The documents, maps, artefacts and descriptions are interesting enough (text available in English), but the mansion alone is worth looking over. It opens from 10 am to 5 pm Tuesday to Saturday, and from 10 am to 2 pm Sunday. Admission is 400 ptas (200 ptas with TITSA Bonobus; 100 ptas for students).

Calle de San Agustín and the surrounding streets are lined with fine old houses. Take a look inside the **Casa del Montañés** at No 16. The patio of No 28, part of the university administration, is equally inspiring. The **Casa de los Capitanes Generales**, next door to the Ayuntamiento (town hall) on Calle del Obispo Rey Redondo, is a little rundown, but quite beautiful. There are others about too, so keep your eyes peeled.

Churches & Convents
Perhaps less enchanting, because less original to the eyes of anyone who has seen the great cathedrals and monasteries of mainland Europe, are La Laguna's contributions to religious architecture.

The **Iglesia de la Concepción** was the island's first, but has undergone many changes. Elements of gothic and plateresque can still be distinguished, and inside the *mudéjar artesonado*, the ceilings are admirable. You can only visit from 10.30 am to 12.30 pm.

A few minutes' walk east, the less interesting **Catedral** was completely rebuilt in 1913. Inside is a fine baroque retablo in the chapel dedicated to the Virgen de los Remedios. The **Iglesia de Santo Domingo** dates to the 17th century and contains some fine canvases by Cristóbal Hernández de Quintana. At the northern end of the casco, the **Iglesia de San Miguel de las Victorias** (or just plain del Cristo to locals), is known for the black gothic wood sculpture of Christ held inside. Visiting hours are from 10 am to 1.30 pm and 4 to 8 pm Tuesday to Friday, and from 10 am to 2 pm Saturday and Sunday.

Of the convents, the most interesting is

La Laguna

0   100   200 m

To Tegina & Taganana

Plaza de San Francisco

Calle de Quintín

Benito

Calle de Cabrera

Pinto

4 ▼

Santiago Cuadrado

Anchieta

Tabares de Cala

Calle de Nava y Grimón

Calle de Pinto Aguéra

★ 3

✚ 5

San Agustín 10

11

12

13

La Palma

Plaza de la Catedral

15

14

Calle de Bencomo

Calle de Nava y Grimón

Calle de San Roque

Deán Palahí

Plaza del Adelantado 18

Mercado de San Miguel

Calle de José C Llarena

16

17

19

Calle del Consistorio

20

22 ▼

21

Calle de la Catedral

23 ●

Plaza de San Cristóbal

Calle del Doctor Zamenhof

24

25

26

Calle de Lucas Vega

✚ 6

7

Plaza de la Concepción

Calle del Capitán Brotóns

8

9

Calle de Manuel de Ossuna

Calle de los Herradores

Calle del Obispo Rey Redondo

Calle de los Hermanos Marrero

Calle de Higuera

Calle de San Juan

Calle del Juego

C de Baltasar Núñez

Avenida de la Trinidad

C de Pablo Iglesias

Calle de Horacio Sánchez

C de Morales

C de Doctor Antonio González

Calle de María del Cristo Ossuna

Delgado Barreto

Avenida de Calvo Sotelo

Barranco Gonzáliánez

To Estación de Guaguas & Puerto de la Cruz

TF-5

Autopista del Norte

Glorieta del Brasil

Universidad de La Laguna

Avenida de Angel Guimerá

To Santa Cruz de Tenerife

TF-5

To Museo de la Historia de Tenerife (Casa Lercaro); Marco de la Ciencia y del Cosmos & Santa Cruz

Calle de los Molinos de Agua

Calle del Obispo Pérez Cáceres

Calle del Dr Marañón

C del Hermano Pedro

C del Padre Herrera

PLACES TO STAY
9 Hotel Aguere
19 Hotel-Apartamentos Nivaria

PLACES TO EAT
2 Restaurante San Antonio
4 Tasca La Laguna
14 Tasca Restaurante
    La Gotera
22 Tasca La Panadería

OTHER
1 Iglesia de San Miguel
   de las Victorias
3 Policía Nacional
5 Centro de Salud
6 Cruz Roja
7 Iglesia de la Concepción
8 Teatro Leal
10 University Building
11 Casa Lercaro (Museo de la
    Historia de Tenerife)
12 Convento de
    Santa Clara
13 Casa del Montañes
15 Catedral
16 Casa de los
    Capitanes Generales
17 Ayuntamiento
18 Tourist Information Kiosk
20 Correos y Telégrafos
21 Iglesia de Santo Domingo
23 TIVE (Student Travel)
24 Blues Bar
25 Azúcar
26 Bars

the **Convento de Santa Clara**, which you can visit from 9.30 am to 1 pm and 3.30 to 5.30 pm. Both it and the closed order in the **Convento de Santa Catalina** are still active.

Museo de la Ciencia y el Cosmos
This is a place for the science buff only, a museum where you push buttons, watch balls and things jiggle around, and muse on the forces of nature. There's also a planetarium here, which is quite interesting. It's on Vía Láctea, south of Avenida de Calvo Sotelo, and opens from 10 am to 10 pm, Tuesday to Sunday. Admission is the same as for the Museo de la Historia de Tenerife. although the planetarium is quite

Special Events
The most important fiestas in La Laguna are the Romería de San Benito Abad on the first Sunday of July, and the Fiesta del Santísimo Cristo, from 7 to 15 September. Carnaval (February) and Corpus Christi (June) are also celebrated with gusto here.

Places to Stay
The sleeping possibilities are extremely limited in La Laguna. The only cheapies are a couple of pensiones in the suburbs. *Pensión Berlín* (☎ 922 25 50 43), Calle de la República de Venezuela 64, has rooms for 3000/4000 ptas. *Pensión Medina* (☎ 922 66 08 48), Calle de Eduardo de Roo 68, is in La Cuesta and charges 2100/3700 ptas.

Back in town, you could try *Hotel Aguere* (☎ 922 25 94 90), Calle del Obispo Rey Redondo 57 (opposite the Teatro Leal), where fine singles/doubles cost 5600/6900 ptas. *Hotel-Apartamentos Nivaria* (☎ 922 26 42 98), Plaza del Adelantado 11, has doubles only for 7940 ptas.

Places to Eat
Restaurante San Antonio, Plaza de San Francisco 6, has a cool bar inside and a leafy courtyard in which to eat your filling meals. You'll spend about 1500 ptas.

Tasca La Laguna, Calle de Juan de Vera 53, is a great spot. The so-called tapas are

actually sizeable portions of mouth-watering food. Try the champiñones empanados (breaded mushrooms).

Tasca La Panadería, Calle de Santo Domingo 24, has a good menú del día for 950 ptas.

More upmarket is the *Tasca Restaurante La Gotera*, Calle de San Agustín 9. The old mansion is lovely and the prices reflect the class of the locale. Mains start at 1500 ptas.

Entertainment
Bars, Pubs & Discos The students provide the nightlife, and the bulk of the bars are concentrated at the university end of Calle del Doctor Antonio González and Calle de Heraclio Sánchez, as well as the cross streets between them. *Blues Bar*, Calle del Doctor Zamenhof 9, sometimes has live music. *Azúcar*, Calle del Doctor Antonio González 11, is a busy place. But you're best off bar-hopping and finding what suits your tastes – you don't have far to hop (or stagger).

Getting There & Away
Bus There is a stream of buses to Santa Cruz (No 015 is best as it takes you to Plaza de España), Puerto de la Cruz (Nos 101 & 102), La Orotava (062) and beyond.

Car & Motorcycle La Laguna is on the TF-5 motorway, making for a fast getaway to either Santa Cruz or Puerto de la Cruz.

THE NORTH-EAST
San Andrés & Around
About 6km north-east of Santa Cruz, the leafy hillside village of San Andrés offers the white sands of the artificial Playa de las Teresitas, an extremely pleasant beach made with sand from the Sahara. The village was once protected by a round tower, which has now crumbled. There's nowhere to stay here, but plenty of good little fish restaurants to choose from.

There are frequent buses (No 910) from Santa Cruz. Bus No 245 goes north to the end of the road, to Igueste de San Andrés, another 6km of beautiful coastline.

ISLA DE TENERIFE

If you have your own transport, you could head down to the secluded Playa de las Gaviotas, about half way from San Andrés.

Taganana & the Anaga Mountains
A spectacular trip leads up the Barranco de las Huertas to cross the Anaga range (geologically the oldest part of the island) and plummet down on the other side to the little hamlet of Taganana. The views to the craggy coast from above the town are quite breathtaking. There's not much to the town, but you can proceed a few more kilometres to the coast and **Roque de las Bodegas**. Local surfers like the beach here (Playa de San Roque), and there are four or five little restaurants and drink stands. *Casa Africa*, on the coast road, is particularly popular. Beyond, the road continues to a couple of minor settlements, Almáciga and Benijo.

Taganana hosts an odd celebration in March-April (the date changes), in which an effigy of Judas Iscariot is burned in a kind of collective purging of the villagers' sins and guilty consciences!

Bus No 246 comes here from Santa Cruz.

If you have your own wheels, backtracking a few kilometres into the Anaga mountain range and heading west at the intersection (follow signs for La Laguna) is a worthwhile excursion. The views from the numerous *miradores* along the way are wonderful.

Bajamar & Punta del Hidalgo
The mountain road drops into a valley on the way to La Laguna. Turn west for Tegueste and after about 10km you reach the local seaside resort of Bajamar (via Tejina). The only swimming is in rock pools awash with Atlantic rollers, but it is popular with Canarios and mainland Spaniards. As 'resorts' go, it's pretty low key. Three kilometres north-east, Punta del Hidalgo is an extension of Bajamar, and local lads try their luck on boogie boards in the surf of Playa de los Troches.

If you want to stay, you'll find a few sets of apartments in both locations. *Apartamentos Bellamar* (☎ 922 54 06 61), Avenida de Rafael González Vernetta, has apartments from 7000 ptas. You could also try the *Hotel Delfín* (☎ 922 54 02 00), Avenida del Sol. Singles/doubles cost up to 7000/ 9500 ptas.

Bus No 105 runs here from Santa Cruz via La Laguna.

Tacoronte & El Sauzal
From Tejina, a 10km jaunt south leads you to Tacoronte. This is one of the island's most important wine regions, and the feast of Cristo de los Dolores is celebrated with the harvest festivities on the first Sunday after 15 September – a good time to be here as much wine-tasting is done.

Downhill from the modern town centre is the **Iglesia de Santa Catalina** (signposted), a bright little grey stone, whitewashed church built in the Canaries colonial style. Around about is a handful of traditional old houses. Otherwise, there really isn't a lot to the place.

A few kilometres on, El Sauzal is another wine-growing community. Down on the coast, the cliffs of El Sauzal and Tacoronte form an impressive buttress against the Atlantic.

Bus No 101 links these towns to Puerto de la Cruz and Santa Cruz.

La Matanza de Acentejo & La Victoria
La Matanza ('the slaughter') is where Bencomo's Guanches inflicted a nasty defeat on Alonso Fernández de Lugo's Spaniards in 1493. Two years later, however, de Lugo was back and this time he had better luck, winning a decisive victory over the Guanches just 3km south of the scene of his earlier defeat. Predictably, the village that eventually sprang up here was known as La Victoria.

Bus No 101 links these towns to Puerto de la Cruz and Santa Cruz.

PUERTO DE LA CRUZ
• *population 25,500*
A coastal paradise, with palms swaying among the banana plantations, black sandy

beaches and a limpid ocean. Oh, and a forest of high-rise hotels, shopping malls, touts, swimming pools, 'traditional Sunday roasts' and street vendors selling Julio Iglesias tapes to sun-scorched pensioners from as far afield as London and Leipzig.

Historically, Puerto de la Cruz was a secondary port much used by English traders. As maritime trade dropped off, it was the English who came to the rescue, erecting the monumental Grand Hotel Taoro as a kind of members' club. This marked the beginning of Puerto de la Cruz's vocation as a tourist recreation destination. It's not all bad news. The older parts of the town centre and toward the west are pretty in places and not so obviously overrun – and you would be hard pressed not to find the natural setting agreeable.

Orientation

The city spreads from east to west along the Atlantic coast. The bus station is in the west, and roughly a 10-minute walk away are some modest hotels and quiet local eateries. The busy Plaza del Charco is a focal point, and most of the town's historic buildings lie in the immediate vicinity. To the east is the more hideous jumble of high-rise hotels, discos and bars, international restaurants and the admittedly very pleasant Lago Martiánez, a watery playground designed by César Manrique.

Information

Tourist Office The Oficina de Información Turística is on Plaza de Europa and opens 9 am to 8 pm Monday to Friday, and 9 am to 1 pm Saturday and Sunday.

Money American Express is represented by Viajes Insular (☎ 922 38 02 62) at Avenida del Generalísimo 20A. Otherwise, the same street is lined with banks and ATMs. Banca March is handy on Plaza del Charco.

Post & Communications The town's main post office is on Calle del Pozo, opposite the bus station. There are telephones on Calle de Mequínez, near the little fishing

port. The postcode for Puerto de la Cruz is 38400.

Emergency The Policía Nacional HQ (☎ 922 38 12 24) is on Avenida de José del Campo Llarena. For an ambulance you can call the Cruz Roja on ☎ 922 38 38 12.

Disabled Travellers Le Ro (☎ 922 37 33 01) is a specialist shop that rents wheelchairs and other appliances for the disabled, as well as offering a repair service. It's on Avenida del Generalísimo in the Apartamentos Martina building.

Things to See & Do

Around Town Created by César Manrique, the **Lago Martiánez** is not an unpleasant diversion. The fountains and layout are attractive, and entry costs 350 ptas.

If you feel that your soul is in danger from the resort end of town, head for the centre and the 17th-century **Iglesia de Nuestra Señora de la Peña de Francia**. The church has a fine mudéjar ceiling and some paintings by Luis de la Cruz in the retablo of the Capilla del Evangelio.

Closer to the waterfront is the **Ayuntamiento**, a fine old building but by no means the only one around here. Across the square is the **Casa de Miranda**, dating from 1730 and now a restaurant (see the following Places to Eat section), and down the narrow Calle de las Lonjas is the **Casa de la Aduana**, the customs house founded in 1620. Another noteworthy old mansion is the **Casa de los Iriarte**, where the family of writers and artists had their family home. The laurels in the nearby **Plaza del Charco** were brought from Cuba in 1852. A block east brings you to the **Iglesia de San Francisco** and **Ermita de San Juan**. The little hermitage was built between 1599 and 1608. Only the **Ermita de San Amaro**, up in the east of town, is older.

Just west of Plaza del Charco, the **Museo Arqueológico** has a modest collection of Guanche artefacts and mummies, along with some other odds and sods. It is open from 10 am to 1 pm and 5 to 9 pm Tuesday

ISLA DE TENERIFE

ISLA DE TENERIFE

PLACES TO STAY
3 Pensión Bunge
9 Pensión Rosamary
11 Pensión Los Geranios
12 Hotel Puerto Azul
13 Residencia Altomar
17 Hotel Marquesa
18 Hotel Monopol
33 Pensión Loly
34 Pensión La Platanera

PLACES TO EAT
2 Marisquería El Pescador
6 Casas Miranda
14 Casa del Pueblo
20 Restaurante Cocina Vasca
21 El Limón
24 Restaurante El Rincón
26 Tapas Arcón
27 Bar Las Portelas

OTHER
1 Le Ro
4 Ayuntamiento
5 Tourist Office
7 Casa de la Aduana
10 Museo Arqueológico
15 Banca March
16 Iglesia de San Francisco
   & Ermita de San Juan
19 Iglesia de Nuestra Señora
   de la Peña de Francia
22 Viajes Insular
23 Canarisub
25 Casa de los Iriarte &
   Restaurant El Rincón
28 Estación de Guaguas
29 Correos y Telégrafos
30 Policía Nacional
31 Castillo de San Felipe
32 Bicicletas Melian
35 Grand Hotel Taoro

ATLANTIC OCEAN

Playa Martiánez

Lago Martiánez

Puerto de la Cruz

Parque Taoro

0   100   200 m

to Saturday, and from 10 am to 1 pm Sunday. At the western edge of town, a little 17th-century fort known as the **Castillo de San Felipe** stands watch over a pretty stretch of beach. It opens only for special exhibitions.

South of the city spreads the majesty of **Parque Taoro**, dominated by the grand old Hotel Taoro – part of which now houses a casino. The Risco Bello Aquatic Gardens, an artificial tropical playground, are situated in the heart of the park.

A good place for views of the town is the **Mirador de la Paz**, near the Ermita de San Amaro, where you can enjoy a drink in one of several bars. Along the road to La Orotava is the 200-year-old **Jardín Botánico**, open from 9 am to 6 pm daily.

Loro Parque The dolphinarium here has a dual tourist and scientific function. One dolphin was actually born in captivity here in 1994. You can see sharks, manta rays and all sorts of other sealife in the aquarium, as well as an assortment of other beasties, including gorillas, crocodiles, tigers and flamingos. Entry costs 2500 ptas and a silly yellow train takes you from the city centre if you don't have your own transport. It's about a five-minute drive to the west of town.

Bananera El Guanche This British operated, and functioning, banana plantation aims to teach visitors the history of the banana trade and how bananas are grown. The place is also bursting with all sorts of other exotic flora.

It's about 2km out of town on the road to the TF-5 motorway (and La Orotava). There's a free bus from the town centre. Entry costs 950 ptas.

Diving You can organise dives and classes at Canarisub (☎ 922 38 30 07), Calle de Esquivel 8.

Places to Stay
Pensión Rosamary (☎ 922 38 32 53), Calle de San Felipe 14, is an immaculately kept little place, where doubles (no singles) with own bath cost 3900 ptas. It's often full.

Pensión La Platanera (☎ 922 38 41 57), Calle de Blanco 29, is a charmless, modern place, but the rooms are clean and comfortable. Singles/doubles go for 3500/4600 ptas. Nearby, *Pensión Loly* (☎ 922 38 36 93), Calle de La Sala 4, has simple doubles, without bath, for 2600 ptas.

Down around the Museo Arqueológico, in a quiet little barrio largely devoid of the tourist trappings, is *Pensión Los Geranios* (☎ 922 38 28 10), Calle del Lomo 14. Double rooms here range up to 3500 ptas with own shower. Up the road, at No 24, *Hotel Puerto Azul* (☎ 922 38 32 13) charges as little as 3500 ptas for doubles with ensuite in off-season, but double from November to April. If they don't suit, try *Residencia Alfomar* (☎ 922 38 06 82), at Calle de la Peñita 6. They only have doubles, which come in at 4500 ptas.

There is no shortage of drab, four and five-star monoliths to stay in, but for a bit of tasteful elegance you can't go past two of the longest established hotels in the town. *Hotel Monopol* (☎ 922 38 46 11), Calle de Quintana 15, dates back to 1742, although its life as a hotel started later. The rooms are exquisitely presented and there is a pool too. In high season you are looking at shelling out 8500/10,500 ptas. At No 11, *Hotel Marquesa* (☎ 922 38 31 51) is in much the same class, if a little cheaper.

Places to Eat
If you must hang out in the eastern end of town (around Avenida del Generalísimo), you could do worse than the seafood at *Marisquería El Pescador*, Avenida de Venezuela 3. There is an infinite number of pizzerias and international food outlets around here.

In a quite different vein are three places along the quiet Calle de Esquivel. *Restaurante El Rincón*, on the corner of Calle de los Iriarte, is a nice spot for local cuisine – the set menu costs 950 ptas. *El Limón*, on the corner with Calle de B. Miranda, is vegetarian, with great 'burgers', soups and fruit

ISLA DE TENERIFE

juices. More expensive is the *Restaurante Cocina Vasca*, Calle de la Hoya 2, where mains cost 1500 ptas.

Bar Las Portelas, Calle de Cupido, is a basic bar/restaurant where you can have papas arrugadas y mojo picón for 600 ptas. They advertise Canarian breakfasts, as if in defiance of the full English-breakfast trend.

Going Bananas

Although bananas had been grown in the Canary Islands for centuries, they only really came into their own as *the* export cash crop around the 1870s. They remained the islands' economic mainstay until WWI, when the British blockade strangled international trade and robbed the islands of their foreign markets.

Conditions improved slowly after the war, and although the banana no longer plays the pre-eminent role it once did in the islands' overall economy, it is still cultivated extensively for export. It remains the single most important crop in the Canaries.

Those who do depend more on the banana are the Latin American heirs of the Canary Islands' banana; it was the early Spanish conquistadores who introduced it to the western hemisphere, starting from Columbus' first landfall at Hispaniola (the Dominican Republic and Haiti), and quickly spreading to other islands and the mainland. Fray Tomás de Berlanga, later Bishop of Panama, took some specimens there in 1516.

To this day the banana remains a central feature of the economies of countries like Panama, the Dominican Republic, Guadeloupe, Jamaica, Costa Rica, Honduras, Guatemala, Brazil, Colombia and Ecuador.

So what's so great about bananas? Easily grown in tropical and sub-tropical environments, the banana is jammed with vitamins A and C, potassium and carbohydrates. People have been raving about bananas since ancient times – Alexander the Great encountered them during his conquests in India, three hundred years before Christ.

The banana plant is actually an outlandishly large herb, comprising an underground stem (or rhizome) from which springs a false trunk that can grow up to 6m. After the first planting, it can take up to 15 months for fruit to appear. The false trunk flowers, and then a bunch of anything up to 150 bananas grows, divided into 'hands' of 10 to 20 pieces of fruit. As each plant only bears one bunch, the false trunk is pruned away to make way for new ones to take its place. The underground stem remains in place. Hundreds of types of banana are scattered across plantations around the world, but one important distinction is between the sweet tasting banana and the starchy plantain, which is always used for cooking.

Tapas Arcón, Calle de Blanco 8, is another unassuming place to get local grub.

The *Casa del Pueblo*, Calle de Pérez Zamora 32, has a courtyard out the back.

Casa de Miranda, on Plaza de Europa, is more than two centuries old and with its low, wooden-beamed ceilings and tasteful period décor, makes for a very romantic place to eat, if a tad pricey.

Entertainment
The bulk of the noisier bars and discos are clustered along and around Avenida del Generalísimo. Take your pick!

Getting There & Away
The Estación de Guaguas is on Calle del Pozo in the west of the town. There are regular departures for Santa Cruz and La Laguna (Nos 101 & 102) and south-west to Icod de los Vinos (No 363) and Playa de las Américas (No 343). The slow 101 (*por Carretera General*) does the scenic tour to Santa Cruz via La Orotava and Tacoronte.

Getting Around
You can hire bicycles at Bicicletas Melian (☎ 922 38 29 17), Centro Comercial Ucanca, Avenida de José del Campo Llarena.

AROUND PUERTO DE LA CRUZ
La Orotava
• *population 32,000*
Just a few kilometres inland from Puerto de la Cruz is one of the prettiest towns on the island. It gives its name to the prosperous valley that spreads out to the west, and the noble mansions which grace the old centre of town seem a reflection of that wealth. The valley was soon settled after the Spanish conquest, and by the 16th-century well-to-do families from La Laguna began building churches and convents, and later their own homes, in this town. The casco is about a five-minute walk west from the Estación de Guaguas.

Information There is a tourist office (☎ 922 27 85 10) at Calle de la Carrera del Escultor Estévenez 2. It opens from 10 am to 6 pm Monday to Friday, and from 10 am to 2 pm Saturday.

The post office is on Calle de Cologan, opposite the Iglesia de la Concepción.

Things to See The **Iglesia de la Concepción** is the Canary Islands' most notable contribution to baroque architecture. Behind it, Calle del Colegio climbs south to become Calle de San Francisco, lined by impressive mansions from the 17th and 18th centuries.

Of the so-called Doce Casas (Twelve Houses), the **Casa de Fonseca** (aka Casa de los Balcones) is perhaps the most outstanding, boasting long and splendidly worked teak balconies. Inside, it opens onto a leafy patio, off which are rooms now used by a research institute on Spanish and Latin American crafts. It is open from 8.30 am to 6.30 pm, Monday to Saturday.

Across the road is the **Casa Molina** (aka Casa del Turista), open from 9 am to 6 pm daily. In both places you can see (and buy) Canarian handicrafts.

Following Calle de San Francisco up (south), you come to the **Iglesia de San Francisco** and **Hospitalito de la Santísima Trinidad**, occupying what was once the Convento de San Lorenzo. The hospital remains in use, so wandering around inside snapping photos is probably not appropriate. Heading further south still, the street name changes to Calle del Doctor Domingo González García, along which (on the east side) is a series of 17th and 18th-century mills once used to make gofio.

To the east, on Calle de Fernando Fuentes, is the 18th-century **Iglesia de San Juan Bautista del Farrobo**, with an outstanding artesonado ceiling. Back towards the centre, next to the Jardín Victoria, the **Iglesia de San Agustín** also boasts a fine artesonado.

Downhill on Calle de Tomás Zerolo, the former **Convento de Santo Domingo** now houses the Museo de Artesanía Iberoamericana, exhibiting handicrafts from Spain and Latin America. It opens from 9.30 am to 6 pm daily except Sunday.

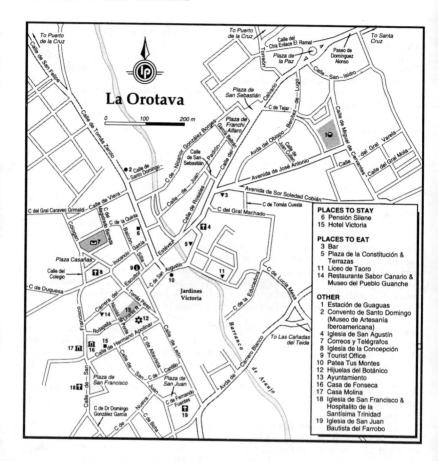

PLACES TO STAY
6 Pensión Silene
15 Hotel Victoria

PLACES TO EAT
3 Bar
5 Plaza de la Constitución &
   Terrazas
11 Liceo de Taoro
14 Restaurante Sabor Canario &
   Museo del Pueblo Guanche

OTHER
1 Estación de Guaguas
2 Convento de Santo Domingo
   (Museo de Artesanía
   Iberoamericana)
4 Iglesia de San Agustín
7 Correos y Telégrafos
8 Iglesia de la Concepción
9 Tourist Office
10 Patea Tus Montes
12 Hijuelas del Botánico
13 Ayuntamiento
16 Casa de Fonseca
17 Casa Molina
18 Iglesia de San Francisco &
   Hospitalito de la
   Santísima Trinidad
19 Iglesia de San Juan
   Bautista del Farrobo

Activities Patea Tus Montes (☎ 922 33 59 03), Calle de San Agustín 9, organises hikes around the island.

Special Event Corpus Christi is celebrated with particular gusto in La Orotava. Tonnes of volcanic earth, flowers, branches and sand are hauled into the centre (especially around the 19th-century Ayuntamiento) to create extraordinary 'carpets' in the streets and plazas.

Places to Stay & Eat It's a good thing La Orotava is an easy day trip from Santa Cruz or Puerto de la Cruz, because accommodation is thin on the ground. You could try *Pensión Silene* (☎ 922 33 01 99), Calle de Tomás Zerolo 9, which has singles/doubles with own shower for 4500/6000 ptas. Otherwise, *Hotel Victoria* (☎ 922 33 16 83), Calle de Hermano Apolinar 8, is an attractive option in a refurbished 400-year old Canarian mansion. The 13 double rooms have all the mod cons if you can afford 12,800/16,000 ptas or more, plus 4.5% taxes (includes breakfast).

Restaurante Sabor Canario, Calle de la Carrera del Escultor Estévenez 17, is part of the Museo del Pueblo Guanche, (more a showcase for handicrafts than a museum). The restaurant is enticing though, especially if you get a seat in the patio. For a bit of a splurge you could eat at the *Hotel Victoria*, also in a patio. Mains start at 1500 ptas.

If you're around for lunch on Sunday, see if the *Liceo de Taoro* has put on its 800 ptas buffet. It's the imposing building on Calle de San Augustín.

For a cheap snack or meal, the more prosaic, nameless bar at Avenida de José Antonio 6 might be the go.

Getting There & Away Bus No 101 comes up from Puerto de la Cruz; No 063 from Santa Cruz and No 062 from La Laguna.

THE NORTH-WEST
Icod de los Vinos
• *population 18,000*
The main attraction in this wine-belt town is its weird tree, the **Drago Milenario**, supposed to be a thousand years old. This, the oldest 'dragon tree' in the islands, appears from a distance for all the world to be a lopsided umbrella.

If you like butterflies, you might want to visit the **Mariposario del Drago**, a tropical garden swarming with *mariposas*. It opens from 10 am to 6 pm daily. Admission is 600 ptas.

Nearby on a shady square, the **Iglesia de San Marcos** is worth a look. Its sober renaissance interior hides within a superb pine artesonado ceiling and silver high altar. A few steps away, **Plaza de la Constitución** (aka Plaza de la Pila) is flanked by some fine old Canarian houses. If you head a little way up Calle de San Antonio, you'll see on the right another dragon tree, the **Drago Chico**. The streets around here, forming the kernel of the old town, are worth a wander.

A few kilometres outside town, you can have a swim at the little beach in the fishing village of **Playa de San Marcos** (bus No 362 from Icod).

Places to Eat If you need a bite to eat, *Restaurante Carmen*, Avenida de las Canarias 1, is not a bad choice. Afterwards, try the *bodegas* on Plaza de la Constitución, where you can sample Icod's wines, particularly the Malvasía for which the volcanic soil around here is well known.

Getting There & Away Bus No 108 goes to Santa Cruz, No 354 heads for Puerto de la Cruz and No 460 to Playa de las Américas.

Garachico
• *population 5900*
It is a real pleasure to simply wander the uneven streets and admire the traditional houses in this whitewashed fishing hamlet. They deserve special admiration, as Garachico has not been the luckiest town. Founded by Genoese merchants who had accompanied and to some extent bankrolled the *conquistadores*, Garachico soon developed into a centre of sugar production.

Its port was for a while the busiest on the island, but the 17th century brought a series of disasters which all but finished the place off. The long-suffering inhabitants were assailed by epidemics, freak storms which destroyed countless ships, fires and finally, in 1706, a major volcanic eruption which buried the town in lava and destroyed the port. In 1905 another earthquake reminded them of the ever-present dangers posed by nature.

Information The small tourist office (☎ 922 83 01 85) at Calle de Estéban de Ponte 5 is open from 10 am to 3 pm Monday to Saturday. The postcode for Garachico is 38450.

Things to See The **Fortaleza de San Miguel**, a stout little portside fort with curious white turrets, erected in the 16th century to protect Garachico from pirates, was one of the few survivors of the 1706 eruption. It is now home to a fossil and rock collection, and is open from 10 am to 6 pm daily. Entry costs 100 ptas.

The **Iglesia de San Francisco**, on the central plaza that is itself a pleasant place to hang around for late afternoon aperitifs, has a fine mudéjar ceiling.

The **Museo de Arte**, Plaza de Santo Domingo, is a modern art collection housed in what was a Dominican monastery. It opens from 9 am to 1 pm and 4 to 7 pm daily. Entry is 100 ptas.

Special Events The Romería de San Roque, held in August (the dates change) is the village's biggest yearly festival and worth being in town for.

Places to Stay & Eat The only cheapie here is in *Pizzeria Il Giardino* (☎ 922 83 02 45), Calle de Estéban de Ponte 8, just behind the waterfront. They have a handful of double rooms ranging in price from 3000 ptas to 5000 ptas (the latter is very nice and has a shower); they also run a dive shop and, of course, serve up pizzas.

A stylish option is the *Hotel San Roque* (☎ 922 13 34 35) on the same street at No 32. The core of this elegant place dates to the 18th century. Singles/doubles cost 12,000 ptas per person. This is something of a surprise packet, as the price includes beautiful rooms equipped with TV, videos, CDs and minibar. Also included in the price are use of the pool, sauna, tennis court and even massages – and breakfast. Add 4.5% tax.

Pretty much the whole waterfront street, the Avenida de Tomé Cano, is taken up with restaurants whose speciality, unsurprisingly enough, is fish. You can eat well for about 1500 ptas.

Getting There & Away Bus No 363 from Buenavista passes through en route to Puerto de la Cruz, as does the less frequent No 107 to Santa Cruz.

El Tanque

Just 10 minutes west of Icod, the village of El Tanque is home to the Camello Center (☎ 922 13 61 91). These people will dress you up as an 'Arab', lead you around for a few kilometres on a camel (with 50 other similarly attired tourists), stick you on a donkey as a follow-up and then pump 'traditional Arabian tea' down your throat in an 'authentic Arabian tent'. Hmm ...

Buenavista del Norte & Punta de Teno

The most north-westerly village on the island, Buenavista has little to recommend it. But if you get this far, you should try to thumb a lift the 10km out to Punta de Teno, a startling spit of volcanic rock leaning out into the ocean. Behind rise pale green, cactus-dotted mountains. You can see La Gomera from here and on a good day sunset is a treat. If you're driving, note that in bad weather the road is prone to mud falls from the cliffs above, and therefore can be quite dangerous.

Bus No 107 goes all the way to Santa Cruz from Buenavista. More frequent is No 363 to Puerto de la Cruz via Icod and Garachico.

PARQUE NACIONAL DE LAS CAÑADAS DEL TEIDE

Declared a national park in 1954 (the third to be established in Spain), the Parque Nacional de las Cañadas del Teide basically takes in an enormous volcanic crater. Covering 13,571 hectares, it is the fifth largest national park in Spain.

In the north rises the great cone that forms the Pico del Teide, at 3718m the highest mountain in all Spain. To the south are the *cañadas*, a series of plains stretching away inside the old crater from the foot of Teide. The huge ancient crater measures 40km in circumference and 14km in diameter.

The park lies about 2000m above sea level, and presents a striking sight. Weird basalt, pumice and obsidian rock formations emerge from the sandy plains. A menacing black lava flow frozen in time reaches all the way down to the only road that crosses the park. The Teleférico (cablecar) ride up to the top of the mountain is an experience in itself – an ascent of some 1200m in eight minutes!

Twenty-one walking trails, of widely varying difficulty, criss-cross the park. If you plan to do any serious hiking, you should get information, at the Centro de Visitantes (see below), about which trails are suitable for your level of skill and fitness. You are not permitted to stray from the marked trails.

Many hikers choose to walk to the peak, starting from El Portillo and passing the Montaña Blanca (four hours) before reaching the overnight stop in the basic ICONA shelter, the *Refugio Altavista*. They complete the hike the following day, and many elect to take the Teleférico back down! This hike, particularly the second part (six hours if you include a diversion around to the Pico Viejo) is not for the faint-hearted. Only experienced walkers with a good nose for direction should do it, and the final ascent should not be attempted in bad weather. Snow and ice can be a problem in winter. The refugio is open from March to October; otherwise, a simple emergency cabin is all you'll find. Bring along your own food and water.

It is also possible to join hikes guided by park staff. You need to book a place in advance: call ICONA on 922 29 01 29 or visit their office at Calle del Pilar 1, Santa Cruz de Tenerife. Most of the hikes are of about four hours' duration, although it may be possible to do the two-day ascent of the peak as a guided walk too.

Approaches to the Park
There are basically four roads approaching the park, of which the C-824 from La Laguna via La Esperanza is by far the prettiest. It joins the C-821 from La Orotava at El Portillo, where there is an information booth and a couple of bar/restaurants. If the booth is shut, proceed half a kilometre along the C-821 towards the peak and you'll reach the Centro de Visitantes, where you can get information, buy books, look at the displays and watch a multilingual video. The centre is open from 9.15 am to 4.15 pm, Monday to Friday. From this point it's another 8km or so across the bizarre vol-canic landscape to the base of the peak and the Teleférico.

The Pico del Teide
You have a couple of choices on how to get to the top of the mountain. Most take the Teleférico, but it is possible to hike up from various points (see above).

The Teleférico takes 8 minutes to lift you from 2356m to 3550m – about 200m short of the lip of the crater. The return trip costs 2100 ptas, or 1300 ptas one way for those planning to hike up but return the easy way. It runs from 9 am to 4 pm (going up) and the last one down leaves at 5 pm. Your maximum time at the top is supposed to be one hour, although it's a little hard to see how this can be policed.

Once at the top, you could be on a stairway to heaven. You can see out to Gran Canaria, La Palma, La Gomera and El Hierro – and even on the cloudiest day down below you will probably be bathed in glorious sunshine at this height. Despite this, however, it can get quite cold, so bring a decent jacket, hiking boots and long trousers – the shorts and flip-flops brigade often look decidedly uncomfortable up here, particularly in winter.

Access to the crater has been closed off for safety reasons, but you can wander along to the Pico Viejo.

Warning Oxygen is a little short up here, so anyone likely to suffer, especially those with cardiovascular problems, should refrain from going up.

Roques de García
A few kilometres south of the peak, a bizarre set of rocks pokes up in an unlikely fashion from the plains around the Parador. Known as the Roques de García, they are the result of erosion on old volcanic dikes. The hard rock of the dikes has been bared while surrounding earth and rock has been gradually swept away. The weirdest of the rocks, the Roque Cinchado, is wearing away faster at the base than above, and one of these days is destined to topple over (so

ISLA DE TENERIFE

Roque Chinchado, part of Los Roques de García – leftovers from erosion of volcanic dykes at the base of Teide mountain

maybe you shouldn't get up too close!). Spreading out to the west are the bald plains of the Llano de Ucanca; the road out to Los Cristianos is to the south-west; and the road to Santiago del Teide is in the north-west.

Places to Stay & Eat
Camping is not allowed in the park. The only place to stay is the *Parador de Cañadas del Teide* (☎/fax 922 38 64 15), where singles/doubles cost from 12,4000/ 15,500 ptas. There is a snack bar at both ends of the Teleférico, and several restaurants are strategically located along the way (from the north). A couple of them are at the small information booth at El Portillo.

Getting There & Away
One bus a day (No 342) leaves Playa de las Américas at 9.15 am (Los Cristianos at 9.30 am) for the Parador, the Teleférico and El Portillo.

The return run leaves the Teleférico at 3.40 pm and the Parador at 4 pm. No 348 from Puerto de la Cruz leaves for the Parador at 9.15 am and returns at 4 pm.

Drivers should follow signs along the C-821 road for the Parque Nacional del Teide.

THE WEST COAST
Santiago del Teide
There's not much to this little town, but you will probably pass through it whether you use the buses or have your own transport. Five kilometres south on a branch road is the sleepy hamlet of **Arguayo**, quite unremarkable but possibly of interest to those who like ceramics; there is a couple of places at the north end of town where local pottery is made and sold.

There are buses from Playa de las Américas, Icod de los Vinos and Buenavista del Norte. Bus No 462 stops in Arguayo en route from Guía de Isora to Santiago and back around to Los Gigantes.

Masca
Six kilometres north-west of Santiago lies a true surprise packet. The narrow road rises steeply to a high ridge, only then to cascade down the other side into the Barranco de Masca in a series of tight switchbacks. The ride alone is a spectacle, and the little farming village is charming. Old stone houses look out across the palm-trees and the ravine walls to the Atlantic Ocean. A couple of restaurants and bars have opened up in strategic bits of the town so that the growing stream of tourists can admire the wonderful views in comfort.

No, Masca is no secret. In the late afternoon the serpentine mountain road seems more like Oxford Street with only two shopping days left until Christmas. How the tour buses even negotiate the curves is as big a mystery as the Immaculate Conception. Just how much the locals appreciate the constant flow of gawking outsiders is equally hard to gauge. If the hordes don't appeal, try to get there early in the morning before the tour buses start to roll in.

If you happen to be around in the first week of December, ask about the Fiesta de la Consolación, a religious festival in which many of the locals wear traditional dress and bring out their timples and other instruments for an evening of Canarian music.

Just outside town on the road to Santiago is a well-placed terraza. With views right down the gorge to the ocean, this must be one of the best seats for sunset on the island.

Hardy walkers could trek down the Barranco de Masca to the sea, but it is a difficult walk for experienced hikers only (allow six hours hiking there and back).

Bus No 355 (two a day to/from Santiago del Teide; four to/from Buenavista del Norte) stops at Masca.

Los Gigantes & Puerto de Santiago
The Acantilados de los Gigantes (Cliffs of the Giants) are remarkably sheer rock walls which plunge into the ocean a quarter of the way down the west coast of Tenerife. Across the small bight lies the little port and resort town of Los Gigantes and, virtually linked to it, Puerto de Santiago.

Both live from tourism, although on a more modest scale than the Playa de las Américas phenomenon. Of the two settlements, Los Gigantes is easily the more pleasant (if you except the presence of a black sand beach in Puerto de Santiago).

Information The Oficina de Turismo (☎ 922 10 03 48), Avenida Marítima 36-37, is actually on the coast at Playa de la Arena, Puerto de Santiago.

Activities The only real attraction here is the cliffs, so most visitors join a boat tour towards them, which usually includes dolphin watching and then a swim off the Barranco de Masca. Excursions to the cliffs can also be joined from Los Cristianos and Playa de las Américas.

Places to Stay & Eat The accommodation possibilities here are largely limited to apartments. A particularly attractive option is the gracefully laid out complex *Aparthotel Poblado Marinero* (☎ 922 86 09 66), right on Los Gigantes port. The best rooms have balconies facing the Los Gigantes

cliffs. Apartments with twin beds, kitchen, bathroom and lounge room cost 8500 ptas for one or two people, 9500 ptas for three.

Eating is also an enjoyable affair down by the same port. Take your pick. Unfortunately, the traditional English breakfast theme is rampant throughout Los Gigantes and Puerto de Santiago.

Getting There & Away Bus Nos 493 and 462 go to Guía de Isora. Otherwise, No 473 goes as far as Las Galletas via Playa de las Américas and Los Cristianios. Up to six buses a day connect with Puerto de la Cruz.

Guía de Isora
There's little reason to call in here, but those using buses in the area may have to change service in Guía de Isora. Frequent buses connect with Playa de las Américas and other destinations in the south.

Adeje & Barranco del Infierno
There's not a great deal to the village of Adeje, but from here you can undertake the hike up one of the most spectacular ravines on the island, the Barranco del Infierno (Hell's Gorge). A narrow path and steps make the 6km trek (there and back) possible for most people of average fitness – reckon on at least four hours. The deeper you get into the gorge, the higher its walls soar up above you as they also close in. Various species of plant native to the island thrive in its shelter, and the end of the path is marked by a waterfall.

Bus No 416 runs to the centre of Adeje from Playa de las Américas.

LOS CRISTIANOS & PLAYA DE LAS AMÉRICAS
• *population (impermanent) 200,000*
What can one say about a place that lives entirely off its reputation as a year-round sun and fun scene? The beaches (although all artificial) are nice enough without being the world's most spectacular, and Playa de las Américas and the adjacent Costa Adeje are an uninterrupted stream of hotel-apartments, pubs, bars, discos, kitsch souvenir

shops and lots of bright lights and noise. Just what you'd expect, and taken in the right spirit, a good laugh – for a while anyway. Los Cristianos is considerably quieter and retains something more of an authentic local identity, but only just.

Information

Tourist Office The main tourist office (☎ 922 75 06 33), Avenida de Rafael Puig 1, is in Playa de las Américas. It opens from 9 am to 2 pm, Monday to Friday.

Money Banks with ATMs abound. If you need to be sent an urgent top-up, you could try Western Union at Mail Boxes Etc, Calle Antigua del General Franco 16, Los Cristianos. American Express is represented by Viajes Insular (☎ 922 79 01 54), at Residencial El Camisón, in Playa de las Américas.

Post & Communications There are several post offices scattered across the area. One is just around the corner from the tourist office. In Los Cristianos there's one on a pedestrian mall off Calle de los Sabandeños. Los Cristianos' postcode is 38650.

Email To send an email, try Atlantis Net, Calle del General Franco 36, in the heart of Los Cristianos.

Bookshops Librería Barbara, Calle de Pablo Abril 36, Los Cristianos, has a stock of German, French and English books. The Book Swop, in the Puerto de Colón shopping complex in Playa de las Américas, concentrates mainly on English language material.

Travel Agents One decent agent in Los Cristianos is Viajes Isla Azul, Calle de Juan XXIII 8. The rule of thumb, however, is to hunt around, as in this part of the Canaries agents abound and deals come and go with amazing rapidity.

Medical Services Medical centres abound (due to the drunken brawls which occasion-

ally cause havoc). There's one next to the tourist office and another, Salus (☎ 922 79 61 61), just off Avenida de Rafael Puig on Calle de la República de Panama.

If you need specific help for handicaps, go to Le Ro (☎ 922 75 02 89), in the same building as Hotel Mar y Sol, Los Cristianos.

Emergency The police (☎ 922 79 78 50) have several stations across the area. One is just around the corner from the tourist office in Playa de las Américas, another on Avenida de Valle Menéndez in Los Cristianos.

The Cruz Roja ambulance service is on ☎ 922 78 07 59. Call ☎ 922 28 24 24 to find out the location of nearest open pharmacy.

Activities

For all of the following and any other activities available, you will find yourself deluged with possibilities, brochures and touts. The shops around Puerto de Colón in Playa de las Américas are a good first stop, but agents bustle up and down the resort and on the waterfront at Los Cristianos too. Shop around.

Diving The Centro de Buceo Los Cristianos (☎ 922 75 13 75), in the Edificio Marina off Avenida Marítima in Los Cristianos, offers introductory dives for 6000 ptas and openwater PADI courses from 45,000 ptas.

Fishing Deep sea fishing trips can start at about 7500 ptas per person for a five-hour jaunt, or 10,000 ptas for a full day.

Sailing You can hire luxury yachts or nippy catamarans, with or without skipper, for day trips or more involved excursions from CCB Yacht Charters (☎ 922 79 44 04), Puerto de Colón, Local 5B, Playa de las Américas. Prices start at 45,000 ptas a day for a small yacht without crew taking up to eight people (you must be fully licensed). Plan well in advance, as you pay half to make a reservation and the rest six weeks *before* you charter. A crewed yacht will cost 120,000 ptas a day.

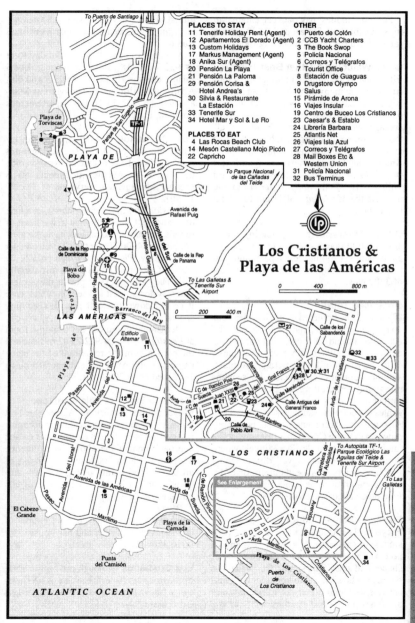

PLACES TO STAY
11 Tenerife Holiday Rent (Agent)
12 Apartamentos El Dorado (Agent)
13 Custom Holidays
17 Markus Management (Agent)
18 Anika Sur (Agent)
20 Pensión La Playa
21 Pensión La Paloma
29 Pensión Corisa &
   Hotel Andrea's
30 Silvia & Restaurante
   La Estación
33 Tenerife Sur
34 Hotel Mar y Sol & Le Ro

PLACES TO EAT
4 Las Rocas Beach Club
14 Mesón Castellano Mojo Picón
22 Capricho

OTHER
1 Puerto de Colón
2 CCB Yacht Charters
3 The Book Swop
5 Policía Nacional
6 Correos y Telégrafos
7 Tourist Office
8 Estación de Guaguas
9 Drugstore Olympo
10 Salus
15 Pirámide de Arona
16 Viajes Insular
19 Centro de Buceo Los Cristianos
23 Caesar's & Establo
24 Librería Barbara
25 Atlantis Net
26 Viajes Isla Azul
27 Correos y Telégrafos
28 Mail Boxes Etc &
   Western Union
31 Policía Nacional
32 Bus Terminus

Los Cristianos & Playa de las Américas

For more modest pay packets, catamaran trips can be had for around 3500 ptas a person for three hours, including food.

Whale Watching & Other Boat Trips You will probably be hounded into taking a tour on one of the many sailing boats and glass-bottomed catamarans which set out in pursuit of whales and dolphins. Your average two-hour jaunt costs 2000 ptas, although some will charge double and throw in some food and drink of dubious value. Among the latter variety are Nautisport (☎ 922 79 14 59). They take you out aboard sailing vessels – the *Jolly Roger* (I kid you not) and the *Meridian* – at 11 am for about five hours.

Other Watersports Waterskiing costs around 5000 ptas a session, or you can go parascending (gliding from a parachute tied to a boat's behind) for 10 minutes at a cost of 3200 ptas.

Organised Tours
If you can't be bothered doing it under your own steam, you can get on a day tour of the island for around 2500 ptas; up to the northern mountain village of Masca (1300 ptas); or to the island of La Gomera (7000 ptas). Another popular excursion is a day's swimming and snorkelling at Los Gigantes, further north along the coast (see the Los Gigantes & Puerto de Santiago section earlier). Also popular with some tourists is a shopping trip to Santa Cruz and an evening at the 'authentic' Castillo de San Miguel, where you can enjoy a 'medieval' dinner whilst watching knights prance about, followed by an evening of dancing to 60s hits sung by a foursome called The Drifters!

Places to Stay – budget
Playa de las Américas There are no pensiones in this area. It's either expensive hotels or apartments, which can come in all shapes and sizes. The simple fact is that the entire area is often full to bursting. If you do arrive and would rather not wander around aimlessly for hours, head straight for the tourist office. They can give you some contacts for agents dealing in apartments and studios.

Among these are: Tenerife Holiday Rent (☎ 922 79 58 18), Edificio Altamar, Local 2-bajo; Custom Holidays (☎ 922 79 60 00), Aparthotel California 6; and Markus Management (☎ 922 75 10 64), Apartamentos Portosin, Local 3.

Los Cristianos For an apartment, try Anika Sur (☎ 922 79 13 77), Apartamentos Azahara, Local 5 & 6, extension of Avenida de Suecia. At Avenida de Suecia 60 is Premier Management Services (☎ 922 79 17 90).

Pensión La Paloma (no phone), in a lane off Calle del General Franco in the heart of town's pedestrian zone, has basic singles/doubles for 4000/6000 ptas – if you can get one. Nearby, *Pensión La Playa* (☎ 922 79 22 64), Calle de la Paloma 9, is also usually full. They charge 3300 ptas a day unless you stay for at least a week, in which case it comes down to 2100 ptas. It's nothing special.

Occasionally you can get a simple room at *Pensión Corisa* (☎ 922 79 07 69), around the corner from the restaurant of the same name at Calle Antigua del General Franco 18. A bed costs 2000 ptas.

Places to Stay – middle & top end
Playa de las Américas Again, the best thing to do if you arrive here without a reservation is first try the tourist office and approach one of the above listed agents. There are at least 100 apartment blocks of all classes and plenty of big hotels – singling them out in the limited scope of this guide is virtually impossible.

By way of example, *Apartamentos El Dorado* (☎ 922 79 05 00) is a couple of blocks from the beach and has doubles for up to 5500 ptas.

Los Cristianos Although not on the scale of Playa de las Américas, there is no shortage of apartments and big hotels in Los Cristianos.

Hotel Andrea's (☎ 922 79 00 12), Avenida de Valle Menéndez, has singles/doubles starting at 4000/6500 ptas. If that fails, you could try the hotel apartment block *Silvia* (☎ 922 79 25 64) next door. You'll pay at least 7000 ptas here for two beds with attached bathroom and kitchen.

A much nicer version of the same thing is *Tenerife Sur* (☎ 922 79 14 74), a block east of Avenida de Los Cristianos. Prices depend on the kind of room and season, starting at 7500 ptas and rising to 18,000 ptas. The apartments are spacious and have balconies. There is also a pool.

Worth noting is *Hotel Mar y Sol* (☎ 922 75 05 40; fax 922 79 05 73), which is at the eastern end of Calle del General Franco. It is one of the few places on the island which caters properly for disabled guests.

Places to Eat
Playa de las Américas The place is awash with restaurants. To name any seems almost churlish. Most fit into a general category of resort 'international' – you are unlikely to get any fine Canarian cuisine here, but Yorkshire pudding and pizza are all very popular.

One pricey, but attractive, spot, is *Las Rocas Beach Club*, whose restaurant has been built out right over the water. It belongs to the Hotel Jardín Tropical, but anyone may dine there.

For good mainland Spanish food, *Mesón Castellano Mojo Picón*, Residencial Las Viñas, is a good, authentic restaurant – something that is hard to come by in this place.

Drugstore Olympo is a 24-hour supermarket for those doing their own grocery shopping. It's on the corner of Avenida de Rafael Puig and Calle de la República de Panama.

Los Cristianos As in Playa de las Américas, the bulk of the restaurants zero in on the lowest common denominator and churn out extremely uninspired stuff to shovel down the unsuspecting foreign masses' throats.

Although nothing to write home about, *Restaurante La Estación*, next door to Hotel Andrea's back entrance at Calle Antigua del General Franco 22, at least has the distinction of being frequented by a largely Spanish clientele. The set menú de la casa is not bad at 900 ptas. For a sandwich and fine fruit shake, try *Capricho* on Calle de Juan XXIII.

Entertainment
Playa de las Américas Where do you start? Squeezed in between all the restaurants is an ocean of bars and discos. At night the streets are awash with young, northern Europeans splayed out in various poses of catatonic splendour. This, apart from the sunshine, is what most of the younger set are here for. But older folk have plenty of pubs of a slightly less hormonal character to choose from. Lots of German lager and fine British bitters (but do they travel well?) to be had.

Dance The Gran Ballet Clásico Español performs at the Pirámide de Arona (☎ 922 79 63 60) Avenida de las Américas, Playa de las Américas. They present some reasonable interpretations of flamenco. The tip is that tickets are more cheaply secured through your hotel than by calling the above number.

Los Cristianos This end of the tourist zone is rather tranquil. In the town centre about the only bars thumping on into the night are *Establo* and *Caesar's*, next door to one another at Calle de Pablo Abril 5.

Getting There & Away
Bus TITSA buses leave from the Estación de Guaguas on the Carretera General in Playa de las Américas. No 111 goes to Santa Cruz and No 487 to Tenerife Sur airport. They both pass through Los Cristianos (the stop is on Carretera de la Autopista). Plenty of other buses run between the two towns as well, en route to destinations like Los Gigantes, Las Galletas, El Médano, Arona and so on.

Sea Los Cristianos is the main jump-off point for ferries to the three westernmost islands.

Trasmediterránea operates one or two car ferries a day to San Sebastián de la Gomera. The one-way fare is 1920 ptas. The competition comes from Líneas Fred Olsen, with four runs and a minifare of 1560 ptas for the 2nd and 3rd departures. Trasmediterránea also operates three to four hydrofoils to San Sebastián (2070 ptas). Three of these proceed to Valle de Gran Rey on the other side of the island (2350 ptas).

Trasmediterránea also has a daily ferry to El Hierro. The more convenient one is the 8.45 am departure on Tuesdays, Thursdays, and weekends. It takes 5¼ hours, stops in San Sebastián and the ticket costs 2350 ptas.

For some reason which escapes human reason, the ferry companies seem intent on discouraging you from getting to Santa Cruz de la Palma. You have the choice of Trasmediterránea's direct service (Thursday and Saturday only), which departs at 8.15 pm and takes four or so hours, or Fred Olsen's daily 8 pm boat via La Gomera, which arrives at 1 am. Everybody's idea of the perfect arrival time is after midnight!

Getting Around
Bus Most of the TITSA buses running between Playa de las Américas and Los Cristianos and to other destinations beyond have the double function of acting as local transport, with various stops along Avenida Litoral in Playa de las Américas. Most places you'll need to get to will be within walking distance, though. The tourist office in Playa de las Américas has a map with bus stops and route numbers marked.

Taxi Watch the taxis here, as some drivers feel tempted to dispense with the meter.

AROUND LOS CRISTIANOS
Parque Ecológico Las Aguilas del Teide
About 3km from Los Cristianos off the road to Arona, this much publicised attraction offers displays of trained eagles flying in low over the crowd as they zero in on morsels held out for them by their trainers. You can also see an odd assortment of other beasties, including hippos and crocodiles. You can organise tickets through assorted agents in Playa de las Américas and Los Cristianos, who will put you on a free bus to get out there.

This is just one of several such attractions put on for the punters in the area. Others include Octopus Park (the biggest fun park in the islands – all sorts of water slides; it's a few minutes' drive outside Playa de las Américas heading for Adeje) and a camel ranch. You will be hard put to avoid brochures on such theme parks, and may well find them a useful distraction for the ankle-biters. In most cases, free buses are arranged to get tourists to and from these attractions.

Las Galletas
A rather hodgepodge array of modern buildings and semi-high rises, it is difficult to see what attracts people here, except for the usual order of sun and sea. Even the black sand and pebble beach seems hardly remarkable. Still, quite a few people end up in this relatively quiet backwater around the coast east from Los Cristianos.

Information Teide Financial SL (☎ 922 78 56 76), Edificio Yaiza, Calle General, is one of the few reps in the islands for Western Union money transfers.

Tenesub Marine (☎ 922 73 16 05), Calle de María del Carmen García 40, organises dive expeditions.

Places to Stay & Eat Tenerife's only fully equipped camping ground, *Camping Nauta* (☎ 922 78 51 18) is at Cañada Blanca, a few kilometres north of Las Galletas, just off the road to Buzanada.

Pensión La Estrella (☎ 922 73 15 62), Carretera General, Km 1, is, as the address suggests, a bit of a walk from central Las Galletas. But the singles/doubles are OK at 2000/2500 ptas, or 3500 ptas for doubles with own bath. Right in town, *Pensión Vitoria* (☎ 922 78 58 03), Calle de Venezuela 4, has simple rooms with own bath for 2500/3500 ptas. Otherwise, you can try at the various apartment blocks.

You'll find any number of waterfront restaurants. *Restaurante Varadero*, on the water where Calle de Fernando Salazar González runs into Calle del Varadero, is a pleasant spot.

THE EAST

Heading south from Santa Cruz, you have two choices: the TF-1 autovía, or the tortuous C-822, which once passed for the main highway along the east coast. The latter is infinitely slower and more scenic, if scenic is the right word to describe the bare, sinuous land cut up by *barrancos* and carved farming terraces, buttressed by rough-hewn stone walls.

Candelaria

Your first stop might be Candelaria, about 15km south of Santa Cruz. The only real sight here is the **Basílica de Nuestra Señora de Candelaria**, the patron saint of the archipelago. According to legend, an image of the Virgin Mary (apparently it was actually a wooden bust from the prow of a wrecked ship) turned up around here in the 1300s, was kept by the local Guanche chief and eventually passed into Spanish hands after the conquest.

A sanctuary was built on this seaside site in 1526, and in the 19th century was replaced by the present church and convent. Although the feast day is 2 February, the official celebrations take place on 15 August (coinciding with the Feast of the Assumption). Pilgrims from all over the island converge on the town for festivities on both holidays. The basilica can be visited daily from 7.30 am to 1 pm and 3 to 7.30 pm.

On the same square as the church, Plaza de la Patrona de Canarias, stands a row of larger-than-life statues of great Guanche leaders; behind them the Atlantic laps the black sandy beach, one of several around Candelaria.

Was He Tossed Off?

A great holiday destination, the Canary Islands make a nice backdrop for a little death, too. And so it is that the corpulent figure of media mogul Robert Maxwell was found washed up on the shores of Gran Canaria on 6 November 1991. He had gone missing the day before from his luxury yacht, off Tenerife. The autopsy was inconclusive, and although many think he committed suicide, the question persists – did he jump or was he pushed?

Why would the apparently successful chief of Maxwell Communications, owner of, among other publishing and printing concerns, London's *Daily Mirror*, kill himself?

Maxwell had made his way to Britain from Czechoslovakia in the early stages of WWII. Most of his family and relatives, all Jewish, would later perish in the Holocaust. After the war, having changed his name from Jan Ludvik Hoch, he got into academic and scientific publishing. He soon proved a dab hand at business, and proceeded to expand his operations until he acquired the Mirror Group in 1984. In the course of the 80s his empire moved into the USA, and in 1990 he launched the Europe-wide paper *The European*.

He had over-extended himself, however. Long suspected to be a shady dealer, he decided that the only way to prop up his top-heavy group was to start siphoning off money from his employees' pension funds. When things improve, he reasoned, I'll pop the money back in, and no-one will be any the wiser. He moved US$1.2 billion from company funds and pensions in this way, but the much hoped-for improvements in business didn't come. For many, therein lies the reason why his luxury Canary Islands cruise ended as it did.

An original eating experience in the area requires your own transport. Head back for the autovía and take exit (*salida*) 9. Follow the C-822 in the direction of Güímar and then the signs for Cuevacitas de Candelaria. *Casa María* (☎ 922 50 46 35) is outside the village in a cave (signposted). The food is good and the locale a one-off!

Candelaria is an easy bus ride from Santa Cruz (Nos 122, 123 & 124).

Güímar

There's not much to this town, although it is one of the oldest in the island. The **Iglesia de San Pedro** is the centrepiece, and a brief stroll in the surrounding streets is pleasant enough. You can pick up a snack and beer in the **Tasca La Zapatería**, Calle de las Canarias 1, a block from the church.

There are plenty of buses from Santa Cruz – No 127 is the slow one that plies the C-822.

South From Güímar

The ride south has its moments. Shortly after Güímar, the **Mirador de Don Martín** offers sweeping views of the coast and across to Gran Canaria. You then pass through farming pueblos like El Escobonal and Fasnia, before hitting upon **Icor**, an even smaller and half abandoned pueblo, interesting because most of the houses are still built of brown stone rather than concrete slabs.

Another 7km south lie **Arico Viejo** and **Arico Nuevo**. Surprisingly, it's the latter that is the most interesting, with pretty little white houses huddled around narrow lanes. From Arico to the end of the road in Los Cristianos/Playa de las Américas there is precious little of interest.

Those with wheels could make a 10km detour to the coast here for **Porís de Abona**, a fishing village which looks set to become a minor tourist resort.

The turn-off north at Granadilla de Abona for the Teide peak makes for a nice drive, passing through the hamlet of **Vilaflor**, known above all for its lacework, similar to that found in Venice.

Closer to Los Cristianos, the town of **Arona** is an agreeable little place. You might like to have a meal in the *Restaurante El Patio Canario*, a charming little French-run restaurant at Calle de Domínguez Alfonso 4, just up the road from the bus stop (No 480 for Los Cristianos).

On the coast, **El Médano** is a rather dumpy sort of town, but the beach is pretty good. Windsurfers are virtually guaranteed good conditions. There's none of the resort racket here either. You'll find a few places to stay, among them *Hostal Carel* (☎ 922 17 60 66), Avenida de los Príncipes 22, where singles/doubles cost up to 4000/5400 ptas with own bathroom.

Right on the beach is the upmarket *Hotel Médano* (☎ 922 17 70 00), where rooms come in at 7000/9000 ptas. A stone's throw from the hotel, three waterfront restaurants line up, each much the same as the other. Several buses leave from here, among them No 470 to Las Galletas and Los Cristianos.

Isla de la Palma

More properly known as San Miguel de la Palma, the north-westernmost island of the archipelago has also long been dubbed the Isla Bonita (Pretty Island), and it's easy enough to see why La Palma got the accolade.

With rainfall and spring water more plentiful here than anywhere else in the Canaries (on average the sun doesn't come out at all 63 days a year!), La Palma's 708 sq km form the greenest island of the Canaries. Its 81,521 inhabitants live fairly well from a combination of agriculture (it's hard to avoid banana plantations), fishing and the still modest tourist business. This comparative prosperity has not, however, been a constant on the island, and Venezuela has traditionally been the emigrant Palmeros' favourite place to escape to. So much so that the Latin American country is often known around here as the 'eighth (Canary) island'.

The flourishing orchards, plantations and forests contrast strikingly with the hostile volcanic heights, which form a kind of mountainous question mark down the middle of the island.

La Palma's most extraordinary feature is the huge horseshoe-shaped rock wall known as the Caldera de Taburiente, composed of the island's highest peaks, including the Roque de los Muchachos (which is also home to one of the world's most important astrophysical observatories). One statistic claims that, relative to its size, La Palma is the hilliest island in the world. It is any case the highest island in the archipelago after Tenerife.

Volcanic activity on the island is far from over, and the last modest eruption in the Canaries took place in the south of La Palma in 1971. The south end of the island is worlds away from the general lushness of La Palma – a black wasteland interspersed with the reds and browns of other volcanic material and the pale green of what little flora attempts to reclaim the land.

HIGHLIGHTS

ATLANTIC OCEAN

La Palma
Tenerife
La Gomera
El Hierro
Gran Canaria
Fuerteventura
Lanzarote
Alegranza
Africa

- Enjoying a *barraquito* on Placeta de Borero in Santa Cruz de la Palma
- Relaxing at the laid-back resort and black-sand beach of Puerto de Naos
- Exploring the Parque Nacional de la Caldera de Taburiente
- Clambering among the southern volcanoes and hiking the ridgeback Ruta de los Volcanes
- The fine old balconies of the old town of Santa Cruz de la Palma

---

The abrupt and often forbidding coastline does not offer the great sandy stretches that attract sun-seekers to La Palma's more easterly neighbours, although the cliffs and rocky outcrops are occasionally interrupted by pleasant little black beaches. For this reason alone the island may be spared the massive influx of tourists seen elsewhere in the Canaries, allowing those who do visit the luxury of exploring the ravines, hamlets and fertile countryside in comparitive peace.

History

La Palma was not incorporated into the Crown of Castilla until 1493, the year after Alonso Fernández de Lugo had finished off the island's native opposition. This he had

219

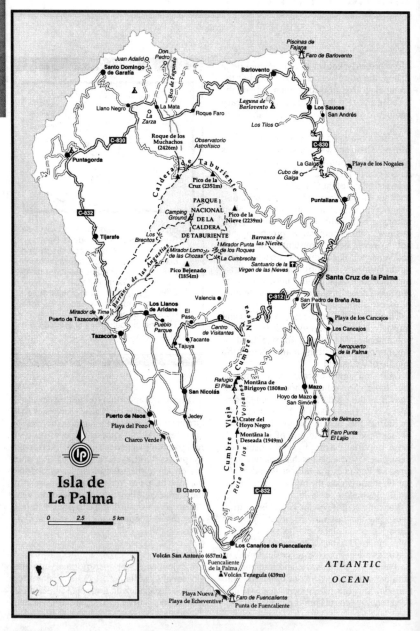

Isla de La Palma

0   2.5   5 km

ATLANTIC OCEAN

achieved only after a stroke of trickery, inviting their leader, Mencey Tanausú, to abandon his impregnable stronghold in the Caldera de Taburiente for talks, only to ambush him and his men at the spot now known as El Riachuelo. Tanausú was shipped to Spain as a slave, but went on hunger strike and never saw the Spanish mainland.

By the following century, the few Guanches (known as Benahoares on this island) who had not been enslaved or wiped out had been joined by a motley assortment of Spanish, Portuguese, Italian and Flemish migrants. The main exports became sugar, *malvasía* (Malmsey wine) and honey. In the meantime, the abundant Canary pine provided timber for burgeoning shipyards. By the late 16th century, as trans-Atlantic trade flourished, Santa Cruz was considered the third most important port of the Spanish empire after Seville and Antwerp (in modern Belgium).

The fortunes of La Palma to this day largely followed those of the other islands, as one cash crop succeeded another. Today, the banana is quite plainly still a mainstay of the local economy, although a wide range of crops are grown for local consumption. The cigars (which seem to be more commonly smoked than cigarettes by the menfolk of the island) are of particular note and concede little to the product of Havana.

Activities

Hiking is the main activity, with the massive depression of the Caldera de Taburiente forming the high point of any visit to the island. Other possible walks would take you south along the volcanic ridge of the Cumbre Vieja in the southern half of the island, while the north, the dense forest of Los Tilos is a green paradise far removed from the sandy resort of the Canaries, and ripe for exploration.

Diving is also a possibility, and you'll find several dive centres around the island. The island does have beaches – a few of them quite pretty – but the black sand puts some people off and, in any case, they are not the endless coastlines that are so popular elsewhere in the Canaries.

Accommodation

Camping Free camping is prohibited on the island. There are a few basic camping grounds, but to use them you need to apply in advance. For the only camping ground inside the Parque Nacional de la Caldera de Taburiente (a 6km hike from Los Brecitos, itself 10km of driveable dirt trail north from Los Llanos de Aridane), call the park authorities at Calle de O'Daly 35 in Santa Cruz (☎ 922 41 31 41) or the park's Centro de Visitantes (☎ 922 49 72 77), 3.5km east of El Paso. The facilities are basic and it has room for 100 people – you need to book well ahead (one month), and pick up the permit in person, preferably from the Centro de Visitantes. The maximum stay is three days.

There are four camping grounds outside the park: outside Puntagorda, around the Laguna de Barlovento, the Refugio El Pilar in the north of the Cumbre Vieja, and at San Antonio, south-east of Santo Domingo de Garafía. For these you need to make a request at the Department of the Environment (Consejería de Política Territorial y Medio Ambiente) in Santa Cruz (☎ 922 41 15 83) or El Paso (☎ 922 48 52 38). You need to apply at least a week in advance and pick up your permit in person at least two days before you intend to be in the camping grounds. The Santa Cruz office is just before the tunnel leading south to the airport.

Hotels & Apartments There is a shortage of standard accommodation such as hotels and pensiones on the island. Resort apartments are spreading in a few areas, notably at Los Cancajos, just south of Santa Cruz, and Puerto de Naos in the west, but these are aimed at pre-booked package tourists, mainly from Germany and Holland.

Casas Rurales Another pleasant option are *casas rurales*, farmhouses done up to cater for city-softies. The Asociación de

Turismo Rural has around 70 such houses scattered across the island, mostly in the north (where alternatives are extremely thin on the ground). Try the central reservations office (☎ 922 43 06 25, fax 922 43 03 08), Casa Luján, El Pósito 3, Puntallana (or write to Apartado de Correos 447, 38700 Santa Cruz de la Palma). There's a Web site at infolapalma.com.

Getting There & Away
Air From La Palma there are frequent connections to Tenerife, but fewer to Gran Canaria. You can also get limited flights to some mainland Spanish cities, while charter flights link the island directly with some European destinations. See Getting There & Away in the following Santa Cruz de la Palma section for more details.

Sea Ferries from Tenerife (Santa Cruz and Los Cristianos) and La Gomera arrive in Santa Cruz de la Palma. See Getting There & Away in the following Santa Cruz de la Palma section for more details.

Getting Around
Bus As with the island of Tenerife, you are better off buying a Bonobus card if you intend using the buses a lot to get around the island. They start at 2000 ptas and represent a discount of about 30% off the normal individual fares. They can be bought at bus stations and various shops such as newsagents. There are 18 bus lines, covering most main destinations, although you may find yourself needing to change buses (for instance, to get from Santa Cruz to the small beach resort of Puerto de Naos, you need to change at Los Llanos de Aridane).

Santa Cruz de la Palma

• *population 17,000*

The row of seemingly modern, gleaming-white buildings that greets the traveller who lands by sea in the harbour of Santa Cruz might seem to promise little. Look inland and, as the waves of white walls give way to the farmers' green terraces and volcanic hills, you may be sorely tempted to strike immediately inland.

But hang on, because hidden from view as you get off the ferry is a quite enchanting old town centre, featuring some fine examples of old Canarian architecture gathered in and around some charming little plazas.

History
The bay that is the town's window on the world was known to the Guanches as Timibucar, and the area around it as Tedote. The island's Spanish conqueror, Alonso Fernández de Lugo, had the first breakwater built, along with the settlement's first public buildings.

As Spain's imperial interests in the Americas grew in the 16th century, so did the fortunes of Santa Cruz, whose dockyards soon acquired a reputation as the best in all the Canary Islands. Such was the town's importance that King Felipe II had the first Juzgado de Indias (Court of the Indias) installed here in 1558.

Of course, such prosperity did not go unnoticed, and Santa Cruz was frequently besieged and occasionally sacked by a succession of pirates, including those under the command of Sir Francis Drake. The worst attack came in 1553, when Jean Paul de Billancourt (also known as Jambe de Bois, or Pegleg) unleashed a merciless assault on the town.

Orientation
Santa Cruz is a fairly small town, and most of what is of interest lies within a few blocks of the waterfront Avenida Marítima, which runs north from the ferry port. It is about a 15-minute walk from the port to the Barranco de las Nieves that virtually marks off the northern confines of the town.

The heart of the old town and the prettiest part of Santa Cruz de la Plam lies around Plaza de España and Calle de O'Daly, known to the Santacruceros as the Calle Real.

Information
Tourist Office The Oficina de Turismo (☎ 922 41 31 41) is at Calle de O'Daly 22, and opens from 8.30 am to 1 pm and 4 to 6 pm Monday to Friday, and from 10 am to 2 pm Saturday.

Consulate Germany has an honorary consulate (☎ 922 42 06 89) at Calle de O'Daly 39.

Money A cluster of banks lines Calle de O'Daly. Western Union has a representative at the airport.

Post & Communications The Correos y Telégrafos is on Plaza de la Constitución. The town centre is loaded with public phones. The postcode for Santa Cruz de la Palma is 38700.

Bookshops You can pick up a wide range of foreign papers at Librería Cervantes, Calle de O'Daly 4. The best bookshop is Librería Trasera, Calle de Álvarez de Abreu 22.

Medical & Emergency The Hospital de Dolores (☎ 922 42 32 62), Calle de Ramón y Cajal s/n, is about halfway between Plaza de España and Plaza de San Francisco. You can call the Cruz Roja (Red Cross; ☎ 922 41 16 95) for an ambulance.

The Policía Nacional (☎ 922 41 12 37) are at Calle de Pérez Galdós 16, and the local Guardia Civil (☎ 922 41 11 00) at La Portada.

The Old Town
The curiously named Calle de O'Daly is the most venerable street in Santa Cruz, dominated by the 17th-century late-renaissance **Palacio de Salazar**, now home to the tourist office. Along both sides of the pedestrianised street is a mix of shops, bars and offices, most of them housed in centuries-old Canarian mansions.

On Plaza de la Constitución stands the post office (a few doors down from the local office of the Falange – the ruling fascist party under Franco), and on the rise behind it (climb the stairs about 100m south of the post office) the modest 16th-century **Ermita de Nuestra Señora de la Luz**, one of a few small chapels in Santa Cruz. It opens for Mass only from 7 to 9 pm on Saturday and from 11 am to 1 pm on Sunday. Another, dedicated to **San Sebastián**, is on the street of the same name behind the Iglesia de San Salvador.

Just north of the Parador on the waterfront is a series of wonderful **old houses**, gaily painted and sporting a very varied series of balconies. Some of these date back to the 16th century. This penchant for balconies came with Andalucían migrants and was modified by Portuguese influences. The style was also exported, and similar balconies can be seen on noble houses in Venezuela, Cuba and Peru, where they came to be part of the so-called 'colonial style' of building.

The fact they are there at all is perhaps more due to luck than anything else. King Felipe II apparently disapproved of balconies, and sent orders to the islands that they be torn down. The ship carrying the royal command apparently never made it to La Palma, and so the good citizens of Santa Cruz maintained their prized balconies, safe in their ignorance.

Plaza de España Wander north along Calle de O'Daly and you end up in the heart of old Santa Cruz. The main façade of the **Ayuntamiento** (town hall) is a 16th-century renaissance creation, and the imposing **Iglesia de San Salvador** dates from the same period. Inside the town hall, there are magnificent tea tree ceilings, or *artesonados*. Much the same can be said for the church, which boasts a fine *mudéjar* ceiling, rich in traditional motifs like the eight-point star whose roots lie in mainland Spain's Moorish period. Noteworthy among the artworks is the 16th-century Flemish carving *Cristo de los Mulatos*.

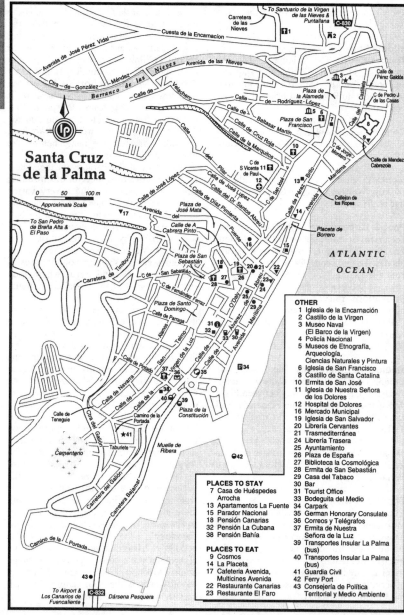

Santa Cruz de la Palma

0   50   100 m
Approximate Scale

ATLANTIC
OCEAN

OTHER
1 Iglesia de la Encarnación
2 Castillo de la Virgen
3 Museo Naval
(El Barco de la Virgen)
4 Policía Nacional
5 Museos de Etnografía,
Arqueología,
Ciencias Naturales y Pintura
6 Iglesia de San Francisco
8 Castillo de Santa Catalina
10 Ermita de San José
11 Iglesia de Nuestra Señora
de los Dolores
12 Hospital de Dolores
16 Mercado Municipal
19 Iglesia de San Salvador
20 Librería Cervantes
21 Trasmediterránea
24 Librería Trasera
25 Ayuntamiento
26 Plaza de España
27 Biblioteca la Cosmológica
28 Ermita de San Sebastián
29 Casa del Tabaco
30 Bar
31 Tourist Office
33 Bodeguita del Medio
34 Carpark
35 German Honorary Consulate
36 Correos y Telégrafos
37 Ermita de Nuestra
Señora de la Luz
39 Transportes Insular La Palma
(bus)
40 Transportes Insular La Palma
(bus)
41 Guardia Civil
42 Ferry Port
43 Consejería de Política
Territorial y Medio Ambiente

PLACES TO STAY
7 Casa de Huéspedes
Arrocha
13 Apartamentos La Fuente
15 Parador Nacional
18 Pensión Canarias
32 Pensión La Cubana
38 Pensión Bahía

PLACES TO EAT
9 Cosmos
14 La Placeta
17 Cafetería Avenida,
Multicines Avenida
22 Restaurante Canarias
23 Restaurante El Faro

Isla de la Gomera
Top Left: Sunset view of Pico del Teide, Tenerife from Alto de Garajonay on La Gomera
Top Right: Playa de Hermigua
Bottom: Agulo

Isla de La Gomera
Left: Terrace farming, Valle de Gran Rey
Top Right: Cemetery on the heights above Alojera
Middle Right: Houses of San Sebastián de la Gomera
Bottom Right: Closed chapel at Mirador del Igualero, south of Parque Nacional de Garajonay

The square itself boasts a fine old fountain and is flanked by grand mansions. You'll see more such noble houses, most of them adorned with balconies in a variety of styles (but considerably more recent than those on Avenida Marítima), as you head north along Calle de Pérez de Brito.

Around the Barranco de las Nieves The **Iglesia de San Francisco** is another renaissance effort, also with mudéjar ceiling and jammed with works of art, the majority of them unmistakably baroque.

The restored convent next door now houses the combined **Museos de Etnografía, Arqueología, Ciencias Naturales y Pintura**. In here you'll find everything from Guanche skulls to cupboards of stuffed animals and fish; shells and corals; traditional household utensils; and a very nice portrait of Franco upstairs in among a fairly dreary collection of generally little-known Spanish artists. The old convent is itself worth the visit though. It is open from 9 am to 2 pm and 4 to 6.30 pm, Monday to Friday. Admission costs 300 ptas.

North across the leafy Plaza de la Alameda (a good place to hover over a beer), it looks as though Columbus' *Santa María* got stranded here. But no, it's actually a rather weird idea for the town's **Museo Naval**! Locals know it as El Barco de la Virgen (the Virgin's Boat). It opens from 9.30 am to 2 pm and 4 to 6.30 pm, Monday to Friday. Admission costs 300 ptas.

On the waterfront, the **Castillo de Santa Catalina** was one of several erected in the 17th century to help fend off pirate raids. Across the ravine and higher is a rather smaller version of the same thing, the **Castillo de la Virgen**, while looming behind it is still another 16th-century church, the **Iglesia de la Encarnación**. That so many grand churches went up in much the same period is eloquent testimony to the prosperity of Santa Cruz at the time.

Cigars If you want to see how these big brown tobacco sticks are handmade, poke your nose in at the **Casa del Tabaco** (☎ 922 42 95 01), Calle de Álvarez de Abreu 37.

Special Events
Every five years (next in the year 2000), Santa Cruz really puts on its party clothes for the June-July celebration of the Bajada de la Virgen de las Nieves (Descent of Our Lady of the Snows). It is the principal fiesta in the whole island – finding a place to stay at this time without having booked in advance will be no easy matter! The high point is the 'dance of the dwarves' which takes place along Calle de O'Daly.

Down this street also march the processions for Carnaval (February) and Easter Week, when members of lay brotherhoods parade in their blood-red robes and tall, pointy hoods (not uncommon in Spanish Easter parades, but chillingly reminiscent of the Ku Klux Klan!).

Places to Stay – budget
Pensión La Cubana (☎ 922 41 13 54), Calle de O'Daly 24, is something of a travellers' hostel and the pick of a small crop. The clean and attractive singles/doubles in this old Santa Cruz house cost 3000/4000 ptas. Unlike most places of this grade, the basins in the rooms even have hot water.

Pensión Canarias (☎ 922 41 31 82), Calle de A. Cabrera Pinto 27, has no charm, but it's OK. Singles/doubles with own bath cost 3000/4300 ptas. Cheaper rooms without own bath cost 2300/4000 ptas.

Pensión Bahía (☎ 922 41 18 46), Calle de la Virgen de la Luz 35, has basic singles/doubles for 2000/3500 ptas. It's across from the Ermita de Nuestra Señora de la Luz.

The *Casa de Huéspedes Arrocha* (☎ 922 41 11 17), Calle de Pérez Brito 79, is about as cheap as they come here, with rooms for 2000/3000 ptas. Only problem is, it seemed very closed at the time of writing!

Places to Stay – middle & top end
Apartamentos La Fuente (☎ 922 41 56 36), Calle de Pérez Brito 49, is a good bet, especially for travellers who come in threes.

There are no singles. Smaller doubles/triples cost 4500/5700 ptas, while bigger ones with balcony and views cost 7500/8700 ptas. The apartments come with kitchen and lounge.

The town's top address is the waterfront *Parador Nacional* (☎ 922 41 23 40; fax 922 41 18 56), Avenida Marítima 34, where rooms cost 7500/11,000 ptas.

Places to Eat

A great little place for a beer and filling arepa is *Cosmos*, Avenida Marítima 70.

If you happen to have a little money in your pockets, you should really spill some of it at *La Placeta*, Placeta de Borrero 1. The restaurant is upstairs and the Canarian/international menu is superb. A main dish will cost upwards of 1500 ptas. If this is too much, come by for breakfast – a barraquito in the little square is a good investment.

Restaurante Canarias, Avenida Marítima 29, is a mid-priced place that offers hearty meals. The meat dishes are good and cost around 1300 ptas. Across the road, at No 27, *Restaurante El Faro* doesn't look like much, but it is popular with Santacruceros especially for lunch.

For a quick burger, pizza (nothing special) or a full meal, the *Cafetería Avenida*, in the same building as the cinema at Avenida del Puente 37, is not bad.

Entertainment

Cinema You can catch movies at the Multicines Avenida complex, Avenida del Puente 37.

Cafés & Bars Avenida Marítima is lined with cafés, *zumerías* (juice bars) and bars of a more nocturnal colouring. The Bodeguita del Medio, Calle de Álvarez de Abreu 58, is a bright little drinkery. Later in the evening, you could move across to the nameless bar at No 65. For discos, you need to head down the coast to Los Cancajos.

Things to Buy

A flea market is held on Sunday at the car park on Avenida Marítima.

Getting There & Away

Air The poor sea links make wings the only sensible alternative for most people – for this reason flights are often booked solid. Binter connects La Palma airport (☎ 922 41 15 40) with Tenerife Norte (eight daily) and Gran Canaria (two daily). Air Europa has scheduled flights to half a dozen mainland Spanish cities, including Madrid and Barcelona. Otherwise, traffic consists of direct charter flights, mostly from Germany, with a few from Amsterdam and Zürich.

The airport is 7km south of Santa Cruz. You'll find several car-rental agents, an exchange bureau (with Western Union money transfer representative) and an ATM there.

Bus There is no bus station. Transportes Insular La Palma buses service most destinations on the island and depart from Carretera Bajamar, virtually on Plaza de la Constitución. The fare to Los Llanos de Aridane is 570 ptas and to Fuencaliente 425 ptas.

Taxi You can use taxis to get around, but they aren't a cheap mode of transport. The trip to Puerto de Naos on the west coast, for example, will burn a 4000 ptas hole in your pocket.

Car & Motorcycle The C-830 heads north out of Santa Cruz for Puntallana and on around the northern half of the island to Puntagorda. For Fuencaliente, follow the short stretch of highway to the airport and follow the signs down the C-832. If you're off to El Paso and on to Los Llanos de Aridane and Tazacorte, you can follow the Fuencaliente road and turn off when you see the appropriate signs, or take the Carretera de Galión for Breña Alta.

Sea Trasmediterránea ferries are few and far between. Two a week (Friday and Sunday) depart at 1 am for Los Cristianos (Tenerife), where they arrive at 8.15 am. The same ferry proceeds then to San Sebastián de la Gomera. The other way, you don't arrive in Santa Cruz until after midnight! Another leaves at 2 pm on Tuesday for Santa Cruz de Tenerife (arrival 8 pm). The minimum fare in either case is 2690 ptas. A bed in a cabin will cost up to 5000 ptas.

A Líneas Fred Olsen ferry departs daily from Los Cristianos at 8 pm, calls in at San Sebastián de la Gomera and then proceeds to Santa Cruz de la Palma, where it arrives around 1 am (must be a conspiracy!). It turns around an hour later for the return journey. The minimum one-way fare is 2690 ptas, or 8800 ptas for a cabin (good for one or two passengers).

You can buy tickets at the port or at travel agents. Trasmediterránea has an office at Calle de O'Daly 2.

Getting Around
To/From the Airport Buses leave every thirty minutes on the quarter hour from the airport and take about 20 minutes, stopping at Los Cancajos and then the port and Parador. The fare is 160 ptas. A taxi will cost about 1000 ptas.

Bus Buses to the beach at Los Cancajos (125 ptas) are fairly frequent, stopping there en route to the airport. It would take you about 40 minutes to walk it.

AROUND SANTA CRUZ DE LA PALMA
Santuario de la Virgen de las Nieves
A 3.5km hike or drive inland from Santa Cruz (follow the signs from the Avenida Marítima where it crosses the Barranco de las Nieves), stands La Palma's main object of pilgrimage.

This modest little 17th-century church is in the fairly standard Canarian colonial style, whitewashed, with tea tree balconies and a fine mudéjar ceiling. Above the altar is placed the image of the Virgin Mary that is brought in grand procession down to Santa Cruz every five years (see Special Events above). The spot is charming, surrounded by green slopes and palm trees, and those who walk up will at least be rewarded by the restaurant bar. Bus No 14 comes up from Santa Cruz.

Los Cancajos
A small strip of black-sand beach forms the nucleus of the east coast resorts. About 40 minutes' walk south of the capital, there's not an awful lot to say about the place – apart from the beach, 16 sets of apartments and a scattering of restaurants, bars and discos. There is also the San Borondon dive centre (☎ 922 18 13 93), Centro Comercial de los Cancajos, Local 27.

Restaurante Tiuna overlooks the beach, and for more traditional dishes try *Mesón Canario*, in Centrocancajos, Local 314.

The two discos, Decada and Guaraná, are the premier nightspots on the whole island.

Around the Island

PARQUE NACIONAL DE LA CALDERA DE TABURIENTE
Scan the enormous and ancient stone walls of this natural fortress from the south and you can see how the terrain presented something of a challenge to the invading Spaniards back in the late 15th century. Here the last of the Benahoares under Mencey Tanausú took refuge and there was precious little Alonso Fernández de Lugo could do to dislodge them. Luckily for him, the chief seemed to have some sort of faith in the honour of his opponents and was induced to abandon his eyrie for 'talks' that proved to be none other than an old-fashioned ambush.

The Parque Nacional de la Caldera de Taburiente was declared a national park in 1954, the fourth in Spain. Its massive, broken wall of volcanic rock is about 10km in diameter, and its only real opening, the aptly named Barranco de las Angustias (Gorge of Fear), lies to the south-west. The walls drop in some places as much as 2000m, and their crests are crenellated by shafts of rock known as *roques*. The park covers 4690 hectares and at its lower levels it is covered in dense thickets of Canary pine.

All may seem impressively still as you

contemplate this extraordinary feat of accidental engineering, but the forces of erosion are hard at work. Landslides and collapsing roques are not infrequent, and some geologists give the caldera only another 5000 years before its last vestiges finally disappear – time enough for us to admire it at leisure.

In 1825 the German geologist, Leopold von Buch, applied the Spanish term 'caldera' (a large, deep pot or cauldron) to what he assumed to be a massive volcanic crater, the Caldera de Taburiente. The term stuck, to be used as a standard term for all such volcanic craters the world over. Problem is, it appears that this caldera, although indeed largely made up of volcanic rock, was not the result of a massive eruption, but has rather been slowly excavated by erosion over the millennia.

Water flows mainly along underground channels but occasionally crashes headlong in waterfalls down the caldera's many steep ravines. It flows to the south-west coast along the Barranco de las Angustias and is siphoned off to irrigate the lowlands beyond the park.

Approaches to the Park

The South No roads run right through the park. From the south you have two possible approaches. The most common is from El Paso, 3.5km east of which lies the park's Centro de Visitantes. It is open from 10 am to 2 pm and 4 to 6 pm Monday to Friday, and from 10 am to 3 pm Saturday. It can help plan walks in the park. Next to the centre is the turn-off north for La Cumbrecita, a 7km drive that takes you to a *mirador* (lookout) and information booth in the southern reaches of the park. That's as far as your motor will get you.

Alternatively, from Los Llanos de Aridane (follow the signs for Los Barrios) a dirt trail leads 10km into the park and ends at Los Brecitos – the trail follows the Barranco de las Angustias in places. From there it is a 6km hike to the park's only camping ground (see Accommodation at the beginning of this chapter).

From both these points several walking trails lead off into the park.

The North A secondary road snakes across this half of the island, and skirts the northern peaks of the caldera. Coming from Santa Cruz, the road is signposted Observatorio Astrofísico del Roque de los Muchachos. You'll need your own vehicle as no buses pass this way.

If you're not keen on long hikes and simply want to get an idea of what this massive eroded wall and its many gorges look like, a drive up this way and a few strategic stops is the best way to approach what is after all the island's star attraction. The most spectacular lookout is from the Roque de los Muchachos (at 2426m the island's highest point), which you can drive to. The turn-off for the Roque is the same as for the observatory, which may *not* be visited. A sign proclaims that only authorised personnel may enter – this appears to refer only to the observatory buildings, although what to make of the barrier across half the road is anyone's guess. Should you wish to avoid all this, there is a spot to leave your car on the main road itself, from where you can scramble up to the same point (ironically right past the observatory buildings) along a clearly marked path. The spot is signposted Mirador de la Caldera de Taburiente and lies a few kilometres east of the turn-off for the observatory and Roque de los Muchachos.

Hiking in the Park

A handy, although far from complete map to pick up if you don't already have a separate walking guide is published by the Ministerio de Medio Ambiente (Environment Ministry) and entitled *Caldera de Taburiente*. It indicates some walking trails and comes with descriptions of the flora and fauna in the park. The information booth at the Mirador de la Cumbrecita sells them for 400 ptas.

The trails aren't in bad shape, but signposting is scarce. Come prepared for all weather extremes – when the sun is shining

Starry Starry Night

When you gaze up into the crystal arch of sky above the Canary Islands, you cannot help but get some sense of what it is that excites astronomers from the world over. The quality of the sky is such that the islands have been singled out as one of the best locations in the world for earth-bound observation of the universe. Madrid even has the Law of the Sky (passed in 1988) in place to protect what it considers an 'astronomical reserve'. The law governs such issues as outdoor lighting and air pollution. In January 1992, the Oficina Técnica para la Protección de la Calidad del Cielo (Technical Office for the Protection of the Sky's Quality), was set up to keep a permanent watch.

For more than 30 years astronomers have been peering into the night firmament here. Their efforts are coordinated by the Instituto de Astrofísica de Canarias (IAC), based at the Universidad de la Laguna on Tenerife. In 1979, Spain agreed to internationalise the effort, signing a protocol that led to the 1985 inauguration of the European Northern Observatory, shared by 12 western European nations. Researchers working on all sorts of projects have to apply for time on the telescopes, with a fifth of the allocations reserved for Spanish scientists.

The IAC has an observatory on the Teide mountain (2400m) at Izaña, and another at Roque de los Muchachos on La Palma. The Teide observatory is used primarily for solar research and has attracted some of the best European telescopes for this kind of work, including the Franco-Italian THEMIS and the German VTT and other solar instruments. Other telescopes are used to train Spanish astronomers and to study the Big Bang.

More famous is the observatory located at an altitude of 2426m, just on the edge of the Parque Nacional de la Caldera de Taburiente on La Palma. And while astronomers at Teide are daylight creatures, their colleagues at the Roque de los Muchachos observatory are very much night owls. Even the locals support the scientists' efforts, with the island's lights being turned off once a year to allow certain experiments to be carried out. Making a virtue out of necessity, the occasion becomes one for impromptu partying – when stumbling in the dark presumably starts well before inebriation sets in.

Current research ranges from the study of the expansion of the universe through to star bursts, the observation of quasars and investigation of 'circumnuclear gas', eruptions of extragalactic supernovae, and studies on telescope making, optics and infrared instrumentation. The most important telescopes here are those of the Isaac Newton Group, whose big gun is the state-of-the-art William Herschel Telescope, an Anglo-Dutch instrument with a 4.2m diameter. It is one of the most advanced telescopes on the planet. The Isaac Newton telescope itself has a diameter of 2.5m.

Among others is a series of new technology telescopes (NTTs), including Italy's Galileo project (3.5m diameter) and the Scandinavian countries' joint effort, the 2.5m Nordic Optical Telescope (NOT).

But the sun will also rise on Roque de los Muchachos, as a new and powerful solar telescope called LEST is planned. Its addition will make the combined IAC observatories the world's leading centre for solar astronomy.

The observatories are not open to the public.

DAMIEN SIMONIS

Observatorio Astrofísico del Roque de los Muchachos

it's hot, but it can easily turn nastily cold. Always take water and, on longer walks, food supplies.

The South From the Mirador de la Cumbrecita you can undertake a couple of short, painless strolls. The first leads 1km along a track west of La Cumbrecita to another lookout, the Mirador Lomo de las Chozas. A little more difficult is the trek north (initially downhill) to the Mirador Punta de los Roques. A more challenging hike strikes out north-north-east to El Escuchadero, up inside the eastern wall of the caldera. Reckon on about two hours each way.

Another possibility, if you have your own wheels (in fact doing anything in the park presupposes that you are independently mobile), is to follow the fork in the road to Valencia from the Centro de Visitantes rather than that to La Cumbrecita. The asphalt road becomes a dirt trail for a bit, then recovers its bitumen covering. Shortly thereafter another track leads off to the left. Follow this for about 10 minutes to a flat section of road, where you'll see a walking trail that heads north (right) to the Pico Bejenado (1854m). This is about an hour's walk, and the reward is one of the most inspiring views out over the caldera.

From the camping ground (itself a 6km trek from Los Brecitos), various walks can be done. They lead north part of the way up some of the ravines sliced into the northern walls of the caldera, and circuits inside its heart below. In summer (June to August), park guides lead day-long excursions from the camping ground. You need to contact the Centro de Visitantes first to book in. Just near the camping ground, the clear water from several barrancos runs together in the so-called Playa de Taburiente, where tired hikers can give themselves a refreshing rinse down.

The North It is possible to walk around much of the length of the top of the rock walls that form the caldera. From Santa Cruz take the approach road described above and leave the car at the turn-off for the Pico de la Nieve (2239m). A 2km stroll brings you to the peak from where you have fine views from east to west across the basin of the caldera. Those who have given themselves the whole day (and arranged for a car to be waiting for them in the car park at the Roque de los Muchachos), can in fact follow a narrow path right around to the Roque. You will then have the extraordinary spectacle of the caldera constantly on the left.

Although not too difficult, this six-hour walk gets hairy at a few points, and a fear of heights is definitely not a recipe for success!

If you don't want to do this whole walk, the drive west affords several opportunities to stop at lookouts and lean out over one of nature's most remarkable balconies. The last of these (heading west) is signposted Mirador de la Caldera de Taburiente. There is room off the road to park about four cars. From here head west about 100m and to the left you'll see a rocky path winding up to the top.

It's a quick 10-minute or so scramble past some of the observatory buildings to a fine lookout over the caldera, and a little further to the distinctive rock figures of the 'lads' (*muchachos*) that constitute the Roque de los Muchachos.

THE NORTH
Puntallana
San Juan de Puntallana still retains some signs of its centuries of inhabitation, among them the **Iglesia de San Juan Bautista**, but there is really not a lot to this small and largely neglected hamlet.

Outside the village, however, is one of those delightful little finds still possible on an island relatively undamaged by mass tourism. **Playa de los Nogales** is a comparatively long stretch of black sandy beach backed by forbidding cliffs that by midday already cast their shadow across the sand. You'll need your own transport to get here. From Puntallana follow signs for the coastal hamlet of Bajamar, and then the turn-off to 'Playa Nogales'. You have to park your vehicle at the top of the cliffs and pick your way down a steep dirt path.

La Galga
Somewhat larger than Puntallana, La Galga is in much the same vein and could be skipped without any great loss. A side road leads 4km west to the **Cubo de la Galga**, a small protected forest.

San Andrés & Los Sauces
Of all the island's villages, San Andrés is one of the best preserved. Walking the uneven cobbled streets is a delight, with its tumbledown houses and a couple of small churches. The Fiesta de San Andrés is celebrated on 30 November.

You can stay in San Andrés at one of a couple of pensiones. *Casa de Huéspedes El Drago* (☎ 922 45 03 50) is on the main road and has singles/doubles with bath for 2000/ 3500 ptas. Nearby, *Pensión Las Lonjas* (☎ 922 45 07 36), Calle de San Sebastián 16, has doubles with bath for 3000 ptas. *Restaurante San Andrés*, Carretera General, is recommended for its traditional local dishes.

Los Sauces is of little interest except for bus connections to Santa Cruz, but if you have a vehicle you could take a nearby back road for **Los Tilos** (the turn-off is about 1km before Los Sauces if you are coming from Santa Cruz), a small subtropical forest in the Barranco del Agua. UNESCO declared it a Biosphere Reserve in 1983, and it contains the biggest concentration of *laurisilva* (laurel forest) on the island (for more about laurisilva, see the La Gomera chapter). The Centro de Visitantes is open from 9 am to 5 pm, Monday to Friday. There are several walking trails through the area. Just behind the Centro de Visitantes, one trail leads upwards (750 steps on the way) to a fine lookout – reckon on about a half hour up. A tougher walk (6km one way) for those used to steep hill-walking leads south-west to the Corderos spring.

Up to six buses a day connect San Andrés and Los Sauces, which is on the main Barlovento-Santa Cruz bus route.

Barlovento
Barlovento is a rather dull farming centre and local transport hub. A few kilometres south is the **Laguna de Barlovento**, an artificial lake created in an extinct volcano.

The rather surprising *Hotel La Palma Romántica* (☎ 922 18 62 21) is on the main road towards the western exit of town. It is the only three-star hotel in the north of the island and singles/doubles cost 9000/12,000 ptas. The *Parrilla La Pradera* is a pleasant spot for grilled dishes. It's on the main road out by the Laguna de Barlovento.

For the so-called **Piscinas de Fajana**, take the Santa Cruz road for a couple of kilometres and then the signposted left turn that leads you 1.5km down to the coast, where Atlantic waves keep a protected rock pool full of refreshing ocean water.

Up to nine buses run between Barlovento (via Los Sauces) and Santa Cruz, although the service drops to four on Sunday.

La Zarza
Less than 1km after the turn-off for the hamlet of La Mata (heading west) you'll see a visitors' centre for La Zarza being built (maybe it will be finished by the time you get there) just off the south side of the highway. Roughly a 15-minute stroll down a trail behind the centre are some of the most remarkable **rock carvings** left behind by the Benahoares, the Guanches of La Palma. No one has been able to decipher the strange circular designs. Hitching or your own wheels are about your only chance of getting here and out again.

Other rock carvings have been found in various locations in the north of the island, including Roque Faro, Don Pedro and Juan Adalid (see also Cueva de Belmaco below).

Santo Domingo de Garafía
This soporific village has little to draw you in for long. It started life as a busy community of Portuguese Jews, who had been expelled from their home country at the end of the 15th century. What little of the old nucleus of the village remains is gathered

around the 16th-century **Iglesia de la Virgen de la Luz**, which was never finished, and the adjacent Plaza de Baltasar Martín.

There's nowhere to stay here, but a few casas rurales are scattered about in neighbouring hamlets. On Plaza de Baltasar Martín there's a bar with tables outside, and the *Restaurante de Santo Domingo*. For Canarian potage and La Palma cheese, head for the *Restaurante San Antonio*, Calle de Díaz y Suárez 3. One bus a day runs between here and Barlovento.

Tijarafe
• *population 2195*

A brief wander around the cobbled streets of the centre of this farming village is a pleasant diversion. The area around it is chopped up by high ridges and deep ravines. On the way south, if you have your own wheels, you could stop at the **Mirador de Time**, where you can enjoy a beer as you contemplate the vistas across the island and ocean.

There's nowhere to stay in Tijarafe. A few buses run south to Los Llanos de Aridane and north to Puntagorda.

THE CENTRE

The C-812 highway climbs from south of Santa Cruz into the Cumbre Nueva ('new summit'), a heavily wooded mountain range that has its continuation in the Cumbre Vieja ('old summit') further south.

The first spot of interest is the Centro de Visitantes for the Parque Nacional de la Caldera de Taburiente (see the relevant section above), 3.5km east of El Paso, and the turn-off for the Mirador de la Cumbrecita inside the park.

A few kilometres before the Centro, another side road branches off south, climbing up into the pine-laden Cumbre Vieja south towards the Refugio El Pilar (a mountain hut for hikers) and a picnic spot. From there a hiking trail leads south along the entire mountain ridge through the heart of the island's volcanic territory towards Fuencaliente. This is a demanding trek for

which you should reckon on six to seven hours one way as far as Canarios de Fuencaliente (from where you can get a bus to Santa Cruz – see below). You'll know you're reaching civilisation again when you spot the TV relay station.

The walk, known locally as the 'Ruta de los Volcanes', should only be attempted in good weather, which will also allow you to enjoy the ever-changing volcanic scenery and the views to both the east and west coasts of the island.

El Paso

Local women of this small town still weave silk and the men folk are mostly busy with farming in the surrounding countryside – bananas (of course), potatoes, tobacco, the vine and several vegetables are all grown in the area.

In the town, the restored 18th-century **Ermita de la Virgen de la Concepción de la Bonanza** (or 'La Bonanza' for short) is a curious looking little place of worship with a wooden balcony above the main entrance. That's about it for curiosity here.

With the exception of a few apartments, there's nowhere (and no real reason) to stay in town. Out across the road from the Centro de Visitantes is *Pensión Nambroque* (☎ 922 48 52 79), where good singles/doubles cost 3500/5000 ptas. About 1km east of town, you can eat well at *Restaurante La Cascada* for about 2000 ptas.

Around El Paso

A few kilometres along the C-812 highway heading towards Los Llanos de Aridane, you'll see signs leading off the highway to **El Paraíso de las Aves** (☎ 922 48 61 60), where you can observe a wide selection of exotic birds and flora. It opens from 10 am to 6 pm daily, and entry costs 1000 ptas.

Los Llanos de Aridane
• *population 16,189*

The central plaza of this, the second major town on the island, is a charming little urban haven in an otherwise dull, modern town. Whether you drive or are catching buses, you are bound to pass through here, so take a half hour to explore the tiny old centre.

Plaza de España is dominated by the gleaming white **Iglesia de Nuestra Señora de los Remedios**, built in the Canarian colonial style. The surrounding streets, particularly Calle de Fernández Taño, still preserve much of their traditional character.

About 500m outside town, on the road to El Paso, is the tourist-oriented **Pueblo Parque La Palma**. This is a mix of botanical garden and cultural centre. More than 6000 species of mostly subtropical plants thrive here, and you can see artisans employed in the traditional business of embroidery, basket weaving and other handicrafts in 'typical Canarian-style' houses. You can wander on your own or take a guided tour, at the end of which is a cafeteria that offers refreshment and respite. The Kulturpark, as it is known in

German (giving an indication of who its main patrons are), opens from 10.30 am to 5 pm, Monday to Saturday. Admission is 1500 ptas.

Places to Stay Should you need to hang about in Los Llanos, *Pensión El Time* (☎ 922 46 09 07), Plaza de España, has basic singles/doubles/triples for 2400/3400/4000 ptas. *Hotel Eden* (☎ 922 46 01 04), at the eastern end of the same square, is also a fairly simple affair, with rooms going for 3000/4400 ptas with own bath. If you require more comfort, *Hotel Valle de Aridane* (☎ 922 46 26 00), Glorieta de Castillo Olivares 5, might be for you, with rooms costing about 5000/6000 ptas.

Places to Eat The passing tourist trade wasn't slow to descend on the bougainvillea-bedecked *La Pérgola*, a pizzeria/restaurant/bar right on Plaza de España. For a filling meal with grilled meat specialities,

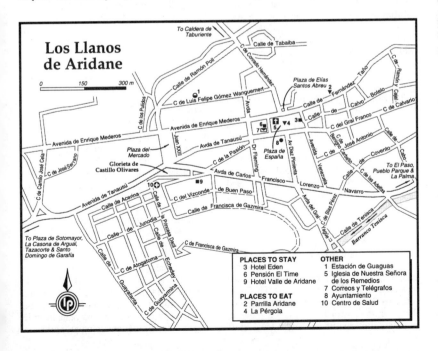

Los Llanos de Aridane

0   150   300 m

PLACES TO STAY
3 Hotel Eden
6 Pensión El Time
9 Hotel Valle de Aridane

PLACES TO EAT
2 Parrilla Aridane
4 La Pérgola

OTHER
1 Estación de Guaguas
5 Iglesia de Nuestra Señora de los Remedios
7 Correos y Telégrafos
8 Ayuntamiento
10 Centro de Salud

you could consider *Parrilla Aridáne*, Calle de Fernández Taño 17. It has a nice patio for lunchtime. In Argual, just west of Los Llanos, *La Casona de Argual*, Llano de San Pedro 6, is a beautiful establishment in a house dating from 1732. You can eat by torchlight in the gardens.

Getting There & Away The Estación de Guaguas is on Calle de Luis F Gómez Wanguemert. Buses to Puerto de Naos (165 ptas) and Tazacorte (125 ptas) run frequently, as do those to Santa Cruz (570 ptas). Buses north to Santo Domingo de Garafía (825 ptas) are less regular.

Tazacorte
• *population 6582*
From Los Llanos de Aridane, the C-812 highway forks south-west towards the banana town of Tazacorte, the spot where the *conquistadores* launched their campaign. The only sight is the **Iglesia de San Miguel Arcángel**, and most people who come here tend to proceed a few kilometres further north-west to Puerto de Tazacorte, which apart from bananas, offers a modest beach and three or four waterfront restaurants. Of the latter, *Restaurante La Gaviota* is reliable and specialises in seafood.

There are no hotels in Tazacorte, but there are several sets of apartments. *Apartamentos Isa* (☎ 922 48 00 52), Lomo Blanco, has doubles for 3700 ptas or 4700 ptas with balcony.

Apart from the eateries on the beach, there's not a lot of choice in the food department. *Bar Bagañate*, Calle del Progreso 17, does poor pizza imitations and a limited menu of standard dishes. Mains start at about 800 ptas.

Puerto de Naos
A side road south from Tazacorte tracks the coast from on high for about 5km before dropping down to the black-sand, palm-shaded beach of Puerto de Naos. This is as close as the west coast comes to a resort. There is no real town here, just a growing population of apartments and a handful of

restaurants and shops aimed at tourists – the great majority of them Germans.

If you have transport or don't mind walking about 20 or 30 minutes, you'll find a couple of other small beaches further south, the second of them comparatively protected from the Atlantic rollers and known as the **Charco Verde** (Green Pond).

Places to Stay & Eat The waterfront of Puerto de Naos is lined with low-level apartment blocks. Among the cheaper ones is *Apartamentos Pedro Martín* (☎ 922 40 80 46). Doubles/triples cost 3500/4500 ptas. More comfortable is *Apartamentos Playa Delphin* (☎ 922 48 01 74), where doubles start at 7000 ptas.

You can eat and drink in any of the terrazas along the waterfront (unless they've been washed away by a winter Atlantic storm!). Less vulnerable is *Ristorante La Scala*, Calle de José Guzmán Pérez 9, which does a fair version of Italian cuisine. A good spot for Canarian, Castilian and Basque cooking is *Restaurante Don Quijote*, Edificio La Palma Beach.

Getting There & Away Buses leave regularly for Los Llanos, although on Sunday and holidays the service is greatly reduced.

THE SOUTH
Mazo
• *population 5069*
A peaceful little spot, you'd barely know it was there as you trundle by on the bus from Santa Cruz, which lies 13km away. The town is known for the production of handmade *puros*, Havana-style cigars, and various other handicrafts. If you are interested in the latter, head for the Escuela Insular de Artesanía. It is signposted downhill off the highway, and opens from 9.30 am to 4.30 pm, Monday to Friday. You can see products being made and buy them.

A block further downhill, the 16th-century **Iglesia de San Blas** looks out over the Atlantic towards Tenerife. Inside, the retablo on the high altar is baroque in style, as are many of the remaining artworks.

Corpus Christi is celebrated here in June with particular gaiety. Arches made of wood and brightly decorated are raised in the streets for the processions.

Places to Stay & Eat Should you want to stay, the choice is down to two sets of apartments run by the same people and for which the same price – 4200 ptas for two – is charged. *Apartamentos Alfa-Alfa* are at Calle de Maximiliano Pérez Díaz 9, while *Apartamentos Su Casa* are at No 79. For information call ☎ 922 44 04 04. *Restaurante Las Toscas*, Carretera General 42 (the main highway), offers cheap, simple meals. For a Swiss touch, try *Restaurante El Elefante*, Calle de Maximiliano Pérez Díaz 4.

Getting There & Away The Línea 8 bus to Fuencaliente calls in here (six a day each way on weekdays; two on Sunday).

Cueva de Belmaco

A little further south from Mazo, and closer to the coast, is an ancient cave once inhabited by Benahoare tribespeople who left behind carvings in the cave walls. The Cueva de Belmaco was the first such site discovered and recorded on the island, back in 1752. There are four sets of engravings, about whose meaning experts remain perplexed. Legend has it that the cave was actually home to the local tribal chief, but there is no hard evidence for this.

The cave is not in any way signposted from the C-832 highway. The best bet is to take the first left after the Mazo exit heading south from Santa Cruz and wind down towards Hoyo de Mazo. From here head south through San Simón – it's another 1km.

You'll see the cave on your right in a bend in the road. Left off the road is an information office and a casa rural, the *Isla Bonita*. The cave and a modest museum were supposed to be open at the time of writing, but a check proved everything to be shut. Well, you could wander in uninvited to get a little closer to the cave, but not close enough to see the rock carvings – you

can see just as much of the cave from the road.

A few buses from Santa Cruz head down this way via Hoyo de Mazo. The nearest bus stop is about 400m south of the cave, just before the Bar Chaplin.

Los Canarios de Fuencaliente

• *population 1731*
The Hoyo de Mazo road eventually rejoins the C-832 south to Fuencaliente. The hot springs from which the area got its name have long since been buried by the anger of the volcanoes that as recently as 1971 were still erupting.

Things to See & Do The attraction here is the volcanoes. From the main settlement, Canarios de Fuencaliente, signs lead you to the first of them – **Volcán San Antonio**. You can follow a path right around the yawning chasm of this great black cone, which last blew in 1949. From here you can walk south (signposted) or drive to the scene of the Canary Islands' most recent eruption, **Volcán Teneguía**. There is nothing to suggest it won't ever repeat its performance, but for now you can scramble up to the shattered rim of the volcano, from where you have views not only into its cone, but back to the higher Volcán San Antonio and out over the ocean to the islands of Tenerife, La Gomera and El Hierro.

If you have wheels and feel like cooling off, **Playa de Echeventive**, down near the lighthouse at the southern tip of the island, is rarely busy. A kiosk sells cool drinks.

Back in Canarios de Fuencaliente, you might want to pop into the **Taller de Artesanía**, where you can see traditional embroidery being done – and buy some. It is at Carretera General No 84.

Places to Stay & Eat Should you want to stay here, *Pensión Los Volcanes* (☎ 922 44 14 64), Carretera General 72, has basic singles/doubles for 2000/2500 ptas. The same people have an apartment for up to three people, with kitchen, for 3500 ptas.

Hotel Central (☎ 922 44 40 18), at No 19, has a range of different rooms and apartments from 2000 ptas to 5000 ptas. They also have rooms at No 84 (called *Pensión Imperial*).

Restaurante Llanovid, Calle de los Canarios s/n, is the best place in town, but mains start at 1200 ptas. Its own local wines are also for sale. You'll find a couple of more modest parrillas (grill places) on the main road in town.

Getting There & Away Six buses a day head north to Santa Cruz (two on Sunday), and five to Los Llanos (two on Sunday).

Fuencaliente to Los Llanos de Aridane

The highway up the west coast of the island rides high above the seemingly limitless expanses of the Atlantic Ocean. The first settlement is **El Charco**, where you can call in at a mirador that is equipped with a small bar.

Another 10km north takes you through the village of **Jedey**, where some of the inhabitants still live in old stone houses. A little further north is a still smaller hamlet, **San Nicolás**. Just before you enter it there is a great place to eat, the sprawling *Bodegón Tamanca* (☎ 922 49 41 55), located in a cave.

Isla de la Gomera

The Canarios call this the *isla redonda* (the round island) and the bulk of tourists to the islands give it little more than a day trip from Tenerife. In one sense this is a shame, as some more inquisitive travellers who hang around longer have found. The mountainous countryside and the ancient laurel forest of the Parque Nacional de Garajonay warrant more peaceful hiking and contemplation than they get.

On the other hand, the island would be hard pressed to deal with too many more tourists – and some locals feel that they have already been overrun. Although the beaches of Valle de Gran Rey and Playa de Santiago are increasingly popular, they are small and, as beaches go, not really anything terribly marvellous – this fact will hopefully put a natural brake on the growth of tourism on La Gomera. If it doesn't, this relatively wild and sparsely populated island could end up losing much of its charm.

A kind of rocky fortress whose precipitous cliffs crash headlong into the ocean, La Gomera is the most 'dormant' of the islands. There has been no volcanic activity here for millions of years, which accounts for the virtual absence of cones, calderas and other geological signs. But evidence of the island's violent past is there – the odd basalt rock formations that pile upward in various spots across La Gomera are the most visible remains of lava fills once hidden inside now eroded volcanic fissures.

Agriculture still plays an important part in the island's economy – 9 million kg of bananas were produced in 1997!

History

La Gomera's history has been largely one of isolation and is as tough as its terrain is difficult. Although the island is comparatively rich in spring water, agriculture has always been a challenge. The soil is poor, and the sinuous, hilly country once made travel an

HIGHLIGHTS

- Exploring the green terraced banana plantations behind the beaches of Valle de Gran Rey
- Hiking through the misty forest of the Parque Nacional de Garajonay
- Taking a boat trip to the weird rock formations of Los Órganos, and seeing dolphins on the way
- Trekking from the heart of the Parque Nacional de Garajonay or Hermigua to El Cedro and the La Boca del Chorro waterfalls, staying in a *casa rural* en route

arduous undertaking. Indeed, until the construction of modern roads, the only access points inland from the coast were the deep *barrancos* (ravines) that radiate like spokes from the peak of Garajonay (1478m) and cut their way down to the small beaches and coves that long served as the only 'gates' to the island.

Spaniards and descendants of the Guanches alike eked out a living farming the terraces that still spread out over much of the island. But the going has always been tough, and Gomeros have a long tradition of emigration; the population peaked at 29,000 in 1940. Although many of those who have left in recent years have merely opted for nearby Tenerife, only 28km away, most left for Venezuela and Uruguay. This is reflected in a variety of ways, for example, a lot of the music played on local radio will transport you to Latin America.

Vestiges of the whistling language of the Gomeros (see Language in the Facts about the Islands chapter), are still kept alive today, almost exclusively for the delight of foreigners. A couple of the more touristy restaurants will put on lunch time performances, and those on a one-day guided tour from Tenerife can just about bank on having a display included in their itinerary.

Activities

One of the pleasures of the island is taking time out to walk it. Material suggesting hiking routes abound, and is best sought at the Centro de Visitantes del Parque Nacional de Garajonay, near Agulo.

Beaches, accessible or otherwise, tend to be of the small, black, pebbly variety. The southern ones are more protected and suitable for swimming. One way to hang out on a beach of your own is to hire a boat and find one – most of beaches are difficult to reach because there are no walking tracks leading to them.

Accommodation

With only 22 hotels and *pensiones* across the island, the bulk of the accommodation is in private apartments and homes, the most tempting of them being the *casas rurales* sprinkled all over the countryside. Many of these are old farmhouses long abandoned by Gomero émigrés, now refurbished and resurrected for a role. The easiest way to rent one of them is to call ahead to the central reservations number – ☎ 922 14 41 01.

During peak periods it can get a little squeezy, so when you arrive go to the tourist office in San Sebastián and arm yourself with all the accommodation lists and phone numbers you can. That way you can call ahead.

Camping is prohibited on the island. That said, there is one camping ground near El Cedro – but to use it you need permission from the island's environment office (Oficina Insular de Medio Ambiente). Enquire at the tourist office.

Getting There & Away

There is no airport on La Gomera, but one is being built in the south of the island. Access is by ferry from Los Cristianos (Tenerife), Santa Cruz de la Palma and El Hierro. Ferries and hydrofoils call at San Sebastián, and the hydrofoils from Los Cristianos also go to Valle de Gran Rey. There is talk of extending the service to Playa de Santiago.

Getting Around

Four daily buses serve all the main destinations on the island.

San Sebastián de la Gomera

• *population 6191*

The capital and main port are the obligatory point of entry to the island. Aside from a small assortment of minor monuments, there is not an awful lot to keep you here, although a stroll around the centre is pleasant enough if you have an eye for the remaining traditional houses squished in between characterless concrete additions of this century.

History

This settlement must have been the scene of much excitement back on 6 September 1492. After loading up with food provisions, timber and water, Christopher Columbus led his three small caravels out of the bay of San Sebastián and embarked on what some must have viewed as a highly risky venture – to sail beyond the end of the known world and head westwards for the Indies.

The town had barely been founded when Columbus sailed in. Five years earlier, there had been a terrible massacre in the wake of the failed uprising against Hernán Peraza, the island's governor. When it was all over, what had been the Villa de las Palmas (on a spot known to the Guanches as Hipalán) was rechristened San Sebastián and began to grow.

The arrival of Columbus, and later the boom in trans-Atlantic trade, helped boost the fortunes of the city, sited on a good sheltered harbour. Nevertheless, its population only passed the 1000 mark at the beginning of the 19th century. The good times also brought dangers, and as with the other islands, San Sebastián was regularly subjected to pirate attack from the English, French and Portuguese. In 1739, the English fleet actually landed an invasion force hoping to capture the island, however the assault was repulsed.

In the 18th century the town was the channel for silk and rum exports to Tenerife, from where it in return received the run-off of products imported from Latin America and Europe. The fate of the town was intimately linked with that of the rest of the island. Its fortunes rose with the cochineal boom in the 19th century and then collapsed with that industry.

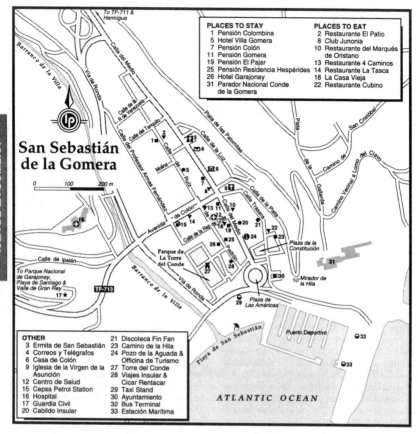

PLACES TO STAY
1 Pensión Colombina
5 Hotel Villa Gomera
7 Pensión Colón
11 Pensión Gomera
19 Pensión El Pajar
25 Pensión Residencia Hespérides
26 Hotel Garajonay
31 Parador Nacional Conde de la Gomera

PLACES TO EAT
2 Restaurante El Patio
8 Club Junonia
10 Restaurante del Marqués de Oristano
13 Restaurante 4 Caminos
14 Restaurante La Tasca
18 La Casa Vieja
22 Restaurante Cubino

OTHER
3 Ermita de San Sebastián
4 Correos y Telégrafos
6 Casa de Colón
9 Iglesia de la Virgen de la Asunción
12 Centro de Salud
15 Cepsa Petrol Station
16 Hospital
17 Guardia Civil
20 Cabildo Insular
21 Discoteca Fin Fan
23 Camino de la Hila
24 Pozo de la Aguada & Officina de Turismo
27 Torre del Conde
28 Viajes Insular & Cicar Rentacar
29 Taxi Stand
30 Ayuntamiento
32 Bus Terminal
33 Estación Marítima

Orientation

You arrive by sea at the shipping terminal at the eastern end of town. From there you can get buses to the rest of the island.

The main road, Calle del Medio, heads off north-west from the port and the small black-sand beach, and along it you'll find the tourist office and other useful offices, as well as the main sights. The bulk of the town's hotels and pensiones are on this street and the Calle de Ruíz de Padrón, which runs parallel.

For nice views of the town, its mountainous backdrop and the fine black-sand beach, walk up to the Mirador de la Hila.

Information

Tourist Office The Oficina de Turismo (☎ 922 14 01 47), is housed on Calle del Medio. It is open from 9 am to 1.30 pm and 3.30 to 6.30 pm Monday to Saturday; from 10 am to 1 pm Sunday.

Money There's are banks along Calle del Medio and Calle de Ruíz de Padrón, most with exchange services and ATMs.

Post & Communications The main post office (Correos y Telégrafos) is on Calle del Medio. You'll find public phones all over the town centre. The postcode for San Sebastián de la Gomera is 38800.

Medical Services The Hospital de Nuestra Señora de Guadelupe (☎ 922 14 02 00) is about a 15-minute walk west of the town centre.

The town's clinic, or Centro de Salud (☎ 922 87 02 86), is at Calle de Ruíz de Padrón 32. The town's four pharmacies take turns in opening for 24 hours.

Emergency The Guardia Civil barracks (☎ 922 87 02 55) is out of the town centre on the highway to Valle de Gran Rey. For an ambulance, call the Cruz Roja (Red Cross) on ☎ 922 87 00 00.

Things to See & Do
The small town centre is dotted with a few charming old mansions, but is fairly short on noteworthy monuments.

Set in a park just back from the beach, the late gothic **Torre del Conde** is where it all began. Beatriz de Bobadilla, the wife of the ill-fated Hernán Peraza, had to barricade herself in this citadel in 1488 until help arrived. The fort had been raised in 1447, the first building of any note to go up on the site of the future San Sebastián. It is about the only one to have been more or less preserved in its original state. It only opens for exhibitions.

ISLA DE LA GOMERA

Murder & Revenge in La Gomera

Love affairs can be a risky business. When, in 1488, Hernán Peraza, the son of the of governor of La Gomera, Diego de Herrera, began to see Yballa, a young local beauty, his wife Beatriz de Bobadilla was probably none too impressed. Even less so was Yballa's Gomero suitor, Hautacuperche, who also saw in this a unique opportunity, and hatched a plan with other tribesmen to seize Peraza and compel him to confess his extramarital activities. Hautacuperche hoped not only to win back Yballa, but also to extract from Peraza a promise of fairer treatment of the islanders by the colonial authorities, who had been particularly harsh with the local populace.

The chance to enact the plan was not long in coming. Tipped off that Peraza and Yballa were to meet clandestinely, Hautacuperche lay in wait. Things didn't quite go according to plan and Hautacuperche ended up fatally spearing Peraza. There may well have been a touch of poetic justice in Peraza's death, since he had stood accused of murdering Juan Rejón, the unloved commander of the 1478 assault on Gran Canaria, in 1481.

Were Peraza and Yballa really lovers? Another version of the story is that Peraza had five Guanche women seized for the benefit of his officers in a wild party. One of them, Yballa, resisted and was publicly mistreated by Peraza. Whichever way it went, Peraza's death unleashed a blood bath. Having killed the governor, the islanders laid siege to Beatriz de Bobadilla and the small Spanish contingent holed up in Villa de las Palmas, the precursor to modern San Sebastián.

Pedro de Vera in Gran Canaria got wind of the uprising and soon arrived to put a stop to it. His ruthlessness was blood-curdling. According to one account, de Vera ordered the execution of all males above the age of 15. In an orgy of wanton violence, islanders were hanged, impaled, decapitated or drowned. Some had their hands and feet lopped off beforehand, just for good measure. The women were parcelled out to the militiamen, and many of the children were bundled off for sale as slaves. To complete the job, de Vera similarly ordered the execution of some 300 Gomeros living on Gran Canaria.

Also worth a visit is the **Iglesia de la Virgen de la Asunción**. The central nave of the original hermitage was begun in 1450, but additions were made to the church, all in gothic style, until well into the 18th century.

The **Casa de Colón**, Calle del Medio 56, is where Columbus supposedly put up before heading off for the New World in 1492. Inside you'll find a few artefacts from Peru, models of Columbus' caravels, and another of Iglesia de la Virgen de la Asunción that is made of sugar! It opens from 10 am to 1 pm and 4 to 6 pm Monday to Friday. Admission is free. On the subject of Columbus, nip out the back of the tourist office to have a look at the **Pozo de la Aguada**. They say that water drawn from this well was used to 'baptise America'.

The tiny **Ermita de San Sebastián**, near the post office, is said to have been the first chapel built on the island.

The black sandy beach isn't bad. If you want something wilder and more secluded, a walking track heads south-west to the hamlet of **El Cabrito** from the TF-713 highway near the hospital. Ask around for it. The walk will take you about two hours, but the beach is quite pretty, with a huddle of houses set among palm trees and the mountainous terrain behind them serving as a colourful backdrop. Bring your own food and water.

Special Events
The Fiesta de San Sebastián, the town's patron saint, is celebrated on 20 January, and Columbus' first voyage is commemorated on 6 September.

Every five years on 5 October (the next in 1998) the city celebrates the Bajada de la Virgen de Gaudelupe with a seaborne *romería* to Puntallana, where fishers take the statue of the Virgin Mary from the hermitage to escort it south to the capital in a flotilla.

Places to Stay – budget
At Calle del Medio 23, the first place you'll come across is *Pensión El Pajar* (☎ 922 87 02 07). It's a charming old Canarian house in a noisy, thin-walled fashion and rooms go for 2500 ptas for one or two – the hot water is only for the quick. They have an outdoor restaurant in the back. Quieter and with a nicer internal garden is *Pensión Gomera* (☎ 922 87 04 17) at No 33, which has rooms for 3000 ptas.

If these are both full (which happens often enough), try the more modern *Pensión Colombina* (☎ 922 87 12 57), Calle de Ruíz de Padrón 83, which has singles/doubles for 2500/4000 ptas with bath. It is charmless but clean and quiet. Otherwise, *Pensión Residencia Hespérides* (☎ 922 87 13 05) at No 42 has rooms for 1800/3500 ptas without bath, or marginally more with.

Pensión Colón (☎ 922 87 02 35), Calle del Medio 59, is not a bad deal and offers comfortable singles/doubles for 2000/3500

DAMIEN SIMONIS

The building of Iglesia de la Virgen de la Asunción commenced in 1450

ptas without own bath, or 4200/5500 ptas with.

You may be met by touts with apartments to rent. They can be a good deal, starting at 4000 ptas a throw for two. Otherwise, keep an eye out for signs around town – there's no shortage of them.

Places to Stay – middle
Of the handful of hotels, the *Hotel Villa Gomera* (☎ 922 87 00 20), Calle de Ruíz de Padrón 68, is unimaginative but comfortable enough, with singles/doubles for 4200/5500 ptas. Much the same is the *Hotel Garajonay* (☎ 922 87 05 50) at No 17. Here you'll be paying 4500/5600 ptas for rooms with an ensuite bathroom.

Places to Stay – top end
The *Parador Nacional Conde de la Gomera* (☎ 922 87 11 00; fax 922 87 11 16) is a graceful four-star Canarian-style mansion. The views to Tenerife from the back garden are breathtaking. Single/double rooms cost 14,000/17,500 ptas. Don't even think about walking up here – get a cab.

Places to Eat
The bulk of the town's restaurants are clustered around the port end of Calle del Medio and Calle de Ruíz de Padrón. *La Casa Vieja*, Calle de la República de Chile 5, is a simple bar where you can get cheap tapas and arepas. Another no-frills joint is *Restaurante Cubino*, Calle Trasera (or Calle de la Virgen de Guadelupe) 2, where most mains cost less than 900 ptas.

A good spot is the *Club Junonia*, Calle del Medio 51, where you can eat well for modest prices in the garden.

Restaurante La Tasca, Calle de Ruíz de Padrón 34, is set in a Canarian house with whitewashed walls. The conejo en salmorejo (marinated rabbit) is nicely washed down with a slightly sweet local house red. Next door at No 36, *Restaurante 4 Caminos* also serves up good food (about 1000 ptas for mains) in intimate surroundings – the upstairs dining area is particularly agreeable, and they do a nice version of gazpacho.

For a slightly classier atmosphere and the option of al fresco dining, try *Restaurante del Marqués de Oristano*, Calle del Medio 24. Mains here cost up to 1500 ptas, and there is music on Saturday evenings.

San Sebastián seems to have more than its fair share of pizzerias. If you are sick of the local fare and want an approximation of Italian food, try *Restaurante El Patio*, Calle de Ruíz de Padrón 86.

For a splurge, head up to the Parador, where a classy meal will cost you around 3500 ptas.

Entertainment
One does not turn up in La Gomera for the rocking nightlife. Some of the restaurants have bars that stay open until about 2 am. The only disco is *Discoteca Fin Fan* at Calle Trasera 7.

Getting There & Away
Bus Three bus lines leave San Sebastián to cover the main destinations across the island. In each case there are four departures a day, all at 11 am, 2, 5.30 and 9.30 pm. Línea 1 goes to Valle de Gran Rey and is the longest of the three routes, taking one hour and 40 minutes (675 ptas). It follows the TF-713 highway, with a detour that takes it just south of the Garajonay peak. Línea 2 follows the same road as far as Las Paredes and then circles south to Playa de Santiago via Alajeró (650 ptas). Línea 3 takes the TF-711 to Vallehermoso via Hermigua and Agulo (550 ptas). The aqua coloured buses of the Servicio Regular Gomero leave from the ferry terminal.

Taxi If money is no object, you can get a taxi (☎ 922 87 05 24) wherever you want. The trip to Valle de Gran Rey will cost up to 6000 ptas, depending on the driver.

Car & Motorcycle With your own wheels you can take the same roads to leave the capital. There is no shortage of car rental offices here. *Cicar* has a desk at the office of Viajes Insular (☎ 922 87 14 50), Calle de Ruíz de Padrón 9. Some companies will let

ISLA DE LA GOMERA

When Columbus Dropped By

When Christopher Columbus drop-ped anchor in the small harbour of San Sebastián de la Gomera in August 1492, he must have been filled with mixed emotions. The tiny Canary Island was his last stop in the known world; after so many years of grim determination and bitter disap-pointment, this was his chance to prove that there was a western sea route to the Orient – and that the world was round!

A Genoese sailor of modest means, Cristoforo Colombo (as he is known in his native Italy) was born in 1451. He went to sea early and was something of a dreamer. Fascinated by Marco Polo's travels in the Orient, he decided early that it must be pos-sible to get there by heading into the sunset. Nice idea, but the rulers of Genoa, a considerable seafaring power, did not see such a dodgy enterprise as worthy of in-vestment. The young Columbus was undeterred and moved to Portugal in 1478, where he continued his career at sea and searched for backers for his idea. At every door he knocked the reaction was always the same, until finally the Catholic mon-archs of Spain, Fernando and Isabel, gave their patronage in 1492.

On 3 August, along with three small caravels – the *Santa María*, the *Pinta* and the *Niña* – Columbus weighed anchor in Palos de la Frontera (Andalucía).

A singled-minded enough chap, Cristóbal Colón (as the Spaniards like to call him) does not seem to have been above distraction. During his stay on La Gomera he took quite a shine to Beatriz de Bobadilla, the widow of the unlamented Hernán Peraza. Still, he finally set sail on 6 September.

Columbus' little flotilla only sighted land on 12 October, just as his restless men were reaching the end of their patience with their commander's whims. They discov-ered several Caribbean islands on this trip, including Haiti and Cuba, and returned to Spain in March of the following year.

On his two subsequent voyages of discovery Columbus chose again to land in San Sebastián, in October 1493 and May 1498. On this latter trip he found that Beatriz was married and some historians surmise that it is no coincidence that he didn't pass this way again on his final voyage in 1502.

Columbus founded Santo Domingo on Hispaniola and charted the coasts of Hon-duras and Venezuela; as an administrator, however, he ran into difficulties and was shipped back to Spain, clapped in irons, in 1500. His name was later cleared, allow-ing him to return to the new colonies.

In 1504 he died a forgotten and embittered man in Valladolid, Spain. To the last he remained convinced he had found a new route to the Orient, rather than discovering an entirely unknown continent – America.

you hire in San Sebastián and drop off in Valle de Gran Rey (or vice versa).

Sea Trasmediterránea and Líneas Fred Olsen between them have up to six car ferries a day to Los Cristianos (Tenerife). A normal one-way fare costs 1920 ptas, although with Fred Olsen there is a minifare of 1560 ptas if you take the 10.45 am or 2.15 pm boats (the same is true of the 12.30 and 4 pm boats the other way). The trip takes about 1½ hours. Trasmediterránea also operates up to four hydrofoils, which take 45 minutes and cost 2070 ptas one way. They continue round the island to Valle de Gran Rey (30 minutes) for 1000 ptas (or a total of 2350 ptas from Los Cristianos). The round trip between San Sebastián and Valle de Gran Rey is 1700 ptas.

Líneas Fred Olsen operates a daily ferry to Santa Cruz de la Palma, leaving at the awkward time of 10 pm and arriving there 3¼ hours later. The cheapest ticket costs 2170 ptas one way (a cabin costs 6300 ptas).

Trasmediterránea's El Hierro ferry departs once a day. Try to get the direct service departing on alternate days at 10.45 am (the trip takes 3¼ hours). If you get the 5 pm every other day, you go first to Los Cristianos and then direct to El Hierro from there – a very long trip! The one-way trip costs 2350 ptas (the same as from Los Cristianos!).

You can buy tickets at the Estación Marítima (ferry terminal).

Getting Around
All you need to get around San Sebastián is two feet (unless you are staying at the Parador, in which case a taxi is preferable!).

Around the Island

PARQUE NACIONAL DE GARAJONAY
La Gomera's outstanding natural attraction is the ancient *laurisilva* (laurel forest) at the heart of the island's national park.

The 4000 hectare park is a haven for some of the planet's most ancient forest land. Although called laurisilva, there is more to it than the several types of laurel that abound. In fact, as many as 400 species of flora, including Canary willows and Canary holly, flourish here. The roof of the island, as it were, it is here that cool Atlantic trade winds clash with warmer breezes, creating a constant ebb and flow of mist through the dense forest. Streams are few and as much precipitation comes from the mist as from rain. Indeed, conservation of the forest is essential to attract the mists and their moisture, which in turn feeds the island's springs. Relatively little light penetrates the canopy, allowing moss and lichen to spread over everything. In the trees you may happen to spot rare laurel and long-toed pigeons.

What you see here was common across the Mediterranean millions of years ago until the frosty fingers of the last Ice age, which never made it as far as the Canaries, wiped it out. Humans have done more damage in the islands than ice, but in this case at least, they have acted to protect a good chunk of unique land before it was too late – the park was designated a World Heritage site by UNESCO in 1981.

Information
Oddly enough, the main visitors' centre for the park is well outside it (see Agulo below) in the north of the island. Pick up a copy of the *Caminos de la Gomera* map (500 ptas) if you don't already have a good walking map/guide to the island. Some hiking guides, mostly in German, are on sale at the centre. The centre also organises guided walks on Saturday, setting off from La Laguna Grande. Call ☎ 922 80 09 93 the day before, if you are interested.

Several trails crisscross the park, most of them roughly from north to south, and it is possible to walk from one coast to the other in a day.

It is forbidden to camp or light fires in the park (except in a few designated areas in the latter case). It can get cold here, and the

ISLA DE LA GOMERA

damp goes right through to the bones, even when it is not raining. Bring hiking boots, warm garments and a rain-proof jacket.

Approaches to the Park

The TF-713 highway cuts east-west right through the park until it meets the TF-711 at the park's western extremity, the latter looping northward and then back to San Sebastián, while the former bends south for Valle de Gran Rey. The four daily buses each way between the capital and Valle de Gran Rey actually make a fascinating detour south along a secondary road, branching off shortly before the Alto de Garajonay (the island's tallest peak) and continuing westwards along a decidedly tortuous route. They stop in such places as Igualero, Chipude, El Cercado and Las Hayas before branching north again to rejoin the main road. At Chipude another road breaks to follow a *barranco* to La Dama on the south coast, but this is for the motorised or those hitching.

Another way to enter the park is from the north-east. Get off the Línea 3 bus at Cruce de El Rejo. From here a secondary road twists and turns its way south about 6km to the TF-713 (bus stop Cruce de la Zarcita). There are some fine lookouts along this road, and off it branches a driveable dirt road (signposted to Caserío de El Cedro) that meanders to El Cedro and then along the northern boundary to Meriga.

A minor asphalted road also connects the visitors' centre at Juego de Bolas in the north of the island to La Laguna Grande, about halfway along the TF-713 from the park's eastern and western boundaries.

In & Around the Park

Most visitors make for the **Alto de Garajonay**, from where you have splendid views over the island. Another favourite stop is **La Laguna Grande**, just off the highway and ideal for picnics if you aren't interested in eating at the restaurant.

There's a popular and well signposted walk up the Alto de Garajonay. Take the first Línea 1 or Línea 2 bus from San Sebas-

tián and get off at the Pajarito stop (where the bus turns south). From here it is about an hour's walk (signposted) to the peak. On a clear day you can see the islands of Tenerife, La Palma, El Hierro and sometimes even Gran Canaria. If you have your own transport or get a taxi, a much shorter trail (1.6km) leads up from the Alto de Contadero to the peak.

From the peak follow the signposted path back down to Contadero. There you will see another track signposted north to Caserío de El Cedro. This is mostly descent and takes about two hours. It takes you through the heart of the park (and is so far the only trail described in a free brochure handed out at the Centro de Visitantes).

On the Línea 1 bus route, the detour along the south of the park is full of interest. **Chipude**, with its 16th-century Iglesia de la Virgen de la Candelaria, and **El Cercado** (known in particular for its pottery production) are intriguing stops. Both villages are situated amid rows of intensively farmed terraces. A dirt track and walking trail of about 3.5km climb from El Cercado to La Laguna Grande in the national park. There is a small pensión (☎ 922 80 41 58), which charges 3600 ptas a double, in Chipude.

The South Coast Those with transport or a will to walk and hitch could follow the steep, serpentine and narrow branch road south to **La Dama** and past the basalt, flat-topped peak of La Fortaleza (the Fortress; 1243m) from the Chipude bus stop. La Dama is little more than a smattering of houses and banana plantations high up above the Atlantic. You might dig up a room in one of a couple of apartments here, but don't bank on it. A few steep kilometres of track separate the town from a black pebbly beach, **Playa de la Rajita**, which is made rather ugly by the disused factory that sits glumly back from the shore. A rather punishing walk inland (unsignposted) and then back down the Barranco de la Negra gets you to a prettier version of the same.

A good but difficult hike runs from La

DAMIEN SIMONIS

Ermita de Nuestra Señora de las Nieves,
La Dama

Rajita north to Arguayoda (2km) and then about 6km eastwards to Alajeró, traversing two ravines in the process. Your orienteering skills need to be in good shape, though. At Alajeró you are on the Línea 2 bus route between San Sebastián and Playa de Santiago. (See the Alajeró entry later in this chapter.)

NORTHERN LA GOMERA
Hermigua
• *population 1500*

Set in territory once known to the Guanches as Mulagua, Hermigua stretches south to north along the bottom of a pretty ravine of the same name, a century-old centre for banana cultivation fed by water coming down from the Parque Nacional de Garajonay. Its small port, a few kilometres north, once made it an important export outlet and many of the island's notable families had their residence here. Although farming has lost much of its importance, the terraces scaling the steep slopes of the barranco are a pretty sight even today. Pretty, yes. But

the peasants of the area long lived in misery, and revolts in 1690 and 1762 were mercilessly suppressed. The original heart of the village, the Valle Alto, is dominated by the **Iglesia de Santo Domingo** and the convent of the same name, completed in 1520.

In September the town is transformed for a week by the crowds who gather from far and wide for the Fiestas de la Encarnación.

Information You'll find several shops, some bars and two banks with ATMs in the valley, as well as a petrol station. The tourist office (☎ 922 14 40 25) is just behind the Iglesia de la Encarnación in the lower part of town.

Just by the convent you'll find a handicrafts workshop, Los Telares, where you can buy handmade rugs and various other souvenirs. It has become something of an obligatory stop for busloads of day-trippers from Tenerife.

The San Sebastián-Vallehermoso bus passes through here four times a day each way.

Rough weather usually makes the nearby stony beaches (Playa de Hermigua, Playa de Santa Catalina) rather unsuitable for swimming and sunbathing. The nicest, Playa de la Caleta, entails about an hour's hike (see the Parque Natural de Majona entry later in this chapter).

Places to Stay & Eat Up and down the valley are scattered 15 casas rurales (each sleeping three to five people). Call the central reservations number at the beginning of this chapter to find out what is available. You'll be looking at around 6000 ptas a double. Another decent option is *Apartamentos Los Telares* (☎ 922 88 07 81), right by the convent. You can get a double with attached kitchenette for as little as 4000 ptas. A pricey and more luxurious option is the *Hotel Rural Ibo Alfaro* (☎ 922 88 01 68), west of the main road about halfway along the valley. Singles/doubles cost 7000/8000 ptas.

Virtually where the village begins at the

southern end of the valley you can eat solidly for about 1500 ptas including wine and a simple dessert at *Restaurante Las Chácaras*. Or for views of the ocean, try *Restaurante El Faro* (at the end of the road marked for the *playa*, or beach).

Around Hermigua

El Cedro A walking track twists its way south from the village of Hermigua up towards the Parque Nacional de Garajonay. On the park borders, El Cedro is a rural hamlet amid farmed terraces and laurel thickets. The ravine and waterfall known as La Boca del Chorro are beautiful. In Hermigua, ask for the *sendero* (trail) to El Cedro – it is about a two-hour hike.

This is as good a spot as any to start hiking in the park too, and the trail heading south from El Cedro leads about 5km south to the Alto de Garajonay, although the mostly uphill walk is easier the other way (see the Parque Nacional de Garajonay section earlier in the chapter). A 1km wander out from the hamlet is the *mudéjar* style Ermita de Nuestra Señora de Lourdes.

In El Cedro itself are four cottages for rent, and the *Restaurante La Vista*.

The hamlet is accessible by dirt road (signposted) off a minor road connecting the TF-711 and TF-713 highways through the eastern end of the national park.

Parque Natural de Majona Clamped in between the craggy coast and the limits of the Garajonay park, this reserve also offers the chance to do some walking and get away from it all. A barely driveable dirt road winds its way from Carrasco, halfway down the valley between Hermigua and the beaches, to eventually loop south and meet the TF-711 to San Sebastián at Las Casetas (there's a bus stop there). Off the dirt track, signposting is nonexistent on the few walking trails, so don't plunge in unless you are confident of your trekking skills.

A branch of the trail leads instead to **Playa de la Caleta**. This represents about an hour's walk from Hermigua. It is one of the prettier black sand-and-pebble beaches

in the north of the island, and there's also a little refreshment stand.

Agulo
• *population 1157*
Five kilometres from Hermigua on the bus route, the village of Agulo was founded early in the 17th century. Along with the picturesque hamlet of Lepe (population 20), it is set on a low platform behind which steeply rises the rugged hinterland that stretches back in towards the Garajonay park. A couple of steep trails from Agulo lead up to a track that cuts in behind the village to the spectacular **Mirador de Abrante**, from where you have magnificent views across the village and ocean to Tenerife. It's a long walk and you can more easily drive around (if you have wheels) from Las Rosas.

Places to Stay & Eat In Lepe you could stay at *Casa de los Delfines* (☎ 922 88 07 81) for 6000 ptas a double – call ahead though, as it is often booked up well in advance. There's nowhere to eat here, so you'll have to head towards Playa Hermigua or into Agulo. In Agulo itself, the *Hotel Rural Casa de los Pérez* (☎ 922 14 61 22) has comfortable singles/doubles for 5000/7000 ptas. *Restaurante Zula*, on the main road, does simple, economical food. Mains cost less than 1000 ptas.

Las Rosas
Next stop on the bus route west is the sprawling hamlet of Las Rosas. Take the turn-off for La Palmita and after a few kilometres you will strike the **Centro de Visitantes del Parque Nacional de Garajonay** at a spot known as Juego de Bolas. It is worth calling in here, as the staff have piles of information on the park and the island in general and interesting gardens containing a microcosm of the Canary Islands' floral riches. There are also handicraft displays. The centre is open from 9.30 am to 4.30 pm daily except Monday. From here a back road and walking trail lead north to the Mirador de Abrante. You can sit

down to a meal at the Centro's bar/restaurant.

From the Centro a minor road leads south to La Laguna Grande, a picnic and play area off the TF-713 in the park. A branch road takes you on a breathtaking drive along a ravine through the hamlets of **La Palmita** and **Meriga**. They are about as faithful a reflection of traditional rural Gomeran living as you will find on the island. It is said the older folk around here still use the Silbo Gomero to communicate.

Casa Luis, Plaza de Santa Rosa de Lima, Las Rosas, is a fine old traditional eatery where you can munch on good tapas. A few kilometres west, back on the main road towards Vallehermoso. is *Restaurante Las Rosas*. It's a bit of a tour-bus favourite, but the views are wonderful.

Vallehermoso
• *population 1800*
The bus from Agulo winds its way 17km westwards to the village of Vallehermoso, passing through traditional farming hamlets like Tamargada along the way. Vallehermoso itself makes a good base for hiking in the area and into the Parque Nacional de Garajonay, with its shops, post office, banks (ATMs), petrol station and so on. The tourist office (☎ 922 80 01 81) is at Avenida de Guillermo Ascanio 18, just off Plaza de la Constitución. It opens from 10 am to 2 pm, Monday to Friday. Just outside the town towers the volcanic monolith of the **Roque Cano**, whose rock walls rise up 250m.

Places to Stay & Eat This isn't the greatest beach territory. Three kilometres north of the village down a palm-studded valley, the rocky Playa de Vallehermoso is a bit of a disappointment.

You'll find a couple of pensiones and a few private houses and apartments to rent in the village. *Pensión Medina Hernández* (☎ 922 80 00 23), just off Plaza de la Constitución, charges 2500 ptas for a double (bathroom in the corridor). Nearby, *Casa Bernardo* (no phone), Calle de Triana 4,

offers simple, clean singles/doubles for 2000/3000 ptas. *Pensión Amaya* (☎ 922 80 00 73), Plaza de la Constitución 2, has basic rooms from 1500/3000 ptas. For 2500/4000 ptas you can up the comfort level with own bath, TV and fridge. The owners also have a couple of apartments.

A good little place to eat with locals is the *Restaurante Triana*, Calle de Triana 19. There's no sign, so look for the green doors.

Around Vallehermoso
Los Órganos To contemplate this extraordinary cliffscape (something like a great sculpted church organ in basalt rising abruptly from the ocean depths), 4km north of Vallehermoso, you'll need to head out to sea. The place to look for boats making the trip is actually Valle de Gran Rey, in the

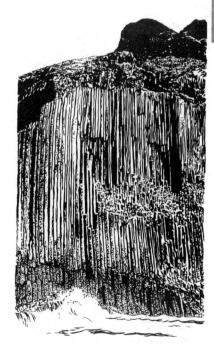

The striking basalt cliff face of Los Órganos, best viewed from the sea south-west of the island (see the Western La Gomera section later in this chapter). The columned cliff face has been battered into its present shape by the ocean.

Alojera The main highway south of Vallehermoso snakes its way along the valley through farming villages (some abandoned) and up into the western extremity of the Parque Nacional de Garajonay. Shortly before the highway enters the park proper, a side road winds out west to Alojera, a sleepy settlement sprawled out above the black pebble Playa de Alojera. Tracks lead north to Tazo (about 5km) and Arguamul (8km). The best part of coming here is the spectacular drive down from the highway. If you want to stay, you should try *Apartamentos Ossorio* (☎ 922 80 03 34), at the entrance to town.

Tazo & Arguamul In and around Tazo are some fine old traditional farm houses. The surrounding area also has the island's most extensive palm grove. The sap is used to make palm honey, a local speciality – the sap is boiled into a kind of thick dark syrup.

After another 3km walk is Arguamul, another tiny hamlet. Walking trails lead on a kilometre to Playa del Remo, and you could also walk south-east up to the ridge dominated by the Teselinde peak (876m) and then follow the Barranco de la Era Nueva down into Vallehermoso.

In dry weather you can get a car down this road: in wet weather it is often impassable.

WESTERN LA GOMERA
Valle de Gran Rey
• *population 3631*

So, how's your German? If Germany-upon-Sea is your idea of fun, then Valle de Gran Rey is for you. The tourists are German, the bar and waiting staff are German, the signs are in German. The Canarios are in there somewhere … Still, it is a far cry from the horrors of lager-lout land in southern Tenerife!

To the extent that tourism on the island has taken off, the Valle de Gran Rey (Valley

of the Great King, known as Orone before the conquest) is where it's at. The majority of La Gomera's accommodation is concentrated in the area, and it is not hard to see why. The valley is an improbably deep gorge carved out from the ancient island rock that fans out in a small fertile delta as it meets the ocean. Forbidding basalt walls tower all around.

The area is one of the island's most prosperous, but farmers have stretched the possible to the limit, planting (bananas and tomatoes especially) in the most unlikely spots, including into the Barranco de Valle de Gran Rey. The terraces cut into the valley walls are vaguely reminiscent of the terraced rice paddies in Bali. Ocean, palm stands, banana and papaya plantations – it is a beautiful valley.

Before you descend into the valley itself, you could stop in **Arure**, where the views from the Mirador del Santo over the ravines and out to La Palma and El Hierro are splendid. There are a few small restaurants in Arure. Before El Retamal, a few kilometres further south, there are several more stunning lookouts along the highway.

Orientation & Information Valle de Gran Rey is really a collection of little hamlets. The high part is known as La Calera. From here the road forks to La Playa (right) and Vueltas (left). Both have small beaches and plenty of accommodation, and Vueltas also serves as the area's harbour.

Street names and numbers are all but nonexistent, so use a map – pick one up from the tourist office (☎ 922 80 54 58) on Calle de la Noria in La Playa. It opens from 9 am to 1.30 pm and 4 to 6.30 pm Monday to Saturday, and from 10 am to 1.30 pm Sunday. An information office directed primarily at German visitors, La Paloma, is in the heart of Vueltas.

The main post office is in Vueltas, while the banks (some with ATMs) and petrol station are in La Calera. There is a Centro de Salud (clinic) at the northern end of La Calera.

If you want to send off an email, try

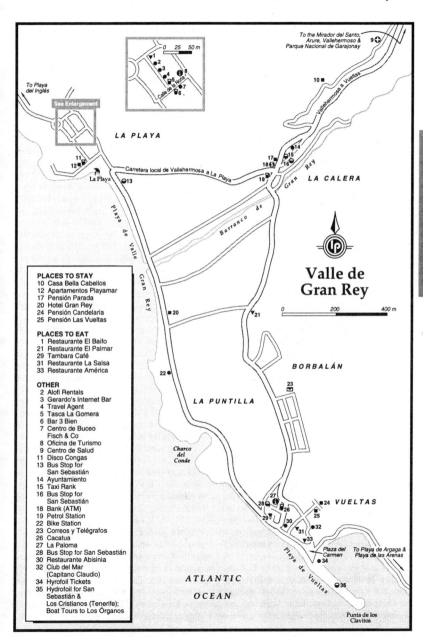

ISLA DE LA GOMERA

Valle de
Gran Rey

PLACES TO STAY
10 Casa Bella Cabellos
12 Apartamentos Playamar
17 Pensión Parada
20 Hotel Gran Rey
24 Pensión Candelaria
25 Pensión Las Vueltas

PLACES TO EAT
1 Restaurante El Baifo
21 Restaurante El Palmar
29 Tambara Café
31 Restaurante La Salsa
33 Restaurante América

OTHER
2 Alofi Rentals
3 Gerardo's Internet Bar
4 Travel Agent
5 Tasca La Gomera
6 Bar 3 Bien
7 Centro de Buceo
   Fisch & Co
8 Oficina de Turismo
9 Centro de Salud
11 Disco Congas
13 Bus Stop for
   San Sebastián
14 Ayuntamiento
15 Taxi Rank
16 Bus Stop for
   San Sebastián
18 Bank (ATM)
19 Petrol Station
22 Bike Station
23 Correos y Telégrafos
26 Cacatua
27 La Paloma
28 Bus Stop for San Sebastián
30 Restaurante Abisinia
32 Club del Mar
   (Capitano Claudio)
34 Hyrofoil Tickets
35 Hydrofoil for San
   Sebastián &
   Los Cristianos (Tenerife);
   Boat Tours to Los Órganos

Gerardo's Internet bar, in the Edificio Normara, La Playa, a few minutes walk from the beach.

Activities Walking up into the valley is pleasant, although it can get pretty hot and you may want to abandon the luxuriant greenery for a dip in the briny. The black sandy stretch of beach at La Playa is quite tiny, but inviting enough and a few steps from several laid-back restaurants and bars. A dirt track leads north to the west-facing Playa del Inglés. The beach at Vueltas is not so pretty, but a dirt road leads east to Playa de Argaga and Playa de las Arenas.

There is a German-run dive centre opposite the tourist office, the *Centro de Buceo Fisch & Co* (☎ 922 80 56 88), Calle de la Noria 5. It is open from 9 am to 1 pm daily except Friday.

You can also join one of several boat excursions. The most common takes you to Los Órganos, a bizarre cliff formation in the island's north (see Around Vallehermoso earlier), where you may also get to see dolphins and have a swim. Sometimes they will take you right around the island. Unfortunately, the success of these expeditions depends on prevailing winds, and operators do not guarantee you'll see either dolphins or Los Órganos, which means that your 5000 ptas a head could go begging. One assumes that, since the operators haven't been boycotted, the success rate is pretty high! Lunch and drinks are included in the price. Departure is at 10.30 am from the Vueltas port.

Whale observing or yachting trips can also be organised. Tickets for the Los Órganos trip can be bought all over the island, but if you want information on other boating activities, go and see Capitano Claudio in the Club del Mar, in Vueltas.

For windsurfing (2500 ptas an hour), ask at Restaurante Abisinia in Vueltas.

Places to Stay About half a dozen pensiones are scattered evenly about Vueltas, La Calera and La Playa. Otherwise, the area is absolutely swarming with apartments –

and more are being built all the time. You may want to get a list from the tourist office.

One of the prettiest places you could possibly choose to stay is *Casa Bella Cabellos* (☎ 922 80 51 82) up in La Calera. It is an enchanting old Canarian house with a dark wooden balcony and is set amid a grove of shady palms, high up the valley. The easiest way to find it is to follow the sign right off the main road to the Centro de Salud as you approach La Calera from the north. The house is a few hundred metres further along on the right. Rooms start at 2500 ptas for a simple double, and there is a studio for 4000 ptas. The owner also has a four-bed apartment across the road for 6000 ptas.

Vueltas seems to be made up of nothing but apartments, and the going prices start at 3000 ptas and head steadily upwards depending on quality, number of beds and whim. If you just want a no-nonsense room, *Pensión Las Vueltas* (☎ 922 80 52 16) has simple but clean and comfortable doubles for 3000 ptas. Just up the hill, *Pensión Candelaria* (☎ 922 80 54 02) has doubles with their own bathroom for 4000 ptas.

Pensión Parada (☎ 922 80 50 52), near the bus stop in La Calera, has uninspiring doubles (communal bathroom) for 3000 ptas.

In La Playa, *Apartamentos Playamar* (☎ 922 80 56 72), on the beach, has small doubles with attached bathroom and kitchenette for as little as 3000 ptas.

If you are looking at going a little upmarket, try *Hotel Gran Rey* (☎ 922 80 58 59), on the waterfront about halfway between La Playa and Vueltas. Singles/doubles cost 7000/10,000 ptas, including breakfast.

Places to Eat When it comes to edible marine life, this is a good place for it. The fresh fish, combined with a good local mojo, is generally great value. Try out *Restaurante El Palmar* in the Borbolán suburb (just off the road linking Vueltas with La Calera). They do a mean atún en mojo for 850 ptas.

In the heart of Vueltas, *Restaurante La Salsa* serves up vegetarian food. For a more Italian slant on your munching, try *Restaurante América*, just off the Plaza del Carmen in Vueltas. A full meal here will cost close to 2000 ptas.

In La Playa, *Restaurante El Baifo* offers an unusual mix of French and South-East Asian dishes (such as gado-gado).

A good place for breakfast is on the balcony of *Tambara Café* in Vueltas, with views over the ocean.

Entertainment There are quite a few cosy little bars open until about 2 am. *Tasca La Gomera* in La Playa is generally busy, as is the nearby *Bar 3 Bien*. In Vueltas, head for *Cacatua*. Later on, the music thumps at *Disco Congas* in La Playa.

Getting There & Away Four buses leave daily for San Sebastián, departing from at least three points (one stop each in Vueltas, La Playa and La Calera). Alternatively, three Trasmediterránea hydrofoils depart for San Sebastián and on to Los Cristianos (Tenerife) from the mole behind Playa de las Vueltas. One way/return to San Sebastián is 1000/1700 ptas, to Los Cristianos the one-way fare is 2350 ptas.

Getting Around You can rent mountain bikes, scooters and motor cycles at Alofi Rentals in La Playa. Bike Station in La Puntilla organises cycle excursions.

SOUTHERN LA GOMERA
Playa de Santiago
• *population 1600*

Until the 1960s Playa de Santiago was one of the busiest centres on the island, with food processing factories, a small shipyard and port facilities for the export of the familiar cash crops – bananas and tomatoes. Crisis hit the farming sector and by the 70s the town had all but shut down, its populace having fled to Tenerife or South America in search of work.

Now tourism is coming to the rescue. Locals hope that their beaches (the playas de Santiago, Tapahuga, Chinguarime and del Medio), a huge tourist hotel built by the Fred Olsen shipping company, the planned airport nearby and claims to the best year-round climate on the island will turn the place around.

The beaches all lie at the end of barrancos, and the last three can be reached on foot or by car from the main village along 1.5km of dirt road up and back down the Barranco de Tapahuga. As elsewhere on the island, you won't be too excited by the beaches – they are the usual narrow strip of black sand, pebble and stone.

Information The tourist office is in the Casa de Cultura on the waterfront Avenida Marítima and opens from 10 am to 2 pm Monday to Friday.

The town has a post office, two banks (ATMs), general stores and a petrol station. The postcode for Playa de Santiago is 38810.

Places to Stay There is no shortage of apartments in and around the village – signs advertising phone numbers abound and you are looking in most cases at around 3000 to 4000 ptas a double. The tourist office can provide a list.

Along Avenida Marítima is a series of perfectly decent pensiones. *Pensión El Carmen* (☎ 922 89 50 28) is a pretty place draped with plants. The rooms are basic but clean, have two beds and cost 2000 ptas. *Pensión Casanova* (☎ 922 89 50 02) is less attractive but similar in quality, with singles/doubles costing 1500/3000 ptas. A step up is *Pensión La Gaviota* (☎ 922 89 51 35). The main difference is that rooms here have their own bathroom. Doubles cost 3000 ptas.

Spread out on the cliffs overlooking the ocean at the eastern side of town is the grand *Hotel Jardín Tecina* (☎/fax 922 89 50 50). Prices vary a lot with the season, but at the time of writing it was a not unreasonable 8400 ptas plus 4.5% IGIC a head in comfortable doubles. The price includes breakfast and dinner.

Places to Eat The waterfront is lined with modest little bars and eateries, and fish is the order of the day. *Restaurante El Paso*, on the corner of Avenida Marítima and Calle de Santiago Apostol (the road that leads to Alajeró), is popular with locals and serves huge portions. Try their ensalada mixta with avocado and asparagus – you'll have little room left for the main course.

For a meal with a view, head uphill towards the Hotel Jardín Tecina (and Playa de Tapahuga) and park yourself in the *Restaurante Tagoror*.

Getting There & Away Four buses a day link Playa de Santiago with the capital, leaving from the little Plaza formed by the junction of Avenida Marítima and Calle de Santiago Apostol. The fare is 650 ptas. There are several car-rental outlets in Playa de Santiago.

Alajeró
• *population 1145*
The only sizeable village outside Playa de Santiago in the south-east of the island, Alajeró is a pretty, palm-tree studded oasis on the road from the fog down to the beach. The modest 16th-century **Iglesia del Salvador** is worth a quick look.

About 1.5km north, at Agalán, you can see the island's only surviving *drago*, or dragon tree – about a 10-minute walk west of the highway (the bus stops here).

In September Gomeros from far and wide converge on Alajeró to celebrate the Fiesta del Paso, a chirpy procession that dances its way down from the mountains.

There are three casas rurales and several apartments in and around the village. You'll also find three modest bar/restaurants, two of them just downhill from the church.

The San Sebastián-Playa de Santiago bus passes through here four times a day.

The Caseríos of La Benchijigua
One of the prettier zones of inland southern Gomera is La Benchijigua, a smattering of half-abandoned hamlets along the northern reaches of the Barranco de Santiago, whose valley butts up against the *meseta* walls that mark the south-eastern boundary of the Parque Nacional de Garajonay.

A couple of trails lead north into the park (going the other way, at least one is marked heading south into the area from the Roque de Agando by the TF-713 highway) and several others trace paths southwards along the ravines to the coast. Increasingly, farmhouses are being converted into pretty lodgings, but as yet the area remains sparse and bereft of the trappings of tourism.

No buses run here, but you could drive or hitch up a minor road as far as Pastrana and hike up from there. Otherwise, take the highway to San Sebastián along the Lomada de Tecina and turn off onto the dirt road at Las Toscas (at the time of writing this highway was closed). You should book your casa rural in advance – call the central reservations number cited at the beginning of this chapter.

Isla de El Hierro

The smallest and westernmost member of the Canaries, El Hierro is known to locals as La Isla Chiquita (the Little Island). In the days when the earth was thought to be flat, the island was said to mark the edge of the world.

Covering only 269 sq km, and with a population of just 8338, it is the least developed and most remote of the Canary Islands – locals often feel they are being ignored by the rest of the archipelago, and the reduction in air and sea links over the years has done nothing to alleviate the rancour.

El Hierro is also about as far as you can get from the stereotypical image of the Canary Islands. This is a rural island largely untouched by tourism. The high country, dripping with a wet swirling mist (which, by the way, can make driving hazardous) and divided up by rough stone walls into a green patchwork quilt of farm and grazing land, is more reminiscent of the Irish west country than a sunny subtropical paradise. Like La Gomera, much of the coastline is rugged and forbidding, while the south is a mix of semi-arid, volcanic landscape and pine forest. The highest peak is the Malpaso (1501m). Scuba diving is possible in the marine park off La Restinga in the south, but there are few beaches to speak of.

History

El Hierro hasn't always been the tiny tot of the Canaries. About 50,000 years ago the area was hit by a quake so massive that a third of the island was ripped off the north side and slipped away beneath the waves, creating the crescent-shaped coast of El Golfo. It must have been a very dramatic event – the ensuing tsunami (tidal wave) may have been more than 100m high and probably crashed as far off as the American coast.

The last eruption was 200 years ago, but the island is littered with about 500 cones

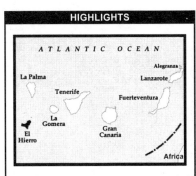

(and 300 more were covered up by lava flows).

How the island got its name is anyone's guess, but there is not a drop of iron (*hierro*) in the place. Perhaps the original inhabitants, the Bimbaches, called it 'milk' (*hero*).

Ptolemy identified the western edge of the island as the end of the known world in the 2nd century AD, and it remained the 'zero meridian' until replaced by the Greenwich version in 1884.

After the Spanish conquest in the 15th century a form of feudalism was introduced with Spanish farmers assimilating with those locals who had not been sold into slavery. In the subsequent quest for farmland much of El Hierro's forests were destroyed.

Today, the island's economy is based on fishing, fruit growing, livestock and tourism.

ISLA DE EL HIERRO

255

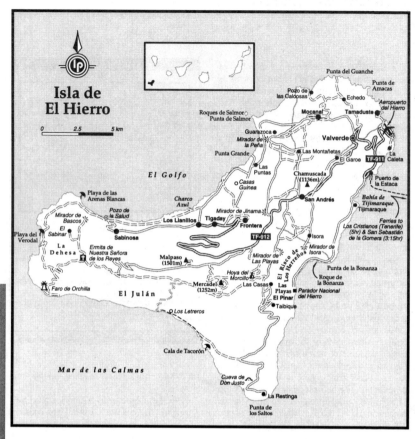

Isla de El Hierro

El Golfo

El Julán

Mar de las Calmas

Bahía de Tijimaraque

Punta del Guanche
Punta de Amacas
Echedo
Aeropuerto del Hierro
Pozo de las Calcosas
Mocanal
Tamaduste
Roques de Salmor
Punta de Salmor
Guarazoca
Valverde
Mirador de la Peña
Las Montañetas
El Garoe
TF-911
La Caleta
Punta Grande
Las Puntas
Chamuscada (1136m)
Puerto de la Estaca
Casas Guinea
Charco Azul
Mirador de Jinama
San Andrés
Playa de las Arenas Blancas
Pozo de la Salud
Los Llanillos
Tigaday
Frontera
TF-912
Ferries to Los Cristianos (Tenerife) (5hr) & San Sebastián de la Gomera (3:15hr)
Mirador de Bascos
El Sabinar
Sabinosa
La Dehesa
Ermita de Nuestra Señora de los Reyes
Isora
Mirador de Isora
Playa del Verodal
Malpaso (1501m)
Mirador de Las Playas
Punta de la Bonanza
Roque de la Bonanza
Hoya del Morcillo
Mercadel (1252m)
Las Casas
Las Playas
El Pinar
Parador Nacional del Hierro
Faro de Orchilla
Taibique
Los Letreros
Cala de Tacorón
Cueva de Don Justo
La Restinga
Punta de los Saltos

0   2.5   5 km

El Risco de Los Herreños

Special Events

The fiesta par excellence on El Hierro is the Bajada de la Virgen de los Reyes, held in early July every four years (the next is in 2001). A procession involving most of the island's population carries a statue of the Virgin from the Ermita de Nuestra Señora de los Reyes in the west of the island right across to Valverde. The festival is accompanied by musicians and dancers dressed in traditional red and white tunics and gaudy caps; celebrations continue for most of the month in villages and hamlets across the island.

Other fiestas of note include:

25 April
   Fiesta de los Pastores (Shepherd's Feast) – La Dehesa
15 May
   Fiesta de San Isidro – Valverde
24 June
   Fiesta de San Juan – La Restinga & Las Puntas
June
   Fiesta de la Apañada (Festival of the Clever!) – San Andrés. Farmers gather for a livestock sale at which everyone extracts a good price.
16 July
   Fiesta de la Virgen del Carmen – La Restinga

DAMIEN SIMONIS

DAMIEN SIMONIS

DAMIEN SIMONIS

Isla del Hierro
Top Left: Stone walls on farm land around Las Montañetas
Top Right: Iglesia de las Concepción & Plaza de Miguel Nuñez, Valverde
Bottom: Military parade, Valverde

DAMIEN SIMONIS

DAMIEN SIMONIS

DAMIEN SIMONIS

Isla del Hierro
Top Left: Woman of Valverde
Top Right: Casa Rosa, Pozo de la Salud (Well of Health), near Sabinosa, El Golfo
Bottom: Playa del Verodal, west coast

August
Fiesta de la Virgen de la Candelaria – Frontera

Accommodation

With about 800 beds available across the island, it is advisable to book ahead in busy periods such as the summer (or during important fiestas such as the Bajada de la Virgen de los Reyes). Winter, traditionally peak season for the invasion of northern Europeans in the other islands, is not so problematic here. There is only one camping ground, at Hoya del Morcillo. Free camping is otherwise prohibited on the island.

Getting There & Away

Flights connect the island with Tenerife and Gran Canaria, and a car ferry with Tenerife and La Gomera.

Getting Around

A limited bus service covers the main destinations on the island. Three buses leave Valverde at noon. One heads north and then west as far as the Mirador de la Peña (125 ptas); a second goes via San Andrés and Frontera (275 ptas) to Sabinosa (300 ptas) in the far west of the island; and the third aims south to La Restinga (300 ptas) via Isora and El Pinar. They all return to Valverde the following day at 7 am.

Drivers should be aware that there are only four petrol stations on the island: two of them are in Valverde, one is in El Pinar and the other is in Tigaday. A full tank should be sufficient to get right around the island.

Valverde

• *population 1600*

The only capital in the Canaries not located on the coast, the straggly white town of Valverde (or to give it its full title, la Villa de Santa María de Valverde) rises 570m above sea level, cradled by what remains of the walls of an ancient volcanic cone. It seems rather like a set of theatre stalls overlooking the ocean. Cloaked in a seemingly permanent mantle of low cloud and Atlantic mist, it is a rather dispiriting theatre and not a great introduction to the island. Luckily, once you've arrived it's not so easy to turn straight around and leave, so get out and see the rest of the island, which makes the melancholy capital well worth suffering.

History

When Jean de Béthencourt landed here with his motley crew in 1405, he wasted little time in defeating the Bimbaches of the area, then known as Armiche. When they surrendered, the intruders rounded them up for sale into slavery. Fortunately, not all the remaining islanders ended up suffering the same fate.

Valverde only really came into being following a devastating hurricane in 1610, when much of the island's populace fled there for shelter. A couple of churches had already been erected in the area and in 1812 the town was made the seat of a *municipio* that covered the whole island, and in 1926 the island's first Cabildo Insular was established here.

Orientation

You'll find it a challenge to get lost here. Approaching from the aerodrome or Puerto de la Estaca, the one-way main street (known for most of its length as Calle de la Constitución) winds its way up (and southwards) through town. On or near it you'll find the post office, banks, travel agencies, a couple of pensiones, car rental firms and an assortment of shops.

Information

Tourist Office The tourist office (☎ 922 55 03 02), is at Calle del Licenciado Bueno 1 (a short strip which connects Calle de la Constitución to Calle de San Francisco, forming the town's main drag) and opens from 8.30 am to 2.30 pm Monday to Friday, and from 9 am to 1.30 pm on Saturday.

ISLA DE EL HIERRO

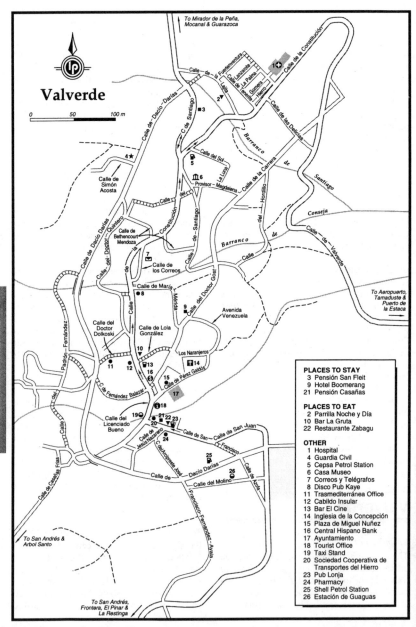

Valverde

To Mirador de la Peña,
Mocanal & Guarazoca

0   50   100 m

Calle de la Fuentenventura

To Aeropuerto,
Tamaduste &
Puerto de
la Estaca

To San Andrés &
Arbol Santo

To San Andrés,
Frontera, El Pinar &
La Restinga

ISLA DE EL HIERRO

PLACES TO STAY
3 Pensión San Fleit
9 Hotel Boomerang
21 Pensión Casañas

PLACES TO EAT
2 Parrilla Noche y Día
10 Bar La Gruta
22 Restaurante Zabagu

OTHER
1 Hospital
4 Guardia Civil
5 Cepsa Petrol Station
6 Casa Museo
7 Correos y Telégrafos
8 Disco Pub Kaye
11 Trasmediterránea Office
12 Cabildo Insular
13 Bar El Cine
14 Inglesia de la Concepción
15 Plaza de Miguel Nuñez
16 Central Hispano Bank
17 Ayuntamiento
18 Tourist Office
19 Taxi Stand
20 Sociedad Cooperativa de
    Transportes del Hierro
23 Pub Lonja
24 Pharmacy
25 Shell Petrol Station
26 Estación de Guaguas

They don't have much, but a booklet listing all the island's accommodation is worth getting hold of.

Medical & Emergency Services The hospital (☎ 922 55 00 79) on Calle de la Constitución is virtually the first major building you pass on your right on the way into town from the port. The handiest pharmacy is on the corner of Calle de San Franciso and Calle de Jesús Nazareno. For an ambulance, call the *Cruz Roja* (Red Cross) on ☎ 922 55 11 36.

The local Guardia Civil (☎ 922 55 01 05) is on Calle de Dacío Darías in the north of the town.

Things to See
Although pleasant enough to wander around for half an hour or so, the town offers few specific noteworthy sites. The 18th century **Iglesia de la Concepción** is a relatively simple three-nave affair, crowned by a bell tower whose railed-off upper level serves as a lookout. Inside, the polychrome *Purísima Concepción* is the town's most prized piece of artwork. A private museum, the **Casa Museo**, Calle del Provisor Magdalena 8, contains an oddball collection of island curios and memorabilia.

Places to Stay
Pensión San Fleit (☎ 922 55 08 57), Calle de Santiago 24, has doubles/singles starting at 1500/2500 ptas without own bath, or 2500/3500 ptas with. More expensive and spotless is the *Pensión Casañas* (☎ 922 55 02 54), Calle de San Francisco 9. Singles/doubles are 2500/3500 ptas, and 100 ptas more for own bathroom.

The town's luxury joint is the *Hotel Boomerang* (☎ 922 55 02 00), Calle del Doctor Gost 1, where singles/doubles cost 4650/6550 ptas.

Places to Eat
For a quick snack or hamburger, you could do worse than *Bar La Gruta*, Calle de Lola González 10. Otherwise it's slim pickings.

Restaurante San Fleit, next door to the pensión of the same name, offers solid meals (basically meat and veg) for around 1100 ptas. Their potaje de lentejas (lentil soup) is good. *Restaurante Zabagu*, Calle de San Francisco 9, is a similar deal – but avoid their pizzas.

Pricier and good for grills is the *Parrilla Noche y Día*, Calle de la Lajita 7. A full meal here will leave you little change from 2000 ptas.

Entertainment
Well, we know you didn't come here for nocturnal entertainment. A capital can't get much quieter than this. The town's two discos are Bar El Cine, Calle del Doctor Quintero 6 (just off Calle de la Constitución) and Disco Pub Kaye, on the corner of Calle de la Constitución and Calle de María Mérida. Or you could try a drink at Pub Lonja, Calle de San Francisco 11. Don't bank on any of them though: a weekend spent in tireless research of Valverde's nightlife revealed that they were all tightly shut!

Getting There & Away
Air The island's aerodrome (☎ 922 55 07 25) lies 10km east of the town. Up to three Binter flights a day connect with Tenerife Norte (7230 ptas), while there is a twice-weekly service to Gran Canaria with Air Atlantic (Friday and Sunday, 9000 ptas). At the airport you'll find car rental offices, a bar and a shop selling local products such as cheese and wine.

Bus The Estación de Guaguas is at the south end of town on Calle del Molino. See the Getting Around section at the beginning of this chapter for full details of island bus services. The latest timetable information can be had at the office of the Sociedad Co-operativa de Transportes del Hierro on Calle de San Francisco.

Taxi Taxis (☎ 922 55 07 29) will take you anywhere you want on the island, but it is cheaper to hire a car instead – there are

ISLA DE EL HIERRO

several car hire firms up and down Calle de la Constitución and Calle de San Francisco. A day tour will cost about 10,000 ptas (so hire a car!).

Sea Trasmediterránea (☎ 922 55 01 29) runs a daily ferry service to Los Cristianos. The direct service leaves at midnight on Monday, Wednesday and Friday (4½ hours; 2350 ptas one way). The rest of the week it leaves at 2.45 pm and takes a little longer because it calls in at San Sebastián de la Gomera (but the fare is the same).

The ferries depart from Puerto de la Estaca, 9km south of the capital. Trasmediterránea has an office at Calle del Doctor Dolkoski 3.

Getting Around

A Sociedad Cooperativa de Transportes minibus leaves at 8 am daily to meet the first flight from Tenerife, and another meets all the ferries. The ticket in both cases is 125 ptas. Otherwise you'll need to take a taxi, for which you'll be charged around 1000 ptas.

AROUND VALVERDE
Echedo

Five kilometres north of Valverde, this tiny settlement is at the heart of wine-growing territory that benefits from the volcanic soil. A track leads west a few kilometres from the village to the **Charco Manso**, natural swimming pools scooped out of the volcanic rock.

Tamaduste & Caleta

About 10km east of Valverde at the end of a side road off the airport highway, **Tamaduste** is little more than a huddle of houses clustered around a relatively calm inlet ideal for swimming in the summer (although the beach is minuscule). Indeed, it is so popular with Herreños that some have started building holiday homes here! Out of the black volcanic soil grow stands of grapevine, thriving in the shadow of the rim of a former volcano.

You could stay at one of several sets of

apartments here. *Apartamentos Boomerang II* (☎ 922 55 02 00), Calle de la Tabaiba 6, is right on the water's edge and has doubles for 8000 ptas. Enquire at the Hotel Boomerang in Valverde.

Another turn-off from the airport road, about 1km further on, leads to **Caleta**, where there are a few houses, a bar and phone box. You can splash around in an ocean rock pool, or follow the steps and little bridge beyond to a basalt rock face bearing what are claimed to be ancient, undeciphered inscriptions – frankly, they look as though anyone could have done them as a hoax just the other day!

South Coast Road

Puerto de la Estaca is a frumpy, dishevelled little place devoid of interest. This is where you'll arrive and leave on the ferry. A secondary road, pushing on down the coast, is overshadowed by a tall and jagged volcanic ridge, and after a couple of kilometres enters a tiny cluster of houses (among them a small pensión) collectively known as **Timijiraque**. The beach isn't bad, but watch the undertow. Another 4km south, the Roque de la Bonanza is a little rocky outcrop rising out of the sea just off the coast.

Another 8km and the road peters out in the grounds of the *Parador Nacional del Hierro* (☎ 922 55 80 36; fax 922 55 80 86), in an area known as **Las Playas**. Singles/doubles with sea views cost 12,400/15,500 ptas a night, making it the island's premier establishment. From here the only way out with wheels is by heading back to Valverde.

Divers should look out for Club de Buceo Hierro Sub (☎ 922 55 04 82), Carretera de las Playas 5, along the road north of the Roque de Bonanza. They offer courses and diving off the coast and/or from a boat all year round.

Around the Island

With your own transport you can rush around pretty much the whole island, backtracking several times along fairly good roads, in one day. Using buses and your own two feet you'll need a lot more time. What follows is a series of routes which, combined, present a roughly counter-clockwise tour around the island, starting from Valverde.

NORTHERN CIRCUIT

Following the TF-911 out of Valverde, you reach **Mocanal** after 5km. This is one of several farming villages you'll encounter along the road. **Guarazoca**, 3km further on, is similar. The surrounding meadows are fertile ground, and the whole area is frequently enveloped in sea mist. A short drive, or rather long and steep walk, down the slopes from Mocanal are the remains of the coastal hamlet of **Pozo de Las Calcosas**, where you will find another ocean-side rock pool and the *Restaurante La Barca*.

Back on the main road, you next arrive at the **Mirador de la Peña**, designed by César Manrique and housing a restaurant from whose tables you can enjoy magnificent views down the length of El Golfo (open at noon for lunch and 7 pm for dinner). You can't take a vehicle down to the coast from here, but there is a walking trail down to Las Puntas (see below). Another track trails off northward to Punta de Salmor, from where you can observe the **Roques de Salmor**, an important nesting spot for several bird species and reputedly a habitat of the primeval *lagarto del Salmor* (lizard of Salmor).

The road doglegs back inland across highland fields. The largely abandoned houses of **Las Montañetas**, one of the island's oldest villages, are scattered about in a bend in the road that leads to **San Andrés**. Although farmers continue to work the land and run small herds of sheep, goats and even some cattle up here, the unpleasantly damp climate has led most of them to move away. Winter at San Andrés, 1100m above sea level and only 8km from Valverde on the TF-912, is no more enticing, but in summer you roast. A couple of places on the main road could make a rea-

sonable lunch stop. Cereal and potato crops, cabbages, almonds, eucalyptus, figs and various fruits all flourish in the rich soil here. The plots are divided up by rough walls of volcanic stone which recall in no small measure some of the wilder country of western Ireland.

The modest peak to the north of San Andrés is the Chamuscada (1136m). About 4km to its north-east, and reached by a dirt track that runs off the San Andrés-Las Montañetas road, you can visit the site of **El Garoé**, the ancient *arbol santo* (holy tree) of the Bimbaches. It was said to spout water, a myth explained perhaps by the mist-induced condensation on the tree's leaves. With patience, small quantities of drinking water could be collected. The ancient tree is long gone, replaced by a new model in 1949.

A couple of kilometres south-west of San Andrés the **Mirador de Jinama** affords magnificent views down over the low fertile plains of El Golfo towards the island of La Palma to the north – mist permitting.

SOUTH TO LA RESTINGA

A walking trail meanders its way south from San Andrés to the cheese-producing village of **Isora**, or you can take the secondary road that branches off the TF-912 highway just north-east of San Andrés. Beyond the village (which has a couple of restaurants and one or two apartments) on the edge of a ridge known as El Risco de los Herreños is the fine **Mirador de Isora**. Looking over Las Playas and to the ocean, it gives you the feeling of staring into infinity. A track allows hikers to descend to the coast here (reckon on about an hour down). Or you can follow another road south-west back on to the La Restinga highway. Turn left (south) and follow the signs for La Restinga. Yet another lookout, the Mirador de las Playas (not signposted) lies off to the left (east).

HOYA DEL MORCILLO

If you want to camp or stop for a picnic, facilities have been laid on at the Hoya del

Morcillo recreation area in the pine forest, a few kilometres west of the highway and just north of El Pinar. The road eventually turns into a dirt track to cross El Julán, a protected pine forest that reaches all the way across to the west of the island. For ecological reasons, you are supposedly only permitted to drive about 12km along this road. The free camping ground has cooking facilities and showers.

Those with an archaeological bent might like to walk about 5km west of the camping ground along the route to the Faro de Orchilla. About a 20-minute rough scramble downhill from that point is the ancient site of **Los Letreros**, the most important rock engravings, or petroglyphs, left behind by the Bimbaches. However, no-one has a clue what they mean. And because they've been vandalised in the past you need written permission to get to them (ask at the tourist office in Valverde).

EL PINAR

Just south of the Hoya del Morcillo turn-off, the highway hits the villages of **Las Casas** and **Taibique** (a biggish settlement with supermarkets, banks – no ATMs – bars and restaurants), collectively known as El Pinar (because of the area's pine forests). You could have a quick look around the private **Museo de Panchillo** (signposted at the northern end of Taibique), full of curios. The town seems to slide precariously down hill, and just before you leave you'll see *Hotel Pinar* (☎ 922 55 80 08), Travesía del Pino 64, where singles/doubles with bath, TV and phone cost 3600/4500 ptas. Next door is a decent restaurant, of which there a couple in town. Head a little way uphill along the main road for a drink with the local good old boys in the *Bar Mentidero*.

From Taibique it's another 15km south to La Restinga. A little over half way is a turn-off westwards for the **Cala de Tacorón**, a set of deserted coves facing the Mar de las Calmas, whose limpid waters are hard to resist. Two kilometres short of La Restinga, cave enthusiasts might like to look out for

the **Cueva Don Justo** (you'll need local help to find it, as there is no sign). With more than 6km of volcanic rock tunnels and passages, it is said to be the sixth largest cavity of its type on the planet.

LA RESTYINGA

Home to the island's fishing fleet, this is also the place to be if you want to do some diving off El Hierro. The Reserva Marina Punta de la Restinga is home to a range of ocean marine life. This is a good thing, because on land there is precious little to occupy your senses in this volcanic desert.

There are two dive centres. The Centro de Buceo El Hierro (☎ 922 55 70 23), Avenida Marítima 16, opens all year and does daily boat dives and night dives. You can rent or buy equipment and do ACUC courses at all levels. El Submarino (☎ 922 55 80 58), Avenida Marítima 2, offers much the same options. You are looking at about 5000 ptas a dive if you have no gear, and from 40,000 ptas for a beginner's course.

There are about a dozen holiday homes and apartments to let in La Restinga, many of them on the waterfront. Aside from them you could try *Pensión Kai Marino* (☎ 922 55 80 34), right on the water's edge, which offers basic singles/doubles for 2000/3000 ptas. The German-run *Pensión Matias I* (☎ 922 55 81 89), Calle del Paral 2 at the entrance to the village, has simple rooms for 1500 ptas a head.

On the stomach front, fish is the predictable cure for hunger pangs. Several waterfront eating houses will oblige. Try *Restaurante Casa Juan*, Calle de Gutiérrez Mont 23, where a meal will come in at around 1500 ptas.

The bus for Valverde leaves at 7 am and costs 300 ptas.

EL GOLFO

To proceed anywhere on wheels from La Restinga, you need to head back north the way you came, as far as the junction with the TF-912, 1km west of San Andrés.

Space Invaders

In early 1996, the first rumours began to circulate of plans to build a rocket-launch pad on El Hierro. Only in December of that year, however, did the Ministry of Defence in Madrid come clean and admit that it was studying such a proposal. The Ministry's Instituto Nacional de Técnica Aeroespacial needs a launch pad for Spain's planned Argos and Capricornio missiles. The projected site is near the Faro de Orchilla in the island's southwest, and would include a space launch centre (Centro de Lanzamiento Espacial). A control centre would also be built on Malpaso, the island's highest peak.

While it became clear that the provincial Canaries government had gone along with the idea, the Cabildo de El Hierro, backed by a good many Herreños, came out against the *lanzadera* (launch pad). For a while, no one took any notice. In March of 1997, the Canaries government set up a commission of inquiry into the viability of the El Hierro rocket centre – and seemed well disposed to the idea.

Reports from the universities of La Laguna and Las Palmas meanwhile condemned the plan, saying that the space centre could 'mortgage the island's future'. By this time, islander opposition was beginning to make itself heard outside Spain. Members of the European Parliament (albeit a rather powerless organisation) took up the cause, claiming that the space centre would violate European directives on environmental and wildlife protection.

The Cabildo de El Hierro voted to oppose construction of the centre, saying that missile and space launches would endanger the environment and disrupt life on the island. At the time of writing, the Ministry of Defence seemed to have backed off somewhat, but most locals fear it will be back to fight again another day. All over the island you'll see graffiti: '*No a la Lanzadera – El Hierro para la Paz!*' ('No to the Launch pad – El Hierro for Peace!').

ISLA DE EL HIERRO

FRONTERA

Those sticking to asphalt roads and/or buses will follow the TF-912 in its sweeping crescent along the crown of the volcanic wall that overlooks El Golfo. The **Malpaso** peak (1501m) is the island's highest. A dirt track known as the Camino de San Salvador (signposted) veers south off the highway and takes you to the foot of the mountain – it's about 5km of dirt track, some of it pretty rough.

The TF-912 then zigzags down into the coastal plain, where the first town you encounter is Frontera, the name also used to cover all the villages looking onto El Golfo. You will find it hard to miss the **Iglesia de Nuestra Señora de Candelaria**, built outside the town in 1818. Its bell tower is a striking, squat three-storey edifice erected on a hill of volcanic ash so that it could be seen from all over the plains.

One kilometre west, **Tigaday** is another major village, with shops, bank, bar/restaurants and a petrol station. Hang a right and follow the road north-east to Las Puntas. On the way, off to the left, are the fully restored cottages of **Casas de Guinea**, another contender for oldest village of El Hierro (along with Las Montañetas). The stone houses have mostly been converted into little *apartamentos*.

Around here is also the **Lagartario** (☎ 922 55 60 62), where you can see a few *lagartos de Salmor*, a rare lizard species found only on El Hierro. It is only open to the public from 11 am to 2 pm public on Thursday.

Another couple of kilometres and you are in **Las Puntas**. The star attraction is the old port building, built in 1884 and now restored and converted into what the Guinness Book of Records considers to be the smallest hotel in the world, the enticing *Hotel Punta Grande* (☎ 922 55 90 81), whose impeccably kept four rooms cost 7000 ptas a night, or 5000 ptas for single occupation. Breakfast is 750 ptas more per person. If you can't get in here, you could try the surrounding apartments. *Apartamentos Los Roques de Salmor* (☎ 922 55 90 16) and *Apartamentos Noemí* (☎ 922 55 92 03) are both close by. The latter charges about 6000 ptas for a double with kitchenette, while the former goes as high as 9000 ptas.

Pensiones and apartments are scattered all over the area. In Tigaday, you could do worse than *Pensión El Guanche* (☎ 922 55 90 65), Calle de la Cruz Alta s/n, where simple, clean rooms will set you back 1500/2500 ptas.

Just west of Tigaday is **Los Llanillos**, an orderly little hamlet which could win any tidy town award. A 10-minute walk to the coast brings you to the Charco Azul (Blue Pond), a swimming pond cut out of the ocean rock.

SABINOSA & AROUND
Six kilometres west of Los Llanillos, Sabinosa marks the western high point of El Golfo. You can stay at the *Pensión Sabinosa* (☎ 922 55 93 55), Calle de Valentina Hernández 7 (doubles cost 3000 ptas), or keep following the road as it winds down to the coast at **Pozo de la Salud** (the Well of Health). The natural sulphurous spring water is used to treat various ailments, and the little well is just outside the *Casa Rosa* (☎ 922 55 90 22), a quaint little hostal with its own restaurant. Rooms with a bath here cost 2000/3000 ptas. About a 45-minute walk westwards, **Playa de las Arenas Blancas** is not a bad beach.

LA DEHESA
Faro de Orchilla
The road from Sabinosa arches right round the west coast of what is known as La Dehesa (the Pasture). You pass a couple of beaches, including the rust-red volcanic **Playa del Verodal**, before reaching the most south-western point of all Spanish territory, the Faro (lighthouse) de Orchilla (the last 2km are dirt track). The coastal drive from Sabinosa on is quite spectacular, culminating in a set of dramatic switchbacks after Verodal.

Although robbed of its status as 'zero meridian' last century when it was transferred to Greenwich in the UK, the lighthouse still marks the first or last contact with land (depending on which way you are going) for mariners plying the rough Atlantic seas between Africa and Europe on the one hand, and the Americas on the other. The couple of kilometres of dirt track down to the lighthouse are exceedingly corrugated and make for a bumpy ride – you want to have a fervent love of lighthouses to bother.

La Ermita de Nuestra Señora de los Reyes
Back on the asphalt road, head inland a few kilometres towards El Julán. The road takes you to an unassuming chapel that contains the image of the Virgen de los Reyes (Madonna of the Kings). In July every four years (the next in 2001), virtually everyone on the island gathers to witness or join the procession in which the image, seated in a sedan chair, is hauled all the way along the Camino de la Virgen to Valverde. The pro-

The Sabina trees of the high west grow into unusual shapes, battered as they are by the prevailing Atlantic winds

cession is known as the Bajada de la Virgen de los Reyes.

El Sabinar

If the dirt track is dry and you have a vehicle, you can continue up this windswept height named after the *sabinas* (junipers) which grow here in such a malformed way. Bending before the ceaseless Atlantic winds, they have become the island's symbol.

To get here, follow the road around the back of the Ermita de los Reyes. It soon turns into a dirt track. After roughly 2km

take the left fork – it's signposted. Back at the fork, you could proceed north a further 2km to reach another spectacular lookout, the **Mirador de Bascos**, from which on a clear day you not only have an uninterrupted view the length of El Golfo, but may even make out the islands of La Palma, La Gomera and Tenerife.

From here you have no real choice but to backtrack to the Ermita. To return to Valverde you really have to retrace the route back via Frontera. You could also hike along here to the camping ground at Hoya del Morcillo.

Glossary

abierto – open
aficionado – enthusiast
apartado de correos – post office box
apnea – snorkelling
artesonado – coffered ceiling
ayuntamiento – town hall

barranco – ravine or gorge. All but the two easternmost islands are rippled by these ravines which cut paths from the mountainous centres to the coast; they often represent the only interruption to long coastlines of rocky bluffs and cliffs.
barrio – district, quarter (of a town or city)
biblioteca – library
buceo – scuba diving

cabildo insular – island government
cajero automático – automatic teller machine (ATM)
Carnaval – festival celebrating the beginning of Lent, 40 days before Easter
casa rural – a village or country house or farmstead with rooms to let
casco – literally, helmet; often used to refer to old centre of town
caserío – traditional farmhouse or hamlet
catedral – cathedral
centro comercial – shopping centre, common in coastal resorts where they usually contain not only shops, but restaurants, bars and other facilities for tourists
cerrado – closed
comedor – dining room
comsaría – National Police station
Corpus Christi – festival in honour of the Eucharist, held eight weeks after Easter
correos – post office
cruz – cross
Cruz Roja – Red Cross

duro – common name for 5 ptas coin (literally 'hard')

east este
entrada – entrance

ermita – hermitage or chapel
estación – terminal
estación de guaguas – bus terminal
estación marítima – ferry terminal

faro – lighthouse
fiesta – festival, public holiday or party
fin de semana – weekend

gofio – ground, roasted grain used in place of bread in Canarian cuisine
guagua – bus

hostal – commercial establishment providing accommodation in the one to three star range; not to be confused with youth hostels, of which there is only one throughout the islands

ICONA – Instituto para la Conservación de la Naturaleza
IGIC – Impuesto General Indirecto Canario (local version of value added tax)
iglesia – church

llegada – arrival
librería – bookshop
lista de correos – poste restante

madrugada – the 'early hours', from around 3 am to dawn; a pretty lively time in the cities and resorts!
marcha – action, nightlife, 'the scene'
mercado – market
meseta – high plateau
mirador – lookout point
muelle – wharf or pier
museo – museum, gallery

norte – north

oeste – west
oficina de turismo – tourist office

piscina – swimming pool
playa – beach

pueblo – village
puerta – door
puerto – port

rastro – flea market
retablo – altarpiece
romería – festive pilgrimage or procession

salida – departure or exit
Semana Santa – Holy Week, the week leading up to Easter
Sida – AIDS

s/n – sin numero (without number); sometimes seen in street addresses
sur – south

tapas – bar snacks traditionally served on saucer or lid (*tapa*)
tarjeta de crédito – credit card
tarjeta telefónica – phonecard
tasca – pub, bar
terraza – terrace; outdoor cafe tables

valle – valley

Index

LONELY PLANET PHRASEBOOKS

Building bridges,
Breaking barriers,
Beyond babble-on

Listen for the gems

Speak your own words

Ask your own
questions

Master of
your
own
image

- handy pocket-sized books
- easy to understand Pronunciation chapter
- clear and comprehensive Grammar chapter
- romanisation alongside script to allow ease of pronunciation
- script throughout so users can point to phrases
- extensive vocabulary sections, words and phrases for every situation
- full of cultural information and tips for the traveller

'...vital for a real DIY spirit and attitude in language learning' – Backpacker

'the phrasebooks have good cultural backgrounders and offer solid advice for challenging situations in remote locations' – San Francisco Examiner

'...they are unbeatable for their coverage of the world's more obscure languages' – The Geographical Magazine

---

Arabic (Egyptian)
Arabic (Moroccan)
Australia
  Australian English, Aboriginal and Torres Strait languages
Baltic States
  Estonian, Latvian, Lithuanian
Bengali
Brazilian
Burmese
Cantonese
Central Asia
Central Europe
  Czech, French, German, Hungarian, Italian and Slovak
Eastern Europe
  Bulgarian, Czech, Hungarian, Polish, Romanian and Slovak
Ethiopian (Amharic)
Fijian
French
German
Greek

Hindi/Urdu
Indonesian
Italian
Japanese
Korean
Lao
Latin American Spanish
Malay
Mandarin
Mediterranean Europe
  Albanian, Croatian, Greek, Italian, Macedonian, Maltese, Serbian and Slovene
Mongolian
Nepali
Papua New Guinea
Pilipino (Tagalog)
Quechua
Russian
Scandinavian Europe
  Danish, Finnish, Icelandic, Norwegian and Swedish

South-East Asia
  Burmese, Indonesian, Khmer, Lao, Malay, Tagalog (Pilipino), Thai and Vietnamese
Spanish (Castilian)
  Basque, Catalan and Galician
Sri Lanka
Swahili
Thai
Thai Hill Tribes
Tibetan
Turkish
Ukrainian
USA
  US English, Vernacular, Native American languages and Hawaiian
Vietnamese
Western Europe
  Basque, Catalan, Dutch, French, German, Irish, Italian, Portuguese, Scottish Gaelic, Spanish (Castilian) and Welsh

---

LONELY PLANET TRAVEL ATLASES

Lonely Planet has long been famous for the number and quality of its guidebook maps. Now we've gone one step further and in conjunction with Steinhart Katzir Publishers produced a handy companion series: Lonely Planet travel atlases – maps of a country produced in book form.

Unlike other maps, which look good but lead travellers astray, our travel atlases have been researched on the road by Lonely Planet's experienced team of writers. All details are carefully checked to ensure the atlas corresponds with the equivalent Lonely Planet guidebook.

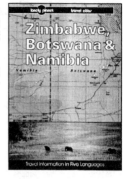

The handy atlas format means no holes, wrinkles, torn sections or constant folding and unfolding. These atlases can survive long periods on the road, unlike cumbersome fold-out maps. The comprehensive index ensures easy reference.

- full-colour throughout
- maps researched and checked by Lonely Planet authors
- place names correspond with Lonely Planet guidebooks
  – no confusing spelling differences
- legend and travelling information in English, French, German, Japanese and Spanish
- size: 230 x 160 mm

Available now:
Chile & Easter Island • Egypt • India & Bangladesh • Israel & the Palestinian Territories •Jordan, Syria & Lebanon • Kenya • Laos • Portugal • South Africa, Lesotho & Swaziland • Thailand • Turkey • Vietnam • Zimbabwe, Botswana & Namibia

---

LONELY PLANET TV SERIES & VIDEOS

Lonely Planet travel guides have been brought to life on television screens around the world. Like our guides, the programmes are based on the joy of independent travel, and look honestly at some of the most exciting, picturesque and frustrating places in the world. Each show is presented by one of three travellers from Australia, England or the USA and combines an innovative mixture of video, Super-8 film, atmospheric soundscapes and original music.

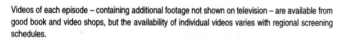

Videos of each episode – containing additional footage not shown on television – are available from good book and video shops, but the availability of individual videos varies with regional screening schedules.

Video destinations include: Alaska • American Rockies • Australia – The South-East • Baja California & the Copper Canyon • Brazil • Central Asia • Chile & Easter Island • Corsica, Sicily & Sardinia – The Mediterranean Islands • East Africa (Tanzania & Zanzibar) • Ecuador & the Galapagos Islands • Greenland & Iceland • Indonesia • Israel & the Sinai Desert • Jamaica • Japan • La Ruta Maya • Morocco • New York • North India • Pacific Islands (Fiji, Solomon Islands & Vanuatu) • South India • South West China • Turkey • Vietnam • West Africa • Zimbabwe, Botswana & Namibia

The Lonely Planet TV series is produced by:
Pilot Productions
The Old Studio
18 Middle Row
London W10 5AT UK

For video availability and ordering information contact your nearest Lonely Planet office.

Music from the TV series is available on CD & cassette.

PLANET TALK

Lonely Planet's FREE quarterly newsletter

We love hearing from you and think you'd like to hear from us.

When...is the right time to see reindeer in Finland?
Where...can you hear the best palm-wine music in Ghana?
How...do you get from Asunción to Areguá by steam train?
What...is the best way to see India?

For the answer to these and many other questions read PLANET TALK.

Every issue is packed with up-to-date travel news and advice including:

- a letter from Lonely Planet co-founders Tony and Maureen Wheeler
- go behind the scenes on the road with a Lonely Planet author
- feature article on an important and topical travel issue
- a selection of recent letters from travellers
- details on forthcoming Lonely Planet promotions
- complete list of Lonely Planet products

To join our mailing list contact any Lonely Planet office.

Also available: Lonely Planet T-shirts. 100% heavyweight cotton.

LONELY PLANET ONLINE

Get the latest travel information before you leave or while you're on the road

Whether you've just begun planning your next trip, or you're chasing down specific info on currency regulations or visa requirements, check out Lonely Planet Online for up-to-the minute travel information.

As well as travel profiles of your favourite destinations (including maps and photos), you'll find current reports from our researchers and other travellers, updates on health and visas, travel advisories, and discussion of the ecological and political issues you need to be aware of as you travel.

There's also an online travellers' forum where you can share your experience of life on the road, meet travel companions and ask other travellers for their recommendations and advice. We also have plenty of links to other online sites useful to independent travellers.

And of course we have a complete and up-to-date list of all Lonely Planet travel products including guides, phrasebooks, atlases, Journeys and videos and a simple online ordering facility if you can't find the book you want elsewhere.

www.lonelyplanet.com
or
AOL keyword: lp

LONELY PLANET PRODUCTS

Lonely Planet is known worldwide for publishing practical, reliable and no-nonsense travel information in our guides and on our web site. The Lonely Planet list covers just about every accessible part of the world. Currently there are nine series: *travel guides, shoestring guides, walking guides, city guides, phrasebooks, audio packs, travel atlases, Journeys – a unique collection of travel writing and Pisces Books - diving and snorkeling guides.*

EUROPE

Amsterdam • Austria • Baltic States phrasebook • Britain • Central Europe on a shoestring • Central Europe phrasebook • Czech & Slovak Republics • Denmark • Dublin • Eastern Europe on a shoestring • Eastern Europe phrasebook • Estonia, Latvia & Lithuania • Finland • France • French phrasebook • Germany • German phrasebook • Greece • Greek phrasebook • Hungary • Iceland, Greenland & the Faroe Islands • Ireland • Italian phrasebook • Italy • Lisbon • London • Mediterranean Europe on a shoestring • Mediterranean Europe phrasebook • Paris • Poland • Portugal • Portugal travel atlas • Prague • Romania & Moldova • Russia, Ukraine & Belarus • Russian phrasebook • Scandinavian & Baltic Europe on a shoestring • Scandinavian Europe phrasebook • Slovenia • Spain • Spanish phrasebook • St Petersburg • Switzerland •Trekking in Spain • Ukrainian phrasebook • Vienna • Walking in Britain • Walking in Italy • Walking in Switzerland • Western Europe on a shoestring • Western Europe phrasebook

Travel Literature: The Olive Grove: Travels in Greece

NORTH AMERICA

Alaska • Backpacking in Alaska • Baja California • California & Nevada • Canada • Chicago • Deep South• Florida • Hawaii • Honolulu • Los Angeles • Mexico • Mexico City • Miami • New England • New Orleans • New York City • New York, New Jersey & Pennsylvania • Pacific Northwest USA • Rocky Mountain States • San Francisco • Southwest USA • USA phrasebook • Washington, DC & the Capital Region

Travel Literature: Drive thru America

CENTRAL AMERICA & THE CARIBBEAN

•Bahamas and Turks & Caicos •Bermuda •Central America on a shoestring • Costa Rica • Cuba •Eastern Caribbean •Guatemala, Belize & Yucatán: La Ruta Maya • Jamaica

SOUTH AMERICA

Argentina, Uruguay & Paraguay • Bolivia • Brazil • Brazilian phrasebook • Buenos Aires • Chile & Easter Island • Chile & Easter Island travel atlas • Colombia Ecuador & the Galápagos Islands • Latin American Spanish phrasebook • Peru • Quechua phrasebook • Rio de Janeiro • South America on a shoestring • Trekking in the Patagonian Andes • Venezuela

Travel Literature: Full Circle: A South American Journey

ISLANDS OF THE INDIAN OCEAN

Madagascar & Comoros • Maldives• Mauritius, Réunion & Seychelles

AFRICA

Africa - the South • Africa on a shoestring • Arabic (Moroccan) phrasebook • Cairo • Cape Town • Central Africa • East Africa • Egypt • Egypt travel atlas• Ethiopian (Amharic) phrasebook • Kenya • Kenya travel atlas • Malawi, Mozambique & Zambia • Morocco • North Africa • South Africa, Lesotho & Swaziland • South Africa, Lesotho & Swaziland travel atlas • Swahili phrasebook • Tunisia Trekking in East Africa • West Africa • Zimbabwe, Botswana & Namibia • Zimbabwe, Botswana & Namibia travel atlas

Travel Literature: The Rainbird: A Central African Journey • Songs to an African Sunset: A Zimbabwean Story

MAIL ORDER

Lonely Planet products are distributed worldwide. They are also available by mail order from Lonely Planet, so if you have difficulty finding a title please write to us. North American and South American residents should write to 150 Linden St, Oakland CA 94607, USA; European and African residents should write to 10a Spring Place, London NW5 3BH; and residents of other countries to PO Box 617, Hawthorn, Victoria 3122, Australia.

NORTH-EAST ASIA

Beijing • Cantonese phrasebook • China • Hong Kong • Hong Kong, Macau & Guangzhou • Japan • Japanese phrasebook • Japanese audio pack • Korea • Korean phrasebook • Mandarin phrasebook • Mongolia • Mongolian phrasebook • North-East Asia on a shoestring • Seoul • Taiwan • Tibet • Tibet phrasebook • Tokyo

Travel Literature: Lost Japan

MIDDLE EAST & CENTRAL ASIA

Arab Gulf States • Arabic (Egyptian) phrasebook • Central Asia • Central Asia phrasebook • Iran • Israel & the Palestinian Territories • Israel & the Palestinian Territories travel atlas • Istanbul • Jerusalem • Jordan & Syria • Jordan, Syria & Lebanon travel atlas • Lebanon • Middle East • Turkey • Turkish phrasebook • Turkey travel atlas • Yemen

Travel Literature: The Gates of Damascus • Kingdom of the Film Stars: Journey into Jordan

ALSO AVAILABLE:

Brief Encounters • Travel with Children • Traveller's Tales

INDIAN SUBCONTINENT

Bangladesh • Bengali phrasebook • Delhi • Goa • Hindi/Urdu phrasebook • India • India & Bangladesh travel atlas • Indian Himalaya • Karakoram Highway • Nepal • Nepali phrasebook • Pakistan • Rajasthan • Sri Lanka • Sri Lanka phrasebook • Trekking in the Indian Himalaya • Trekking in the Karakoram & Hindukush • Trekking in the Nepal Himalaya

Travel Literature: In Rajasthan • Shopping for Buddhas

SOUTH-EAST ASIA

Bali & Lombok • Bangkok • Burmese phrasebook • Cambodia • Ho Chi Minh City • Indonesia • Indonesian phrasebook • Indonesian audio pack • Jakarta • Java • Laos • Lao phrasebook • Laos travel atlas • Malay phrasebook • Malaysia, Singapore & Brunei • Myanmar (Burma) • Philippines • Pilipino phrasebook • Singapore • South-East Asia on a shoestring • South-East Asia phrasebook • Thailand • Thailand's Islands & Beaches • Thailand travel atlas • Thai phrasebook • Thai audio pack • Thai Hill Tribes phrasebook • Vietnam • Vietnamese phrasebook • Vietnam travel atlas

AUSTRALIA & THE PACIFIC

Australia • Australian phrasebook • Bushwalking in Australia • Bushwalking in Papua New Guinea • Fiji • Fijian phrasebook • Islands of Australia's Great Barrier Reef • Melbourne • Micronesia • New Caledonia • New South Wales • New Zealand • Northern Territory • Outback Australia • Papua New Guinea • Papua New Guinea phrasebook • Queensland • Rarotonga & the Cook Islands • Samoa • Solomon Islands • South Australia • Sydney • Tahiti & French Polynesia • Tasmania • Tonga • Tramping in New Zealand • Vanuatu • Victoria • Western Australia

Travel Literature: Islands in the Clouds • Sean & David's Long Drive

ANTARCTICA

Antarctica

THE LONELY PLANET STORY

Lonely Planet published its first book in 1973 in response to the numerous 'How did you do it?' questions Maureen and Tony Wheeler were asked after driving, bussing, hitching, sailing and railing their way from England to Australia.

Written at a kitchen table and hand collated, trimmed and stapled, *Across Asia on the Cheap* became an instant local bestseller, inspiring thoughts of another book.

Eighteen months in South-East Asia resulted in their second guide, *South-East Asia on a shoestring*, which they put together in a backstreet Chinese hotel in Singapore in 1975. The 'yellow bible', as it quickly became known to backpackers around the world, soon became *the* guide to the region. It has sold well over half a million copies and is now in its 9th edition, still retaining its familiar yellow cover.

Today there are over 240 titles, including travel guides, walking guides, language kits & phrasebooks, travel atlases and travel literature. The company is the largest independent travel publisher in the world. Although Lonely Planet initially specialised in guides to Asia, today there are few corners of the globe that have not been covered.

The emphasis continues to be on travel for independent travellers. Tony and Maureen still travel for several months of each year and play an active part in the writing, updating and quality control of Lonely Planet's guides.

They have been joined by over 70 authors and 170 staff at our offices in Melbourne (Australia), Oakland (USA), London (UK) and Paris (France). Travellers themselves also make a valuable contribution to the guides through the feedback we receive in thousands of letters each year and on our web site.

The people at Lonely Planet strongly believe that travellers can make a positive contribution to the countries they visit, both through their appreciation of the countries' culture, wildlife and natural features, and through the money they spend. In addition, the company makes a direct contribution to the countries and regions it covers. Since 1986 a percentage of the income from each book has been donated to ventures such as famine relief in Africa; aid projects in India; agricultural projects in Central America; Greenpeace's efforts to halt French nuclear testing in the Pacific; and Amnesty International.

'I hope we send people out with the right attitude about travel. You realise when you travel that there are so many different perspectives about the world, so we hope these books will make people more interested in what they see. Guidebooks can't really guide people. All you can do is point them in the right direction.'

– **Tony Wheeler**

LONELY PLANET PUBLICATIONS

Australia
PO Box 617, Hawthorn 3122, Victoria
tel: (03) 9819 1877 fax: (03) 9819 6459
e-mail: talk2us@lonelyplanet.com.au

USA
150 Linden St
Oakland, CA 94607
tel: (510) 893 8555 TOLL FREE: 800 275-8555
fax: (510) 893 8563
e-mail: info@lonelyplanet.com

UK
10a Spring Place,
London NW5 3BH
tel: (0171) 428 4800 fax: (0171) 428 4828
e-mail: go@lonelyplanet.co.uk

France:
71 bis rue du Cardinal Lemoine, 75005 Paris
tel: 01 44 32 06 20 fax: 01 46 34 72 55
e-mail: bip@lonelyplanet.fr

World Wide Web: http://www.lonelyplanet.com
or *AOL keyword: lp*